Mercedes Of Castile;
Or,
The Voyage To Cathay

by

J. Fenimore Cooper

Double 9
BOOKS

Mercedes Of Castile;
Or,
The Voyage To Cathay
Translated Into English Verse
by J. Fenimore Cooper

ISBN: 978-93-59951-85-0

Published by

DOUBLE 9 BOOKS

2/13-B, Ansari Road
Daryaganj, New Delhi – 110002
info@double9books.com
www.double9books.com
Tel. 011-40042856

ABOUT THE AUTHOR

James Fenimore Cooper (September 15, 1789 – September 14, 1851) was an American writer of the first half of the nineteenth century, best known for his historical romances depicting colonial and indigenous characters from the 17th to the 19th centuries. He spent much of his childhood and the last fifteen years of his life at Cooperstown, New York, which was founded on land owned by his father, William Cooper. Cooper joined the Episcopal Church soon before his death and gave liberally to it. He spent three years at Yale University, where he was a member of the Linonian Society. Cooper enlisted in the United States Navy as a midshipman after a period on a commercial voyage, where he studied the mechanics of handling sailing vessels, which heavily affected many of his novels and other writings. The Spy, a story about espionage set during the American Revolutionary War and published in 1821, established his career. He also wrote American marine tales. His best-known works are the Leatherstocking Tales, a series of five historical frontier novels written between 1823 and 1841 that established the famous American frontier scout, Natty Bumppo.

CONTENTS

PREFACE

So much has been written of late years, touching the discovery of America, that it would not be at all surprising should there exist a disposition in a certain class of readers to deny the accuracy of all the statements in this work. Some may refer to history, with a view to prove that there never were such persons as our hero and heroine, and fancy that by establishing these facts, they completely destroy the authenticity of the whole book. In answer to this anticipated objection, we will state, that after carefully perusing several of the Spanish writers—from Cervantes to the translator of the journal of Columbus, the Alpha and Omega of peninsular literature—and after having read both Irving and Prescott from beginning to end, we do not find a syllable in either of them, that we understand to be conclusive evidence, or indeed to be any evidence at all, on the portions of our subject that are likely to be disputed. Until some solid affirmative proof, therefore, can be produced against us, we shall hold our case to be made out, and rest our claims to be believed on the authority of our own statements. Nor do we think there is any thing either unreasonable or unusual in this course, as perhaps the greater portion of that which is daily and hourly offered to the credence of the American public, rests on the same species of testimony—with the trifling difference that we state truths, with a profession of fiction, while the great moral caterers of the age state fiction with the profession of truth. If any advantage can be fairly obtained over us, in consequence of this trifling discrepancy, we must submit.

There is one point, notwithstanding, concerning which it may be well to be frank at once. The narrative of the "Voyage to Cathay," has been written with the journal of the Admiral before us; or, rather, with all of that journal that has been given to the world through the agency of a very incompetent and meagre editor. Nothing is plainer than the general fact that this person did not always understand his author, and in one particular circumstance he has written so obscurely, as not a little to embarrass even a novelist, whose functions naturally include an entire familiarity with the thoughts, emotions, characters, and, occasionally, with the unknown fates of the subjects of his pen. The nautical day formerly commenced at meridian, and, with all our native ingenuity and high professional prerogatives, we have not been able to discover whether the editor of the journal has adopted that mode of counting time, or whether he has condescended to use the more vulgar and irrational practice of landsmen. It is our opinion, however, that in the spirit of impartiality which becomes an historian, he has adopted both. This little peculiarity might possibly embarrass a superficial critic; but accurate critics being so very common, we feel no concern on this head, well knowing that they will be much more apt to wink at these minor inconsistencies, than to pass over an error of the press, or a comma with a broken tail. As we wish to live on good terms with this useful class of our fellow-creatures, we have directed the printers to mis-spell some eight or ten words for their convenience, and to save them from headaches, have honestly stated this principal difficulty ourselves.

Should the publicity which is now given to the consequences of commencing a day in the middle have the effect to induce the government to order that it shall, in future, with all American seamen, commence at one of its ends, something will be gained in the way of simplicity, and the writing of novels will, in-so-much, be rendered easier and more agreeable.

As respects the minor characters of this work, very little need be said. Every one knows that Columbus had seamen in his vessels, and that he brought some of the natives of the islands he had discovered, back with him to Spain. The reader is now made much more intimately acquainted with certain of these individuals, we will venture to say, than he can be possibly by the perusal of any work previously written. As for the subordinate incidents connected with the more familiar events of the age, it is hoped they will be found so completely to fill up this branch of the subject, as to render future investigations unnecessary.

CHAPTER I

"There was knocking that shook the marble floor,
And a voice at the gate, which said—
'That the Cid Ruy Diez, the Campeador,
Was there in his arms array'd.'" — —

Mrs. Hemans.

Whether we take the pictures of the inimitable Cervantes, or of that scarcely less meritorious author from whom Le Sage has borrowed his immortal tale, for our guides; whether we confide in the graver legends of history, or put our trust in the accounts of modern travellers, the time has scarcely ever existed when the inns of Spain were good, or the roads safe. These are two of the blessings of civilization which the people of the peninsula would really seem destined never to attain; for, in all ages, we hear, or have heard, of wrongs done the traveller equally by the robber and the host. If such are the facts to-day, such also were the facts in the middle of the fifteenth century, the period to which we desire to carry back the reader in imagination.

At the commencement of the month of October, in the year of our Lord 1469, John of Trastamara reigned in Aragon, holding his court at a place called Zaragosa, a town lying on the Ebro, the name of which is supposed to be a corruption of Cæsar Augustus, and a city that has become celebrated in our own times, under the more Anglicised term of Saragossa, for its deeds in arms. John of Trastamara, or, as it was more usual to style him, agreeably to the nomenclature of kings, John II., was one of the most sagacious monarchs of his age; but he had become impoverished by many conflicts with the turbulent, or, as it may be more courtly to say, the liberty-loving Catalonians; had frequently enough to do to maintain his seat on the throne; possessed a party-colored empire that included within its sway, besides his native Aragon with its dependencies of Valencia and Catalonia, Sicily and the Balearic Islands, with some very questionable rights in Navarre. By the will of his elder brother and predecessor, the crown of Naples had descended to an illegitimate son of the latter, else would that kingdom have been added to the list. The King of Aragon had seen a long and troubled reign, and, at this very moment, his treasury was nearly exhausted by his efforts to subdue the truculent Catalans, though he was nearer a triumph than he could then foresee, his competitor, the Duke of Lorraine, dying suddenly, only two short months after the precise period chosen for the commencement of our tale. But it is denied to man to look into the future, and on the 9th of the month just mentioned, the ingenuity of the royal treasurer was most sorely taxed, there having arisen an unexpected demand for a considerable sum of money, at the very moment that the army was about to disband itself for the want of pay, and the public coffers contained only the very moderate sum of three hundred *Enriques*, or Henrys—a gold coin named after a previous monarch, and which had a value not far from that of the modern ducat, or our own quarter eagle. The matter, however, was too pressing to be deferred, and even the objects of the war were considered as secondary to those connected with this suddenly-conceived, and more private enterprise. Councils were held, money-dealers were cajoled or frightened, and the confidants of the court were very manifestly in a state of great and earnest excitement. At length, the time of preparation appeared to be passed and the instant of action arrived. Curiosity was relieved, and the citizens of Saragossa were permitted to know that their sovereign was about to send a solemn embassy, on matters of high moment, to his neighbor, kinsman, and ally, the monarch of Castile. In 1469, Henry, also of Trastamara, sat upon the throne of the adjoining kingdom, under the title of Henry IV. He was the grandson, in the male line, of the brother of John II.'s father, and, consequently, a first-cousin once removed, of the monarch of Aragon. Notwithstanding this affinity, and the strong family interests that might be supposed to unite them, it required many friendly embassies to preserve the peace between the two monarchs; and the announcement of that which was about to depart, produced more satisfaction than wonder in the streets of the town.

Henry of Castile, though he reigned over broader and richer peninsular territories than his relative of Aragon, had his cares and troubles, also. He had been twice married, having repudiated his first consort, Blanche of Aragon, to wed Joanna of Portugal, a princess of a levity of character so marked, as not only to bring great scandal on the court generally, but to throw so much distrust on the birth of her only child, a daughter, as to push discontent to disaffection, and eventually to deprive the infant itself of the rights of royalty. Henry's father, like himself, had been twice married, and the issue of the second union was a son and a daughter, Alfonso and Isabella; the latter becoming subsequently illustrious, under the double titles of the Queen of Castile, and of the Catholic. The luxurious impotency of Henry, as a monarch, had driven a portion of his subjects into open rebellion. Three years preceding that selected for our opening, his brother Alfonso had been proclaimed king in his stead, and a civil war had raged throughout his provinces. This war had been recently terminated by the death of Alfonso, when the peace of the kingdom was temporarily restored by a treaty, in which Henry consented to the setting aside of his own daughter—or rather of the daughter of Joanna of Portugal—and to the recognition of his half-sister Isabella, as the rightful heiress of the throne. The last concession was the result of dire necessity, and, as might have been expected, it led to many secret and violent measures, with a view to defeat its objects. Among the other expedients adopted by the king—or, it might be better to say, by his favorites, the inaction and indolence of the self-indulgent but kind-hearted prince being proverbial—with a view to counteract the probable consequences of the expected accession of Isabella, were various schemes to control her will, and guide her policy, by giving her hand, first to a subject, with a view to reduce her power, and subsequently to various foreign princes, who were thought to be more or less suited to the furtherance of such schemes. Just at this moment, indeed, the marriage of the princess was one of the greatest objects of Spanish prudence. The son of the King of Aragon was one of the suitors for the hand of Isabella, and most of those who heard of the intended departure of the embassy, naturally enough believed that the mission had some connection with that great stroke of Aragonese policy.

Isabella had the reputation of learning, modesty, discretion, piety, and beauty, besides being the acknowledged heiress of so enviable a crown; and there were many competitors for her hand. Among them were to be ranked French, English, and Portuguese princes, besides him of Aragon to whom we have already alluded. Different favorites supported different pretenders, struggling to effect their several purposes by the usual intrigues of courtiers and partisans; while the royal maiden, herself, who was the object of so much competition and rivalry, observed a discreet and womanly decorum, even while firmly bent on indulging her most womanly and dearest sentiments. Her brother, the king, was in the south, pursuing his pleasures, and, long accustomed to dwell in comparative solitude, the princess was earnestly occupied in arranging her own affairs, in a way that she believed would most conduce to her own happiness. After several attempts to entrap her person, from which she had only escaped by the prompt succor of the forces of her friends, she had taken refuge in Leon, in the capital of which province, or kingdom as it was sometimes called, Valladolid, she temporarily took up her abode. As Henry, however, still remained in the vicinity of Granada, it is in that direction we must look for the route taken by the embassy.

The cortège left Saragossa, by one of the southern gates, early in the morning of a glorious autumnal day. There was the usual escort of lances, for this the troubled state of the country demanded; bearded nobles well mailed—for few, who offered an inducement to the plunderer, ventured on the highway without this precaution; a long train of sumpter mules, and a host of those who, by their guise, were half menials and half soldiers. The gallant display drew crowds after the horses' heels, and, together with some prayers for success, a vast deal of crude and shallow conjecture, as is still the practice with the uninstructed and gossiping, was lavished on the probable objects and results of the journey. But curiosity has its limits, and even the gossip occasionally grows weary; and by the time the sun was setting, most of the multitude had already forgotten to think and speak of the parade of the morning. As the night drew on, however, the late pageant was still the subject of discourse between two soldiers, who belonged to the guard of the western gate, or that which opened on the road to the province of Burgos. These worthies were loitering away the hours, in the listless manner common to men on watch, and the spirit of discussion and of critical censure had survived the thoughts and bustle of the day.

"If Don Alonso de Carbajal thinketh to ride far in that guise," observed the elder of the two idlers, "he would do well to look sharp to his followers, for the army of Aragon never sent forth a more scurvily-appointed guard than that he hath this day led through the southern gate, notwithstanding the glitter of housings, and the clangor of trumpets. We could have furnished lances from Valencia more befitting a king's embassy, I tell thee, Diego; ay, and worthier knights to lead them, than these of Aragon. But if the king is content, it ill becomes soldiers, like thee and me, to be dissatisfied."

"There are many who think, Roderique, that it had been better to spare the money lavished in this courtly letter-writing, to pay the brave men who so freely shed their blood in order to subdue the rebellious Barcelans."

"This is always the way, boy, between debtor and creditor. Don John owes you a few maravedis, and you grudge him every Enrique he spends on his necessities. I am an older soldier, and have learned the art of paying myself, when the treasury is too poor to save me the trouble."

"That might do in a foreign war, when one is battling against the Moor, for instance; but, after all, these Catalans are as good Christians as we are ourselves; some of them are as good subjects; and it is not as easy to plunder a countryman as to plunder an Infidel."

"Easier by twenty fold; for the one expects it, and, like all in that unhappy condition, seldom has any thing worth taking, while the other opens his stores to you as freely as he does his heart—but who are these, setting forth on the highway, at this late hour?"

"Fellows that pretend to wealth, by affecting to conceal it. I'll warrant you, now, Roderique, that there is not money enough among all those varlets to pay the laquais that shall serve them their boiled eggs, to-night."

"By St. Iago, my blessed patron!" whispered one of the leaders of a small cavalcade, who, with a single companion rode a little in advance of the others, as if not particularly anxious to be too familiar with the rest, and laughing, lightly, as he spoke: "Yonder vagabond is nearer the truth than is comfortable! We may have sufficient among us all to pay for an olla-podrida and its service, but I much doubt whether there will be a dobla left, when the journey shall be once ended."

A low, but grave rebuke, checked this inconsiderate mirth; and the party, which consisted of merchants, or traders, mounted on mules, as was evident by their appearance, for in that age the different classes were easily recognized by their attire, halted at the gate. The permission to quit the town was regular, and the drowsy and consequently surly gate-keeper slowly undid his bars, in order that the travellers might pass.

While these necessary movements were going on, the two soldiers stood a little on one side, coolly scanning the group, though Spanish gravity prevented them from indulging openly in an expression of the scorn that they actually felt for two or three Jews who were among the traders. The merchants, moreover, were of a better class, as was evident by a follower or two, who rode in their train, in the garbs of menials, and who kept at a respectful distance while their masters paid the light fee that it was customary to give on passing the gates after nightfall. One of these menials, capitally mounted on a tall, spirited mule, happened to place himself so near Diego, during this little ceremony, that the latter, who was talkative by nature, could not refrain from having his say.

"Prithee, Pepe," commenced the soldier, "how many hundred doblas a year do they pay, in that service of thine, and how often do they renew that fine leathern doublet?"

The varlet, or follower of the merchant, who was still a youth, though his vigorous frame and embrowned cheek denoted equally severe exercise and rude exposure, started and reddened at this free inquiry, which was enforced by a hand slapped familiarly on his knee, and such a squeeze of the leg as denoted the freedom of the camp. The laugh of Diego probably suppressed a sudden outbreak of anger, for the soldier was one whose manner indicated too much good-humor easily to excite resentment.

"Thy gripe is friendly, but somewhat close, comrade," the young domestic mildly observed; "and if thou wilt take a friend's counsel, it will be, never to indulge in too great familiarity, lest some day it lead to a broken pate."

"By holy San Pedro!—I should relish—"

It was too late, however; for his master having proceeded, the youth pushed a powerful rowel into the flank of his mule, and the vigorous animal dashed ahead, nearly upsetting Diego, who was pressing hard on the pommel of the saddle, by the movement.

"There is mettle in that boy," exclaimed the good-natured soldier, as he recovered his feet. "I thought, for one moment, he was about to favor me with a visitation of his hand."

"Thou art wrong—and too much accustomed to be heedless, Diego," answered his comrade; "and it had been no wonder had that youth struck thee to the earth, for the indignity thou putt'st upon him."

"Ha! a hireling follower of some cringing Hebrew! He dare to strike a blow at a soldier of the king!"

"He may have been a soldier of the king himself, in his day. These are times when most of his frame and muscle are called on to go in harness. I think I have seen that face before; ay, and that, too, where none of craven hearts would be apt to go."

"The fellow is a mere varlet, and a younker that has just escaped from the hands of the women."

"I'll answer for it, that he hath faced both the Catalan and the Moor in his time, young as he may seem. Thou knowest that the nobles are wont to carry their sons, as children, early into the fight, that they may learn the deeds of chivalry betimes."

"The nobles!" repeated Diego, laughing. "In the name of all the devils, Roderique, of what art thou thinking, that thou likenest this knave to a young noble? Dost fancy him a Guzman, or a Mendoza, in disguise, that thou speakest thus of chivalry?"

"True—it doth, indeed, seem silly—and yet have I before met that frown in battle, and heard that sharp, quick voice, in a rally. By St. Iago de Compostello! I have it! Harkee, Diego!—a word in thy ear."

The veteran now led his more youthful comrade aside, although there was no one near to listen to what he said; and looking carefully round, to make certain that his words would not be overheard, he whispered, for a moment, in Diego's ear.

"Holy Mother of God!" exclaimed the latter, recoiling quite three paces, in surprise and awe. "Thou canst not be right, Roderique!"

"I will place my soul's welfare on it," returned the other, positively. "Have I not often seen him with his visor up, and followed him, time and again, to the charge?"

"And he setting forth as a trader's varlet! Nay, I know not, but as the servitor of a Jew!"

"Our business, Diego, is to strike without looking into the quarrel; to look without seeing, and to listen without hearing. Although his coffers are low, Don John is a good master, and our anointed king; and so we will prove ourselves discreet soldiers."

"But he will never forgive me that gripe of the knee, and my foolish tongue. I shall never dare meet him again."

"Humph!—It is not probable thou ever wilt meet him at the table of the king, and, as for the field, as he is wont to go first, there will not be much temptation for him to turn back in order to look at thee."

"Thou thinkest, then, he will not be apt to know me again?"

"If it should prove so, boy, thou need'st not take it in ill part; as such as he have more demands on their memories than they can always meet."

"The Blessed Maria make thee a true prophet!—else would I never dare again to appear in the ranks. Were it a favor I conferred, I might hope it would be forgotten; but an indignity sticks long in the memory."

Here the two soldiers moved away, continuing the discourse from time to time, although the elder frequently admonished his loquacious companion of the virtue of discretion.

In the mean time, the travellers pursued their way, with a diligence that denoted great distrust of the roads, and as great a desire to get on. They journeyed throughout the night, nor did there occur any relaxation in their speed, until the return of the sun exposed them again to the observations of the curious, among whom were thought to be many emissaries of Henry of Castile, whose agents were known to be particularly on the alert, along all the roads that communicated between the capital of Aragon and Valladolid, the city in which his royal sister had then, quite recently, taken refuge. Nothing remarkable occurred, however, to distinguish this journey from any other of the period. There was nothing about the appearance of the travellers—who soon entered the territory of Soria, a province of Old Castile, where armed parties of the monarch were active in watching the passes—to attract the attention of Henry's soldiers; and as for the more vulgar robber, he was temporarily driven from the highways by the presence of those who acted in the name of the prince. As respects the youth who had given rise to the discourse between the two soldiers, he rode diligently in the rear of his master, so long as it pleased the latter to remain in the saddle; and during the few and brief pauses that occurred in the travelling, he busied himself, like the other menials, in the duties of his proper vocation. On the evening of the second day, however, about an hour after the party had left a hostelry, where it had solaced itself with an olla-podrida and some sour wine, the merry young man who has already been mentioned, and who still kept his place by the side of his graver and more aged companion in the van, suddenly burst into a fit of loud laughter, and, reining in his mule he allowed the whole train to pass him, until he found himself by the side of the young menial already so particularly named. The latter cast a severe and rebuking glance at his reputed master, as he dropped in by his side, and said, with a sternness that ill comported with their apparent relations to each other—

"How now, Master Nuñez! what hath called thee from thy position in the van, to this unseemly familiarity with the varlets in the rear?"

"I crave ten thousand pardons, honest Juan," returned the master, still laughing, though he evidently struggled to repress his mirth, out of respect to the other; "but here is a calamity befallen us, that outdoes those of the fables and legends of necromancy and knight-errantry. The worthy Master Ferreras, yonder, who is so skilful in handling gold, having passed his whole life in buying and selling barley and oats, hath actually mislaid the purse, which it would seem he hath forgotten at the inn we have quitted, in payment of some very stale bread and rancid oil. I doubt if there are twenty reals left in the whole party!"

"And is it a matter of jest, Master Nuñez," returned the servant, though a slight smile struggled about his mouth, as if ready to join in his companion's merriment; "that we are penniless? Thank Heaven! the Burgo of Osma cannot be very distant; and we may have less occasion for gold. And now, master of mine, let me command thee to keep thy proper place in this cavalcade, and not to forget thyself by such undue familiarity with thy inferiors. I have no farther need of thee, and therefore hasten back to Master Ferreras and acquaint him with my sympathy and grief."

The young man smiled, though the eye of the pretended servant was averted, as if he cared to respect his own admonitions; while the other evidently sought a look of recognition and favor. In another minute, the usual order of the journey was resumed.

As the night advanced, and the hour arrived when man and beast usually betray fatigue, these travellers pushed their mules the hardest; and about midnight, by dint of hard pricking, they came under the principal gate of a small walled town, called Osma, that stood not far from the boundary of the province of Burgos, though still in that of Soria. No sooner was his mule near enough to the gate to allow of the freedom, than the young merchant in advance dealt sundry blows on it with his staff, effectually apprising those within of his presence. It required no strong pull of the reins to stop the mules of those behind; but the pretended varlet now pushed ahead, and was about to assume his place among the principal personages near the gate, when a heavy stone, hurled from the battlements, passed so close to his head, as vividly to remind him how near he might be to making a hasty journey to another world. A cry arose in the whole party, at this narrow escape; nor were loud imprecations on the hand that had cast the missile spared. The youth, himself, seemed the least disturbed of them all; and though his voice was sharp and authoritative, as he raised it in remonstrance, it was neither angry nor alarmed.

"How now!" he said; "is this the way you treat peaceful travellers; merchants, who come to ask hospitality and a night's repose at your hands?"

"Merchants and travellers!" growled a voice from above—"say, rather, spies and agents of King Henry. Who are ye? Speak promptly, or ye may expect something sharper than stones, at the next visit."

"Tell me," answered the youth, as if disdaining to be questioned himself—"who holds this borough? Is it not the noble Count of Treviño?"

"The very same, Señor," answered he above, with a mollified tone: "but what can a set of travelling traders know of His Excellency? and who art thou, that speakest up as sharply and as proudly as if thou wert a grandee?"

"I am Ferdinand of Trastamara—the Prince of Aragon—the King of Sicily. Go! bid thy master hasten to the gate."

This sudden announcement, which was made in the lofty manner of one accustomed to implicit obedience, produced a marked change in the state of affairs. The party at the gate so far altered their several positions, that the two superior nobles who had ridden in front, gave place to the youthful king; while the group of knights made such arrangements as showed that disguise was dropped, and each man was now expected to appear in his proper character. It might have amused a close and philosophical observer to note the promptitude with which the young cavaliers, in particular, rose in their saddles, as if casting aside the lounging mien of grovelling traders, in order to appear what they really were, men accustomed to the tourney and the field. On the ramparts the change was equally sudden and great.

All appearance of drowsiness vanished; the soldiers spoke to each other in suppressed but hurried voices; and the distant tramp of feet announced that messengers were dispatched in various directions. Some ten minutes elapsed in this manner, during which an inferior officer showed himself on the ramparts, and apologized for a delay that arose altogether from the force of discipline, and on no account from any want of respect. At length a bustle on the wall, with the light of many lanterns, betrayed the approach of the governor of the town; and the impatience of the young men below, that had begun to manifest itself in half-uttered execrations, was put under a more decent restraint for the occasion.

"Are the joyful tidings that my people bring me true?" cried one from the battlements; while a lantern was lowered from the wall, as if to make a closer inspection of the party at the gate: "Am I really so honored, as to receive a summons from Don Ferdinand of Aragon, at this unusual hour?"

"Cause thy fellow to turn his lantern more closely on my countenance," answered the king, "that thou may'st make thyself sure. I will cheerfully overlook the disrespect, Count of Treviño, for the advantage of a more speedy admission."

"'Tis he!" exclaimed the noble: "I know those royal features, which bear the lineaments of a long race of kings, and that voice have I heard, often, rallying the squadrons of Aragon, in their onsets against the Moor. Let the trumpets speak up, and proclaim this happy arrival; and open wide our gates, without delay."

This order was promptly obeyed, and the youthful king entered Osma, by sound of trumpet, encircled by a strong party of men-at-arms, and with half of the awakened and astonished population at his heels.

"It is lucky, my Lord King," said Don Andres de Cabrera, the young noble already mentioned, as he rode familiarly at the side of Don Ferdinand, "that we have found these good lodgings without cost; it being a melancholy truth, that Master Ferreras hath, negligently enough, mislaid the only purse there was among us. In such a strait, it would not have been easy to keep up the character of thrifty traders much longer; for, while the knaves higgle at the price of every thing, they are fond of letting their gold be seen."

"Now that we are in thine own Castile, Don Andres," returned the king, smiling, "we shall throw ourselves gladly on thy hospitality, well knowing that thou hast two most beautiful diamonds always at thy command."

"I, Sir King! Your Highness is pleased to be merry at my expense, although I believe it is, just now, the only gratification I can pay for. My attachment for the Princess Isabella hath driven me from my lands; and even the humblest cavalier in the Aragonese army is not, just now, poorer than I. What diamonds, therefore, can I command?"

"Report speaketh favorably of the two brilliants that are set in the face of the Doña Beatriz de Bobadilla; and I hear they are altogether at thy disposal, or as much so as a noble maiden's inclinations can leave them with a loyal knight."

"Ah! my Lord King! if indeed this adventure end as happily as it commenceth, I may, indeed, look to your royal favor, for some aid in that matter."

The king smiled, in his own sedate manner; but the Count de Treviño pressing nearer to his side at that moment, the discourse was changed. That night Ferdinand of Aragon slept soundly; but with the dawn, he and his followers were again in the saddle. The party quitted Osma, however, in a manner very different from that in which it had approached its gate. Ferdinand now appeared as a knight, mounted on a noble Andalusian charger; and all his followers had still more openly assumed their proper characters. A strong body of lancers, led by the Count of Treviño in person, composed the escort; and on the 9th of the month, the whole cavalcade reached Dueñas, in Leon, a place quite near to Valladolid. The disaffected nobles crowded about the prince to pay their court, and he was received as became his high rank and still higher destinies.

Here the more luxurious Castilians had an opportunity of observing the severe personal discipline by which Don Ferdinand, at the immature years of eighteen, for he was scarcely older, had succeeded in hardening his body and in stringing his nerves, so as to be equal to any deeds in arms. His delight was found in the rudest military exercises; and no knight of Aragon could better direct his steed in the tourney or in the field. Like most of the royal races of that period, and indeed of this, in despite of the burning sun under which he dwelt, his native complexion was brilliant, though it had already become embrowned by exposure in the chase, and in the martial occupations of his boyhood. Temperate as a Mussulman, his active and well-proportioned frame seemed to be early indurating, as if Providence held him in reserve for some of its own dispensations, that called for great bodily vigor as well as for deep forethought and a vigilant sagacity. During the four or five days that followed, the noble Castilians who listened to his discourse, knew not of which most to approve, his fluent eloquence, or a wariness of thought and expression, which, while they might have been deemed prematurely worldly and cold-blooded, were believed to be particular merits in one destined to control the jarring passions, deep deceptions, and selfish devices of men.

CHAPTER II

"Leave to the nightingale her shady wood:
A privacy of glorious light is thine;
Whence thou dost pour upon the world a flood
Of harmony, with rapture more divine;
Type of the wise, who soar, but never roam;
True to the kindred points of Heaven and Home."

Wordsworth.

While John of Aragon had recourse to such means to enable his son to escape the vigilant and vindictive emissaries of the King of Castile, there were anxious hearts in Valladolid, awaiting the result with the impatience and doubt that ever attend the execution of hazardous enterprises. Among others who felt this deep interest in the movements of Ferdinand of Aragon and his companions, were a few whom it has now become necessary to introduce to the reader.

Although Valladolid had not then reached the magnificence it subsequently acquired as the capital of Charles V., it was an ancient, and, for the age, a magnificent and luxurious town, possessing its palaces, as well as its more inferior abodes. To the principal of the former, the residence of John de Vivero—a distinguished noble of the kingdom—we must repair in imagination; where companions more agreeable than those we have just quitted, await us, and who were then themselves awaiting, with deep anxiety, the arrival of a messenger with tidings from Dueñas. The particular apartment that it will be necessary to imagine, had much of the rude splendor of the period, united to that air of comfort and fitness that woman seldom fails to impart to the portion of any edifice that comes directly under her control. In the year 1469, Spain was fast approaching the termination of that great struggle which had already endured seven centuries, and in which the Christian and the Mussulman contended for the mastery of the peninsula. The latter had long held sway in the southern parts of Leon, and had left behind him, in the palaces of this town, some of the traces of his barbaric magnificence. The lofty and fretted ceilings were not as glorious as those to be found further south, it is true; still, the Moor had been here, and the name of Veled Vlid—since changed to Valladolid—denotes its Arabic connection. In the room just mentioned, and in the principal palace of this ancient town—that of John de Vivero—were two females, in earnest and engrossing discourse. Both were young, and, though in very different styles, both would have been deemed beautiful in any age or region of the earth. One, indeed, was surpassingly lovely. She had just reached her nineteenth year—an age when the female form has received its full development in that generous climate; and the most imaginative poet of Spain—a country so renowned for beauty of form in the sex—could not have conceived of a person more symmetrical. The hands, feet, bust, and all the outlines, were those of feminine loveliness; while the stature, without rising to a height to suggest the idea of any thing masculine, was sufficient to ennoble an air of quiet dignity. The beholder, at first, was a little at a loss to know whether the influence to which he submitted, proceeded most from the perfection of the body itself, or from the expression that the soul within imparted to the almost faultless exterior. The face was, in all respects, worthy of the form. Although born beneath the sun of Spain, her lineage carried her back, through a long line of kings, to the Gothic sovereigns; and its frequent intermarriages with foreign princesses, had produced in her countenance that intermixture of the brilliancy of the north with the witchery of the south, that probably is nearest to the perfection of feminine loveliness.

Her complexion was fair, and her rich locks had that tint of the auburn which approaches as near as possible to the more marked color that gives it warmth, without attaining any of the latter's distinctive hue. "Her mild blue eyes," says an eminent historian, "beamed with intelligence and sensibility." In these indexes to the soul, indeed, were to be found her highest claims to loveliness, for they bespoke no less the beauty within, than the beauty without; imparting to features of exquisite delicacy and symmetry, a serene expression of dignity and moral excellence, that was remarkably softened by a modesty that seemed as much allied to the sensibilities of a woman, as to the purity of an angel. To add to all these charms, though of royal blood, and educated in a court, an earnest, but meek sincerity presided over every look and thought—as thought was betrayed in the countenance—adding the illumination of truth to the lustre of youth and beauty.

The attire of this princess was simple, for, happily, the taste of the age enabled those who worked for the toilet to consult the proportions of nature; though the materials were rich, and such as became her high rank. A single cross of diamonds sparkled on a neck of snow, to which it was attached by a short string of pearls; and a few rings, decked with stones of price, rather cumbered than adorned hands that needed no ornaments to rivet the gaze. Such was Isabella of Castile, in her days of maiden retirement and maiden pride—while waiting the issues of those changes that were about to put their seal on her own future fortunes, as well as on those of posterity even to our own times.

Her companion was Beatriz de Bobadilla, the friend of her childhood and infancy, and who continued, to the last, the friend of her prime, and of her death-bed. This lady, a little older than the princess, was of more decided Spanish mien, for, though of an ancient and illustrious house, policy and necessity had not caused so many foreign intermarriages in her race, as had been required in that of her royal mistress. Her eyes were black and sparkling, bespeaking a generous soul, and a resolution so high that some commentators have termed it valor; while her hair was dark as the raven's wing. Like that of her royal mistress, her form exhibited the grace and loveliness of young womanhood, developed by the generous warmth of Spain; though her stature was, in a slight degree, less noble, and the outlines of her figure, in about an equal proportion, less perfect. In short, nature had drawn some such distinction between the exceeding grace and high moral charms that encircled the beauty of the princess, and those which belonged to her noble friend, as the notions of men had established between their respective conditions; though, considered singly, as women, either would have been deemed pre-eminently winning and attractive.

At the moment we have selected for the opening of the scene that is to follow, Isabella, fresh from the morning toilet, was seated in a chair, leaning lightly on one of its arms, in an attitude that interest in the subject she was discussing, and confidence in her companion, had naturally produced; while Beatriz de Bobadilla occupied a low stool at her feet, bending her body in respectful affection so far forward, as to allow the fairer hair of the princess to mingle with her own dark curls, while the face of the latter appeared to repose on the head of her friend. As no one else was present, the reader will at once infer, from the entire absence of Castilian etiquette and Spanish reserve, that the dialogue they held was strictly confidential, and that it was governed more by the feelings of nature, than by the artificial rules that usually regulate the intercourse of courts.

"I have prayed, Beatriz, that God would direct my judgment in this weighty concern," said the princess, in continuation of some previous observation; "and I hope I have as much kept in view the happiness of my future subjects, in the choice I have made, as my own."

"None shall presume to question it," said Beatriz de Bobadilla; "for had it pleased you to wed the Grand Turk, the Castilians would not gainsay your wish, such is their love!"

"Say, rather, such is thy love for me, my good Beatriz, that thou fanciest this," returned Isabella, smiling, and raising her face from the other's head.

"Our Castilians might overlook such a sin, but I could not pardon myself for forgetting that I am a Christian. Beatriz, I have been sorely tried, in this matter!"

"But the hour of trial is nearly passed. Holy Maria! what lightness of reflection, and vanity, and misjudging of self, must exist in man, to embolden some who have dared to aspire to become your husband! You were yet a child when they betrothed you to Don Carlos, a prince old enough to be your father; and then, as if that were not sufficient to warm Castilian blood, they chose the King of Portugal for you, and he might well have passed for a generation still more remote! Much as I love you, Doña Isabella, and my own soul is scarce dearer to me than your person and mind, for nought do I respect you more, than for the noble and princely resolution, child as you then were, with which you denied the king, in his wicked wish to make you Queen of Portugal."

"Don Enriquez is my brother, Beatriz; and thine and my royal master."

"Ah! bravely did you tell them all," continued Beatriz de Bobadilla, with sparkling eyes, and a feeling of exultation that caused her to overlook the quiet rebuke of her mistress; "and worthy was it of a princess of the royal house of Castile! 'The Infantas of Castile,' you said, 'could not be disposed of, in marriage, without the consent of the nobles of the realm;' and with that fit reply they were glad to be content."

"And yet, Beatriz, am I about to dispose of an Infanta of Castile, without even consulting its nobles."

"Say not that, my excellent mistress. There is not a loyal and gallant cavalier between the Pyrenees and the sea, who will not, in his heart, approve of your choice. The character, and age, and other qualities of the suitor, make a sensible difference in these concerns. But unfit as Don Alfonso of Portugal was, and is, to be the wedded husband of Doña Isabella of Castile, what shall we say to the next suitor who appeared as a pretender to your royal hand—Don Pedro Giron, the Master of Calatrava! truly a most worthy lord for a maiden of the royal house! Out upon him! A Pachecho might think himself full honorably mated, could he have found a damsel of Bobadilla to elevate his race!"

"That ill-assorted union was imposed upon my brother by unworthy favorites; and God, in his holy providence, saw fit to defeat their wishes, by hurrying their intended bridegroom to an unexpected grave!"

"Ay! had it not pleased his blessed will so to dispose of Don Pedro, other means would not have been wanting!"

"This little hand of thine, Beatriz," returned the princess, gravely, though she smiled affectionately on her friend as she took the hand in question, "was not made for the deed its owner menaced."

"That which its owner menaced," replied Beatriz, with eyes flashing fire, "this hand would have executed, before Isabella of Castile should be the doomed bride of the Grand Master of Calatrava. What! was the purest, loveliest virgin of Castile, and she of royal birth—nay, the rightful heiress of the crown—to be sacrificed to a lawless libertine, because it had pleased Don Henry to forget his station and duties, and make a favorite of a craven miscreant!"

"Thou always forgettest, Beatriz, that Don Enriquez is our lord the king, and my royal brother."

"I do not forget, Señora, that you are the royal sister of our lord the king, and that Pedro de Giron, or Pachecho, whichever it might suit the ancient Portuguese page to style him, was altogether unworthy to sit in your presence, much less to become your wedded husband. Oh! what days of anguish were those, my gracious lady, when your knees ached with bending in prayer, that this might not be! But God would not permit it—neither would I! That dagger should have pierced his heart, before ear of his should have heard the vows of Isabella of Castile!"

"Speak no more of this, good Beatriz, I pray thee," said the princess, shuddering, and crossing herself; "they were, in sooth, days of anguish; but what were they in comparison with the passion of the Son of God, who gave himself a sacrifice for our sins! Name it not, then; it was good for my soul to be thus tried; and thou knowest that the evil was turned from me—more, I doubt not, by the efficacy of our prayers, than by that of thy dagger. If thou wilt speak of my suitors, surely there are others better worthy of the trouble."

A light gleamed about the dark eye of Beatriz, and a smile struggled toward her pretty mouth; for well did she understand that the royal, but bashful maiden, would gladly hear something of him on whom her choice had finally fallen. Although ever disposed to do that which was grateful to her mistress, with a woman's coquetry, Beatriz determined to approach the more pleasing part of the subject coyly, and by a regular gradation of events, in the order in which they had actually occurred.

"Then, there was Monsieur de Guienne, the brother of King Louis of France," she resumed, affecting contempt in her manner; "*he* would fain become the husband of the future Queen of Castile! But even our most unworthy Castilians soon saw the unfitness of that union. Their pride was unwilling to run the chance of becoming a fief of France."

"That misfortune could never have befallen our beloved Castile," interrupted Isabella with dignity; "had I espoused the King of France himself, he would have learned to respect me as the Queen Proprietor of this ancient realm, and not have looked upon me as a subject."

"Then, Señora," continued Beatriz, looking up into Isabella's face, and laughing—"was your own royal kinsman, Don Ricardo of Gloucester; he that they say was born with teeth, and who carries already a burthen so heavy on his back, that he may well thank his patron saint that he is not also to be loaded with the affairs of Castile." [1]

"Thy tongue runneth riot, Beatriz. They tell me that Don Ricardo is a noble and aspiring prince; that he is, one day, likely to wed some princess, whose merit may well console him for his failure in Castile. But what more hast thou to offer concerning my suitors?"

"Nay, what more can I say, my beloved mistress? We have now reached Don Fernando, literally the first, as he proveth to be the last, and as we know him to be, the best of them all."

"I think I have been guided by the motives that become my birth and future hopes, in choosing Don Ferdinand," said Isabella, meekly, though she was uneasy in spite of her royal views of matrimony; "since nothing can so much tend to the peace of our dear kingdom, and to the success of the great cause of Christianity, as to unite Castile and Aragon under one crown."

"By uniting their sovereigns in holy wedlock," returned Beatriz, with respectful gravity, though a smile again struggled around her pouting lips. "What if Don Fernando is the most youthful, the handsomest, the most valiant, and the most agreeable prince in Christendom, it is no fault of yours, since you did not make him, but have only accepted him for a husband!"

"Nay, this exceedeth discretion and respect, my good Beatriz," returned Isabella, affecting to frown, even while she blushed deeply at her own emotions, and looked gratified at the praises of her betrothed. "Thou knowest that I have never beheld my cousin, the King of Sicily."

"Very true, Señora; but Father Alonso de Coca hath—and a surer eye, or truer tongue than his, do not exist in Castile."

"Beatriz, I pardon thy license, however unjust and unseemly, because I know thou lovest me, and lookest rather at mine own happiness, than at that of my people," said the princess, the effect of whose gravity now was not diminished by any betrayal of natural feminine weakness—for she felt slightly offended. "Thou knowest, or ought'st to know, that a maiden of royal birth is bound principally to consult the interests of the state, in bestowing her hand, and that the idle fancies of village girls have little in common with her duties. Nay, what virgin of noble extraction, like thyself, even, would dream of aught else than of submitting to the counsel of her family, in taking a husband? If I have selected Don Fernando of Aragon, from among many princes, it is, doubtless, because the alliance is more suited to the interests of Castile, than any other that hath offered. Thou seest, Beatriz, that the Castilians and the Aragonese spring from the same source, and have the same habits and prejudices. They speak the same language" —

"Nay, dearest lady, do not confound the pure Castilian with the dialect of the mountains!"

"Well, have thy fling, wayward one, if thou wilt; but we can easier teach the nobles of Aragon our purer Spanish, than we can teach it to the Gaul. Then, Don Fernando is of my own race; the House of Trastamara cometh of Castile and her monarchs, and we may at least hope that the King of Sicily will be able to make himself understood."

"If he could not, he were no true knight! The man whose tongue should fail him, when the stake was a royal maiden of a beauty surpassing that of the dawn—of an excellence that already touches on heaven—of a crown" —

"Girl, girl, thy tongue is getting the mastery of thee—such discourse ill befitteth thee and me."

"And yet, Doña Ysabel, my tongue is close bound to my heart."

"I do believe thee, my good Beatriz; but we should bethink us both of our last shrivings, and of the ghostly counsel that we then received. Such nattering discourse seemeth light, when we remember our manifold transgressions, and our many occasions for forgiveness. As for this marriage, I would have thee think that it has been contracted on my part, with the considerations and motives of a princess, and not through any light indulgence of my fancies. Thou knowest that I have never beheld Don Fernando, and that he hath never even looked upon me."

"Assuredly, dearest lady and honored mistress, all this I know, and see, and believe; and I also agree that it were unseemly and little befitting her birth, for even a noble maiden to contract the all-important obligations of marriage, with no better motive than the light impulses of a country wench. Nothing is more just than that we are alike bound to consult our own dignity, and the wishes of kinsmen and friends; and that our duty, and the habits of piety and submission in which we have been reared, are better pledges for our connubial affection than any caprices of a girlish imagination. Still, my honored lady, it is most fortunate that your high obligations point to one as youthful, brave, noble, and chivalrous, as is the King of Sicily, as we well know, by Father Alonso's representations, to be the fact; and that all my friends unite in saying that Don Andres de Cabrera, madcap and silly as he is, will make an exceedingly excellent husband for Beatriz de Bobadilla!"

Isabella, habitually dignified and reserved as she was, had her confidants and her moments for unbending; and Beatriz was the principal among the former, while the present instant was one of the latter. She smiled, therefore, at this sally; and parting, with her own fair hand, the dark locks on the brow of her friend, she regarded her much as the mother regards her child, when sudden passages of tenderness come over the heart.

"If madcap should wed madcap, *thy* friends, at least, have judged rightly," answered the princess. Then, pausing an instant, as if in deep thought, she continued in a graver manner, though modesty shone in her tell-tale complexion, and the sensibility that beamed in her eyes betrayed that she now felt more as a woman than as a future queen bent only on the happiness of her people: "As this interview draweth near, I suffer an embarrassment I had not thought it easy to inflict on an Infanta of Castile. To thee, my faithful Beatriz, I will acknowledge, that were the King of Sicily as old as Don Alfonso of Portugal, or were he as effeminate and unmanly as Monsieur of Guienne; were he, in sooth, less engaging and young, I should feel less embarrassment in meeting him, than I now experience."

"This is passing strange, Señora! Now, I will confess that I would not willingly abate in Don Andres, one hour of his life, which has been sufficiently long as it is; one grace of his person, if indeed the honest cavalier hath any to boast of; or one single perfection of either body or mind."

"Thy case is not mine, Beatriz. Thou knowest the Marquis of Moya; hast listened to his discourse, and art accustomed to his praises and his admiration."

"Holy St. Iago of Spain! Do not distrust any thing, Señora, on account of unfamiliarity with such matters—for, of all learning, it is easiest to learn to relish praise and admiration!"

"True, daughter"—(for so Isabella often termed her friend, though her junior: in later life, and after the princess had become a queen, this, indeed, was her usual term of endearment)—"true, daughter, when praise and admiration are freely given and fairly merited. But I distrust, myself, my claims to be thus viewed, and the feelings with which Don Fernando may first behold me. I know—nay, I *feel* him to be graceful, and noble, and valiant, and generous, and good; comely to the eye, and strict of duty to our holy religion; as illustrious in qualities as in birth; and I tremble to think of my own unsuitableness to be his bride and queen."

"God's Justice!—I should like to meet the impudent Aragonese noble that would dare to hint as much as this! If Don Fernando is noble, are you not nobler, Señora, as coming of the senior branch of the same house; if he is young, are you not equally so; if he is wise, are you not wiser; if he is comely, are you not more of an angel than a woman; if he is valiant, are you not virtuous; if he is graceful, are you not grace itself; if he is generous, are you not good, and what is more, are you not the very soul of generosity; if he is strict of duty in matters of our holy religion, are you not an angel?"

"Good sooth—good sooth—Beatriz, thou art a comforter! I could reprove thee for this idle tongue, but I know thee honest."

"This is no more than that deep modesty, honored mistress, which ever maketh you quicker to see the merits of others, than to perceive your own. Let Don Fernando look to it! Though he come in all the pomp and glory of his many crowns, I warrant you we find him a royal maiden in Castile, who shall abash him and rebuke his vanity, even while she appears before him in the sweet guise of her own meek nature!"

"I have said naught of Don Fernando's vanity, Beatriz—nor do I esteem him in the least inclined to so weak a feeling; and as for pomp, we well know that gold no more abounds at Zaragosa than at Valladolid, albeit he hath many crowns, in possession, and in reserve. Notwithstanding all thy foolish but friendly tongue hath uttered, I distrust myself, and not the King of Sicily. Methinks I could meet any other prince in Christendom with indifference—or, at least, as becometh my rank and sex; but I confess, I tremble at the thought of encountering the eyes and opinions of my noble cousin."

Beatriz listened with interest; and when her royal mistress ceased speaking, she kissed her hand affectionately, and then pressed it to her heart.

"Let Don Fernando tremble, rather, Señora, at encountering yours," she answered.

"Nay, Beatriz, we know that he hath nothing to dread, for report speaketh but too favorably of him. But, why linger here in doubt and apprehension, when the staff on which it is my duty to lean, is ready to receive its burthen: Father Alonso doubtless waiteth for us, and we will now join him."

The princess and her friend now repaired to the chapel of the palace, where her confessor celebrated the daily mass. The self-distrust which disturbed the feelings of the modest Isabella was appeased by the holy rites, or, rather, it took refuge on that rock where she was accustomed to place all her troubles, with her sins. As the little assemblage left the chapel, one, hot with haste, arrived with the expected, but still doubted tidings, that the King of Sicily had reached Dueñas in safety, and that, as he was now in the very centre of his supporters, there could no longer be any reasonable distrust of the speedy celebration of the contemplated marriage.

Isabella was much overcome with this news, and required more than usual of the care of Beatriz de Bobadilla, to restore her to that sweet serenity of mind and air, which ordinarily rendered her presence as attractive as it was commanding. An hour or two spent in meditation and prayer, however, finally produced a gentle calm in her feelings, and these two friends were again alone, in the very apartment where we first introduced them to the reader.

"Hast thou seen Don Andres de Cabrera?" demanded the princess, taking a hand from a brow which had been often pressed in a sort of bewildered recollection

Beatriz de Bobadilla blushed—and then she laughed outright, with a freedom that the long-established affection of her mistress did not rebuke.

"For a youth of thirty, and a cavalier well hacked in the wars of the Moors, Don Andres hath a nimble foot," she answered. "He brought hither the tidings of the arrival; and with it he brought his own delightful person, to show it was no lie. For one so experienced, he hath a strong propensity to talk; and so, in sooth, while you, my honored mistress, would be in your closet alone, I could but listen to all the marvels of the journey. It seems, Señora, that they did not reach Dueñas any too soon; for the only purse among them was mislaid, or blown away by the wind on account of its lightness."

"I trust this accident hath been repaired. Few of the house of Trastamara have much gold at this trying moment, and yet none are wont to be entirely without it."

"Don Andres is neither beggar nor miser. He is now in our Castile, where I doubt not he is familiar with the Jews and money-lenders; as these last must know the full value of his lands, the King of Sicily will not want. I hear, too, that the Count of Treviño hath conducted nobly with him."

"It shall be well for the Count of Treviño that he hath had this liberality. But, Beatriz, bring forth the writing materials; it is meet that I, at once, acquaint Don Enriquez with this event, and with my purpose of marriage."

"Nay, dearest mistress, this is out of all rule. When a maiden, gentle or simple, intendeth marriage against her kinsmen's wishes, it is the way to wed first, and to write the letter and ask the blessing when the evil is done."

"Go to, light-of-speech! Thou hast spoken; now bring the pens and paper. The king is not only my lord and sovereign, but he is my nearest of kin, and should be my father."

"And Doña Joanna of Portugal, his royal consort, and our illustrious queen, should be your mother; and a fitting guide would she be to any modest virgin! No—no—my beloved mistress; your royal mother was the Doña Isabella of Portugal—and a very different princess was she from this, her wanton niece."

"Thou givest thyself too much license, Doña Beatriz, and forgettest my request. I desire to write to my brother the king."

It was so seldom that Isabella spoke sternly, that her friend started, and the tears rushed to her eyes at this rebuke; but she procured the writing materials, before she presumed to look into Isabella's face, in order to ascertain if she were really angered. There all was beautiful serenity again; and the Lady of Bobadilla, perceiving that her mistress's mind was altogether occupied with the matter before her, and that she had already forgotten her displeasure, chose to make no further allusion to the subject.

Isabella now wrote her celebrated letter, in which she appeared to forget all her natural timidity, and to speak solely as a princess. By the treaty of Toros de Guisando, in which, setting aside the claims of Joanna of Portugal's daughter, she had been recognized as the heiress of the throne, it had been stipulated that she should not marry without the king's consent; and she now apologized for the step she was about to take, on the substantial plea that her enemies had disregarded the solemn compact entered into not to urge her into any union that was unsuitable or disagreeable to herself. She then alluded to the political advantages that would follow the union of the crowns of Castile and Aragon, and solicited the king's approbation of the step she was about to take. This letter, after having been submitted to John de Vivero, and others of her council, was dispatched by a special messenger—after which act the arrangements necessary as preliminaries to a meeting between the betrothed were entered into. Castilian etiquette was proverbial, even in that age; and the discussion led to a proposal that Isabella rejected with her usual modesty and discretion.

"It seemeth to me," said John de Vivero, "that this alliance should not take place without some admission, on the part of Don Fernando, of the inferiority of Aragon to our own Castile. The house of the latter kingdom is but a junior branch of the reigning House of Castile, and the former territory of old was admitted to have a dependency on the latter."

This proposition was much applauded, until the beautiful and natural sentiments of the princess, herself, interposed to expose its weakness and its deformities.

"It is doubtless true," she said, "that Don Juan of Aragon is the son of the younger brother of my royal grandfather; but he is none the less a king. Nay, besides his crown of Aragon—a country, if thou wilt, which is inferior to Castile—he hath those of Naples and Sicily; not to speak of Navarre, over which he ruleth, although it may not be with too much right. Don Fernando even weareth the crown of Sicily, by the renunciation of Don Juan; and shall he, a crowned sovereign, make concessions to one who is barely a princess, and whom it may never please God to conduct to a throne? Moreover, Don John of Vivero, I beseech thee to remember the errand that bringeth the King of Sicily to Valladolid. Both he and I have two parts to perform, and two characters to maintain—those of prince and princess, and those of Christians wedded and bound by holy marriage ties. It would ill become one that is about to take on herself the duties and obligations of a wife, to begin the intercourse with exactions that should be humiliating to the pride and self-respect of her lord. Aragon may truly be an inferior realm to Castile—but Ferdinand of Aragon is even now every way the equal of Isabella of Castile; and when he shall receive my vows, and, with them, my duty and my affections"—Isabella's color deepened, and her mild eye lighted with a sort of holy enthusiasm—"as befitteth a woman, though an infidel, he would become, in some particulars, my superior. Let me, then, hear no more of this; for it could not nearly as much pain Don Fernando to make the concessions ye require, as it paineth me to hear of them."

CHAPTER III

"Nice customs curt'sy to great kings. Dear Kate, you and
.I cannot be confined within the weak list of a country's
fashion. We are the makers of manners; and the liberty that
follows our places, stops the mouths of all fault-finders." —
Henry V.

Notwithstanding her high resolution, habitual firmness, and a serenity of mind, that seemed to pervade the moral system of Isabella, like a deep, quiet current of enthusiasm, but which it were truer to assign to the high and fixed principles that guided all her actions, her heart beat tumultuously, and her native reserve, which almost amounted to shyness, troubled her sorely, as the hour arrived when she was first to behold the prince she had accepted for a husband. Castilian etiquette, no less than the magnitude of the political interests involved in the intended union, had drawn out the preliminary negotiations several days; the bridegroom being left, all that time, to curb his impatience to behold the princess, as best he might.

On the evening of the 15th of October, 1469, however, every obstacle being at length removed, Don Fernando threw himself into the saddle, and, accompanied by only four attendants, among whom was Andres de Cabrera, he quietly took his way, without any of the usual accompaniments of his high rank, toward the palace of John of Vivero, in the city of Valladolid. The Archbishop of Toledo was of the faction of the princess, and this prelate, a warlike and active partisan, was in readiness to receive the accepted suitor, and to conduct him to the presence of his mistress.

Isabella, attended only by Beatriz de Bobadilla, was in waiting for the interview, in the apartment already mentioned; and by one of those mighty efforts that even the most retiring of the sex can make, on great occasions, she received her future husband with quite as much of the dignity of a princess as of the timidity of a woman. Ferdinand of Aragon had been prepared to meet one of singular grace and beauty; but the mixture of angelic modesty with a loveliness that almost surpassed that of her sex, produced a picture approaching so much nearer to heaven than to earth, that, though one of circumspect behavior, and much accustomed to suppress emotion, he actually started, and his feet were momentarily riveted to the floor, when the glorious vision first met his eye. Then, recovering himself, he advanced eagerly, and taking the little hand which neither met nor repulsed the attempt, he pressed it to his lips with a warmth that seldom accompanies the first interviews of those whose passions are usually so factitious.

"This happy moment hath at length arrived, my illustrious and beautiful cousin!" he said, with a truth of feeling that went directly to the pure and tender heart of Isabella; for no skill in courtly phrases can ever give to the accents of deceit, the point and emphasis that belong to sincerity. "I have thought it would never arrive; but this blessed moment—thanks to our own St. Iago, whom I have not ceased to implore with intercessions—more than rewards me for all anxieties."

"I thank my Lord the Prince, and bid him right welcome," modestly returned Isabella. "The difficulties that have been overcome, in order to effect this meeting, are but types of the difficulties we shall have to conquer as we advance through life."

Then followed a few courteous expressions concerning the hopes of the princess that her cousin had wanted for nothing, since his arrival in Castile, with suitable answers; when Don Ferdinand led her to an armed-chair, assuming himself the stool on which Beatriz de Bobadilla was wont to be seated, in her familiar intercourse with her royal mistress. Isabella, however, sensitively alive to the pretensions of the Castilians, who were fond of asserting the superiority of their own country over that of Aragon, would not quietly submit to this arrangement, but declined to be seated, unless her suitor would take the chair prepared for him also, saying—

"It ill befitteth one who hath little more than some royalty of blood, and her dependence on God, to be thus placed, while the King of Sicily is so unworthily bestowed."

"Let me entreat that it may be so," returned the king. "All considerations of earthly rank vanish in this presence; view me as a knight, ready and desirous of proving his fealty in any court or field of Christendom, and treat me as such."

Isabella, who had that high tact which teaches the precise point where breeding becomes neuter and airs commence, blushed and smiled, but no longer declined to be seated. It was not so much the mere words of her cousin that went to her heart, as the undisguised admiration of his looks, the animation of his eye, and the frank sincerity of his manner. With a woman's instinct she perceived that the impression she had made was favorable, and, with a woman's sensibility, her heart was ready, under the circumstances, to dissolve in tenderness at the discovery. This mutual satisfaction soon opened the way to a freer conversation; and, ere half an hour was passed, the archbishop—who, though officially ignorant of the language and wishes of lovers, was practically sufficiently familiar with both—contrived to draw the two or three courtiers who were present, into an adjoining room, where, though the door continued open, he placed them with so much discretion that neither eye nor ear could be any restraint on what was passing. As for Beatriz de Bobadilla, whom female etiquette required should remain in the same room with her royal mistress, she was so much engaged with Andres de Cabrera, that half a dozen thrones might have been disposed of between the royal pair, and she none the wiser.

Although Isabella did not lose that mild reserve and feminine modesty that threw so winning a grace around her person, even to the day of her death, she gradually grew more calm as the discourse proceeded; and, falling back on her self-respect, womanly dignity, and, not a little, on those stores of knowledge that she had been diligently collecting, while others similarly situated had wasted their time in the vanities of courts, she was quickly at her ease, if not wholly in that tranquil state of mind to which she had been accustomed.

"I trust there can now be no longer any delay to the celebration of our union by holy church," observed the king, in continuation of the subject. "All that can be required of us both, as those entrusted with the cares and interests of realms, hath been observed, and I may have a claim to look to my own happiness. We are not strangers to each other, Doña Isabella; for our grandfathers were brothers, and from infancy up, have I been taught to reverence thy virtues, and to strive to emulate thy holy duty to God."

"I have not betrothed myself lightly, Don Fernando," returned the princess, blushing, even while she assumed the majesty of a queen; "and with the subject so fully discussed, the wisdom of the union so fully established, and the necessity of promptness so apparent, no idle delays shall proceed from me. I had thought that the ceremony might be had on the fourth day from this, which will give us both time to prepare for an occasion so solemn, by suitable attention to the offices of the church."

"It must be as thou wiliest," said the king, respectfully bowing; "and now there remaineth but a few preparations, and we shall have no reproaches of forgetfulness. Thou knowest, Doña Isabella, how sorely my father is beset by his enemies, and I need scarce tell thee that his coffers are empty. In good sooth, my fair cousin, nothing but my earnest desire to possess myself, at as early a day as possible, of the precious boon that Providence and thy goodness"—

"Mingle not, Don Fernando, any of the acts of God and his providence, with the wisdom and petty expedients of his creatures," said Isabella, earnestly.

"To seize upon the precious boon, then, that Providence appeared willing to bestow," rejoined the king, crossing himself, while he bowed his head, as much, perhaps, in deference to the pious feelings of his affianced wife, as in deference to a higher Power—"would not admit of delay, and we quitted Zaragosa better provided with hearts loyal toward the treasures we were to find in Valladolid, than with gold. Even that we had, by a mischance, hath gone to enrich some lucky varlet in an inn."

"Doña Beatriz de Bobadilla hath acquainted me with the mishap," said Isabella, smiling; "and truly we shall commence our married lives with but few of the goods of the world in present possession. I have little more to offer thee, Fernando, than a true heart, and a spirit that I think may be trusted for its fidelity."

"In obtaining thee, my excellent cousin, I obtain sufficient to satisfy the desires of any reasonable man. Still, something is due to our rank and future prospects, and it shall not be said that thy nuptials passed like those of a common subject."

"Under ordinary circumstances it might not appear seemly for one of my sex to furnish the means for her own bridal," answered the princess, the blood stealing to her face until it crimsoned even her brow and temples; maintaining, otherwise, that beautiful tranquillity of mien which marked her ordinary manner—"but the well-being of two states depending on our union, vain emotions must be suppressed. I am not without jewels, and Valladolid hath many Hebrews: thou wilt permit me to part with the baubles for such an object."

"So that thou preservest for me the jewel in which that pure mind is encased," said the King of Sicily, gallantly, "I care not if I never see another. But there will not be this need; for our friends, who have more generous souls than well-filled coffers too, can give such warranty to the lenders as will procure the means. I charge myself with this duty, for henceforth, my cousin—may I not say my betrothed!" —

"The term is even dearer than any that belongeth to blood, Fernando," answered the princess, with a simple sincerity of manner that set at nought the ordinary affectations and artificial feelings of her sex, while it left the deepest reverence for her modesty—"and we might be excused for using it. I trust God will bless our union, not only to our own happiness, but to that of our people."

"Then, my betrothed, henceforth we have but a common fortune, and thou wilt trust in me for the provision for thy wants."

"Nay, Fernando," answered Isabella, smiling, "imagine what we will, we cannot imagine ourselves the children of two hidalgos about to set forth in the world with humble dowries. Thou art a king, even now; and by the treaty of Toros de Guisando, I am solemnly recognized as the heiress of Castile. We must, therefore, have our separate means, as well as our separate duties, though I trust hardly our separate interests."

"Thou wilt never find me failing in that respect which is due to thy rank, or in that duty which it befitteth me to render thee, as the head of our ancient House, next to thy royal brother, the king."

"Thou hast well considered, Don Fernando, the treaty of marriage, and accepted cheerfully, I trust, all of its several conditions?"

"As becometh the importance of the measures, and the magnitude of the benefit I was to receive."

"I would have them acceptable to thee, as well as expedient; for, though so soon to become thy wife, I can never cease to remember that I shall be Queen of this country."

"Thou mayest be assured, my beautiful betrothed, that Ferdinand of Aragon will be the last to deem thee aught else."

"I look on my duties as coming from God, and on myself as one rigidly accountable to him for their faithful discharge. Sceptres may not be treated as toys, Fernando, to be trifled with; for man beareth no heavier burden, than when he beareth a crown."

"The maxims of our House have not been forgotten in Aragon, my betrothed—and I rejoice to find that they are the same in both kingdoms."

"We are not to think principally of ourselves in entering upon this engagement," continued Isabella, earnestly—"for that would be supplanting the duties of princes by the feelings of the lover. Thou hast frequently perused, and sufficiently conned the marriage articles, I trust?"

"There hath been sufficient leisure for that, my cousin, as they have now been signed these nine months."

"If I may have seemed to thee exacting in some particulars," continued Isabella, with the same earnest and beautiful simplicity as usually marked her deportment in all the relations of life—"it is because the duties of a sovereign may not be overlooked. Thou knowest, moreover, Fernando, the influence that the husband is wont to acquire over the wife, and wilt feel the necessity of my protecting my Castilians, in the fullest manner, against my own weaknesses."

"If thy Castilians do not suffer until they suffer from that cause, Doña Isabella, their lot will indeed be blessed."

"These are words of gallantry, and I must reprove their use on an occasion so serious, Fernando. I am a few months thy senior, and shall assume an elder sister's rights, until they are lost in the obligations of a wife. Thou hast seen in those articles, how anxiously I would protect my Castilians against any supremacy of the stranger. Thou knowest that many of the greatest of this realm are opposed to our union, through apprehension of Aragonese sway, and wilt observe how studiously we have striven to appease their jealousies."

"Thy motives, Doña Isabella, have been understood, and thy wishes in this and all other particulars shall be respected."

"I would be thy faithful and submissive wife," returned the princess, with an earnest but gentle look at her betrothed; "but I would also that Castile should preserve her rights and her independence. What will be thy influence, the maiden that freely bestoweth her hand, need hardly say; but we must preserve the appearance of separate states."

"Confide in me, my cousin. They who live fifty years hence will say that Don Fernando knew how to respect his obligations and to discharge his duty."

"There is the stipulation, too, to war upon the Moor. I shall never feel that the Christians of Spain have been true to the faith, while the follower of the arch-imposter of Mecca remaineth in the peninsula."

"Thou and thy archbishop could not have imposed a more agreeable duty, than to place my lance in rest against the infidels. My spurs have been gained in those wars, already; and no sooner shall we be crowned, than thou wilt see my perfect willingness to aid in driving back the miscreants to their original sands."

"There remaineth but one thing more upon my mind, gentle cousin. Thou knowest the evil influence that besets my brother, and that it hath disaffected a large portion of his nobles as well as of his cities. We shall both be sorely tempted to wage war upon him, and to assume the sceptre before it pleaseth God to accord it to us, in the course of nature. I would have thee respect Don Enriquez, not only as the head of our royal house, but as my brother and anointed master. Should evil counsellors press him to attempt aught against our persons or rights, it will be lawful to resist; but I pray thee, Fernando, on no excuse seek to raise thy hand in rebellion against my rightful sovereign."

"Let Don Enriquez, then, be chary of his Beltraneja!" answered the prince with warmth. "By St. Peter! I have rights of mine own that come before those of that ill-gotten mongrel! The whole House of Trastamara hath an interest in stifling that spurious scion which hath been so fraudulently engrafted on its princely stock!"

"Thou art warm, Don Fernando, and even the eye of Beatriz de Bobadilla reproveth thy heat. The unfortunate Joanna never can impair our rights to the throne, for there are few nobles in Castile so unworthy as to wish to see the crown bestowed where it is believed the blood of Pelayo doth not flow."

"Don Enriquez hath not kept faith with thee, Isabella, since the treaty of Toros de Guisando!"

"My brother is surrounded by wicked counsellors—and then, Fernando,"—the princess blushed crimson as she spoke—"neither have we been able rigidly to adhere to that convention, since one of its conditions was that my hand should not be bestowed without the consent of the king."

"He hath driven us into this measure, and hath only to reproach himself with our failure on this point."

"I endeavor so to view it, though many have been my prayers for forgiveness of this seeming breach of faith. I am not superstitious, Fernando, else might I think God would frown on a union that is contracted in the face of pledges like these. But, it is well to distinguish between motives, and we have a right to believe that He who readeth the heart, will not judge the well-intentioned severely. Had not Don Enriquez attempted to seize my person, with the plain purpose of forcing me to a marriage against my will, this decisive step could not have been necessary, and would not have been taken."

"I have reason to thank my patron saint, beautiful cousin, that thy will was less compliant than thy tyrants had believed."

"I could not plight my troth to the King of Portugal, or to Monsieur de Guienne, or to any that they proposed to me, for my future lord," answered Isabella, ingenuously. "It ill befitted royal or noble maidens to set up their own inexperienced caprices in opposition to the wisdom of their friends, and the task is not difficult for a virtuous wife to learn to love her husband, when nature and opinion are not too openly violated in the choice; but I have had too much thought for my soul to wish to expose it to so severe a trial, in contracting the marriage duties."

"I feel that I am only too unworthy of thee, Isabella—but thou must train me to be that thou wouldst wish; I can only promise thee a most willing and attentive scholar."

The discourse now became more general, Isabella indulging her natural curiosity and affectionate nature, by making many inquiries concerning her different relatives in Aragon. After the interview had lasted two hours or more, the King of Sicily returned to Dueñas, with the same privacy as he had observed in entering the town. The royal pair parted with feelings of increased esteem and respect, Isabella indulging in those gentle anticipations of domestic happiness that more properly belong to the tender nature of woman.

The marriage took place, with suitable pomp, on the morning of the 19th October, 1469, in the chapel of John de Vivero's palace; no less than two thousand persons, principally of condition, witnessing the ceremony. Just as the officiating priest was about to commence the offices, the eye of Isabella betrayed uneasiness, and turning to the Archbishop of Toledo, she said —

"Your grace hath promised that there should be nothing wanting to the consent of the church on this solemn occasion. It is known that Don Fernando of Aragon and I stand within the prohibited degrees."

"Most true, my Lady Isabella," returned the prelate, with a composed mien and a paternal smile. "Happily, our Holy Father Pius hath removed this impediment, and the church smileth on this blessed union in every particular."

The archbishop then took out of his pocket a dispensation, which he read, in a clear, sonorous, steady voice; when every shade disappeared from the serene brow of Isabella, and the ceremony proceeded. Years elapsed before this pious and submissive Christian princess discovered that she had been imposed on, the bull that was then read having been an invention of the old King of Aragon and the prelate, not without suspicions of a connivance on the part of the bridegroom. This deception had been practised from a perfect conviction that the sovereign pontiff was too much under the influence of the King of Castile, to consent to bestow the boon in opposition to that monarch's wishes. It was several years before Sixtus IV. repaired this wrong, by granting a more genuine authority.

Nevertheless, Ferdinand and Isabella became man and wife. What followed in the next twenty years must be rather glanced at than related. Henry IV. resented the step, and vain attempts were made to substitute his supposititious child, La Beltraneja, in the place of his sister, as successor to the throne. A civil war ensued, during which Isabella steadily refused to assume the crown, though often entreated; limiting her efforts to the maintenance of her rights as heiress presumptive. In 1474, or five years after her marriage, Don Henry died, and she then became Queen of Castile, though her spurious niece was also proclaimed by a small party among her subjects. The war of the succession, as it was called, lasted five years longer, when Joanna, or La Beltraneja, assumed the veil, and the rights of Isabella were generally acknowledged. About the same time, died Don John II., when Ferdinand mounted the throne of Aragon. These events virtually reduced the sovereignties of the peninsula, which had so long been cut up into petty states, to four, viz., the possessions of Ferdinand and Isabella, which included Castile, Leon, Aragon, Valencia, and many other of the finest provinces of Spain; Navarre, an insignificant kingdom in the Pyrenees; Portugal, much as it exists to-day; and Granada, the last abiding-place of the Moor, north of the strait of Gibraltar.

Neither Ferdinand, nor his royal consort, was forgetful of that clause in their marriage contract, which bound the former to undertake a war for the destruction of the Moorish power. The course of events, however, caused a delay of many years, in putting this long-projected plan in execution; but when the time finally arrived, that Providence which seemed disposed to conduct the pious Isabella, through a train of important incidents, from the reduced condition in which we have just described her to have been, to the summit of human power, did not desert its favorite. Success succeeded success—and victory, victory; until the Moor had lost fortress after fortress, town after town, and was finally besieged in his very capital—his last hold in the peninsula. As the reduction of Granada was an event that, in Christian eyes, was to be ranked second only to the rescuing of the holy sepulchre from the hands of the Infidels, so was it distinguished by some features of singularity, that have probably never before marked the course of a siege. The place submitted on the 25th November, 1491—twenty-two years after the date of the marriage just mentioned, and, it may not be amiss to observe, on the very day of the year that has become memorable in the annals of this country, as that on which the English, three centuries later, reluctantly yielded their last foothold on the coast of the republic.

In the course of the preceding summer, while the Spanish forces lay before the town, and Isabella, with her children, were anxious witnesses of the progress of events, an accident occurred that had well nigh proved fatal to the royal family, and brought destruction on the Christian arms. The pavillion of the queen took fire, and was consumed, placing the whole encampment in the utmost jeopardy. Many of the tents of the nobles were also destroyed, and much treasure, in the shape of jewelry and plate, was lost, though the injury went no further. In order to guard against the recurrence of such an accident, and probably viewing the subjection of Granada as the great act of their mutual reign—for, as yet, Time threw his veil around the future, and but one human eye foresaw the greatest of all the events of the period, which was still in reserve—the sovereigns resolved on attempting a work that, of itself, would render this siege memorable. The plan of a regular town was made, and laborers set about the construction of good substantial edifices, in which to lodge the army; thus converting the warfare into that of something like city against city. In three months this stupendous work was completed, with its avenues, streets, and squares, and received the name of Santa Fé, or Holy Faith—an appellation quite as well suited to the zeal which could achieve such a work, in the heat of a campaign, as to that general reliance on the providence of God which animated the Christians in carrying on the war. The construction of this place struck terror into the hearts of the Moors, for they considered it a proof that their enemies intended to give up the conflict only with their lives; and it is highly probable that it had a direct and immediate influence on the submission of Boabdil, the King of Granada, who yielded the Alhambra a few weeks after the Spaniards had taken possession of their new abodes.

Santa Fé still exists, and is visited by the traveller as a place of curious origin; while it is rendered remarkable by the fact—real or assumed—that it is the only town of any size in Spain, that has never been under Moorish sway.

The main incidents of our tale will now transport us to this era, and to this scene; all that has been related as yet, being merely introductory matter, to prepare the reader for the events that are to follow.

CHAPTER IV

"What thing a right line is,—the learned know;
But how availes that him, who in the right
Of life and manners doth desire to grow?
What then are all these humane arts, and lights,
But seas of errors? In whose depths who sound,
Of truth finde only shadowes, and no ground."

Human Learning.

The morning of the 2d of January, 1492, was ushered in with a solemnity and pomp that were unusual even in a court and camp as much addicted to religious observances and royal magnificence, as that of Ferdinand and Isabella. The sun had scarce appeared, when all in the extraordinary little city of Santa Fé were afoot, and elate with triumph. The negotiations for the surrender of Granada, which had been going on secretly for weeks, were terminated; the army and nation had been formally apprised of their results, and this was the day set for the entry of the conquerors.

The court had been in mourning for Don Alonso of Portugal, the husband of the Princess Royal of Castile, who had died a bridegroom; but on this joyous occasion the trappings of woe were cast aside, and all appeared in their gayest and most magnificent apparel. At an hour that was still early, the Grand Cardinal moved forward, ascending what is called the Hill of Martyrs, at the head of a strong body of troops, with a view to take possession. While making the ascent, a party of Moorish cavaliers was met; and at their head rode one in whom, by the dignity of his mien and the anguish of his countenance, it was easy to recognize the mental suffering of Boabdil, or Abdallah, the deposed monarch. The cardinal pointed out the position occupied by Ferdinand, who, with that admixture of piety and worldly policy which were so closely interwoven in his character, had refused to enter within the walls of the conquered city, until the symbol of Christ had superseded the banners of Mahomet; and who had taken his station at some distance from the gates, with a purpose and display of humility that were suited to the particular fanaticism of the period. As the interview that occurred has often been related, and twice quite recently by distinguished writers of our own country, it is unnecessary to dwell on it here. Abdallah next sought the presence of the purer-minded and gentle

Isabella, where his reception, with less affection of the character, had more of the real charity and compassion of the Christian; when he went his way toward that pass in the mountains that has ever since been celebrated as the point where he took his last view of the palaces and towers of his fathers, from which it has obtained the poetical and touching name of El Ultimo Suspiro Del Moro.

Although the passage of the last King of Granada, from his palace to the hills, was in no manner delayed, as it was grave and conducted with dignity, it consequently occupied some time. These were hours in which the multitude covered the highways, and the adjacent fields were garnished with a living throng, all of whom kept their eyes riveted on the towers of the Alhambra, where the signs of possession were anxiously looked for by every good Catholic who witnessed the triumph of his religion.

Isabella, who had made this conquest a condition in the articles of marriage—whose victory in truth it was—abstained, with her native modesty, from pressing forward on this occasion. She had placed herself at some distance in the rear of the position of Ferdinand. Still—unless, indeed, we except the long-coveted towers of the Alhambra—she was the centre of attraction. She appeared in royal magnificence, as due to the glory of the occasion; her beauty always rendered her an object of admiration; her mildness, inflexible justice, and unyielding truth, had won all hearts; and she was really the person who was most to profit by the victory, Granada being attached to her own crown of Castile, and not to that of Aragon, a country that possessed little or no contiguous territory.

Previously to the appearance of Abdallah, the crowd moved freely, in all directions; multitudes of civilians having flocked to the camp to witness the entry. Among others were many friars, priests, and monks—the war, indeed, having the character of a crusade. The throng of the curious was densest near the person of the queen, where, in truth, the magnificence of the court was the most imposing. Around this spot, in particular, congregated most of the religious, for they felt that the pious mind of Isabella created a sort of moral atmosphere in and near her presence, that was peculiarly suited to their habits, and favorable to their consideration. Among others, was a friar of prepossessing mien, and, in fact, of noble birth, who had been respectfully addressed as Father Pedro, by several grandees, as he made his way from the immediate presence of the queen, to a spot where the circulation was easier. He was accompanied by a youth of an air so much superior to that of most of those who did not appear that day in the saddle, that he attracted general attention. Although not more than twenty, it was evident, from his muscular frame, and embrowned but florid cheeks, that he was acquainted with exposure; and by his bearing, many thought, notwithstanding he did not appear in armor on an occasion so peculiarly military, that both his mien and his frame had been improved by familiarity with war. His attire was simple, as if he rather avoided than sought observation, but it was, nevertheless, such as was worn by none but the noble. Several of those who watched this youth, as he reached the less confined portions of the crowd, had seen him received graciously by Isabella, whose hand he had even been permitted to kiss, a favor that the formal and fastidious court of Castile seldom bestowed except on the worthy, or on those, at least, who were unusually illustrious from their birth. Some whispered that he was a Guzman, a family that was almost royal; while others thought that he might be a Ponce, a name that had got to be one of the first in Spain, through the deeds of the renowned Marquis-Duke of Cadiz, in this very war; while others, again, affected to discern in his lofty brow, firm step, and animated eye, the port and countenance of a Mendoza.

It was evident that the subject of all these commentaries was unconscious of the notice that was attracted by his vigorous form, handsome face, and elastic, lofty tread; for, like one accustomed to be observed by inferiors, his attention was confined to such objects as amused his eye, or pleased his fancy, while he lent a willing ear to the remarks that, from time to time, fell from the lips of his reverend companion.

"This is a most blessed and glorious day for Christianity!" observed the friar, after a pause a little longer than common. "An impious reign of seven hundred years hath expired, and the Moor is at length lowered from his pride; while the cross is elevated above the banners of the false prophet. Thou hast had ancestors, my son, who might almost arise from their tombs, and walk the earth in exultation, if the tidings of these changes were permitted to reach the souls of Christians long since departed."

"The Blessed Maria intercede for them, father, that they may not be disturbed, even to see the Moor unhoused; for I doubt much, agreeable as the Infidel hath made it, if they find Granada as pleasant as Paradise."

"Son Don Luis, thou hast got much levity of speech, in thy late journeyings; and I doubt if thou art as mindful of thy paters and confessions, as when under the care of thy excellent mother, of sainted memory!"

This was not only said reprovingly, but with a warmth that amounted nearly to anger.

"Chide me not so warmly, father, for a lightness of speech that cometh of youthful levity, rather than of disrespect for holy church. Nay, thou rebukest warmly, and then, as I come like a penitent to lay my transgressions before thee, and to seek absolution, thou fastenest thine eye on vacancy, and gazest as if one of the spirits of which thou so lately spokest actually had arisen and come to see the Moor crack his heart strings at quitting his beloved Alhambra!"

"Dost see that man, Luis!" demanded the friar, still gazing in a fixed direction, though he made no gesture to indicate to which particular individual of the many who were passing in all directions, he especially alluded.

"By my veracity, I see a thousand, father, though not one to fasten the eye as if he were fresh from Paradise. Would it be exceeding discretion to ask who or what hath thus riveted thy gaze?"

"Dost see yonder person of high and commanding stature, and in whom gravity and dignity are so singularly mingled with an air of poverty; or, if not absolutely of poverty—for he is better clad, and, seemingly, in more prosperity now, than I remember ever to have seen him—still, evidently not of the rich and noble; while his bearing and carriage would seem to bespeak him at least a monarch?"

"I think I now perceive him thou meanest, father; a man of very grave and reverend appearance, though of simple deportment. I see nothing extravagant, or ill-placed, either in his attire, or in his bearing."

"I mean not that; but there is a loftiness in his dignified countenance that one is not accustomed to meet in those who are unused to power."

"To me, he hath the air and dress of a superior navigator, or pilot—of a man accustomed to the seas—ay, he hath sundry symbols about him that bespeak such a pursuit."

"Thou art right, Don Luis, for such is his calling. He cometh of Genoa, and his name is Christoval Colon; or, as they term it in Italy, Christoforo Colombo."

"I remember to have heard of an admiral of that name, who did good service in the wars of the south, and who formerly led a fleet into the far east."

"This is not he, but one of humbler habits, though possibly of the same blood, seeing that both are derived from the identical place. This is no admiral, though he would fain become one—ay, even a king!"

"The man is, then, either of a weak mind, or of a light ambition."

"He is neither. In mind, he hath outdone many of our most learned churchmen; and it is due to his piety to say that a more devout Christian doth not exist in Spain. It is plain, son, that thou hast been much abroad, and little at court, or thou wouldst have known the history of this extraordinary being, at the mention of his name, which has been the source of merriment for the frivolous and gay this many a year, and which has thrown the thoughtful and prudent into more doubts than many a fierce and baneful heresy."

"Thou stirrest my curiosity, father, by such language. Who and what is the man?"

"An enigma, that neither prayers to the Virgin, the learning of the cloisters, nor a zealous wish to reach the truth, hath enabled me to read. Come hither, Luis, to this bit of rock, where we can be seated, and I will relate to thee the opinions that render this being so extraordinary. Thou must know, son, it is now seven years since this man first appeared among us. He sought employment as a discoverer, pretending that, by steering out into the ocean, on a western course, for a great and unheard-of distance, he could reach the farther Indies, with the rich island of Cipango, and the kingdom of Cathay, of which one Marco Polo hath left us some most extraordinary legends!"

"By St. James of blessed memory! the man must be short of his wits!" interrupted Don Luis, laughing. "In what way could this thing be, unless the earth were round—the Indies lying east, and not west of us?"

"That hath been often objected to his notions; but the man hath ready answers to much weightier arguments."

"What weightier than this can be found? Our own eyes tell us that the earth is flat."

"Therein he differeth from most men—and to own the truth, son Luis, not without some show of reason. He is a navigator, as thou wilt understand, and he replies that, on the ocean, when a ship is seen from afar, her upper sails are first perceived, and that as she draweth nearer, her lower sails, and finally her hull cometh into view. But thou hast been over sea, and may have observed something of this?"

"Truly have I, father. While mounting the English sea, we met a gallant cruiser of the king's, and, as thou said'st, we first perceived her upper sail, a white speck upon the water; then followed sail after sail, until we came nigh and saw her gigantic hull, with a very goodly show of bombards and cannon—some twenty at least, in all."

"Then thou agreest with this Colon, and thinkest the earth round?"

"By St. George of England! not I. I have seen too much of the world, to traduce its fair surface in so heedless a manner. England, France, Burgundy, Germany, and all those distant countries of the north, are just as level and flat as our own Castile."

"Why, then, didst thou see the upper sails of the Englishman first?"

"Why, father—why—because they were first visible. Yes, because they came first into view."

"Do the English put the largest of their sails uppermost on the masts?"

"They would be fools if they did. Though no great navigators—our neighbors the Portuguese, and the people of Genoa, exceeding all others in that craft—though no great navigators, the English are not so surpassingly stupid. Thou wilt remember the force of the winds, and understand that the larger the sail the lower should be its position."

"Then how happened it that thou sawest the smaller object before the larger?"

"Truly, excellent Fray Pedro, thou hast not conversed with this Christoforo for nothing! A question is not a reason."

"Socrates was fond of questions, son; but *he* expected answers."

"*Peste!* as they say at the court of King Louis. I am not Socrates, my good father, but thy old pupil and kinsman, Luis de Bobadilla, the truant nephew of the queen's favorite, the Marchioness of Moya, and as well-born a cavalier as there is in Spain—though somewhat given to roving, if my enemies are to be believed."

"Neither thy pedigree, thy character, nor thy vagaries, need be given to me, Don Luis de Bobadilla, since I have known thee and thy career from childhood. Thou hast one merit that none will deny thee, and that is, a respect for truth; and never hast thou more completely vindicated thy character, in this particular, than when thou saidst thou were not Socrates."

The worthy friar's good-natured smile, as he made this sally, took off some of its edge; and the young man laughed, as if too conscious of his own youthful follies to resent what he heard.

"But, dear Fray Pedro, lay aside thy government, for once, and stoop to a rational discourse with me on this extraordinary subject. *Thou*, surely, wilt not pretend that the earth is round?"

"I do not go as far as some, on this point, Luis, for I see difficulties with Holy Writ, by the admission. Still, this matter of the sails much puzzleth me, and I have often felt a desire to go from one port to another, by sea, in order to witness it. Were it not for the exceeding nausea that I ever feel in a boat, I might attempt the experiment."

"That would be a worthy consummation of all thy wisdom!" exclaimed the young man, laughing. "Fray Pedro de Carrasca turned rover, like his old pupil, and that, too, astride a vagary! But set thy heart at rest, my honored kinsman and excellent instructor, for I can save thee the trouble. In all my journeyings, by sea and by land—and thou knowest that, for my years, they have been many—I have ever found the earth flat, and the ocean the flattest portion of it, always excepting a few turbulent and uneasy waves."

"No doubt it so seemeth to the eye; but this Colon, who hath voyaged far more than thou, thinketh otherwise. He contendeth that the earth is a sphere, and that, by sailing west, he can reach points that have been already attained by journeying east."

"By San Lorenzo! but the idea is a bold one! Doth the man really propose to venture out into the broad Atlantic, and even to cross it to some distant and unknown land?"

"That is his very idea; and for seven weary years hath he solicited the court to furnish him with the means. Nay, as I hear, he hath passed much more time—other seven years, perhaps—in urging his suit in different lands."

"If the earth be round," continued Don Luis, with a musing air, "what preventeth all the water from flowing to the lower parts of it? How is it, that we have any seas at all? and if, as thou hast hinted, he deemeth the Indies on the other side, how is it that their people stand erect?—it cannot be done without placing the feet uppermost."

"That difficulty hath been presented to Colon, but he treateth it lightly. Indeed, most of our churchmen are getting to believe that there is no up, or down, except as it relateth to the surface of the earth; so that no great obstacle existeth in that point."

"Thou would'st not have me understand, father, that a man can walk on his head—and that, too, with the noble member in the air? By San Francisco! thy men of Cathay must have talons like a cat, or they would be falling, quickly!"

"Whither, Luis?"

"Whither, Fray Pedro?—to Tophet, or the bottomless pit. It can never be that men walk on their heads, heels uppermost, with no better foundation than the atmosphere. The caravels, too, must sail on their masts—and that would be rare navigation! What would prevent the sea from tumbling out of its bed, and falling on the Devil's fires and extinguishing them?"

"Son Luis," interrupted the monk, gravely, "thy lightness of speech is carried too far. But, if thou so much deridest the opinion of this Colon, what are thine own notions of the formation of this earth, that God hath so honored with his spirit and his presence?"

"That it is as flat as the buckler of the Moor I slew in the last sortie, which is as flat as steel can hammer iron."

"Dost thou think it hath limits?"

"That do I—and please heaven, and Doña Mercedes de Valverde, I will see them before I die!"

"Then thou fanciest there is an edge, or precipice, at the four sides of the world, which men may reach, and where they can stand and look off, as from an exceeding high platform?"

"The picture doth not lose, father, for the touch of thy pencil! I have never bethought me of this before; and yet some such spot there must be, one would think. By San Fernando, himself! that would be a place to try the metal of even Don Alonso de Ojeda, who might stand on the margin of the earth, put his foot on a cloud, and cast an orange to the moon!"

"Thou hast bethought thee little of any thing serious, I fear, Luis; but to me, this opinion and this project of Colon are not without merit. I see but two serious objections to them, one of which is, the difficulty connected with Holy Writ; and the other, the vast and incomprehensible, nay, useless, extent of the ocean that must necessarily separate us from Cathay; else should we long since have heard from that quarter of the world."

"Do the learned favor the man's notions?"

"The matter hath been seriously argued before a council held at Salamanca, where men were much divided upon it. One serious obstacle is the apprehension that should the world prove to be round, and could a ship even succeed in getting to Cathay by the west, there would be great difficulty in her ever returning, since there must be, in some manner, an ascent and a descent. I must say that most men deride this Colon; and I fear he will never reach his island of Cipango, as he doth not seem in the way even to set forth on the journey. I marvel that he should now be here, it having been said he had taken his final departure for Portugal."

"Dost thou say, father, that the man hath long been in Spain?" demanded Don Luis, gravely, with his eye riveted on the dignified form of Columbus, who stood calmly regarding the gorgeous spectacle of the triumph, at no great distance from the rock where the two had taken their seats.

"Seven weary years hath he been soliciting the rich and the great to furnish him with the means of undertaking his favorite voyage."

"Hath he the gold to prefer so long a suit?"

"By his appearance, I should think him poor—nay, I know that he hath toiled for bread, at the occupation of a map-maker. One hour he hath passed in arguing with philosophers and in soliciting princes, while the next hath been occupied in laboring for the food that he hath taken for sustenance."

"Thy description, father, hath whetted curiosity to so keen an edge, that I would fain speak with this Colon. I see he remaineth yonder, in the crowd, and will go and tell him that I, too, am somewhat of a navigator, and will extract from him a few of his peculiar ideas."

"And in what manner wilt thou open the acquaintance, son?"

"By telling him that I am Don Luis de Bobadilla, the nephew of the Doña Beatriz of Moya, and a noble of one of the best houses of Castile."

"And this, thou thinkest, will suffice for thy purpose, Luis!" returned the friar, smiling. "No—no—my son; this may do with most map-sellers, but it will not effect thy wishes with yonder Christoval Colon. That man is so filled with the vastness of his purposes; is so much raised up with the magnitude of the results that his mind intently contemplateth, day and night; seemeth so conscious of his own powers, that even kings and princes can, in no manner, lessen his dignity. That which thou proposest, Don Fernando, our honored master, might scarcely attempt, and hope to escape without some rebuke of manner, if not of tongue."

"By all the blessed saints! Fray Pedro, thou givest an extraordinary account of this man, and only increasest the desire to know him. Wilt thou charge thyself with the introduction?"

"Most willingly, for I wish to inquire what hath brought him back to court, whence, I had understood, he lately went, with the intent to go elsewhere with his projects. Leave the mode in my hands, son Luis, and we will see what can be accomplished."

The friar and his mercurial young companion now arose from their seats on the rock, and threaded the throng, taking the direction necessary to approach the man who had been the subject of their discourse, and still remained that of their thoughts. When near enough to speak, Fray Pedro stopped, and stood patiently waiting for a moment when he might catch the navigator's eye. This did not occur for several minutes, the looks of Colon being riveted on the towers of the Alhambra, where, at each instant, the signal of possession was expected to appear; and Luis de Bobadilla, who, truant, and errant, and volatile, and difficult to curb, as he had proved himself to be, never forgot his illustrious birth and the conventional distinctions attached to personal rank, began to manifest his impatience at being kept so long dancing attendance on a mere map-seller and a pilot.

He in vain urged his companion to advance, however; but one of his own hurried movements at length drew aside the look of Columbus, when the eyes of the latter and of the friar met, and being old acquaintances, they saluted in the courteous manner of the age.

"I felicitate you, Señor Colon, on the glorious termination of this siege, and rejoice that you are here to witness it, as I had heard affairs of magnitude had called you to another country."

"The hand of God, father, is to be traced in all things. You perceive in this success the victory of the cross; but to me it conveyeth a lesson of perseverance, and sayeth as plainly as events can speak, that what God hath decreed, must come to pass."

"I like your application, Señor; as, indeed, I do most of your thoughts on our holy religion. Perseverance is truly necessary to salvation; and I doubt not that a fitting symbol to the same may be found in the manner in which our pious sovereigns have conducted this war, as well as in its glorious termination."

"True, father; and also doth it furnish a symbol to the fortunes of all enterprises that have the glory of God and the welfare of the church in view," answered Colon, or Columbus, as the name has been Latinized; his eye kindling with that latent fire which seems so deeply seated in the visionary and the enthusiast. "It may seem out of reason to you, to make such applications of these great events; but the triumph of their Highnesses this day, marvellously encourageth me to persevere, and not to faint, in my own weary pilgrimage, both leading to triumphs of the cross."

"Since you are pleased to speak of your own schemes, Señor Colon," returned the friar, ingenuously, "I am not sorry that the matter hath come up between us; for here is a youthful kinsman of mine, who hath been somewhat of a rover, himself, in the indulgence of a youthful fancy, that neither friends nor yet love could restrain; and having heard of your noble projects, he is burning with a desire to learn more of them from your own mouth, should it suit your condescension so to indulge him."

"I am always happy to yield to the praiseworthy wishes of the young and adventurous, and shall cheerfully communicate to your young friend all he may desire to know," answered Columbus, with a simplicity and dignity that at once put to flight all the notions of superiority and affability with which Don Luis had intended to carry on the conversation, and which had the immediate effect to satisfy the young man that he was to be the obliged and honored party, in the intercourse that was to follow. "But, Señor, you have forgotten to give me the name of the cavalier."

"It is Don Luis de Bobadilla, a youth whose best claims to your notice, perhaps, are, a most adventurous and roving spirit, and the fact that he may call your honored friend, the Marchioness of Moya, his aunt."

"Either would be sufficient, father. I love the spirit of adventure in the youthful; for it is implanted, no doubt, by God, in order that they may serve his all-wise and beneficent designs; and it is of such as these that my own chief worldly stay and support must be found. Then, next to Father Juan Perez de Marchena and Señor Alonzo de Quintanilla, do I esteem Doña Beatriz, among my fastest friends; her kinsman, therefore, will be certain of my esteem and respect."

All this sounded extraordinary to Don Luis; for, though the dress and appearance of this unknown stranger, who even spoke the Castilian with a foreign accent, were respectable, he had been told he was merely a pilot, or navigator, who earned his bread by toil; and it was not usual for the noblest of Castile to be thus regarded, as it might be, with a condescending favor, by any inferior to those who could claim the blood and lineage of princes. At first he was disposed to resent the words of the stranger; then to laugh in his face; but, observing that the friar treated him with great deference, and secretly awed by the air of the reputed projector, he was not only successful in maintaining a suitable deportment, but he made a proper and courteous reply, such as became his name and breeding. The three then retired together, a little aloof from the thickest of the throng, and found seats, also, on one of the rocks, of which so many were scattered about the place.

"Don Luis hath visited foreign lands, you say, father," said Columbus, who did not fail to lead the discourse, like one entitled to it by rank, or personal claims, "and hath a craving for the wonders and dangers of the ocean?"

"Such hath been either his merit or his fault, Señor; had he listened to the wishes of Doña Beatriz, or to my advice, he would not have thrown aside his knightly career for one so little in unison with his training and birth."

"Nay, father, you treat the youth with unmerited severity; he who passeth a life on the ocean, cannot be said to pass it in either an ignoble or a useless manner. God separated different countries by vast bodies of water, not with any intent to render their people strangers to each other, but, doubtless, that they might meet amid the wonders with which he hath adorned the ocean, and glorify his name and power so much the more. We all have our moments of thoughtlessness in youth—a period when we yield to our impulses rather than to our reason; and as I confess to mine, I am little disposed to bear too hard on Señor Don Luis, that he hath had his."

"You have probably battled with the Infidel, by sea, Señor Colon," observed the young man, not a little embarrassed as to the manner in which he should introduce the subject he most desired.

"Ay, and by land, too, son"—the familiarity startled the young noble, though he could not take offence at it—"and by land, too. The time hath been, when I had a pleasure in relating my perils and escapes, which have been numerous, both from war and tempests; but, since the power of God hath awakened my spirit to mightier things, that his will may be done, and his word spread throughout the whole earth, my memory ceaseth to dwell on them." Fray Pedro crossed himself, and Don Luis smiled and shrugged his shoulders, as one is apt to do when he listens to any thing extravagant; but the navigator proceeded in the earnest, grave manner that appeared to belong to his character. "It is now very many years since I was engaged in that remarkable combat between the forces of my kinsman and namesake, the younger Colombo, as he was called, to distinguish him from his uncle, the ancient admiral of the same name, which took place not far north from Cape St. Vincent. On that bloody day, we contended with the foe—Venetians, richly laden—from morn till even, and yet the Lord carried me through the hot contest unharmed. On another occasion, the galley in which I fought was consumed by fire, and I had to find my way to land—no trifling distance—by the aid of an oar. To me, it seemeth that the hand of God was in this, and that he would not have taken so signal and tender a care of one of his insignificant creatures, unless to use him largely for his own honor and glory."

Although the eye of the navigator grew brighter as he uttered this, and his cheek flushed with a species of holy enthusiasm, it was impossible to confound one so grave, so dignified, so measured even in his exaggerations (if such they were), with the idle and light-minded, who mistake momentary impulses for indelible impressions, and passing vanities for the convictions that temper character. Fray Pedro, instead of smiling, or in any manner betraying that he regarded the other's opinions lightly, devoutly crossed himself again, and showed by the sympathy expressed in his countenance, how much he entered into the profound religious faith of the speaker.

"The ways of God are often mysterious to his creatures," said the friar; "but we are taught that they all lead to the exaltation of his name and to the glory of his attributes."

"It is so that I consider it, father; and with such views have I always regarded my own humble efforts to honor him. We are but instruments, and useless instruments, too, when we look at how little proceedeth from our own spirits and power."

"There cometh the blessed symbol that is our salvation and guide!" exclaimed the friar, holding out both arms eagerly, as if to embrace some distant object in the heavens, immediately falling to his knees, and bowing his shaven and naked head, in deep humility, to the earth.

Columbus turned his eyes in the direction indicated by his companion's gestures, and he beheld the large silver cross that the sovereigns had carried with them throughout the late war, as a pledge of its objects, glittering on the principal tower of the Alhambra. At the next instant, the banners of Castile and of St. James were unfolded from other elevated places. Then came the song of triumph, mingled with the chants of the church. Te Deum was sung, and the choirs of the royal chapel chanted in the open fields the praises of the Lord of Hosts. A scene of magnificent religious pomp, mingled with martial array, followed, that belongs rather to general history than to the particular and private incidents of our tale.

CHAPTER V

"Who hath not proved how feebly words essay
To fix one spark of beauty's heavenly ray?
Who doth not feel, until his failing sight
Faints into dimness with its own delight,
His changing cheek, his sinking heart confess
The might—the majesty of loveliness!"

Byron.

That night the court of Castile and Aragon slept in the palace of the Alhambra. As soon as the religious ceremony alluded to in the last chapter had terminated, the crowd rushed into the place, and the princes followed, with a dignity and state better suited to their high character. The young Christian nobles, accompanied by their wives and sisters—for the presence of Isabella, and the delay that attended the surrender, had drawn together a vast many of the gentler sex, in addition to those whose duty it was to accompany their royal mistress—hurried eagerly through the celebrated courts and fretted apartments of this remarkable residence; nor was curiosity appeased even when night came to place a temporary stay to its indulgence. The Court of the Lions in particular, a place still renowned throughout Christendom for its remains of oriental beauty, had been left by Boabdil in the best condition; and, although it was midwinter, by the aid of human art it was even then gay with flowers; while the adjacent halls, those of the Two Sisters and of Abencerrages, were brilliant with light, and alive with warriors and courtiers, dignified priests and luxuriant beauty.

Although no Spanish eye could be otherwise than familiar with the light peculiar graces of Moorish architecture, these of the Alhambra so much surpassed those of any other palace which had been erected by the Mussulman dynasties of that part of the world, that their glories struck the beholders with the freshness of novelty, as well as with the magnificence of royalty. The rich conceits in stucco, an art of eastern origin then little understood in Christendom; the graceful and fanciful arabesques—which, improved on by the fancies of some of the greatest geniuses the world ever saw, have descended to our own times, and got to be so familiar in Europe, though little known on this side of the Atlantic—decorated the walls, while brilliant fountains cast their waters into the air, and fell in glittering spray, resembling diamonds.

Among the throng that moved through this scene of almost magical beauty, was Beatriz de Bobadilla, who had long been the wife of Don Andres de Cabrera, and was now generally known as the Marchioness of Moya; the constant, near, and confidential friend of the queen, a character she retained until her royal mistress was numbered with the dead. On her arm leaned lightly a youthful female, of an appearance so remarkable, that few strangers would have passed her without turning to take a second look at features and a countenance that were seldom seen and forgotten. This was Doña Mercedes de Valverde, one of the noblest and richest heiresses of Castile; the relative, ward, and adopted daughter of the queen's friend—favorite being hardly the term one would apply to the relation in which Doña Beatriz stood toward Isabella. It was not the particular beauty of Doña Mercedes, however, that rendered her appearance so remarkable and attractive; for, though feminine, graceful, of exquisite form, and even of pleasing features, there were many in that brilliant court who would generally be deemed fairer. But no other maiden of Castile had a countenance so illuminated by the soul within, or no other female face habitually wore so deep an impression of sentiment and sensibility; and the professed physiognomist would have delighted to trace the evidences of a deeply-seated, earnest, but unobtrusive enthusiasm, which even cast a shade of melancholy over a face that fortune and the heart had equally intended should be sunny and serene. Serene it was, notwithstanding; the shadow that rested on it seeming to soften and render interesting its expression, rather than to disturb its tranquillity or to cloud its loveliness.

On the other side of the noble matron walked Luis de Bobadilla, keeping a little in advance of his aunt, in a way to permit his own dark, flashing looks to meet, whenever feeling and modesty would allow it, the fine, expressive blue eyes of Mercedes. The three conversed freely, for the royal personages had retired to their private apartments, and each group of passengers was so much entranced with the novelty of its situation and its own conversation, as to disregard the remarks of others.

"This is a marvel, Luis," observed Doña Beatriz, in continuation of a subject that evidently much interested them all, "that thou, a truant and a rover thyself, should now have heard for the first time of this Colon! It is many years since he has been soliciting their Highnesses for their royal aid in effecting his purposes. The matter of his schemes was solemnly debated before a council at Salamanca; and he hath not been without believers at the Court itself."

"Among whom is to be classed Doña Beatriz de Cabrera," said Mercedes, with that melancholy smile that had the effect to bring out glimpses of all the deep but latent feeling that lay concealed beneath the surface: "I have often heard Her Highness declare that Colon hath no truer friend in Castile."

"Her Highness is seldom mistaken, child—and never in my heart. I do uphold the man; for to me he seemeth one fitted for some great and honorable undertaking; and surely none greater hath ever been proposed or imagined by human mind, than this he urgeth. Think of our becoming acquainted with the nations of the other side of the earth, and of finding easy and direct means of communicating with them, and of imparting to them the consolations of Holy Church!"

"Ay, Señora my aunt," cried Luis, laughing, "and of walking in their delightful company with all our heels in the air, and our heads downward! I hope this Colon hath not neglected to practice a little in the art, for it will need some time to gain a sure foot, in such circumstances. He might commence on the sides of these mountains, by way of a horn-book, throwing the head boldly off at a right-angle; after which, the walls and towers of this Alhambra would make a very pretty grammar, or stepping-stone to new progress."

Mercedes had unconsciously but fervently pressed the arm of her guardian, as Doña Beatriz admitted her interest in the success of the great project; but at this sally of Don Luis, she looked serious, and threw a glance at him, that he himself felt to be reproachful. To win the love of his aunt's ward was the young man's most ardent wish; and a look of dissatisfaction could at any moment repress that exuberance of spirits which often led him into an appearance of levity that did injustice to the really sterling qualities of both his heart and mind. Under the influence of that look, then, he was not slow to repair the wrong he had done himself, by adding almost as soon as he had ceased to speak—

"The Doña Mercedes is of the discovering party, too, I see; this Colon appeareth to have had more success with the dames of Castile than with her nobles"—

"Is it extraordinary, Don Luis," interrupted the pensive-looking girl, "that women should have more confidence in merit, more generous impulses, more zeal for God, than men?"

"It must be even so, since you and my aunt, Doña Beatriz, side with the navigator. But I am not always to be understood in the light I express myself;" Mercedes now smiled, but this time it was archly—"I have never studied with the minstrels, nor, sooth to say, deeply with the churchmen. To be honest with you, I have been much struck with this noble idea; and if Señor Colon doth, in reality, sail in quest of Cathay and the Indies, I shall pray their Highnesses to let me be one of the party, for, now that the Moor is subdued, there remaineth little for a noble to do in Spain."

"If thou should'st really go on this expedition," said Doña Beatriz, with grave irony, "there will, at least, be one human being topsy-turvy, in the event of thy reaching Cathay. But yonder is an attendant of the court; I doubt if Her Highness doth not desire my presence."

The Lady of Moya was right—the messenger coming to announce to her that the queen required her attendance. The manners of the day and country rendered it unseemly that Doña Mercedes should continue her promenade accompanied only by Don Luis, and the marchioness led the way to her own apartments, where a saloon suitable to her rank and to her favor with the queen, had been selected for her from among the numberless gorgeous rooms of the Moorish kings. Even here, the marchioness paused a moment, in thought, before she would leave her errant nephew alone with her ward.

"Though a rover, he is no troubadour, and cannot charm thy ear with false rhymes. It were better, perhaps, that I sent him beneath thy balcony, with his guitar; but knowing so well his dulness, I will confide in it, and leave him with thee, for the few minutes that I shall be absent. A cavalier who hath so strong a dislike to reversing the order of nature, will not surely condescend to go on his knees, even though it be to win a smile from the sweetest maiden in all Castile."

Don Luis laughed; Doña Beatriz smiled, as she kissed her ward, and left the room; while Doña Mercedes blushed, and riveted her gaze on the floor. Luis de Bobadilla was the declared suitor and sworn knight of Mercedes de Valverde; but, though so much favored by birth, fortune, affinity, and figure, there existed some serious impediments to his success. In all that was connected with the considerations that usually decide such things, the union was desirable; but there existed, nevertheless, a strong influence to overcome, in the scruples of Doña Beatriz, herself. High-principled, accustomed to the just-minded views of her royal mistress, and too proud to do an unworthy act, the very advantages that a marriage with her ward offered to her nephew, had caused the marchioness to hesitate. Don Luis had little of the Castilian gravity of character—and, by many, his animal spirits were mistaken for lightness of disposition and levity of thought. His mother was a woman of a very illustrious French family; and national pride had induced most observers to fancy that the son inherited a constitutional disposition to frivolity, that was to be traced to the besetting weakness of a whole people. A consciousness of his being so viewed at home, had, indeed, driven the youth abroad; and as, like all observant travellers, he was made doubly sensible of the defects of his own state of society on his return, a species of estrangement had grown up between him and his natural associates that had urged the young man, again and again, to wander into foreign lands. Nothing, indeed, but his early and constantly increasing passion for Mercedes had induced him to return; a step that, fortunately for himself, he had last taken in time to assist in the reduction of Granada. Notwithstanding these traits, which, in a country like Castile, might be properly enough termed peculiarities, Don Luis de Bobadilla was a knight worthy of his lineage and name. His prowess in the field and in the tourney, indeed, was so very marked as to give him a high military character, in despite of what were deemed his failings; and he passed rather as an inconsiderate and unsafe young man, than as one who was either debased or wicked. Martial qualities, in that age in particular, redeemed a thousand faults; and Don Luis had even been known to unhorse, in the tourney, Alonzo de Ojeda, then the most expert lance in Spain. Such a man could not be despised, though he might be distrusted. But the feeling which governed his aunt, referred quite as much to her own character as to his. Deeply conscientious, while she understood her nephew's real qualities much better than mere superficial observers, she had her doubts about the propriety of giving the rich heiress who was entrusted to her care, to so near a relative, when all could not applaud the act. She feared, too, that her own partiality might deceive her, and that Luis might in truth be the light and frivolous being he sometimes appeared to be in Castilian eyes, and that the happiness of her ward would prove the sacrifice of the indiscretion. With these doubts, then, while she secretly desired the union, she had in public looked coldly on her nephew's suit; and, though unable, without a harshness that circumstances would not warrant, to prevent all intercourse, she had not only taken frequent occasions to let Mercedes understand her distrust, but she had observed the precaution not to leave so handsome a suitor, notwithstanding he was often domiciliated in her own house, much alone with her ward.

The state of Mercedes' feelings was known only to herself. She was beautiful, of an honorable family, and an heiress; and as human infirmities were as besetting beneath the stately mien of the fifteenth century as they are to-day, she had often heard the supposed faults of Don Luis' character sneered at, by those who felt distrustful of his good looks and his opportunities. Few young females would have had the courage to betray any marked preference under such circumstances, until prepared to avow their choice, and to take sides with its subject against the world; and the quiet but deep enthusiasm that prevailed in the moral system of the fair young Castilian, was tempered by a prudence that prevented her from running into most of its lighter excesses. The forms and observances that usually surround young women of rank, came in aid of this native prudence; and even Don Luis himself, though he had watched the countenance and emotions of her to whom he had so long urged his suit, with a lover's jealousy and a lover's instincts, was greatly in doubt whether he had succeeded in the least in touching her heart. By one of those unlooked-for concurrences of circumstances that so often decide the fortunes of men, whether as lovers or in more worldly-minded pursuits, these doubts were now about to be unexpectedly and suddenly removed.

The triumph of the Christian arms, the novelty of her situation, and the excitement of the whole scene, had aroused the feelings of Mercedes from that coy concealment in which they usually lay smothered beneath the covering of maiden diffidence; and throughout the evening her smile had been more open, her eye brighter, and her cheeks more deeply flushed, than was usual even with one whose smiles were always sweet, whose eyes were never dull, and whose cheeks answered so sensitively to the varying impulses within.

As his aunt quitted the room, leaving him alone with Mercedes for the first time since his return from his last ramble, Don Luis eagerly threw himself on a stool that stood near the feet of his adored, who placed herself on a sumptuous couch, that, twenty-four hours before, had held the person of a princess of Abdallah's family.

"Much as I honor and reverence Her Highness," the young man hurriedly commenced, "my respect and veneration are now increased ten-fold! Would that she might send for my beloved aunt thrice where she now wants her services only once! and may her presence become so necessary to her sovereign that the affairs of Castile cannot go on without her counsel, if so blessed an opportunity as this, to tell you all I feel, Doña Mercedes, is to follow her obedience!"

"It is not they who are most fluent of speech, or the most vehement, who always feel the deepest, Don Luis de Bobadilla."

"Nor do they feel the least. Mercedes, thou canst not doubt my love! It hath grown with my growth—increased with each increase of my ideas—until it hath got to be so interwoven with my mind itself, that I can scarce use a faculty that thy dear image doth not mingle with it. In all that is beautiful, I behold thee; if I listen to the song of a bird, it is thy carol to the lute; or if I feel the gentle south wind from the fragrant isles fanning my cheek, I would fain think it thy sigh."

"You have dwelt so much among the light conceits of the French court, Don Luis, you appear to have forgotten that the heart of a Castilian girl is too true, and too sincere, to meet such rhapsodies with favor."

Had Don Luis been older, or more experienced in the sex, he would have been flattered by this rebuke—for he would have detected in the speaker's manner, both feeling of a gentler nature than her words expressed, and a tender regret.

"If thou ascribest to me rhapsodies, thou dost me great injustice. I may not do credit to my own thoughts and feelings; but never hath my tongue uttered aught to thee, Mercedes, that the heart hath not honestly urged. Have I not loved thee since thou and I were children? Did I ever fail to show my preference for thee when we were boy and girl, in all the sports and light-hearted enjoyments of that guileless period?"

"Guileless, truly," answered Mercedes, her look brightening as it might be with agreeable fancies and a flood of pleasant recollections—doing more, in a single instant, to break down the barriers of her reserve, than years of schooling had effected toward building them up. "Thou wert then, at least, sincere, Luis, and I placed full faith in thy friendship, and in thy desire to please."

"Bless thee, bless thee, for these precious words, Mercedes! for the first time in two years, hast thou spoken to me as thou wert wont to do, and called me Luis without that courtly, accursed, Don."

"A noble Castilian should never regard his honors lightly, and he oweth it to his rank to see that others respect them, too;" answered our heroine, looking down, as if she already half repented of the familiarity. "You are quick to remind me of my forgetfulness, Don Luis de Bobadilla."

"This unlucky tongue of mine can never follow the path that its owner wisheth! Hast thou not seen in all my looks—all my acts—all my motives—a desire to please thee, and thee alone, lovely Mercedes? When Her Highness gave her royal approbation of my success, in the last tourney, did I not seek thine eye, in order to ask if thou notedst it? Hast thou ever expressed a wish, that I have not proved an eager desire to see it accomplished?"

"Nay, now, Luis, thou emboldenest me to remind thee that I expressed a wish that thou wouldst not go on thy last voyage to the north, and yet thou didst depart! I felt that it would displease Doña Beatriz; thy truant disposition having made her uneasy lest thou shouldst get altogether into the habits of a rover, and into disfavor with the queen."

"It was for this that thou madst the request, and it wounded my pride to think that Mercedes de Valverde should so little understand my character, as to believe it possible a noble of my name and lineage could so far forget his duties as to sink into the mere associate of pilots and adventurers."

"Thou didst not know that I believed this of thee."

"Hadst thou asked of me, Mercedes, to remain for thy sake—nay, hadst thou imposed the heaviest services on me, as thy knight, or as one who enjoyed the smallest degree of thy favor—I would have parted with life sooner than I would have parted from Castile. But not even a look of kindness could I obtain, in reward for all the pain I had felt on thy account"—

"Pain, Luis!"

"Is it not pain to love to the degree that one might kiss the earth that received the foot-print of its object—and yet to meet with no encouragement from fair words, no friendly glance of the eye, nor any sign or symbol to betoken that the being one hath enshrined in his heart's core, ever thinketh of her suitor except as a reckless rover and a hair-brained adventurer?"

"Luis de Bobadilla, no one that really knoweth thy character, can ever truly think thus of thee."

"A million of thanks for these few words, beloved girl, and ten millions for the gentle smile that hath accompanied them! Thou mightst mould me to all thy wishes"—

"My wishes, Don Luis?"

"To all thy severe opinions of sobriety and dignity of conduct, wouldst thou but feel sufficient interest in me to let me know that my acts can give thee either pain or pleasure."

"Can it be otherwise? Could'st thou, Luis, see with indifference the proceedings of one thou hast known from childhood, and esteemed as a friend?"

"Esteem! Blessed Mercedes! dost thou own even that little in my favor?"

"It is not little, Luis, to esteem—but much. They who prize virtue never esteem the unworthy; and it is not possible to know thy excellent heart and manly nature, without esteeming thee. Surely I have never *concealed* my *esteem* from thee or from any one else."

"Hast thou *concealed* aught? Ah! Mercedes, complete this heavenly condescension, and admit that one—as lightly as thou wilt—but that one soft sentiment hath, at times, mingled with this esteem."

Mercedes blushed brightly, but she would not make the often-solicited acknowledgment. It was some little time before she answered at all. When she did speak, it was hesitatingly, and with frequent pauses, as if she distrusted the propriety or the discretion of that which she was about to utter.

"Thou hast travelled much and far, Luis," she said; "and hast lost some favor on account of thy roving propensities; why not regain the confidence of thy aunt by the very means through which it has been lost?"

"I do not comprehend thee. This is singular counsel to come from one like thee, who art prudence itself!"

"The prudent and discreet think well of their acts and words, and are the more to be confided in. Thou seemest to have been struck with these bold opinions of the Señor Colon; and while thou hast derided them, I can see that they have great weight on thy mind."

"I shall, henceforth, regard thee with ten-fold respect, Mercedes; for thou hast penetrated deeper than my foolish affectation of contempt, and all my light language, and discovered the real feeling that lieth underneath. Ever since I have heard of this vast project, it hath, indeed, haunted my imagination; and the image of the Genoese hath constantly stood beside thine, dearest girl, before my eyes, if not in my heart. I doubt if there be not some truth in his opinions; so noble an idea cannot be wholly false!"

The fine, full eye of Mercedes was fastened intently on the countenance of Don Luis; and its brilliancy increased as some of that latent enthusiasm which dwelt within, kindled and began to glow at this outlet of the feelings of the soul.

"There *is*," she answered, solemnly—"there *must* be truth in it! The Genoese hath been inspired of Heaven, with his sublime thoughts, and he will live, sooner or later, to prove their truth. Imagine this earth fairly encircled by a ship; the farthest east, the land of the heathen, brought in close communion with ourselves, and the cross casting its shadows under the burning sun of Cathay! These are glorious, heavenly anticipations, Luis, and would it not be an imperishable renown, to share in the honor of having aided in bringing about so great a discovery?"

"By Heaven! I will see the Genoese as soon as the morrow's sun shall appear, and offer to make one in his enterprise. He shall not need for gold, if that be his only want."

"Thou speakest like a generous, noble-minded, fearless young Castilian, as thou art!" said Mercedes, with an enthusiasm that set at naught the usual guards of her discretion and her habits, "and as becometh Luis de Bobadilla. But gold is not plenty with any of us at this moment, and it will surpass the power of an ordinary subject to furnish that which will be necessary. Nor is it meet than any but sovereigns should send forth such an expedition, as there may be vast territories to govern and dispose of, should Colon succeed. My powerful kinsman—the Duke of Medina Celi—hath had this matter in close deliberation, and he viewed it favorably, as is shown by his letters to Her Highness; but even he conceived it a matter too weighty to be attempted by aught but a crowned head, and he hath used much influence with our mistress, to gain her over to the opinion of the Genoese's sagacity. It is idle to think, therefore, of aiding effectually in this noble enterprise, unless it be through their Highnesses."

"Thou knowest, Mercedes, that I can do naught for Colon, with the court. The king is the enemy of all who are not as wary, cold, and as much given to artifice as himself"—

"Luis! thou art in his palace—beneath his roof, enjoying his hospitality and protection, at this very moment!"

"Not I," answered the young man, with warmth—"this is the abode of my royal mistress, Doña Isabella; Granada being a conquest of Castile, and not of Aragon. Touching the queen, Mercedes, thou shalt never hear disrespectful word from me, for, like thyself, she is all that is virtuous, gentle, and kind in woman; but the king hath many of the faults of us corrupt and mercenary men. Thou canst not tell me of a young, generous, warm-blooded cavalier, even among his own Aragonese, who truly and confidingly loveth Don Fernando; whilst all of Castile adore the Doña Isabella."

"This may be true in part, Luis, but it is altogether imprudent. Don Fernando is a king, and I fear me, from the little I have seen while dwelling in a court, that they who manage the affairs of mortals must make large concessions to their failings, or human depravity will thwart the wisest measures that can be devised. Moreover, can one truly love the wife and not esteem the husband? To me it seemeth that the tie is so near and dear as to leave the virtues and the characters of a common identity."

"Surely, thou dost not mean to compare the modest piety, the holy truth, the sincere virtue, of our royal mistress, with the cautious, wily policy of our scheming master!"

"I desire not to make comparisons between them, Luis. We are bound to honor and obey both; and if Doña Isabella hath more of the confiding truth and pure-heartedness of her sex, than His Highness, is it not ever so as between man and woman?"

"If I could really think that thou likenest me, in any way, with that managing and false-faced King of Aragon, much as I love thee, Mercedes, I would withdraw, forever, in pure shame."

"No one will liken thee, Luis, to the false-tongued or the double-faced; for it is thy failing to speak truth when it might be better to say nothing, as witness the present discourse, and to look at those who displease thee, as if ever ready to point thy lance and spur thy charger in their very teeth."

"My looks have been most unfortunate, fair Mercedes, if they have left such memories in thee!" answered the youth, reproachfully.

"I speak not in any manner touching myself, for to me, Luis, thou hast ever been gentle and kind," interrupted the young Castilian girl, with a haste and earnestness that hurried the blood to her cheeks a moment afterward; "but solely that thou mayst be more guarded in thy remarks on the king."

"Thou beganst by saying that I was a rover" —

"Nay, I have used no such term of reproach. Don Luis; thy aunt may have said this, but it could have been with no intent to wound. I said that thou hadst travelled *far* and *much*."

"Well—well—I merit the title, and shall not complain of my honors. Thou saidst that I had travelled *far* and *much*, and thou spokest approvingly of the project of this Genoese. Am I to understand, Mercedes, it is thy wish that I should make one of the adventurers?"

"Such was my meaning, Luis, for I have thought it an emprise fitting thy daring mind and willing sword; and the glory of success would atone for a thousand trifling errors, committed under the heat and inconsideration of youth."

Don Luis regarded the flushed cheek and brightened eyes of the beautiful enthusiast nearly a minute, in silent but intense observation; for the tooth of doubt and jealousy had fastened on him, and, with the self-distrust of true affection, he questioned how far he was worthy to interest so fair a being, and had misgivings concerning the motive that induced her to wish him to depart.

"I wish I could read thy heart, Doña Mercedes," he at length resumed; "for, while the witching modesty and coy reserve of thy sex, serve but to bind us so much the closer in thy chains, they puzzle the understanding of men more accustomed to rude encounters in the field than to the mazes of their ingenuity. Dost thou desire me to embark in an adventure that most men, the wise and prudent Don Fernando at their head—he whom thou so much esteemest, too—look upon as the project of a visionary, and as leading to certain destruction? Did I think this, I would depart to-morrow, if it were only that my hated presence should never more disturb thy happiness."

"Don Luis, you have no justification for this cruel suspicion," said Mercedes, endeavoring to punish her lover's distrust by an affectation of resentment, though the tears struggled through her pride, and fell from her reproachful eyes. "You know that no one, here or elsewhere, hateth you; you know that you are a general favorite, though Castilian prudence and Castilian reserve may not always view your wandering life with the same applause as they give to the more attentive courtier and rigidly observant knight."

"Pardon me, dearest, most beloved Mercedes; thy coldness and aversion sometime madden me."

"Coldness! aversion! Luis de Bobadilla! When hath Mercedes de Valverde ever shown either, to *thee*?"

"I fear that Doña Mercedes de Valverde is, even now, putting me to some such proof."

"Then thou little knowest her motives, and ill appreciatest her heart. No, Luis, I am not averse, and would not appear cold, to *thee*. If thy wayward feelings get so much the mastery, and pain thee thus, I will strive to be more plain. Yes! rather than thou shouldst carry away with thee the false notion, and perhaps plunge, again, into some unthinking sea-adventure, I will subdue my maiden pride, and forget the reserve and caution that best become my sex and rank, to relieve thy mind. In advising thee to attach thyself to this Colon, and to enter freely into his noble schemes, I had thine own happiness in view, as thou hast, time and again, sworn to me, thy happiness *could* only be secured" —

"Mercedes! what meanest thou? My happiness can only be secured by a union with thee!"

"And thy union with me can only be secured by thy ennobling that besetting propensity to roving, by some act of worthy renown, that shall justify Doña Beatriz in bestowing her ward on a truant nephew, and gain the favor of Doña Isabella."

"And thou!—would this adventure win thee, too, to view me with kindness?"

"Luis, if thou *wilt* know all, I am won already—nay—restrain this impetuosity, and hear all I have to say. Even while I confess so much more than is seemly in a maiden, thou art not to suppose I can further forget myself. Without the cheerful consent of my guardian, and the gracious approbation of Her Highness, I will wed no man—no, not even *thee*, Luis de Bobadilla, dear as I acknowledge thee to be to my heart"—the ungovernable emotions of female tenderness caused the words to be nearly smothered in tears—"would I wed, without the smiles and congratulations of all who have a right to smile, or weep, for any of the house of Valverde. Thou and I cannot marry like a village hind and village girl; it is suitable that we stand before a prelate, with a large circle of approving friends to grace our union. Ah! Luis, thou hast reproached me with coldness and indifference to thee"—sobs nearly stifled the generous girl—"but others have not been so blind—nay, speak not, but suffer me, now that my heart is overflowing, to unburden myself to thee, entirely, for I fear that shame and regret will come soon enough to cause repentance for what I now confess—but all have not been blind as thou. Our gracious queen well understandeth the female heart, and that thou hast been so slow to discover, she hath long seen; and her quickness of eye and thought hath alone prevented me from saying to thee, earlier, a part at least of that which I now reluctantly confess"—

"How! Is Doña Isabella, too, my enemy? Have I Her Highness' scruples to overcome, as well as those of my cold-hearted and prudish aunt?"

"Luis, thy intemperance causeth thee to be unjust. Doña Beatriz of Moya is neither cold-hearted nor prudish, but all that is the reverse. A more generous or truer spirit never sacrificed self to friendship, and her very nature is frankness and simplicity. Much of that I so love in thee, cometh of her family, and *thou* shouldst not reproach her for it. As for Her Highness, certes, it is not needed that I should proclaim her qualities. Thou knowest that she is deemed the mother of her people; that she regardeth the interests of all equally, or so far as her knowledge will allow; and that what she doth for any, is ever done with true affection, and a prudence that I have heard the cardinal say, seemeth to be inspired by infinite wisdom."

"Ay, it is not difficult, Mercedes, to seem prudent, and benevolent, and inspired, with Castile for a throne, and Leon, with other rich provinces, for a footstool!"

"Don Luis, if you would retain my esteem," answered the single-minded girl, with a gravity that had none of her sex's weakness in it, though much of her sex's truth—"speak not lightly of my royal mistress. Whatever she may have done in this matter, hath been done with a mother's feelings and a mother's kindness—thy injustice maketh me almost to apprehend, with a mother's wisdom."

"Forgive me, adored beloved Mercedes! a thousand times more adored and loved than ever, now that thou hast been so generous and confiding. But I cannot rest in peace until I know what the queen hath said and done, in any thing that toucheth thee and me."

"Thou knowest how kind and gracious the queen hath ever been to me, Luis, and how much I have reason to be grateful for her many condescensions and favors. I know not how it is, but, while thy aunt hath never seemed to detect my feelings, and all those related to me by blood have appeared to be in the same darkness, the royal eye hath penetrated a mystery that, at the moment, I do think, was even concealed from myself. Thou rememberest the tourney that took place just before thou left us on thy last mad expedition?"

"Do I not? Was it not thy coldness after my success in that tourney, and when I even wore thy favors, that not only drove me out of Spain, but almost drove me out of the world?"

"If the world could impute thy acts to such a cause, all obstacles would at once be removed, and we might be happy without further efforts. But," and Mercedes smiled, archly, though with great tenderness in her voice and looks, as she added, "I fear thou art much addicted to these fits of madness, and that thou wilt never cease to wish to be driven to the uttermost limits of the world, if not fairly out of it."

"It is in thy power to make me as stationary as the towers of this Alhambra. One such smile, daily, would chain me like a captive Moor at thy feet, and take away all desire to look at other objects than thy beauty. But Her Highness—thou hast forgotten to add what Her Highness hath said and done."

"In that tourney thou wert conqueror, Luis! The whole chivalry of Castile was in the saddle, that glorious day, and yet none could cope with thee! Even Alonzo de Ojeda was unhorsed by thy lance, and all mouths were filled with thy praises; all memories—perhaps, it would be better to say that all memories but one—forgot thy failings."

"And that one was thine, cruel Mercedes."

"Thou knowest better, unkind Luis! That day I remembered nothing but thy noble, generous heart, manly bearing in the tilt-yard, and excellent qualities. The more mindful memory was the queen's, who sent for me, to her closet, when the festivities were over, and caused me to pass an hour with her, in gentle, affectionate discourse, before she touched at all on the real object of her command. She spoke to me, Luis, of our duties as Christians, of our duties as females, and, most of all, of the solemn obligations that we contract in wedlock, and of the many pains that, at best, attend that honored condition. When she had melted me to tears, by an affection that equalled a mother's love, she made me promise—and I confirmed it with a respectful vow—that I would never appear at the altar, while she lived, without her being present to approve of my nuptials; or, if prevented by disease or duty, at least not without a consent given under her royal signature."

"By St. Denis of Paris! Her Highness endeavored to influence thy generous and pure mind against me!"

"Thy name was not even mentioned, Luis. nor would it have been in any way concerned in the discourse, had not my unbidden thoughts turned anxiously toward thee. What Her Highness meditated, I do not even now know, but it was the manner in which my own sensitive feelings brought up thy image, that hath made me, perhaps idly, fancy the effect might be to prevent me from wedding thee, without Doña Isabella's consent. But, knowing, as I well do, her maternal heart and gentle affections, how can I doubt that she will yield to my wishes, when she knoweth that my choice is not really unworthy, though it may seem to the severely prudent in some measure indiscreet."

"But thou thinkest—thou feelest, Mercedes, that it was in fear of me that Her Highness extorted the vow?"

"I apprehended it, as I have confessed, with more readiness than became a maiden's pride, because thou wert uppermost in my mind. Then thy triumphs throughout the day, and the manner in which thy name was in all men's mouths, might well tempt the thoughts to dwell on thy person."

"Mercedes, thou canst not deny that thou believest Her Highness extorted that vow in dread of me?"

"I wish to deny nothing that is true, Don Luis; and you are early teaching me to repent of the indiscreet avowal I have made. That it was in *dread* of you that Her Highness spoke, I do deny; for I cannot think she has any such feelings toward *you*. She was full of maternal affection for *me*, and I think, for I will conceal naught that I truly believe, that apprehension of thy powers to please, Luis, may have induced her to apprehend that an orphan girl, like myself, might possibly consult her fancy more than her prudence, and wed one who seemed to love the uttermost limits of the earth so much better than his own noble castles and his proper home."

"And thou meanest to respect this vow!"

"Luis! thou scarce reflectest on thy words, or a question so sinful would not be put to me! What Christian maiden ever forgets her vows, whether of pilgrimage. penitence, or performance—and why should I be the first to incur this disgraceful guilt? Besides, had I not vowed, the simple wish of the queen, expressed in her own royal person, would have been enough to deter me from wedding any. She is my sovereign, mistress, and, I might almost say, mother; Doña Beatriz herself scarce manifesting greater interest in my welfare. Now, Luis, thou must listen to my suit, although I see thou art ready to exclaim, and protest, and invoke; but I have heard thee patiently some years, and it is now my turn to speak and thine to listen. I do not think the queen had thee in her mind on the occasion of that vow, which was *offered* freely by me, rather than *extorted*, as thou seemest to think, by

Her Highness. I *do*, then, believe that Doña Isabella supposed there might be a danger of my yielding to thy suit, and that she had apprehensions that one so much given to roving, might not bring, or keep, happiness in the bosom of a family. But, Luis, if Her Highness hath not done thy noble, generous heart, justice; if she hath been deceived by appearances, like most of those around her; if she hath not known thee, in short, is it not thine own fault? Hast thou not been a frequent truant from Castile; and, even when present, hast thou been as attentive and assiduous in thy duties at court, as becometh thy high birth and admitted claims? It is true, Her Highness, and all others who were present, witnessed thy skill in the tourney, and in these wars thy name hath had frequent and honorable mention for prowess against the Moor; but while the female imagination yields ready homage to this manliness, the female heart yearneth for other, and gentler, and steadier virtues, at the fireside and in the circle within. This, Doña Isabella hath seen, and felt, and knoweth, happy as hath been her own marriage with the King of Aragon; and is it surprising that she hath felt this concern for me? No, Luis; feeling hath made thee unjust to our royal mistress, whom it is now manifestly thy interest to propitiate, if thou art sincere in thy avowed desire to obtain my hand."

"And how is this to be done, Mercedes? The Moor is conquered, and I know not that any knight would meet me to do battle for thy favor."

"The queen wisheth nothing of this sort—neither do I. We both know thee as an accomplished Christian knight already, and, as thou hast just said, there is no one to meet thy lance, for no one hath met with the encouragement to justify the folly. It is through this Colon that thou art to win the royal consent."

"I believe I have, in part, conceived thy meaning; but would fain hear thee speak more plainly."

"Then I will tell thee in words as distinct as my tongue can utter them," rejoined the ardent girl, the tint of tenderness gradually deepening on her cheek to the flush of a holy enthusiasm, as she proceeded: "Thou knowest already the general opinions of the Señor Colon, and the mode in which he proposeth to effect his ends. I was still a child when he first appeared in Castile, to urge the court to embark in this great enterprise, and I can see that Her Highness hath often been disposed to yield her aid, when the coldness of Don Fernando, or the narrowness of her ministers, hath diverted her mind from the object. I think she yet regardeth the scheme with favor; for it is quite lately that Colon, who had taken leave of us all, with the intent to quit Spain and seek elsewhere for means, was summoned to return, through the influence of Fray Juan Perez, the ancient confessor of

Her Highness. He is now here, as thou hast seen, waiting impatiently for an audience, and it needeth only to quicken the queen's memory, to obtain for him that favor. Should he get the caravels he asketh, no doubt many of the nobles will feel a desire to share in an enterprise that will confer lasting honor on all concerned, if successful; and thou mightst make one."

"I know not how to regard this solicitude, Mercedes, for it seemeth strange to wish to urge those we affect to value, to enter on an expedition whence they may never return."

"God will protect thee!" answered the girl, her face glowing with pious ardour: "the enterprise will be undertaken for his glory, and his powerful hand will guide and shield the caravels."

Don Luis de Bobadilla smiled, having far less religious faith and more knowledge of physical obstacles than his mistress. He did full justice to her motives, notwithstanding his hastily expressed doubts; and the adventure was of a nature to arouse his constitutional love of roving, and his desire for encountering dangers. Both he and Mercedes well knew that he had fairly earned no small part of that distrust of his character, which alone thwarted their wishes; and, quick of intellect, he well understood the means and manner by which he was to gain Doña Isabella's consent. The few doubts that he really entertained were revealed by the question that succeeded.

"If Her Highness is disposed to favor this Colon," he asked, "why hath the measure been so long delayed?"

"This Moorish war, an empty treasury, and the wary coldness of the king, have prevented it."

"Might not Her Highness look upon all the followers of the man, as so many vain schemers, should we return without success, as will most likely be the case—if, indeed, we ever return?"

"Such is not Doña Isabella's character. She will enter into this project, in honor of God, if she entereth into it at all; and she will regard all who accompany Colon voluntarily, as so many crusaders, well entitled to her esteem. Thou wilt not return unsuccessful, Luis; but with such credit as will cause thy wife to glory in her choice, and to be proud of thy name."

"Thou art a most dear enthusiast, beloved girl! If I could take thee with me, I would embark in the adventure, with no other companion."

A fitting reply was made to this gallant, and, at the moment, certainly sincere speech, after which the matter was discussed between the two, with greater calmness and far more intelligibly. Don Luis succeeded in restraining his impatience; and the generous confidence with which Mercedes gradually got to betray her interest in him, and the sweet, holy earnestness with which she urged the probability of success, brought him at length to view the enterprise as one of lofty objects, rather than as a scheme which flattered his love of adventure.

Doña Beatriz left the lovers alone for quite two hours, the queen requiring her presence all that time; and soon after she returned, her reckless, roving, indiscreet, but noble-hearted and manly nephew, took his leave. Mercedes and her guardian, however, did not retire until midnight; the former laying open her whole heart to the marchioness, and explaining all her hopes as they were connected with the enterprise of Colon. Doña Beatriz was both gratified and pained by this confession, while she smiled at the ingenuity of love, in coupling the great designs of the Genoese with the gratification of its own wishes. Still she was not displeased. Luis de Bobadilla was the son of an only and much-beloved brother, and she had transferred to her nephew most of the affection she had felt for the father. All who knew him, indeed, were fond of the handsome and gallant young cavalier, though the prudent felt compelled to frown on his indiscretions; and he might have chosen a wife, at will, from among the fair and high-born of Castile, with the few occasional exceptions that denote the circumspection and reserve of higher principles than common, and a forethought that extends beyond the usual considerations of marriage. The marchioness, therefore, was not an unwilling listener to her ward; and ere they separated for the night, the ingenuous but modest confessions, the earnest eloquence, and the tender ingenuity, of Mercedes, had almost made a convert of Doña Beatriz.

CHAPTER VI

"Looke back, who list, unto the former ages,
And call to count, what is of them become,
Where be those learned wits and antique sages,
Which of all wisdom knew the perfect somme?
Where those great warriors which did overcome
The world with conquest of their might and maine,
And made one meare of th'earth and of their raigne."

Ruins of Time.

Two or three days had passed before the Christians began to feel at home in the ancient seat of Mahommedan power. By that time, however, the Alhambra and the town got to be more regulated than they were during the hurry, delight, and grief, of taking possession and departing; and as the politic and far from ill-disposed Ferdinand had issued strict orders that the Moors should not only be treated with kindness, but with delicacy, the place gradually settled down into tranquillity, and men began to fall into their ancient habits and to interest themselves in their customary pursuits.

Don Fernando was much occupied with new cares, as a matter of course; but his illustrious consort, who reserved herself for great occasions, exercising her ordinary powers in the quiet, gentle manner that became her sex and native disposition, her truth and piety, had already withdrawn, as far as her high rank and substantial authority would allow, from the pageantry and martial scenes of a warlike court, and was seeking, with her wonted readiness, the haunts of private affection, and that intercourse which is most congenial to the softer affections of a woman. Her surviving children were with her, and they occupied much of her maternal care; but she had also many hours for friendship, and for the indulgence of an affection that appeared to include all her subjects within the ties of family.

On the morning of the third day that succeeded the evening of the interview related in the preceding chapter, Doña Isabella had collected about her person a few of those privileged individuals who might be said to have the entrée to her more private hours; for while that of Castile was renowned among Christian courts for etiquette, habits that it had probably derived from the stately oriental usages of its Mahommedan neighbors, the affectionate nature of the queen had cast a halo around her own private circle, that at once rendered it graceful as well as delightful to all who enjoyed the high honor of entering it. At that day, churchmen enjoyed a species of exclusive favor, mingling with all the concerns of life, and not unfrequently controlling them. While we are quick to detect blemishes of this sort among foreign nations, and are particularly prone to point out the evils that have flowed from the meddling of the Romish divines, we verify the truth of the venerable axiom that teaches us how much easier it is to see the faults of others than to discover our own; for no people afford stronger evidences of the existence of this control, than the people of the United States, more especially that portion of them who dwell in places that were originally settled by religionists, and which still continue under the influence of the particular sects that first prevailed; and perhaps the strongest national trait that exists among us at this moment—that of a disposition to extend the control of society beyond the limits set by the institutions and the laws, under the taking and plausible appellation of Public Opinion—has its origin in the polity of churches of a democratic character, that have aspired to be an *imperium in imperio*, confirmed and strengthened by their modes of government and by provincial habits. Be the fact as it may among ourselves, there is no question of the ascendency of the Catholic priesthood throughout Christendom, previously to the reformation; and Isabella was too sincerely devout, too unostentatiously pious, not to allow them every indulgence that comported with her own sense of right, and among others, that of a free access to her presence, and an influence on all her measures.

On the occasion just named, among others who were present was Fernando de Talavera, a prelate of high station, who had just been named to the new dignity of Archbishop of Granada, and the Fray Pedro de Carrascal, the former teacher of Luis de Bobadilla, an unbeneficed divine, who owed his favor to great simplicity of character, aided by his high birth. Isabella, herself, was seated at a little table, where she was employed with her needle, the subject of her toil being a task as homely as a shirt for the king, it being a part of her womanly propensities to acquit herself of this humble duty, as scrupulously as if she had been the wife of a common tradesman of her own capital. This was one of the habits of the age, however, if not a part of the policy of princes; for most travellers have seen the celebrated saddle of the Queen of Burgundy, with a place arranged for the distaff, that, when its owner rode forth, she might set an example of thrift to her admiring subjects; and with our own eyes, in these luxurious times, when few private ladies even condescend to touch any thing as useful as the garment that occupied the needle of Isabella of Castile, we have seen a queen, seated amid her royal daughters, as diligently employed with the needle as if her livelihood depended on her industry. But Doña Isabella had no affectations. In feelings, speech, nature, and acts, she was truth itself; and matrimonial tenderness gave her a deeply felt pleasure in thus being occupied for a husband whom she tenderly loved as a man, while it was impossible she could entirely conceal from herself all his faults as a monarch. Near her sat the companion of her girlish days, the long-tried and devoted Beatriz de Cabrera. Mercedes occupied a stool, at the feet of the Infanta Isabella, while one or two other ladies of the household were placed at hand, with such slight distinctions of rank as denoted the presence of royalty, but with a domestic freedom that made these observances graceful without rendering them fatiguing. The king himself was writing at a table, in a distant corner of the vast apartment; and no one, the newly-created archbishop not excepted, presumed to approach that side of the room. The discourse was conducted in a tone a little lower than common; even the queen, whose voice was always melody, modulating its tones in a way not to interfere with the train of thought into which her illustrious consort appeared to be profoundly plunged. But, at the precise moment that we now desire to present to the reader, Isabella had been deeply lost in reflection for some time, and a general silence prevailed in the female circle around the little work-tables.

"Daughter-Marchioness"—for so the queen usually addressed her friend—"Daughter-Marchioness," said Isabella, arousing herself from the long silence, "hath aught been seen or heard of late of the Señor Colon, the pilot who hath so long urged us on the subject of this western voyage?"

The quick, hurried glance of intelligence and gratification, that passed between Mercedes and her guardian, betrayed the interest they felt in this question, while the latter answered, as became her duty and her respect for her mistress—

"You remember, Señora, that he was written for, by Fray Juan Perez, Your Highness' ancient confessor, who journeyed all the way from his convent of Santa Maria de Rabida, in Andalusia, to intercede in his behalf, that his great designs might not be lost to Castile."

"Thou thinkest his designs, then, great, Daughter-Marchioness?"

"Can any think them otherwise, Señora? They seem reasonable and natural, and if just, is it not a great and laudable undertaking to extend the bounds of the church, and to confer honor and wealth on one's own country? My enthusiastic ward, Mercedes de Valverde, is so zealous in behalf of this navigator's great project, that, next to her duty to her God, and her duty to her sovereigns, it seemeth to make the great concern of her life."

The queen turned a smiling face toward the blushing girl who was the subject of this remark, and she gazed at her, for an instant, with the expression of affection that was so wont to illuminate her lovely countenance when dwelling on the features of her own daughters.

"Dost thou acknowledge this, Doña Mercedes?" she said; "hath Colon so convinced thee, that thou art thus zealous in his behalf?"

Mercedes arose, respectfully, when addressed by the queen, and she advanced a step or two nearer to the royal person before she made any reply.

"It becometh me to speak modestly, in this presence," said the beautiful girl; "but I shall not deny that I feel deep concern for the success of the Señor Colon. The thought is so noble, Señora, that it were a pity it should not be just."

"This is the reasoning of the young and generous-minded; and I confess myself, Beatrice, almost as childish as any, on this matter, at times—Colon, out of question, is still here?"

"Indeed he is, Señora," answered Mercedes, eagerly, and with a haste she immediately repented, for the inquiry was not made directly to herself; "I know of one who hath seen him as lately as the day the troops took possession of the town."

"Who is that person?" asked the queen, steadily, but not severely, her eye having turned again to the face of the girl, with an interest that continued to increase as she gazed.

Mercedes now bitterly regretted her indiscretion, and, in spite of a mighty effort to repress her feelings, the tell-tale blood mounted to her temples, ere she could find resolution to reply.

"Don Luis de Bobadilla, Señora, the nephew of my guardian, Doña Beatriz," she at length answered; for the love of truth was stronger in this pure-hearted young creature, even, than the dread of shame.

"Thou art particular, Señorita," Isabella observed calmly, severity seldom entering into her communication with the just-minded and good; "Don Luis cometh of too illustrious a house to need a herald to proclaim his alliances. It is only the obscure that the world doth not trouble itself about. Daughter-Marchioness," relieving Mercedes from a state scarcely less painful than the rack, by turning her eyes toward her friend, "this nephew of thine is a confirmed rover—but I doubt if he could be prevailed on to undertake an expedition like this of Colon's, that hath in view the glory of God and the benefit of the realm."

"Indeed, Señora"—Mercedes repressed her zeal by a sudden and triumphant effort.

"Thou wert about to speak, Doña Mercedes," gravely observed the queen.

"I crave Your Highness' forgiveness. It was improperly, as your own words were not addressed to me."

"This is not the court of the Queen of Castile, daughter, but the private room of Isabella de Trastamara," said the queen, willing to lessen the effect of what had already passed. "Thou hast the blood of the Admiral of Castile in thy veins, and art even akin to our Lord the King. Speak freely, then."

"I know your gracious goodness to me, Señora, and had nearly forgotten myself, under its influence. All I had to say was, that Don Luis de Bobadilla desireth exceedingly that the Señor Colon might get the caravels he seeketh, and that he himself might obtain the royal permission to make one among the adventurers."

"Can this be so, Beatriz?"

"Luis is a truant, Señora, beyond a question, but it is not with ignoble motives. I have heard him ardently express his desire to be one of Colon's followers, should that person be sent by Your Highness in search of the land of Cathay."

Isabella made no reply, but she laid her homely work in her lap, and sat musing, in pensive silence, for several minutes. During this interval, none near her presumed to speak, and Mercedes retired, stealthily, to her stool, at the feet of the Infanta. At length the queen arose, and, crossing the room, she approached the table where Don Fernando was still busily engaged with the pen. Here she paused a moment, as if unwilling to disturb him; but soon, laying a hand kindly on his shoulder, she drew his attention to herself. The king, as if conscious whence such familiarity could alone proceed, looked around immediately, and, rising from his chair, he was the first to speak.

"These Moriscoes need looking to," he said, betraying the direction that his thoughts had so early taken toward the increase of his power—"I find we have left Abdallah many strongholds in the Apulxarras, that may make him a troublesome neighbor, unless we can push him across the Mediterranean"—

"Of this, Fernando, we will converse on some other opportunity," interrupted the queen, whose pure mind disliked every thing that even had an approach to a breach of faith. "It is hard enough for those who control the affairs of men, always to obey God and their own consciences, without seeking occasions to violate their faith. I have come to thee, on another matter. The hurry of the times, and the magnitude of our affairs, have caused us to overlook the promise given to Colon, the navigator" —

"Still busied with thy needle, Isabella, and for my comfort," observed the king, playing with the shirt that his royal consort had unconsciously brought in her hand; "few subjects have wives as considerate and kind as thou!"

"Thy comfort and happiness stand next to my duty to God and the care of my people," returned Isabella, gratified at the notice the King of Aragon had taken of this little homage of her sex, even while she suspected that it came from a wish to parry the subject that was then uppermost in her thoughts. "I would do naught in this important concern, without thy fullest approbation, if that may be had; and I think it toucheth our royal words to delay no longer. Seven years are a most cruel probation, and, unless we are active, we shall have some of the hot-blooded young nobles of the kingdom undertaking the matter, as their holiday sports."

"Thou say'st true, Señora, and we will refer the subject, at once, to Fernando de Talavera, yonder, who is of approved discretion, and one to be relied on." As the king spoke, he beckoned to the individual named, who immediately approached the royal pair. "Archbishop of Granada," continued the wily king, who had as many politic arts as a modern patriot intently bent on his own advancement—"Archbishop of Granada, our royal consort hath a desire that this affair of Colon should be immediately inquired into, and reported on to ourselves. It is our joint command that you, and others, take the matter, before the next twenty-four hours shall pass, into mature consideration and inquiry, and that you lay the result before ourselves. The names of your associates shall be given to you in the course of the day."

While the tongue of Ferdinand was thus instructing the prelate, the latter read in the expression of the monarch's eye, and in the coldness of his countenance, a meaning that his quick and practiced wits were not slow in interpreting. He signified his dutiful assent, however; received the names of his associates in the commission, of whom Isabella pointed out one or two, and then waited to join in the discourse.

"This project of Colon's is worthy of being more seriously inquired into," resumed the king, when these preliminaries were settled, "and it shall be our care to see that he hath all consideration. They tell me the honest navigator is a good Christian."

"I think him devotedly so, Don Fernando. He hath a purpose, should God prosper his present undertaking, to join in a new effort to regain the holy sepulchre."

"Umph! Such designs may be meritorious, but ours is the true way to advance the faith—this conquest of our own. We have raised the cross, my wife, where the ensigns of infidelity were lately seen, and Granada is so near Castile that it will not be difficult to maintain our altars. Such, at least, are the opinions of a layman—holy prelate—on these matters."

"And most just and wise opinions are they, Señor," returned the archbishop. "That which can be retained, it is wisest to seek, for we lose our labors in gaining things that Providence hath placed so far beyond our control, that they do not seem designed for our purposes."

"There are those, my Lord Archbishop," observed the queen, "who might argue against all attempts to recover the holy sepulchre, hearing opinions like these, from so high authority!"

"Then, Señora, they would misconceive that authority," the politic prelate hurriedly replied. "It is well for all Christendom, to drive the Infidels from the Holy Land; but for Castile it is better to dispossess them of Granada. The distinction is a very plain one, as every sound casuist must admit."

"This truth is as evident to our reason," added Ferdinand, casting a look of calm exultation out at a window, "as that yonder towers were once Abdallah's, and that they are now our own!"

"Better for Castile!" repeated Isabella, in the tones of one who mused. "For her worldly power better, perhaps, but not better for the souls of those who achieve the deed—surely, not better for the glory of God!"

"My much-honored wife, and beloved consort"—said the king.

"Señora"—added the prelate.

But Isabella walked slowly away, pondering on principles, while the eyes of the two worldings she left behind her, met, with the sort of free-masonry that is in much request among those who are too apt to substitute the expedient for the right. The queen did not return to her seat, but she walked up and down that part of the room which the archbishop had left vacant when he approached herself and her husband. Here she remained alone for several minutes, even Ferdinand holding her in too much reverence to presume to disturb her meditations, uninvited. The queen several times cast glances at Mercedes, and, at length, she commanded her to draw near.

"Daughter," said Isabella, who frequently addressed those she loved by this endearing term, "thou hast not forgotten thy freely-offered vow?"

"Next to my duty to God, Señora, I most consider my duty to my sovereign."

Mercedes spoke firmly, and in those tones that seldom deceive. Isabella riveted her eyes on the pale features of the beautiful girl, and when the words just quoted were uttered, a tender mother could not have regarded a beloved child with stronger proofs of affection.

"Thy duty to God overshadoweth all other feelings, daughter, as is just," answered the queen; "thy duty to me is secondary and inferior. Still, thou and all others, owe a solemn duty to your sovereign, and I should be unfit for the high trust that I have received from Providence, did I permit any of these obligations to lessen. It is not I that reign in Castile, but Providence, through its humble and unworthy instrument. My people are my children, and I often pray that I may have heart enough to hold them all. If princes are sometimes obliged to frown on the unworthy, it is but in humble and distant imitation of that Power which cannot smile on evil."

"I hope, Señora," said the girl, timidly, observing that the queen paused, "I have not been so unfortunate as to displease you; a frown from Your Highness would indeed be a calamity!"

"Thou? No, daughter; I would that all the maidens of Castile, noble and simple, were of thy truth, and modesty, and obedience. But we cannot permit thee to become the victim of the senses. Thou art too well taught, Doña Mercedes, not to distinguish between that which is brilliant and that which is truly virtuous" —

"Señora!" cried Mercedes, eagerly—then checking herself, immediately, for she felt it was a disrespect to interrupt her sovereign.

"I listen to what thou wouldst say, daughter," Isabella answered, after pausing for the frightened girl to continue. "Speak freely; thou addressest a parent."

"I was about to say, Señora, that if all that is brilliant is not virtuous, neither is all that is unpleasant to the sight, or what prudence might condemn, actually vicious."

"I understand thee, Señorita, and the remark hath truth in it. Now, let us speak of other things. Thou appearest to be friendly to the designs of this navigator, Colon?"

"The opinion of one untaught and youthful as I, can have little weight with the Queen of Castile, who can ask counsel of prelates and learned churchmen, besides consulting her own wisdom;" Mercedes modestly answered.

"But thou thinkest well of his project; or have I mistaken thy meaning?"

"No, Señora, I *do* think well of Colon's scheme; for to me it seemeth of that nobleness and grandeur that Providence would favor, for the good of man and the advancement of the church."

"And thou believest that nobles and cavaliers can be found willing to embark with this obscure Genoese, in his bold undertaking?"

The queen felt the hand that she affectionately held in both her own, tremble, and when she looked at her companion she perceived that her face was crimsoned and her eyes lowered. But the generous girl thought the moment critical for the fortunes of her lover, and she rallied all her energies in order to serve his interests.

"Señora, I do," she answered, with a steadiness that both surprised and pleased the queen, who entered into and appreciated all her feelings; "I think Don Luis de Bobadilla will embark with him; since his aunt hath conversed freely with him on the nature and magnitude of the enterprise, his mind dwelleth on little else. He would be willing to furnish gold for the occasion, could his guardians be made to consent "

"Which any guardian would be very wrong to do. We may deal freely with our own, but it is forbidden to jeopard the goods of another. If Don Luis de Bobadilla persevere in this intention, and act up to his professions, I shall think more favorably of his character than circumstances have hitherto led me to do."

"Señora!"

"Hear me, daughter; we cannot now converse longer on this point, the council waiting my presence, and the king having already left us. Thy guardian and I will confer together, and thou shalt not be kept in undue suspense; but Mercedes de Valverde" —

"My Lady the Queen" —

"Remember thy vow, daughter. It was freely given, and must not be hastily forgotten."

Isabella now kissed the pale cheek of the girl and withdrew, followed by all the ladies; leaving the half-pleased and yet half-terrified Mercedes standing in the centre of the vast apartment, resembling a beautiful statue of Doubt.

CHAPTER VII

"He that of such a height hath built his mind,
And reared the dwelling of his thoughts so strong
As neither fear nor hope can shake the frame
Of his resolved powers."

Daniel.

The following day the Alhambra was crowded with courtiers as usual; applicants for favors, those who sought their own, and those who solicited the redress of imaginary wrongs. The ante-chambers were thronged, and the different individuals in waiting jealously eyed each other, as if to inquire how far their neighbors would be likely to thwart their several views or to advance their wishes. Men bowed, in general, coldly and with distrust; and the few that did directly pass their greetings, met with the elaborated civility that commonly characterizes the intercourse of palaces.

While curiosity was active in guessing at the business of the different individuals present, and whispers, nods, shrugs of the shoulders, and meaning glances, passed among the old stagers, as they communicated to each other the little they knew, or thought they knew, on different subjects, there stood in the corner of the principal apartment, one in particular, who might be distinguished from all around him, by his stature, the gravity and dignity of his air, and the peculiar sort of notice that he attracted. Few approached him, and they that did, as they turned their backs, cast those glances of self-sufficiency and ridicule about them, that characterize the vulgar-minded when they fancy that they are deriding or sneering in consonance with popular opinion. This was Columbus, who was very generally regarded by the multitude as a visionary schemer, and who necessarily shared in that sort of contemptuous obloquy that attaches itself to the character. But even the wit and jokes of the crowd had been expended upon this subject, and the patience of those who danced attendance was getting to be exhausted, when a little stir at the door announced the approach of some new courtier. The manner in which the throng quickly gave way, denoted the presence of some one of high rank, and presently Don Luis de Bobadilla stood in the centre of the room.

"It is the nephew of Her Highness' favorite," whispered one.

"A noble of one of the most illustrious families of Castile," said another; "but a fitting associate of this Colon, as neither the authority of his guardians, the wishes of the queen, nor his high station, can keep him from the life of a vagabond."

"One of the best lances in Spain, if he had the prudence and wisdom to turn his skill to profit," observed a third.

"That is the youthful knight who hath so well deported himself in this last campaign," growled an inferior officer of the infantry, "and who unhorsed Don Alonso de Ojeda in the tourney; but his lance is as unsteady in its aim, as it is good in the rest. They tell me he is a rover."

As if purposely to justify this character, Luis looked about him anxiously a moment, and then made his way directly to the side of Colon. The smiles, nods, shrugs, and half-suppressed whispers that followed, betrayed the common feeling; but a door on the side of the closet opening, all eyes were immediately bent in that direction, and the little interruption just mentioned was as soon forgotten.

"I greet you, Señor," said Luis, bowing respectfully to Columbus. "Since our discourse of last evening I have thought of little besides its subject, and have come hither to renew it."

That Columbus was pleased by this homage, appeared in his eye, his smile, and the manner in which he raised his body, as if full of the grandeur of his own designs; but he was compelled to defer the pleasure that it always gave him to dilate on his enterprise.

"I am commanded hither, noble Señor," he answered, cordially, "by the holy Archbishop of Granada, who, it seemeth, hath it in charge from their Highnesses, to bring my affair to a speedy issue, and who hath named this very morning for that purpose. We touch upon the verge of great events: the day is not distant, when this conquest of Granada will be forgotten, in the greater importance of the mighty things that God hath held in reserve!"

"By San Pedro, my new patron! I do believe you, Señor. Cathay must lie at or near the spot you have named, and your own eyes shall not see it, and its gorgeous stories of wealth, sooner than mine. Remember Pedro de Muños, I pray you, Señor Colon."

"He shall not be forgotten, I promise you, young lord; and all the great deeds of your ancestors will be eclipsed by the glory achieved by their son. But I hear my name called; we will talk of this anon."

"El Señor Christoval Colon!" was called by one of the pages, in a loud authoritative voice, and the navigator hurried forward, buoyed up with hope and joy.

The manner in which one so generally regarded with indifference, if not with contempt, had been selected from all that crowd of courtiers, excited some surprise; but as the ordinary business of the antechamber went on, and the subordinates of office soon appeared in the rooms, to hear solicitations and answer questions, the affair was quickly forgotten. Luis withdrew disappointed, for he had hoped to enjoy another long discourse with Columbus, on a subject which, as it was connected with his dearest hopes, now occupied most of his thoughts. We shall leave him, however, and all in the ante-chambers, to follow the great navigator further into the depths of the palace.

Fernando de Talavera had not been unmindful of his orders. Instead, however, of associating with this prelate, men known to be well disposed to listen to the propositions of Columbus, the king and queen had made the mistake of choosing some six or eight of their courtiers, persons of probity and of good general characters, but who were too little accustomed to learned research, properly to appreciate the magnitude of the proposed discoveries. Into the presence of these distinguished nobles and churchmen was Columbus now ushered, and among them is the reader to suppose him seated. We pass over the customary ceremonies of the introduction, and proceed at once to the material part of the narrative. The Archbishop of Granada was the principal speaker on the part of the commissioners.

"We understand, Señor Colon," continued the prelate, "should you be favored by their Highnesses' power and authority, that you propose to undertake a voyage into the unknown Atlantic, in quest of the land of Cathay and the celebrated island of Cipango?"

"That is my design, holy and illustrious prelate. The matter hath been so often up between the agents of the two sovereigns and myself, that there is little occasion to enlarge on my views."

"These were fully discussed at Salamanca, of a verity, where many learned churchmen were of your way of thinking, Señor, though more were against it. Our Lord the King, and our Lady the Queen, however, are disposed to view the matter favorably, and this commission hath been commanded that we might arrange all previous principles, and determine the rights of the respective parties. What force in vessels and equipments do you demand, in order to achieve the great objects you expect, under the blessing of God, to accomplish?"

"You have well spoken, Lord Archbishop; it will be by the blessing of God, and under his especial care, that all will be done, for his glory and worship are involved in the success. With so good an ally on my side, little worldly means will be necessary. Two caravels of light burden are all I ask, with the flag of the sovereigns, and a sufficiency of mariners."

The commissioners turned toward each other in surprise, and while some saw in the moderate request the enthusiastic heedlessness of a visionary, others detected the steady reliance of faith.

"That is not asking much, truly," observed the prelate, who was among the first; "and, though these wars have left us of Castile with an exhausted treasury, we could compass that little without the aid of a miracle. The caravels might be found, and the mariners levied, but there are weighty points to determine before we reach that concession. You expect, Señor, to be intrusted with the command of the expedition, in your own person?"

"Without that confidence I could not be answerable for success. I ask the full and complete authority of an admiral, or a sea-commander, of their Highnesses. The force employed will be trifling in appearance, but the risks will be great, and the power of the two crowns must completely sustain that of him on whose shoulders will rest the entire weight of the responsibility."

"This is but just, and none will gainsay it. But, Señor, have you thought maturely on the advantages that are to accrue to the sovereigns, should they sustain you in this undertaking?"

"Lord Archbishop, for eighteen years hath this subject occupied my thoughts, and employed my studies, both by day and by night. In the whole of that long period have I done little that hath not had a direct bearing on the success of this mighty enterprise. The advantages to all concerned, that will flow from it, have, therefore, scarce been forgotten."

"Name them, Señor "

"First, then, as is due to his all-seeing and omnipotent protection, glory will be given to the Almighty, by the spreading of his church and the increase of his worshippers." Fernando de Talavera and all the churchmen present piously crossed themselves, an act in which Columbus himself joined. "Their Highnesses, as is meet, will reap the next advantages, in the extension of their empire and in the increase of their subjects. Wealth will flow in upon Castile and Aragon, in a rapid stream, His Holiness freely granting to Christian monarchs the thrones and territories of all infidel princes whose possessions may be discovered, or people converted to the faith, through their means."

"This is plausible, Señor," returned the prelate, "and founded on just principles. His Holiness certainly is entrusted with that power, and hath been known to use it, for the glory of God. You doubtless know, Señor Colon, that Don John of Portugal hath paid great attention to these matters already, and that he and his predecessors have probably pushed discovery to the verge of its final limits. His enterprise hath also obtained from Rome certain privileges that may not be meddled with."

"I am not ignorant of the Portuguese enterprise, holy prelate, nor of the spirit with which Don John hath exercised his power. His vessels voyage along the western shore of Africa, and in a direction altogether different from that I propose to take. My purpose is to launch forth, at once, into the broad Atlantic, and by following the sun toward his place of evening retirement, reach the eastern bounds of the Indies, by a road that will lessen the journey many months."

Although the archbishop and most of his coadjutors belonged to the numerous class of those who regarded Columbus as a brain-heated visionary, the earnest, but lofty dignity, with which he thus simply touched upon his projects; the manner in which he quietly smoothed down his white locks, when he had spoken; and the enthusiasm that never failed to kindle in his eye, as he dwelt on his noble designs, produced a deep impression on all present, and there was a moment when the general feeling was to aid him to the extent of the common means. It was a singular and peculiar proof of the existence of this transient feeling that one of the commissioners immediately inquired—

"Do you propose, Señor Colon, to seek the court of Prestor John?"

"I know not, noble Señor, that such a potentate hath even an existence," answered Columbus, whose notions had got the fixed and philosophical bias that is derived from science, and who entered little into the popular fallacies of the day, though necessarily subject to much of the ignorance of the age; "I find nothing to establish the truth of there being such a monarch at all, or such territories."

This admission did not help the navigator's cause; for to affirm that the earth was a sphere, and that Prestor John was a creature of the imagination, was abandoning the marvellous to fall back on demonstration and probabilities—a course that the human mind, in its uncultivated condition, is not fond of taking.

"There are men who will be willing to put faith in the truth of Prestor John's power and territories," interrupted one of the commissioners, who was indebted to his present situation purely to King Ferdinand's policy, "who will flatly deny that the earth is round; since we all know that there are kings, and territories, and Christians, while we see that the earth and the ocean are plains."

This opinion was received with an assenting smile by most present, though Fernando de Talavera had doubts of its justice.

"Señor," answered Columbus, mildly, "if all in this world was in truth what it seemeth, confessions would be little needed, and penance would be much lighter."

"I esteem you a good Christian, Señor Colon," observed the archbishop, sharply.

"I am such as the grace of God and a weak nature have made me, Lord Archbishop; though I humbly trust that when I shall have achieved this great end, that I may be deemed more worthy of the divine protection, as well as of the divine favor."

"It hath been said that thou deemest thyself especially set apart by Providence for this work."

"I feel that within me, holy prelate, that encourageth such a hope; but I build naught on mysteries that exceed my comprehension."

It would be difficult to say whether Columbus lost or gained in the opinions of his auditors, by this answer. The religious feeling of the age was in perfect consonance with the sentiment; but, to the churchmen present, it seemed arrogant in a humble and unknown layman, even to believe it possible that he could be the chosen vessel, when so many who appeared to have higher claims were rejected. Still no expression of this feeling was permitted, for it was then, as it is now—he who seemed to rely on the power of God, carrying with him a weight and an influence that ordinarily checked rebukes.

"You propose to endeavor to reach Cathay by means of sailing forth into the broad Atlantic," resumed the archbishop, "and yet you deny the existence of Prestor John."

"Your pardon, holy prelate—I do propose to reach Cathay and Cipango in the mode you mention, but I do not absolutely deny the existence of the monarch you have named. For the probability of the success of my enterprise, I have already produced my proofs and reasons, which have satisfied many learned churchmen; but evidence is wanting to establish the last."

"And yet Giovanni di Montecorvino, a pious bishop of our holy church, is said to have converted such a prince to the true faith, nearly two centuries since."

"The power of God can do any thing, Lord Archbishop, and I am not one to question the merits of his chosen ministers. All I can answer on this point is, to say that I find no scientific or plausible reasons to justify me in pursuing what may prove to be as deceptive as the light which recedes before the hand that would touch it. As for Cathay and its position and its wonders, we have the better established evidence of the renowned Venetians, Marco and Nicolo Polo, who not only travelled in those territories, but sojourned years at the court of their monarch. But, noble gentlemen, whether there is a Prestor John, or a Cathay, there is certainly a limit to the western side of the Atlantic, and that limit I am ready to seek."

The archbishop betrayed his incredulity in the upward turn of his eyes; but having his commands from those who were accustomed to be obeyed, and knowing that the theory of Columbus had been gravely heard and reported on, years before, at Salamanca, he determined prudently to keep within his proper sphere, and to proceed at once to that into which it was his duty to inquire.

"You have set forth the advantages that you think may be derived to the sovereigns, should your project succeed, Señor," he said, "and truly they are not light, if all your brilliant hopes may be realized; but it now remaineth to know what conditions you reserve for yourself, as the reward of all your risks and many years of anxious labor."

"All that hath been duly considered, illustrious archbishop, and you will find the substance of my wishes set forth in this paper, though many of the smaller provisions will remain to be enumerated."

As Columbus spoke he handed the paper in question to Ferdinand of Talavera. The prelate ran his eyes over it hastily at first, but a second time with more deliberation, and it would be difficult to say whether ridicule or indignation was most strongly expressed in his countenance, as he deridingly threw the document on a table. When this act of contempt was performed, he turned toward Columbus, as if to satisfy himself that the navigator was not mad.

"Art thou serious in demanding these terms, Señor?" he asked sternly, and with a look that would have caused most men, in the humble station of the applicant, to swerve from their purpose.

"Lord Archbishop," answered Columbus, with a dignity that was not easily disturbed, "this matter hath now occupied my mind quite eighteen years. During the whole of this long period I have thought seriously of little else, and it may be said to have engaged my mind sleeping and waking. I saw the truth early and intensely, but every day seems to bring it brighter and brighter before my eyes. I feel a reliance on success, that cometh from dependence on God. I think myself an agent, chosen for the accomplishment of great ends, and ends that will not be decided by the success of this one enterprise. There is more beyond, and I must retain the dignity and the means necessary to accomplish it. I cannot abate, in the smallest degree, the nature or the amount of these conditions."

Although the manner in which these words were uttered lent them weight, the prelate fancied that the mind of the navigator had got to be unsettled by his long contemplation of a single subject. The only things that left any doubt concerning the accuracy of this opinion, were the method and science with which he had often maintained, even in his own presence, the reasonableness of his geographical suppositions; arguments which, though they had failed to convince one bent on believing the projector a visionary, had, nevertheless, greatly puzzled the listener. Still, the demands he had just read seemed so extravagant, that, for a single instant, a sentiment of pity repressed the burst of indignation to which he felt disposed to give vent.

"How like ye, noble lords," he cried, sarcastically, turning to two or three of his fellow-commissioners, who had eagerly seized the paper and were endeavoring to read it, and all at the same moment, "the moderate and modest demands of the Señor Christoval Colon, the celebrated navigator who confounded the Council of Salamanca! Are they not such as becometh their Highnesses to accept on bended knees, and with many thanks?"

"Read them, Lord Archbishop," exclaimed several in a breath. "Let us first know their nature."

"There are many minor conditions that might be granted, as unworthy of discussion," resumed the prelate, taking the paper; "but here are two that must give the sovereigns infinite satisfaction. The Señor Colon actually satisfieth himself with the rank of Admiral and Viceroy over all the countries he may discover; and as for gains, one-tenth—the church's share, my brethren—yea, even one-tenth, one *humble* tenth of the proceeds and customs, will content him!"

The general murmur that passed among the commissioners, denoted a common dissatisfaction, and at that instant Columbus had not a true supporter in the room.

"Nor is this all, illustrious nobles, and holy priests," continued the archbishop, following up his advantage as soon as he believed his auditors ready to hear him—"nor is this all; lest these high dignities should weary their Highnesses' shoulders, and those of their royal progeny, the liberal Genoese actually consenteth to transmit them to his own posterity, in all time to come; converting the kingdom of Cathay into a realm for the uses of the house of Colon, to maintain the dignity of which, the tenth of all the benefits are to be consigned to its especial care!"

There would have been an open laugh at this sally, had not the noble bearing of Columbus checked its indulgence; and even Ferdinand of Talavera, under the stern rebuke of an eye and mien that carried with them a grave authority, began to think he had gone too far.

"Your pardon, Señor Colon," he immediately and more courteously added; "but your conditions sounded so lofty that they have quite taken me by surprise. You cannot seriously mean to maintain them?"

"Not one jot will I abate, Lord Priest: that much will be my due; and he that consenteth to less than he deserveth, becometh an instrument of his own humiliation. I shall give to the sovereigns an empire that will far exceed in value all their other possessions, and I claim my reward. I tell you, moreover, reverend prelate, that there is much in reserve, and that these conditions will be needed to fulfil the future."

"These are truly modest proposals for a nameless Genoese!" exclaimed one of the courtiers, who had been gradually swelling with disgust and contempt. "The Señor Colon will be certain of commanding in the service of their Highnesses, and if nothing is done he will have that high honor without cost; whereas, should this most improbable scheme lead to any benefits, he will become a vice-king, humbly contenting himself with the church's revenue!"

This remark appeared to determine the wavering, and the commissioners rose, in a body, as if the matter were thought to be unworthy of further discussion. With the view to preserve at least the appearance of impartiality and discretion, however, the archbishop turned once more toward Columbus, and now, certain of obtaining his ends, he spoke to him in milder tones.

"For the last time, Señor," he said, "I ask if you still insist on these unheard-of terms?"

"On them, and on no other," said Columbus, firmly. "I know the magnitude of the services I shall perform, and will not degrade them—will in no manner lessen their dignity, by accepting aught else. But, Lord Archbishop, and you, too, noble Señor, that treateth my claims so lightly, I am ready to add to the risk of person, life, and name, that of gold. I will furnish one-eighth of the needful sums, if ye will increase my benefits in that proportion."

"Enough, enough," returned the prelate, preparing to quit the room; "we will make our report to the sovereigns, this instant, and thou shalt speedily know their pleasure."

Thus terminated the conference. The courtiers left the room, conversing earnestly among themselves, like men who did not care to repress their indignation; while Columbus, filled with the noble character of his own designs, disappeared in another direction, with the bearing of one whose self-respect was not to be lessened by clamor, and who appreciated ignorance and narrowness of views too justly to suffer them to change his own high purposes.

Ferdinand of Talavera was as good as his word. He was the queen's confessor, and, in virtue of that holy office, had at all times access to her presence. Full of the subject of the late interview, he took his way directly to the private apartments of the queen, and, as a matter of course, was at once admitted. Isabella heard his representations with mortification and regret, for she had begun to set her heart on the sailing of this extraordinary expedition. But the influence of the archbishop was very great, for his royal penitent knew the sincerity and devotedness of his heart.

"This carrieth presumption to insolence, Señora," continued the irritated churchman; "have we not here a mendicant adventurer demanding honors and authority that belong only to God and his anointed, the princes of the earth? Who is this Colon?—a nameless Genoese, without rank, services, or modesty, and yet doth he carry his pretensions to a height that might cause even a Guzman to hesitate."

"He is a good Christian, holy prelate," Isabella meekly answered, "and seemeth to delight in the service and glory of God, and to wish to favor the extension of his visible and Catholic church."

"True, Señora, and yet may there be deceit in this" —

"Nay, Lord Archbishop, I do not think that deceit is the man's failing, for franker speech and more manly bearing it is not usual to see, even in the most powerful. He hath solicited us for years, and yet no act of meanness may be fairly laid to his charge."

"I shall not judge the heart of this man harshly, Doña Isabella, but we may judge of his actions and his pretensions, and how far they may be suitable to the dignity of the two crowns, freely and without censure. I confess him grave, and plausible, and light of neither discourse nor manner, virtues certainly, as the world moveth in courts"—Isabella smiled, but she said nothing, for her ghostly counsellor was wont to rebuke with freedom, and she to listen with humility—"where the age is not exhibiting its purest models of sobriety of thought and devotion, but even these may exist without the spirit that shall be fitted for heaven. But what are gravity and decorum, if sustained by an inflated pride and inordinate rapacity? ambition being a term too lofty for such a craving. Reflect, Señora, on the full nature of these demands. This Colon requireth to be established, forever, in the high state of a substitute for a king, not only for his own person, but for those of his descendants throughout all time, with the title and authority of Admiral over all adjacent seas, should he discover any of the lands he so much exalts, before he will consent to enter into the command of certain of Your Highnesses' vessels, a station of itself only too honorable for one of so little note! Should his most extravagant pretensions be realized—and the probabilities are that they will entirely fail—his demands would exceed his services; whereas, in the case of failure, the Castilian and Aragonese names would be covered with ridicule, and a sore disrespect would befal the royal dignity for having been thus duped by an adventurer. Much of the glory of this late conquest would be tarnished, by a mistake so unfortunate."

"Daughter-Marchioness," observed the queen, turning toward the faithful, and long-tried friend who was occupied with her needle near her own side—"these conditions of Colon do, truly, seem to exceed the bounds of reason."

"The enterprise also exceedeth all the usual bounds of risks and adventures, Señora," was the steady reply of Doña Beatriz, as she glanced toward the countenance of Mercedes. "Noble efforts deserve noble rewards."

The eye of Isabella followed the glance of her friend, and it remained fixed for some time on the pale, anxious features of her favorite's ward. The beautiful girl herself was unconscious of the attention she excited; but one who knew her secret might easily detect the intense feeling with which she awaited the issue. The opinions of her confessor had seemed so reasonable, that Isabella was on the point of assenting to the report of the commissioners, and of abandoning altogether the secret hopes and expectations she had begun to couple with the success of the navigator's schemes, when a gentler feeling, one that belonged peculiarly to her own feminine heart, interposed to give the mariner another chance. It is seldom that woman is dead to the sympathies connected with the affections, and the wishes that sprang from the love of Mercedes de Valverde were the active cause of the decision that the Queen of Castile came to at that critical moment.

"We must be neither harsh nor hasty with this Genoese, Lord Archbishop," she said, turning again to the prelate. "He hath the virtues of devoutness and fair-dealing, and these are qualities that sovereigns learn to prize. His demands no doubt have become somewhat exaggerated by long brooding, in his thoughts, on a favorite and great scheme; but kind words and reason may yet lead him to more moderation. Let him, then, be tried with propositions of our own, and doubtless, his necessities, if not a sense of justice, will cause him to accept them. The viceroyalty doth, indeed, exceed the usual policy of princes, and, as you say, holy prelate, the tenth is the church's share; but the admiral's rank may be fairly claimed. Meet him, then, with these moderated proposals, and substitute a fifteenth for a tenth; let him be a viceroy in his own person, during the pleasure of Don Fernando and myself, but let him relinquish the claim for his posterity."

Fernando de Talavera thought even these concessions too considerable, but, while he exercised his sacred office with a high authority, he too well knew the character of Isabella to presume to dispute an order she had once issued, although it was in her own mild and feminine manner. After receiving a few more instructions, therefore, and obtaining the counsel of the king, who was at work in an adjoining cabinet, the prelate went to execute this new commission.

Two or three days now passed before the subject was finally disposed of, and Isabella was again seated in the domestic circle, when admission was once more demanded in behalf of her confessor. The archbishop entered with a flushed face, and his whole appearance was so disturbed that it must have been observed by the most indifferent person.

"How now, holy archbishop,"—demanded Isabella—"doth thy new flock vex thy spirit, and is it so very hard to deal with an infidel?"

"'Tis naught of that, Señora—'tis naught relating to my new people. I find even the followers of the false prophet more reasonable than some who exult in Christ's name and favor. This Colon is a madman, and better fitted to become a saint in Mussulmans' eyes, than even a pilot in Your Highness' service."

At this burst of indignation, the queen, the Marchioness of Moya, and Doña Mercedes de Valverde, simultaneously dropped their needle-work, and sat looking at the prelate, with a common concern. They had all hoped that the difficulties which stood in the way of a favorable termination to the negotiation would be removed, and that the time was at hand, when the being who, in spite of the boldness and unusual character of his projects, had succeeded in so signally commanding their respect, and in interesting their feelings, was about to depart, and to furnish a practical solution to problems that had as much puzzled their reasons as they had excited their curiosity. But here was something like a sudden and unlooked-for termination to all their expectations; and while Mercedes felt something like despair chilling her heart, the queen and Doña Beatriz were both displeased.

"Didst thou duly explain to Señor Colon, the nature of our proposals, Lord Archbishop?" the former asked, with more severity of manner than she was accustomed to betray; "and doth he still insist on the pretensions to a vice-regal power, and on the offensive condition in behalf of his posterity?"

"Even so, Your Highness; were it Isabella of Castile treating with Henry of England or Louis of France, the starving Genoese could not hold higher terms or more inflexible conditions. He abateth nothing. The man deemeth himself chosen of God, to answer certain ends, and his language and conditions are such as one who felt a holy impulse to his course, could scarcely feel warranted in assuming."

"This constancy hath its merit," observed the queen; "but there is a limit to concession. I shall urge no more in the navigator's favor, but leave him to the fortune that naturally followeth self-exaltation and all extravagance of demand."

This speech apparently sealed the fate of Columbus in Castile. The archbishop was appeased, and, first holding a short private conference with his royal penitent, he left the room. Shortly after, Christoval Colon, as he was called by the Spaniards—Columbus, as he styled himself in later life—received, for a definite answer, the information that his conditions were rejected, and that the negotiation for the projected voyage to the Indies was finally at an end.

CHAPTER VIII

"Oh! ever thus, from childhood's hour,
I've seen my fondest hopes decay;
I never loved a tree or flower,
But 'twas the first to fade away."

Lalla Rookh.

The season had now advanced to the first days of February, and, in that low latitude, the weather was becoming genial and spring-like. On the morning succeeding that of the interview just related, some six or eight individuals, attracted by the loveliness of the day, and induced morally by a higher motive, were assembled before the door of one of those low dwellings of Santa Fé that had been erected for the accommodation of the conquering army. Most of these persons were grave Spaniards of a certain age, though young Luis de Bobadilla was also there, and the tall, dignified form of Columbus was in the group. The latter was equipped for the road, and a stout, serviceable Andalusian mule stood ready to receive its burden, near at hand. A charger was by the side of the mule, showing that the rider of the last was about to have company. Among the Spaniards were Alonzo de Quintanilla, the accountant-general of Castile, a firm friend of the navigator, and Luis de St. Angel, the receiver of the ecclesiastical revenues of Aragon, who was one of the firmest converts that Columbus had made to the philosophical accuracy of his opinions and to the truth of his vast conceptions.

The two last had been in earnest discourse with the navigator, but the discussion had closed, and Señor de St. Angel, a man of generous feelings and ardent imagination, was just expressing himself warmly, in the following words—

"By the lustre of the two crowns!" he cried, "this ought not to come to pass. But, adieu, Señor Colon—God have you in his holy keeping, and send you wiser and less prejudiced judges, hereafter. The past can only cause us shame and grief, while the future is in the womb of time."

The whole party, with the exception of Luis de Bobadilla, then took their leave. As soon as the place was clear, Columbus mounted, and passed through the thronged streets, attended by the young noble on his charger. Not a syllable was uttered by either, until they were fairly on the plain, though Columbus often sighed like a man oppressed with grief. Still, his mien was calm, his bearing dignified, and his eye lighted with that unquenchable fire which finds its fuel in the soul within.

When fairly without the gates, Columbus turned courteously to his young companion and thanked him for his escort; but, with a consideration for the other that was creditable to his heart, he added—

"While I am so grateful for this honor, coming from one so noble and full of hopes, I must not forget your own character. Didst thou not remark, friend Luis, as we passed through the streets, that divers Spaniards pointed at me, as the object of scorn?"

"I did, Señor," answered Luis, his cheek glowing with indignation, "and had it not been that I dreaded your displeasure, I would have trodden the vagabonds beneath my horse's feet, failing of a lance to spit them on!"

"Thou hast acted most wisely in showing forbearance. But these are men, and their common judgment maketh public opinion; nor do I perceive that the birth, or the opportunities, causeth material distinctions between them, though the manner of expression vary. There are vulgar among the noble, and noble among the lowly. This very act of kindness of thine, will find its deriders and contemners in the court of the two sovereigns."

"Let him look to it, who presumeth to speak lightly of you, Señor, to Luis de Bobadilla! We are not a patient race, and Castilian blood is apt to be hot blood."

"I should be sorry that any man but myself should draw in my quarrel. But, if we take offence at all who think and speak folly, we may pass our days in harness. Let the young nobles have their jest, if it give them pleasure—but do not let me regret my friendship for thee."

Luis promised fairly, and then, as if his truant thoughts would revert to the subject unbidden, he hastily resumed—

"You speak of the noble as of a class different from your own—surely, Señor Colon, thou art noble?"

"Would it make aught different in thy opinions and feelings, young man, were I to answer no?"

The cheek of Don Luis flushed, and, for an instant, he repented of his remark; but falling back on his own frank and generous nature, he answered immediately, without reservation or duplicity—

"By San Pedro, my new patron! I could wish you were noble, Señor, if it were merely for the honor of the class. There are so many among us who do no credit to their spurs, that we might gladly receive such an acquisition."

"This world is made up of changes, young Señor," returned Columbus, smiling. "The seasons undergo their changes; night follows day; comets come and go; monarchs become subjects, and subjects monarchs; nobles lose the knowledge of their descent, and plebeians rise to the rank of nobles. There is a tradition among us, that we were formerly of the privileged class; but time and our unlucky fortune have brought us down to humble employments. Am I to lose the honor of Don Luis de Bobadilla's company in the great voyage, should I be more fortunate in France than I have been in Castile, because his commander happeneth to have lost the evidences of his nobility?"

"That would be a most unworthy motive, Señor, and I hasten to correct your mistake. As we are now about to part for some time, I ask permission to lay bare my whole soul to you. I confess that when first I heard of this voyage, it struck me as a madman's scheme" —

"Ah! friend Luis," interrupted Columbus, with a melancholy shake of the head, "this is the opinion of but too many! I fear Don Ferdinand of Aragon, as well as that stern prelate, his namesake, who hath lately disposed of the question, thinketh in the same manner."

"I crave your pardon, Señor Colon, if I have uttered aught to give you pain; but if I have once done you injustice, I am ready enough to expiate the wrong, as you will quickly see. Thinking thus, I entered into discourse with you, with a view to amuse myself with fancied ravings; but, though no immediate change of opinion followed as to the truth of the theory, I soon perceived that a great philosopher and profound reasoner had the matter in hand. Here my judgment might have rested, and my opinion been satisfied, but for a circumstance of deep moment to myself. You must know, Señor, though come of the oldest blood of Spain, and not without fair possessions, that I may not always have answered the hopes of those who have been charged with the care of my youth" —

"This is unnecessary, noble sir" —

"Nay, by St. Luke! it shall be said. Now, I have two great and engrossing passions, that sometimes interfere with each other. The one is a love for rambling—a burning desire to see foreign lands, and this, too, in a free and roving fashion—with a disposition for the sea and the doings of havens; and the other is a love for Mercedes de Valverde, the fairest, gentlest, most affectionate, warmest-hearted, and truest maiden of Castile!"

"Noble, withal," put in Columbus, smiling.

"Señor," answered Luis, gravely, "I jest not concerning my guardian angel. She is not only noble, and every way fitted to honor my name, but she hath the blood of the Guzmans, themselves, in her veins. But I have lost favor with others, if not with my lovely mistress, in yielding to this rambling inclination; and even my own aunt, who is her guardian, hath not looked smilingly on my suit. Doña Isabella, whose word is law among all the noble virgins of the court, hath also her prejudices, and it hath become necessary to regain her good opinion, to win the Doña Mercedes. It struck me" — Luis was too manly to betray his mistress by confessing that the thought was hers — "it struck me, that if my rambling tastes took the direction of some noble enterprise, like this you urge, that what hath been a demerit might be deemed a merit in the royal eyes, which would be certain soon to draw all other eyes after them. With this hope, then, I first entered into the present intercourse, until the force of your arguments hath completed my conversion, and now no churchman hath more faith in the head of his religion, than I have that the shortest road to Cathay is athwart the broad Atlantic; or no Lombard is more persuaded that his Lombardy is flat, than I feel convinced that this good earth of ours is a sphere."

"Speak reverently of the ministers of the altar, young Señor," said Columbus, crossing himself, "for no levity should be used in connection with their holy office. It seemeth, then," he added, smiling, "I owe my disciple to the two potent agents of love and reason; the former, as most potent, overcoming the first obstacles, and the latter getting uppermost at the close of the affair, as is wont to happen — love, generally, triumphing in the onset, and reason, last."

"I'll not deny the potency of the power, Señor, for I feel it too deeply to rebel against it. You now know my secret, and when I have made you acquainted with my intentions, all will be laid bare. I here solemnly vow" — Don Luis lifted his cap and looked to heaven, as he spoke — "to join you in this voyage, on due notice, sail from whence you may, in whatever bark you shall choose, and whenever you please. In doing this, I trust, first to serve God and his church; secondly, to visit Cathay and those distant and wonderful lands; and lastly, to win Doña Mercedes de Valverde."

"I accept the pledge, young sir," rejoined Columbus, struck by his earnestness, and pleased with his sincerity — "though it might have been a more faithful representation of your thoughts had the order of the motives been reversed."

"In a few months I shall be master of my own means," continued the youth, too intent on his own purposes to heed what the navigator had said —

"and then, nothing but the solemn command of Doña Isabella, herself, shall prevent our having one caravel, at least; and the coffers of Bobadilla must have been foully dealt by, during their master's childhood, if they do not afford two. I am no subject of Don Fernando's, but a servant of the elder branch of the House of Trastamara; and the cold judgment of the king, even, shall not prevent it."

"This soundeth generously, and thy sentiments are such as become a youthful and enterprising noble; but the offer cannot be accepted. It would not become Columbus to use gold that came from so confiding a spirit and so inexperienced a head; and there are still greater obstacles than this. My enterprise must rest on the support of some powerful prince. Even the Guzman hath not deemed himself of sufficient authority to uphold a scheme so large. Did we make the discoveries without that sanction, we should be toiling for others, without security for ourselves, since the Portuguese or some other monarch would wrong us of our reward. That I am destined to effect this great work, I feel, and it must be done in a manner suited to the majesty of the thought and to the magnitude of the subject. And, here, Don Luis, we must part. Should my suit be successful at the court of France, thou shalt hear from me, for I ask no better than to be sustained by hearts and hands like thine. Still, thou must not mar thy fortunes unheedingly, and I am now a fallen man in Castile. It may not serve thee a good turn, to be known to frequent my company any longer—and I again say, here we must part."

Luis de Bobadilla protested his indifference to what others might think; but the more experienced Columbus, who rose so high above popular clamor in matters that affected himself, felt a generous reluctance to permit this confiding youth to sacrifice his hopes, to any friendly impressions in his own favor. The leave-taking was warm, and the navigator felt a glow at his heart, as he witnessed the sincere and honest emotions that the young man could not repress at parting. They separated, however, about half a league from the town, and each bent his way in his own direction; Don Luis de Bobadilla's heart swelling with indignation at the unworthy treatment that there was, in sooth, so much reason for thinking his new friend had received.

Columbus journeyed on, with very different emotions. Seven weary years had he been soliciting the monarchs and nobles of Spain to aid him in his enterprise. In that long period, how much of poverty, contempt, ridicule, and even odium, had he not patiently encountered, rather than abandon the slight hold that he had obtained on a few of the more liberal and enlightened minds of the nation! He had toiled for bread while soliciting the great to aid themselves in becoming still more powerful; and each ray of hope, however feeble, had been eagerly caught at with joy, each disappointment borne with a constancy that none but the most exalted spirit could sustain. But he was now required to endure the most grievous of all his pains. The recall of Isabella had awakened within him a confidence to which he had long been a stranger; and he awaited the termination of the siege with the calm dignity that became his purpose, no less than his lofty philosophy. The hour of leisure had come, and it produced a fatal destruction to all his buoyant hopes. He had thought his motives understood, his character appreciated, and his high objects felt; but he now found himself still regarded as a visionary projector, his intentions distrusted, and his promised services despised. In a word, the bright expectations that had cheered his toil for years, had vanished in a day, and the disappointment was all the greater for the brief, but delusive hopes produced by his recent favor.

It is not surprising, therefore, that, when left alone on the highway, even the spirit of this extraordinary man grew faint within him, and he had to look to the highest power for succor. His head dropped upon his breast, and one of those bitter moments occurred, in which the past and the future, crowd the mind, painfully as to sufferings endured, cheerlessly as to hope. The time wasted in Spain seemed a blot in his existence, and then came the probability of another long and exhausting probation, that, like this, might lead to nothing. He had already reached the lustrum that would fill his threescore years, and life seemed slipping from beneath him, while its great object remained unachieved. Still the high resolution of the man sustained him. Not once did he think of a compromise of what he felt to be his rights — not once did he doubt of the practicability of accomplishing the great enterprise that others derided. His heart was full of courage, even while his bosom was full of grief. "There is a wise, a merciful, and omnipotent God!" he exclaimed, raising his eyes to heaven. "He knoweth what is meet for his own glory, and in him do I put my trust." There was a pause, and the eyes kindled, while a scarcely perceptible smile lighted the grave face, and then were murmured the words—"Yea, he taketh his time, but the Infidel shall be enlightened, and the blessed sepulchre redeemed!"

After this burst of feeling, the grave-looking man, whose hairs had already become whitened to the color of snow, by cares, and toils, and exposures, pursued his way, with the quiet dignity of one who believed that he was not created for naught, and who trusted in God for the fulfilment of his destiny. If quivering sighs occasionally broke out of his breast, they did not disturb the placidity of his venerable countenance; if grief and disappointment still lay heavy on his heart, they rested on a base that was able to support them. Leaving Columbus to follow the common mule-track across the Vega, we will now return to Santa Fé, where Ferdinand and

Isabella had re-established their court, after the few first days that succeeded the possession of their new conquest.

Luis de St. Angel was a man of ardent feelings and generous impulses. He was one of those few spirits who live in advance of their age, and who permitted his reason to be enlightened and cheered by his imagination, though it was never dazzled by it. As he and his friend Alonzo de Quintanilla, after quitting Columbus as already related, walked toward the royal pavillion, they conversed freely together concerning the man, his vast conceptions, the treatment he had received, and the shame that would alight on Spain in consequence, were he suffered thus to depart forever. Blunt of speech, the receiver of the ecclesiastical revenues did not measure his terms, every syllable of which found an echo in the heart of the accountant-general, who was an old and fast friend of the navigator. In short, by the time they reached the pavilion, they had come to the resolution to make one manly effort to induce the queen to yield to Columbus' terms and to recall him to her presence.

Isabella was always easy of access to such of her servants as she knew to be honest and zealous. The age was one of formality, and, in many respects, of exaggeration, while the court was renowned for ceremony; but the pure spirit of the queen threw a truth and a natural grace around all that depended on her, which rendered mere forms, except as they were connected with delicacy and propriety, useless, and indeed impracticable. Both the applicants for the interview enjoyed her favor, and the request was granted with that simple directness that this estimable woman loved to manifest, whenever she thought she was about to oblige any whom she esteemed.

The queen was surrounded by the few ladies among whom she lived in private, as Luis de St. Angel and Alonzo de Quintanilla entered. Among them, of course, were the Marchioness of Moya and Doña Mercedes de Valverde. The king, on this occasion, was in an adjoining closet, at work, as usual, with his calculations and orders. Official labor was Ferdinand's relaxation, and he seldom manifested more happiness than when clearing off a press of affairs that most men would have found to the last degree burdensome. He was a hero in the saddle, a warrior at the head of armies, a sage in council, and respectable, if not great, in all things but motives.

"What has brought the Señor St. Angel and the Señor Quintanilla, as suitors, so early to my presence?" asked Isabella, smiling in a way to assure both that the boon would be asked of a partial mistress. "Ye are not wont to be beggars, and the hour is somewhat unusual."

"All hours are suitable, gracious lady, when one cometh to *confer* and not to *seek* favor," returned Luis de St. Angel, bluntly. "We are not here to solicit for ourselves, but to show Your Highness the manner in which the crown of Castile may be garnished with brighter jewels than any it now possesseth."

Isabella looked surprised, both at the words of the speaker, and at his hurried earnestness, as well as his freedom of speech. Accustomed, however, to something of the last, her own calm manner was not disturbed, nor did she even seem displeased.

"Hath the Moor another kingdom of which to be despoiled," she asked; "or would the receiver of the church's revenues have us war upon the Holy See?"

"I would have Your Highness accept the boons that come from God, with alacrity and gratitude, and not reject them unthankfully," returned de St. Angel, kissing the queen's offered hand with a respect and affection that neutralized the freedom of his words. "Do you know, my gracious mistress, that the Señor Christoval Colon, he from whose high projects we Spaniards have hoped so much, hath actually taken mule and quitted Santa Fé?"

"I expected as much, Señor, though I was not apprized that it had actually come to pass. The king and I put the matter into the hands of the Archbishop of Granada, with other trusty counsellors, and they have found the terms of the Genoese arrogant; so full of exceeding and unreasonable extravagance, that it ill befitted our dignity, and our duty to ourselves, to grant them. One who hath a scheme of such doubtful results, ought to manifest moderation in his preliminaries. Many even believe the man a visionary."

"It is unlike an unworthy pretender, Señora, to abandon his hopes before he will yield his dignity. This Colon feeleth that he is treating for empires, and he negotiates like one full of the importance of his subject."

"He that lightly valueth himself, in matters of gravity, hath need to expect that he will not stand high in the estimation of others," put in Alonzo de Quintanilla.

"And, moreover, my gracious and beloved mistress," added de St. Angel, without permitting Isabella even to answer, "the character of the man, and the value of his intentions, may be appreciated by the price he setteth on his own services. If he succeed, will not the discovery eclipse all others that have been made since the creation of the world? Is it nothing to circle the earth, to prove the wisdom of God by actual experiment, to follow the sun in its daily track, and imitate the motions of that glorious moving mass? And then the benefits that will flow on Castile and Aragon—are they not incalculable? I marvel that a princess who hath shown so high and rare a spirit on all other occasions, should shrink from so grand an enterprise as this!"

"Thou art earnest, my good de St. Angel," returned Isabella, with a smile that betrayed no anger; "and when there is much earnestness there is sometimes much forgetfulness. If there were honor and profit in success, what would there be in failure? Should the king and myself send out this Colon, with a commission to be our viceroy, forever, over undiscovered lands, and no lands be discovered, the wisdom of our councils might be called in question, and the dignity of the two crowns would be fruitlessly and yet deeply committed."

"The hand of the Lord Archbishop is in this! This prelate hath never been a believer in the justice of the navigator's theories, and it is easy to raise objections when the feelings lean against an enterprise. No glory is obtained without risk. Look, Your Highness, at our neighbors, the Portuguese—how much have discoveries done for that kingdom, and how much more may it do for us! We know, my honored mistress, that the earth is round"—

"Are we quite certain of that important fact, Señor," asked the king, who, attracted by the animated and unusual tones of the speaker, had left his closet, and approached unseen. "Is that truth established? Our doctors at Salamanca were divided on that great question, and, by St. James! I do not see that it is so very clear."

"If not round, my Lord the King," answered de St. Angel, turning quickly to face this new opponent, like a well-drilled corps wheeling into a new front, "of what form *can* it be? Will any doctor, come he of Salamanca, or come he from elsewhere, pretend that the earth is a plain, and that it hath limits, and that one may stand on these limits and jump down upon the sun as he passeth beneath at night—is this reasonable, honored Señor, or is it in conformity with scripture?"

"Will any one, doctor of Salamanca, or elsewhere," rejoined the king, gravely, though it was evident his feelings were little interested in the discussion, "allege that there are nations who forever walk with their heads downward, where the rain falleth upward, and where the sea remaineth in its bed, though its support cometh from above, and is not placed beneath?"

"It is to explain these great mysteries, Señor Don Fernando, my gracious master, that I would have this Colon at once go forth. We may see, nay, we have demonstration, that the earth is a sphere, and yet we do not see that the waters fall from its surface any where. The hull of a ship is larger than her top-masts, and yet the last are first visible on the ocean, which proveth that the body of the vessel is concealed by the form of the water. This being so, and all who have voyaged on the ocean know it to be thus, why doth not the water flow into a level, here, on our own shores? If the earth be round, there must be means to encircle it by water, as well as by land—to complete the entire journey, as well as to perform a part. Colon proposeth to open the way to this exploit, and the monarch that shall furnish the means will live in the memories of our descendants, as one far greater than a conqueror. Remember, illustrious Señor, that all the east is peopled with Infidels, and that the head of the church freely bestoweth their lands on any Christian monarch that may drag them from their benighted condition, into the light of God's favor. Believe me, Doña Isabella, should another sovereign grant the terms Colon requireth, and reap the advantages that are likely to flow from such discoveries, the enemies of Spain would make the world ring with their songs of triumph, while the whole peninsula would mourn over this unhappy decision."

"Whither hath the Señor Colon sped?" demanded the king, quickly; all his political jealousies being momentarily aroused by the remarks of his receiver-general: "He hath not gone again to Don John of Portugal?"

"No, Señor, my master, but to King Louis of France, a sovereign whose love for Aragon amounteth to a proverb."

The king muttered a few words between his teeth, and he paced the apartment, to and fro, with a disturbed manner; for, while no man living cared less to hazard his means, without the prospect of a certain return, the idea of another's reaping an advantage that had been neglected by himself, brought him at once under the control of those feelings that always influenced his cold and calculating policy. With Isabella the case was different. Her pious wishes had ever leaned toward the accomplishment of Columbus' great project, and her generous nature had sympathized deeply with the noble conception, vast moral results, and the glory of the enterprise. Nothing but the manner in which her mind, as well as her religious aspirations, had been occupied by the war in Granada, had prevented her from entering earlier into a full examination of the navigator's views; and she had yielded to the counsel of her confessor, in denying the terms demanded by Columbus, with a reluctance it had not been easy to overcome. Then the gentler feelings of her sex had their influence, for, while she too reflected on what had just been urged, her eye glanced around the room and rested on the beautiful face of Mercedes, who sat silent from diffidence, but whose pale, eloquent countenance betrayed all the pleadings of the pure, enthusiastic love of woman.

"Daughter-Marchioness," asked the queen, turning as usual to her tried friend, in her doubts, "what thinkest thou of this weighty matter? Ought we so to humble ourselves as to recal this haughty Genoese?"

"Say not haughty, Señora, for to me he seemeth much superior to any such feeling; but rather regard him as one that hath a just appreciation of that he hath in view. I agree fully with the receiver-general in thinking that Castile will be much discredited, if, in sooth, a new world should be discovered, and they who favored the enterprise could point to this court and remind it that the glory of the event was in its grasp, and that it threw it away, heedlessly"—

"And this, too, on a mere point of dignity, Señora," put in St. Angel—"on a question of parchment and of sound."

"Nay, nay"—retorted the queen—"there are those who think the honors claimed by Colon would far exceed the service, even should the latter equal all the representations of the Genoese himself."

"Then, my honored mistress, they know not at what the Genoese aims. Reflect, Señora, that it will not be an every-day deed to prove that this earth is a sphere, by actual measurement, whatever we may know in theories. Then cometh the wealth and benefits of those eastern possessions, a quarter of the world whence all riches flow—spices, pearls, silks, and the most precious metals. After these, again, cometh the great glory of God, which crowneth and exceedeth all."

Isabella crossed herself, her cheek flushed, her eye kindled, and her matronly but fine form seemed to tower with the majesty of the feelings that these pictures created.

"I do fear, Don Fernando," she said, "that our advisers have been precipitate, and that the magnitude of this project may justify more than common conditions!"

But the king entered little into the generous emotions of his royal consort; feeling far more keenly the stings of political jealousy, than any promptings of a liberal zeal for either the church or science. He was generally esteemed a wise prince, a title that would seem to infer neither a generous nor a very just one. He smiled at the kindling enthusiasm of his wife, but continued to peruse a paper that had just been handed to him by a secretary.

"Your Highness feels as Doña Isabella of Castile ought to feel when the glory of God and the honor of her crown are in question," added Beatriz de Cabrera, using that freedom of speech that her royal mistress much encouraged in their more private intercourse. "I would rather hear you utter the words of recall to this Colon, than again listen to the shouts of our late triumph over the Moor."

"I know that thou lovest me, Beatriz!" exclaimed the queen: "if there is not a true heart in that breast of thine, the fallen condition of man does not suffer the gem to exist!"

"We all love and reverence Your Highness," continued de St. Angel, "and we wish naught but your glory. Fancy, Señora, the page of history open, and this great exploit of the reduction of the Moor succeeded by the still greater deed of a discovery of an easy and swift communication with the Indies, the spread of the church, and the flow of inexhaustible wealth into Spain! This Colon cannot be supported by the colder and more selfish calculations of man, but his very enterprise seeks the more generous support of her who can risk much for God's glory and the good of the church."

"Nay, Señor de St. Angel, thou flatterest and offendest in the same breath."

"It is an honest nature pouring out its disappointment, my beloved mistress, and a tongue that hath become bold through much zeal for Your Highnesses' fame. Alas! alas! should King Louis grant the terms we have declined, poor Spain will never lift her head again for very shame!"

"Art certain, St. Angel, that the Genoese hath gone for France?" suddenly demanded the king, in his sharp, authoritative voice.

"I have it, Your Highness, from his own mouth. Yes, yes, he is at this moment striving to forget our Castilian dialect, and endeavoring to suit his tongue to the language of the Frenchman. They are bigots and unreflecting disciples of musty prejudices, Señora, that deny the theories of Colon. The old philosophers have reasoned in the same manner; and though it may seem to the timid an audacious and even a heedless adventure to sail out into the broad Atlantic, had not the Portuguese done it he would never have found his islands. God's truth! it maketh my blood boil, when I bethink me of what these Lusitanians have done, while we of Aragon and Castile have been tilting with the Infidels for a few valleys and mountains, and contending for a capital!"

"Señor, you are forgetful of the honor of the sovereigns, as well as of the service of God," interrupted the Marchioness of Moya, who had the tact to perceive that the receiver-general was losing sight of his discretion, in the magnitude of his zeal. "This conquest is one of the victories of the church, and will add lustre to the two crowns in all future ages. The head of the church, himself, hath so recognized it, and all good Christians should acknowledge its character."

"It is not that I undervalue this success, but that I consider the conquest that Colon is likely to achieve over so many millions, that I have thus spoken, Doña Beatriz."

The marchioness, whose spirit was as marked as her love for the queen, made a sharp reply, and, for a few minutes, she and Luis de St. Angel, with Alonzo de Quintanilla, maintained the discussion by themselves, while Isabella conversed apart, with her husband, no one presuming to meddle with their private conference. The queen was earnest, and evidently much excited, but Ferdinand maintained his customary coolness and caution, though his manner was marked with that profound respect which the character of Isabella had early inspired, and which she succeeded in maintaining throughout her married life. This was a picture familiar to the courtiers, one of the sovereigns being as remarkable for his wily prudence, as was the other for her generous and sincere ardor, whenever impelled by a good motive. This divided discourse lasted half an hour, the queen occasionally pausing to listen to what was passing in the other group, and then recurring to her own arguments with her husband.

At length Isabella left the side of Ferdinand, who coldly resumed the perusal of a paper, and she moved slowly toward the excited party, that was now unanimous and rather loud in the expression of its regrets—loud for even the indulgence of so gentle a mistress. Her intention to repress this ardor by her own presence, however, was momentarily diverted from its object by a glimpse of the face of Mercedes, who sat alone, her work lying neglected in her lap, listening anxiously to the opinions that had drawn all her companions to the general circle.

"Thou takest no part in this warm discussion, child," observed the queen, stopping before the chair of our heroine, and gazing an instant into her eloquently expressive face. "Hast thou lost all interest in Colon?"

"I speak not, Señora, because it becometh youth and ignorance to be modest; but though silent, I *feel* none the less."

"And what are thy feelings, daughter? Dost thou, too, think the services of the Genoese cannot be bought at too high a price?"

"Since Your Highness doth me this honor," answered the lovely girl, the blood gradually flushing her pale face, as she warmed with the subject—"I will not hesitate to speak. I do believe this great enterprise hath been offered to the sovereigns, as a reward for all that they have done and endured for religion and the church. I do think that Colon hath been guided to this court by a divine hand, and by a divine hand hath he been kept here, enduring the long servitude of seven years, rather than abandon his object; and I do think that this late appeal in his favor cometh of a power and spirit that should prevail."

"Thou art an enthusiast, daughter, more especially in this cause," returned the queen, smiling kindly on the blushing Mercedes. "I am greatly moved by thy wishes to aid in this enterprise!"

Thus spoke Isabella, at a moment when she had neither the leisure nor the thought to analyze her own feelings, which were influenced by a variety of motives, rather than by any single consideration. Even this passing touch of woman's affections, however, contributed to give her mind a new bias, and she joined the group, which respectfully opened as she advanced, greatly disposed to yield to de St. Angel's well-meant though somewhat intemperate entreaties. Still she hesitated, for her wary husband had just been reminding her of the exhausted state of the two treasuries, and the impoverished condition in which both crowns had been left by the late war.

"Daughter-Marchioness," said Isabella, slightly answering the reverences of the circle, "dost thou still think this Colon expressly called of God, for the high purposes to which he pretendeth?"

"Señora, I say not exactly that, though I believe the Genoese hath some such opinion of himself. But this much I do think—that Heaven beareth in mind its faithful servitors, and when there is need of important actions, suitable agents are chosen for the work. Now, we do know that the church, at some day, is to prevail throughout the whole world; and why may not this be the allotted time, as well as another? God ordereth mysteriously, and the very adventure that so many of the learned have scoffed at, may be intended to hasten the victory of the church. We should remember, Your Highness, the humility with which this church commenced; how few of the seemingly wise lent it their aid; and the high pass of glory to which it hath reached. This conquest of the Moor savoreth of a fulfilment of time, and his reign of seven centuries terminated, may merely be an opening for a more glorious future."

Isabella smiled upon her friend, for this was reasoning after her own secret thoughts; but her greater acquirements rendered her more discriminating in her zeal, than was the case with the warm-hearted and ardent Marchioness.

"It is not safe to affix the seal of Providence to this or that enterprise, Daughter-Marchioness"—she answered—"and the church alone may say what are intended for miracles, and what is left for human agencies. What sum doth Colon need, Señor de St. Angel, to carry on the adventure in a manner that will content him?"

"He asketh but two light caravels, my honored mistress, and three thousand crowns—a sum that many a young spendthrift would waste on his pleasures, in a few short weeks."

"It is not much, truly," observed Isabella, who had been gradually kindling with the thoughts of the nobleness of the adventure; "but, small as it is, my Lord the King doubteth if our joint coffers can, at this moment, well bear the drain."

"Oh! it were a pity that such an occasion to serve God, such an opportunity to increase the Christian sway, and to add to the glory of Spain, should be lost for this trifle of gold!" exclaimed Doña Beatriz.

"It would be, truly," rejoined the queen, whose cheek now glowed with an enthusiasm little less obvious than that which shone so brightly in the countenance of the ardent Mercedes. "Señor de St. Angel, the king cannot be prevailed on to enter into this affair, in behalf of Aragon; but I take it on myself, as Queen of Castile, and, so far as it may properly advance human interests, for the benefit of my own much-beloved people. If the royal treasury be drained, my private jewels should suffice for that small sum, and I will freely pledge them as surety for the gold, rather than let this Colon depart without putting the truth of his theories to the proof. The result, truly, is of too great magnitude, to admit of further discussion."

An exclamation of admiration and delight escaped those present, for it was not a usual thing for a princess to deprive herself of personal ornaments in order to advance either the interests of the church or those of her subjects. The receiver-general, however, soon removed all difficulties on the score of money, by saying that his coffers could advance the required sum, on the guarantee of the crown of Castile, and that the jewels so freely offered, might remain in the keeping of their royal owner.

"And now to recall Colon," observed the queen, as soon as these preliminaries had been discussed. "He hath already departed, you say, and no time should be lost in acquainting him with this new resolution."

"Your Highness hath here a willing courier, and one already equipped for the road, in the person of Don Luis de Bobadilla," cried Alonzo de Quintanilla, whose eye had been drawn to a window by the trampling of a horse's foot; "and the man who will more joyfully bear these tidings to the Genoese cannot be found in Santa Fé."

"'Tis scarce a service suited to one of his high station," answered Isabella, doubtingly; "and yet we should consider every moment of delay a wrong to Colon"—

"Nay, Señora, spare not my nephew," eagerly interposed Doña Beatriz; "he is only too happy at being employed in doing Your Highness' pleasure."

"Let him, then, be summoned to our presence without another instant's delay. I scarce seem to have decided, while the principal personage of the great adventure is journeying from the court."

A page was immediately despatched in quest of the young noble, and in a few minutes the footsteps of the latter were heard in the antechamber. Luis entered the presence, flushed, excited, and with feelings not a little angered, at the compelled departure of his new friend. He did not fail to impute the blame of this occurrence to those who had the power to prevent it; and when his dark, expressive eye met the countenance of his sovereign, had it been in her power to read its meaning, she would have understood that he viewed her as a person who had thwarted his hopes on more than one occasion. Nevertheless, the influence of Doña Isabella's pure character and gentle manners was seldom forgotten by any who were permitted to approach her person; and his address was respectful, if not warm.

"It is Your Highness' pleasure to command my presence," said the young man, as soon as he made his reverences to the queen.

"I thank you for this promptitude, Don Luis, having some need of your services. Can you tell us what hath befel the Señor Christoval Colon, the Genoese navigator, with whom, they inform me, you have some intimacy?"

"Forgive me, Señora, if aught unbecoming escape me; but a full heart must be opened lest it break. The Genoese is about to shake the dust of Spain from his shoes, and, at this moment, is on his journey to another court, to proffer those services that this should never have rejected."

"It is plain, Don Luis, that all thy leisure time hath not been passed in courts," returned the queen, smiling; "but we have now service for thy roving propensities. Mount thy steed, and pursue the Señor Colon, with the tidings that his conditions will be granted, and a request that he will forthwith return. I pledge my royal word, to send him forth on this enterprise, with as little delay as the necessary preparations and a suitable prudence will allow."

"Señora! Doña Isabella! My gracious queen! Do I hear aright?"

"As a sign of the fidelity of thy senses, Don Luis, here is the pledge of my hand."

This was said kindly, and the gracious manner in which the hand was offered, brought a gleam of hope to the mind of the lover, which it had not felt since he had been apprized that the queen's good opinion was necessary to secure his happiness. Kneeling respectfully, he kissed the hand of his sovereign, after which, without changing his attitude, he desired to know if he should that instant depart on the duty she had named.

"Rise, Don Luis, and lose not a moment to relieve the loaded heart of the Genoese—I might almost say, to relieve ours, also; for, Daughter-Marchioness, since this holy enterprise hath broken on my mind with a sudden and almost miraculous light, it seemeth that a mountain must lie on my breast until the Señor Christoval shall learn the truth!"

Luis de Bobadilla did not wait a second bidding, but hurried from the presence, as fast as etiquette would allow, and the next minute he was in the saddle. At his appearance, Mercedes had shrunk into the recess of a window, where she now, luckily, commanded a view of the court. As her lover gained his seat, he caught a glimpse of her form; and though the spurs were already in his charger's flanks, the rein tightened, and the snorting steed was thrown suddenly on his haunches. So elastic are the feelings of youth, so deceptive and flattering the hopes of those who love, that the glances which were exchanged were those of mutual delight. Neither thought of all the desperate chances of the contemplated voyage; of the probability of its want of success; or of the many motives which might still induce the queen to withhold her consent. Mercedes awoke first from the short trance that succeeded, for, taking the alarm at Luis' indiscreet delay, she motioned him hurriedly to proceed. Again the rowels were buried in the flanks of the noble animal; fire flashed beneath his armed heels, and, at the next minute, Don Luis de Bobadilla had disappeared.

In the mean time Columbus had pursued his melancholy journey across the Vega. He travelled slowly, and several times even after his companion had left him, did he check his mule, and sit, with his head dropped upon his breast, lost in thought, the very picture of woe. The noble resignation that he manifested in public, nearly gave way in private, and he felt, indeed, how hard his disappointments were to be borne. In this desultory manner of travelling he had reached the celebrated pass of the Bridge of Piños, the scene of many a sanguinary combat, when the sound of a horse's hoofs first overtook his ear. Turning his head, he recognized Luis de Bobadilla in hot pursuit, with the flanks of his horse dyed in blood, and his breast white with foam.

"Joy! joy! a thousand times, joy, Señor Colon," shouted the eager youth, even before he was near enough to be distinctly heard. "Blessed Maria be praised! Joy! Señor, joy! and naught but joy!"

"This is unexpected, Don Luis," exclaimed the navigator, "What meaneth thy return!"

Luis now attempted to explain his errand, but eagerness and the want of breath rendered his ideas confused and his utterance broken and imperfect.

"And why should I return to a hesitating, cold, and undecided court?" demanded Columbus. "Have I not wasted years in striving to urge it to its own good? Look at these hairs, young Señor, and remember that I have lost a time that nearly equals all thy days, in striving uselessly to convince the rulers of this peninsula that my project is founded on truth."

"At length you have succeeded. Isabella, the true-hearted and never-deceiving Queen of Castile, herself hath awoke to the importance of thy scheme, and pledges her royal word to favor it."

"Is this true? *Can* this be true, Don Luis?"

"I am sent to you express, Señor, to urge your immediate return."

"By whom, young Lord?"

"By Doña Isabella, my gracious mistress, through her own personal commands."

"I cannot forego a single condition already offered."

"It is not expected, Señor. Our excellent and generous mistress granteth all you ask, and hath nobly offered, as I learn, to pledge her private jewels, rat'ier than that the enterprise fail."

Columbus was deeply touched with this information, and, removing his cap, he concealed his face with it for a moment, as if ashamed to betray the weakness that came over him. When he uncovered his face it was radiant with happiness, and every doubt appeared to have vanished. Years of suffering were forgotten in that moment of joy, and he immediately signified his readiness to accompany the youth back to Santa Fé.

CHAPTER IX

"How beautiful is genius when combined
With holiness! Oh! how divinely sweet
The tones of earthly harp, whose cords are touch'd
By the soft hand of Piety, and hung
Upon Religion's shrine, there vibrating
With solemn music in the air of God!"

John Wilson.

Columbus was received by his friends, Luis de St. Angel and Alonzo de Quintanilla, with a gratification they found it difficult to express. They were loud in their eulogiums on Isabella, and added to the assurances of Don Luis, such proofs of the seriousness of the queen's intentions, as to remove all doubts from the mind of the navigator. He was then, without further delay, conducted to the presence.

"Señor Colon," said Isabella, as the Genoese advanced and knelt at her feet, "you are welcome back again. All our misunderstandings are finally removed, and henceforth, I trust that we shall act cheerfully and unitedly to produce the same great end. Rise, Señor, and receive this as a gage of my support and friendship."

Columbus saluted the offered hand, and arose from his knees. At that instant, there was probably no one present whose feelings were not raised to the buoyancy of hope; for it was a peculiarity connected with the origin and execution of this great enterprise, that, after having been urged for so long a period, amid sneers, and doubts, and ridicule, it was at first adopted with something very like enthusiasm.

"Señora," returned Columbus, whose grave aspect and noble mien contributed not a little to the advancement of his views—"Señora, my heart thanks you for this kindness—so welcome because so little hoped for this morning—and God will reward it. We have great things in reserve, and I devoutly wish we may all be found equal to our several duties. I hope my Lord the King will not withhold from my undertaking the light of his gracious countenance."

"You are a servitor of Castile, Señor Colon, though little is attempted for even this kingdom, without the approbation and consent of the King of Aragon. Don Fernando hath been gained over to our side, though his greater caution and superior wisdom have not as easily fallen into the measure, as woman's faith and woman's hopes."

"I ask no higher wisdom, no truer faith than those of Isabella's," said the navigator, with a grave dignity that rendered the compliment so much the more acceptable, by giving it every appearance of sincerity. "Her known prudence shall turn from me the derision of the light-minded and idle, and on her royal word I place all my hopes. Henceforth, and I trust forever, I am Your Highness' subject and servant."

The queen was deeply impressed with the air of lofty truth that elevated the thoughts and manners of the speaker. Hitherto she had seen but little of the navigator, and never before under circumstances that enabled her so thoroughly to feel the influence of his air and deportment. Columbus had not the finish of manner that it is fancied courts only can bestow, and which it would be more just to refer to lives devoted to habits of pleasing; but the character of the man shone through the exterior, and, in his case, all that artificial training could supply fell short of the noble aspect of nature, sustained by high aspirations. To a commanding person, and a gravity that was heightened by the loftiness of his purposes, Columbus added the sober earnestness of a deeply-seated and an all-pervading enthusiasm, which threw the grace of truth and probity on what he said and did. No quality of his mind was more apparent than its sense of right, as right was then considered in connection with the opinions of the age; and it is a singular circumstance that the greatest adventure of modern times was thus confided by Providence, as it might be with especial objects, to the care of a sovereign and to the hands of an executive leader, who were equally distinguished by the possession of so rare a characteristic.

"I thank you, Señor, for this proof of confidence," returned the queen, both surprised and gratified; "and so long as God giveth me power to direct, and knowledge to decide, your interests as well as those of this long-cherished scheme, shall be looked to. But we are not to exclude the king from our confederacy, since he hath been finally gained to our opinions, and no doubt now as anxiously looketh forward to success as we do ourselves."

Columbus bowed his acquiescence, and the conjugal affection of Isabella was satisfied with this concession to her husband's character and motives; for, while it was impossible that one so pure and ardent in the cause of virtue, and as disinterested as the queen, should not detect some of the selfishness of Ferdinand's cautious policy, the feelings of a wife so far prevailed in her breast over the sagacity of the sovereign, as to leave her blind to faults that the enemies of Aragon were fond of dwelling on. All admitted the truth of Isabella, but Ferdinand had far less credit with his contemporaries, either on the score of faith or on that of motives. Still he might have been ranked among the most upright of the reigning princes of Europe, his faults being rendered more conspicuous, perhaps, from being necessarily placed in such close connection with, and in such vivid contrast to, the truer virtues of the queen. In short, these two sovereigns, so intimately united by personal and political interests, merely exhibited on their thrones a picture that may be seen, at any moment, in all the inferior gradations of the social scale, in which the worldly views and meretricious motives of man serve as foils to the truer heart, sincerer character, and more chastened conduct of woman.

Don Fernando now appeared, and he joined in the discourse in a manner to show that he considered himself fully committed to redeem the pledges given by his wife. The historians have told us that he had been won over by the intercessions of a favorite, though the better opinion would seem to be that deference for Isabella, whose pure earnestness in the cause of virtue often led him from his more selfish policy, lay at the bottom of his compliance. Whatever may have been the motive, however, it is certain that the king never entered into the undertaking with the ardent, zealous endeavors to insure success, which from that moment distinguished the conduct of his royal consort.

"We have recovered our truant," said Isabella, as her husband approached, her eyes lighting and her cheeks flushed with a pious enthusiasm, like those of Mercedes de Valverde, who was an entranced witness of all that was passing. "We have recovered our truant, and there is not a moment of unnecessary delay to be permitted, until he shall be sent forth on this great voyage. Should he truly attain Cathay and the Indies, it will be a triumph to the church even exceeding this conquest of the territories of the Moor."

"I am pleased to see the Señor Colon at Santa Fé, again," courteously returned the king, "and if he but do the half of that thou seemest to expect, we shall have reason to rejoice that our countenance hath not been withheld. He may not render the crown of Castile still more powerful, but he may so far enrich himself that, as a subject, he will have difficulty in finding the proper uses for his gold."

"There will always be a use for the gold of a Christian," answered the navigator, "while the Infidel remaineth the master of the Holy Sepulchre."

"How is this!" exclaimed Ferdinand, in his quick, sharp voice: "dost thou think, Señor, of a crusade, as well as of discovering new regions?"

"Such, Your Highness, it hath long been my hope, would be the first appropriation of the wealth that will, out of question, flow from the discovery of a new and near route to the Indies. Is it not a blot on Christendom that the Mussulman should be permitted to raise his profane altars on the spot that Christ visited on earth; where, indeed he was born, and where his holy remains lay until his glorious resurrection? This foul disgrace there are hearts and swords enough ready to wipe out; all that is wanted is gold. If the first desire of my heart be to become the instrument of leading the way to the East, by a western and direct passage, the second is, to see the riches that will certainly follow such a discovery, devoted to the service of God, by rearing anew his altars and reviving his worship, in the land where he endured his agony and gave up the ghost for the sins of men."

Isabella smiled at the navigator's enthusiasm, though, sooth to say, the sentiment found something of an echo in her pious bosom; albeit the age of crusades appeared to have gone by. Not so exactly with Ferdinand. He smiled also, but no answering sentiment of holy zeal was awakened within him. He felt, on the contrary, a strong distrust of the wisdom of committing the care of even two insignificant caravels, and the fate of a sum as small as three thousand crowns, to a visionary, who had scarcely made a commencement in one extremely equivocal enterprise, before his thoughts were running on the execution of another, that had baffled the united efforts and pious constancy of all Europe. To him, the discovery of a western passage to the Indies, and the repossession of the holy sepulchre, were results that were equally problematical, and it would have been quite sufficient to incur his distrust, to believe in the practicability of either. Here, however, was a man who was about to embark in an attempt to execute the first, holding in reserve the last, as a consequence of success in the undertaking in which he was already engaged.

There were a few minutes, during which Ferdinand seriously contemplated the defeat of the Genoese's schemes, and had the discourse terminated here, it is uncertain how far his cool and calculating policy might have prevailed over the good faith, sincere integrity, and newly awakened enthusiasm of his wife. Fortunately, the conversation had gone on while he was meditating on this subject, and when he rejoined the circle he found the queen and the navigator pursuing the subject with an earnestness that had entirely overlooked his momentary absence.

"I shall show Your Highness all that she demandeth," continued Columbus, in answer to a question of the queen's. "It is my expectation to reach the territories of the Great Khan, the descendant of the monarch who was visited by the Polos, a century since; at which time a strong desire to embrace the religion of Christ was manifested by many in that gorgeous court, the sovereign included. We are told in the sacred books of prophecy, that the day is to arrive when the whole earth will worship the true and living God; and that time, it would seem, from many signs and tokens that are visible to those who seek them, draweth near, and is full of hope to such as honor God and seek his glory. To bring all those vast regions in subjection to the church, needeth but a constant faith, sustained by the delegated agencies of the priesthood, and the protecting hands of princes."

"This hath a seeming probability," observed the queen, "and Providence so guide us in this mighty undertaking, that it may come to pass! Were those Polos pious missionaries, Señor?"

"They were but travellers; men who sought their own advantage, while they were not altogether unmindful of the duties of religion. It may be well, Señora, first to plant the cross in the islands, and thence to spread the truth over the main land. Cipango, in particular, is a promising region for the commencement of the glorious work, which, no doubt, will proceed with all the swiftness of a miracle."

"Is this Cipango known to produce spices, or aught that may serve to uphold a sinking treasury, and repay us for so much cost and risk?" asked the king, a little inopportunely for the zeal of the two other interlocutors.

Isabella looked pained, the prevailing trait in Ferdinand's character often causing her to feel as affectionate wives are wont to feel when their husbands forget to think, act, or speak up to the level of their own warm-hearted and virtuous propensities; but she suffered no other sign of the passing emotions to escape her.

"According to the accounts of Marco Polo, Your Highness," answered Columbus, "earth hath no richer island. It aboundeth especially in gold; nor are pearls and precious stones at all rare. But all that region is a quarter of infinite wealth and benighted infidelity. Providence seemeth to have united the first with the last, as a reward to the Christian monarch who shall use his power to extend the sway of the church. The sea, thereabouts, is covered with smaller islands, Marco telling us that no less than seven thousand four hundred and forty have been enumerated, not one of all which doth not produce some odoriferous tree, or plant of delicious perfume. It is then, thither, gracious Lord and Lady, my honored sovereigns, that I propose to proceed at once, leaving all meaner objects, to exalt the two kingdoms and to serve the church. Should we reach Cipango in safety, as, by the blessing of God, acting on a zeal and faith that are not easily shaken, I trust we shall be able to do, in the course of two months' diligent navigation, it will be my next purpose to pass over to the continent, and seek the Khan himself, in his kingdom of Cathay. The day that my foot touches the land of Asia will be a glorious day for Spain, and for all who have had a part in the accomplishment of so great an enterprise!"

Ferdinand's keen eyes were riveted on the navigator, as he thus betrayed his hopes with the quiet but earnest manner of deep enthusiasm, and he might have been at a loss, himself, just at that moment, to have analyzed his own feelings. The picture of wealth that Columbus had conjured to his imagination, was as enticing, as his cold and calculating habits of distrust and caution rendered it questionable. Isabella heard only, or thought only, of the pious longings of her pure spirit for the conversion and salvation of the Infidels, and thus each of the two sovereigns had a favorite impulse to bind him, or her, to the prosecution of the voyage.

After this, the conversation entered more into details, and the heads of the terms demanded by Columbus were gone over again, and approved of by those who were most interested in the matter. All thought of the archbishop and his objections was momentarily lost, and had the Genoese been a monarch, treating with monarchs, he could not have had more reason to be satisfied with the respectful manner in which his terms were heard. Even his proposal to receive one-eighth of the profits of this, and all future expeditions to the places he might discover, on condition of his advancing an equal proportion of the outfits, was cheerfully acceded to; making him, at once, a partner with the crown, in the risks and benefits of the many undertakings that it was hoped would follow from the success of this.

Luis de St. Angel and Alonzo de Quintanilla quitted the royal presence, in company with Columbus. They saw him to his lodgings, and left him with a respect and cordiality of manner, that cheered a heart which had lately been so bruised and disappointed. As they walked away in company, the former, who, notwithstanding the liberality of his views and his strong support of the navigator, was not apt to suppress his thoughts, opened a dialogue in the following manner.

"By all the saints! friend Alonzo," he exclaimed, "but this Colon carrieth it with a high hand among us, and in a way, sometimes, to make me doubt the prudence of our interference. He hath treated with the two sovereigns like a monarch, and like a monarch hath he carried his point!"

"Who hath aided him more than thyself, friend Luis?" returned

Alonzo de Quintanilla; "for, without thy bold assault on Doña Isabella's patience, the matter had been decided against this voyage, and the Genoese would still be on his way to the court of King Louis."

"I regret it not; the chance of keeping the Frenchman within modest bounds being worth a harder effort. Her Highness—Heaven and all the saints unite to bless her for her upright intentions and generous thoughts—will never regret the trifling cost, even though bootless, with so great an aim in view. But now the thing is done, I marvel, myself, that a Queen of Castile and a King of Aragon should grant such conditions to an unknown and nameless sea-farer; one that hath neither services, family, nor gold, to recommend him!"

"Hath he not had Luis de St. Angel of his side?"

"That hath he," returned the receiver-general, "and that right stoutly, too; and for good and sufficient cause. I only marvel at our success, and at the manner in which this Colon hath borne himself in the affair. I much feared that the high price he set upon his services might ruin all our hopes."

"And yet thou didst reason with the queen, as if thou thoughtst it insignificant, compared with the good that would come of the voyage."

"Is there aught wonderful in this, my worthy friend? We consume our means in efforts to obtain our ends, and, while suffering under the exhaustion, begin first to see the other side of the question. I am chiefly surprised at mine own success! As for this Genoese, he is, truly, a most wonderful man, and, in my heart, I think him right in demanding such high conditions. If he succeed, who so great as he? and, if he fail, the conditions will do him no good, and Castile little harm."

"I have remarked, Señor de St Angel, that when grave men set a light value on themselves, the world is apt to take them at their word, though willing enough to laugh at the pretensions of triflers. After all, the high demands of Colon may have done him much service, since their Highnesses could not but feel that they were negotiating with one who had faith in his own projects."

"It is much as thou sayest, Alonzo; men often prizing us as we seem to prize ourselves, so long as we act at all up to the level of our pretensions. But there is sterling merit in this Colon to sustain him in all that he sayeth and doth; wisdom of speech, dignity and gravity of mien, and nobleness of feeling and sentiment. Truly, I have listened to the man when he hath seemed inspired!"

"Well, he hath now good occasion to manifest whether this inspiration be of the true quality or not," returned the other. "Of a verity, I often distrust the wisdom of our own conclusions."

In this manner did even these two zealous friends of Columbus discuss his character and chances of success; for, while they were among the most decided of his supporters, and had discovered the utmost readiness to uphold him when his cause seemed hopeless, now that the means were likely to be afforded to allow him to demonstrate the justice of his opinions, doubts and misgivings beset their minds. Such is human nature. Opposition awakens our zeal, quickens our apprehension, stimulates our reason, and emboldens our opinions; while, thrown back upon ourselves for the proofs of what we have been long stoutly maintaining under the pressure of resistance, we begin to distrust the truth of our own theories and to dread the demonstrations of a failure. Even the first disciples of the Son of God faltered most in their faith as his predictions were being realized; and most reformers are never so dogmatical and certain as when battling for their principles, or so timid and wavering as when they are about to put their own long-cherished plans in execution. In all this we might see a wise provision of Providence, which gives us zeal to overcome difficulties, and prudence when caution and moderation become virtues rather than faults.

Although Luis de St. Angel and his friend conversed thus freely together, however, they did not the less continue true to their original feelings. Their doubts were transient and of little account; and it was remarked of them, whenever they were in the presence of Columbus himself, that the calm, steady, but deeply seated enthusiasm of that extraordinary man, did not fail to carry with him the opinions, not only of these steady supporters, but those of most other listeners.

CHAPTER X

—"Song is on thy hills:
Oh, sweet and mournful melodies of Spain,
That lull'd my boyhood, how your memory thrills
The exile's heart with sudden-wakening pain."

The Forest Sanctuary.

From the moment that Isabella pledged her royal word to support Columbus in his great design, all reasonable doubts of the sailing of the expedition ceased, though few anticipated any results of importance. Of so much greater magnitude, indeed, did the conquest of the kingdom of Granada appear, at that instant, than any probable consequences which could follow from this novel enterprise, that the latter was almost overlooked in the all-absorbing interest that was connected with the former.

There was one youthful and generous heart, however, all of whose hopes were concentrated in the success of the great voyage. It is scarcely necessary to add, we mean that of Mercedes de Valverde. She had watched the recent events as they occurred, with an intensity of expectation that perhaps none but the youthful, fervent, inexperienced, and uncorrupted, can feel: and now that all her hopes were about to be realized, a tender and generous joy diffused itself over her whole moral system, in a way to render her happiness, for the time, even blissful. Although she loved so truly and with so much feminine devotedness, nature had endowed this warm-hearted young creature with a sagacity and readiness of apprehension, which, when quickened by the sentiments that are so apt to concentrate all the energies of her sex, showed her the propriety of the distrust of the queen and her guardian, and fully justified their hesitation in her eyes, which were rather charmed than blinded by the ascendency of her passion. She knew too well what was due to her virgin fame, her high expectations, her great name, and her elevated position near the person, and in the immediate confidence of Isabella, even to wish her hand unworthily bestowed; and while she deferred, with the dignity and discretion of birth and female decorum, to all that opinion and prudence could have a right to ask of a noble maiden, she confided in her lover's power to justify her choice, with the boundless confidence of a woman. Her aunt had taught her to believe that this voyage of the Genoese was likely to lead to great events, and her religious enthusiasm, like that of the queen's, led her to expect most of that which she so fervently wished.

During the time it was known to those near the person of Isabella, that the conditions between the sovereigns and the navigators were being reduced to writing and were receiving the necessary forms, Luis neither sought an interview with his mistress, nor was accidentally favored in that way; but, no sooner was it understood Columbus had effected all that he deemed necessary in this particular, and had quitted the court for the coast, than the young man threw himself, at once, on the generosity of his aunt, beseeching her to favor his views now that he was about to leave Spain on an adventure that most regarded as desperate. All he asked was a pledge of being well received by his mistress and her friends, on his return successful.

"I see that thou hast taken a lesson from this new master of thine," answered the high-souled but kind-hearted Beatriz, smiling—"and would fain have thy terms also. But thou knowest, Luis, that Mercedes de Valverde is no peasant's child to be lightly cared for, but that she cometh of the noblest blood of Spain, having had a Guzman for a mother, and Mendozas out of number among her kinsmen. She is, moreover, one of the richest heiresses of Castile; and it would ill become her guardian to forget her watchfulness, under such circumstances, in behalf of one of the idle wanderers of Christendom, simply because he happeneth to be her own beloved brother's son."

"And if the Doña Mercedes be all thou sayest, Señora—and thou hast not even touched upon her highest claims to merit, her heart, her beauty, her truth, and her thousand virtues—but if she be all that thou sayest, Doña Beatriz, is a Bobadilla unworthy of her?"

"How! if she be, moreover, all *thou* sayest too, Don Luis! The heart, the truth, and the thousand virtues! Methinks a shorter catalogue might content one who is himself so great a rover, lest some of these qualities be lost in his many journeys!"

Luis laughed, in spite of himself, at the affected seriousness of his aunt; and then successfully endeavoring to repress a little resentment that her language awakened, he answered in a way to do no discredit to a well-established reputation for good-nature.

"I cannot call thee 'Daughter-Marchioness,' in imitation of Her Highness," he answered, with a coaxing smile, so like that her deceased brother was wont to use when disposed to wheedle her out of some concession, that it fairly caused Doña Beatriz to start—"but I can say with more truth, 'Aunt-Marchioness,'—and a very dear aunt, too—wilt thou visit a little youthful indiscretion so severely? I had hoped, now Colon was about to set forth, that all was forgotten in the noble and common end we have in view."

"Luis," returned the aunt, regarding her nephew with the severe resolution that was so often exhibited in her acts as well as in her words, "dost think that a mere display of courage will prove sufficient to win Mercedes from me? to put to sleep the vigilance of her friends? to gain the approbation of her guardian? Learn, too confident boy, that Mercedes de Guzman was the companion of my childhood; my warmest, dearest friend, next to Her Highness; and that she put all faith in my disposition to do full justice by her child. She died by slow degrees, and the fate of the orphan was often discussed between us. That she could ever become the wife of any but a Christian noble, neither of us imagined possible; but there are so many different characters under the same outward professions, that names deceived us not. I do believe that poor woman bethought her more of her child's future worldly fortunes than of her own sins, and that she prayed oftener for the happy conclusion of the first than for the pardon of the last! Thou knowest little of the strength of a mother's love, Luis, and canst not understand all the doubts that beset the heart, when the parent is compelled to leave a tender plant, like Mercedes, to the cold nursing of a selfish and unfeeling world."

"I can readily fancy the mother of my love fitted for heaven without the usual interpositions of masses and paters, Doña Beatriz; but have aunts no consideration for nephews, as well as mothers for children?"

"The tie is close and strong, my child, and yet is it not parental; nor art thou a sensitive, true-hearted, enthusiastic girl, filled with the confidence of thy purity, and overflowing with the affections that, in the end, make mothers what they are."

"By San Iago! and am I not the very youth to render such a creature happy? I, too, am sensitive—too much so, in sooth, for my own peace; I, too, am true-hearted, as is seen by my having had but this one love, when I might have had fifty; and if I am not exactly overflowing with the confidence of purity, I have the confidence of youth, health, strength, and courage, which is quite as useful for a cavalier; and I have abundance of the affection that makes good fathers, which is all that can reasonably be asked of a man."

"Thou, then, thinkest thyself, truant, every way worthy to be the husband of Mercedes de Valverde?"

"Nay, aunt of mine, thou hast a searching way with thy questions! Who is, or can be, exactly worthy of so much excellence? I may not be altogether *deserving* of her, but then again, I am not altogether *undeserving* of her. I am quite as noble, nearly as well endowed with estates, of suitable years, of fitting address as a knight, and love her better than I love my own soul. Methinks the last should count for something, since he that loveth devotedly, will surely strive to render its object happy."

"Thou art a silly, inexperienced boy, with a most excellent heart, a happy, careless disposition, and a head that was made to hold better thoughts than commonly reside there!" exclaimed the aunt, giving way to an impulse of natural feeling, even while she frowned on her nephew's folly. "But, hear me, and for once think gravely, and reflect on what I say. I have told thee of the mother of Mercedes, of her dying doubts, her anxiety, and of her confidence in me. Her Highness and I were alone with her, the morning of the day that her spirit took its flight to heaven; and then she poured out all her feelings, in a way that has left on us both an impression that can never cease, while aught can be done by either for the security of the daughter's happiness. Thou hast thought the queen unkind. I know not but, in thy intemperate speech, thou hast dared to charge Her Highness with carrying her care for her subjects' well-being beyond a sovereign's rights" —

"Nay, Doña Beatriz," hastily interrupted Luis, "herein thou dost me great injustice. I may have felt—no doubt I have keenly, bitterly, felt the consequences of Doña Isabella's distrust of my constancy; but never has rebel thought of mine even presumed to doubt her right to command all our services, as well as all our lives. This is due to her sacred authority from all; but we, who so well know the heart and motives of the queen, also know that she doth naught from caprice or a desire to rule; while she doth so much from affection to her people."

As Don Luis uttered this with an earnest look, and features flushed with sincerity, it was impossible not to see that he meant as much as he said. If men considered the consequences that often attend their lightest words, less levity of speech would be used, and the office of tale-bearer, the meanest station in the whole catalogue of social rank, would become extinct for want of occupation. Few cared less, or thought less, about the consequences of what they uttered, than Luis de Bobadilla; and yet this hasty but sincere reply did him good service with more than one of those who exercised a material influence over his fortunes. The honest praise of the queen went directly to the heart of the Marchioness, who rather idolized than loved her royal mistress, the long and close intimacy that had existed between them having made her thoroughly acquainted with the pure and almost holy character of Isabella; and when she repeated the words of her nephew to the latter, her own well-established reputation for truth caused them to be implicitly believed. Whatever may be the correctness of our views in general, one of the most certain ways to the feelings is the assurance of being respected and esteemed; while, of all the divine mandates, the most difficult to find obedience is that which tells us to "love those who hate" us. Isabella, notwithstanding her high destiny and lofty qualities, was thoroughly a woman; and when she discovered that, in spite of her own coldness to the youth, he really entertained so much profound deference for her character, and appreciated her feelings and motives in a way that conscience told her she merited, she was much better disposed to look at his peculiar faults with indulgence, and to ascribe that to mere animal spirits, which, under less favorable auspices, might possibly have been mistaken for ignoble propensities.

But this is a little anticipating events. The first consequence of Luis' speech was a milder expression in the countenance of his aunt, and a disposition to consider his entreaties to be admitted to a private interview with Mercedes, with more indulgence.

"I may have done thee injustice in this, Luis," resumed Doña Beatriz, betraying in her manner the sudden change of feeling mentioned; "for I do think thee conscious of thy duty to Her Highness, and of the almost heavenly sense of justice that reigneth in her heart, and through that heart, in Castile. Thou hast not lost in my esteem by thus exhibiting thy respect and love for the queen, for it is impossible to have any regard for female virtue, and not to manifest it to its best representative."

"Do I not, also, dear aunt, in my attachment to thy ward? Is not my very choice, in some sort, a pledge of the truth and justice of my feelings in these particulars?"

"Ah! Luis de Bobadilla, it is not difficult to teach the heart to lean toward the richest and the noblest, when she happeneth also to be the fairest, maiden of Spain!"

"And am I a hypocrite, Marchioness? Dost thou accuse the son of thy brother of being a feigner of that which he doth not feel?—one influenced by so mean a passion as the love of gold and of lands?"

"Foreign lands, heedless boy," returned the aunt, smiling, "but not of others' lands. No, Luis, none that know thee will accuse thee of hypocrisy. We believe in the truth and ardor of thy attachment, and it is for that very cause that we most distrust thy passion."

"How! Are feigned feelings of more repute with the queen and thyself, than real feelings? A spurious and fancied love, than the honest, downright, manly passion."

"It is this genuine feeling, this honest, downright, manly passion, as thou termest it, which is most apt to awaken sympathy in the tender bosom of a young girl. There is no truer touch-stone, by which to try the faithfulness of feelings, than the heart, when the head is not turned by vanity; and the more unquestionable the passion, the easier is it for its subject to make the discovery. Two drops of water do not glide together more naturally than two hearts, nephew, when there is a strong affinity between them. Didst thou not really love Mercedes, as my near and dear relative, thou mightst laugh and sing in her company at all times that should be suitable for the dignity of a maiden, and it would not cause me an uneasy moment."

"I am thy near and dear relative, aunt of mine, with a miracle! and yet it is more difficult for me to get a sight of thy ward" —

"Who is the especial care of the Queen of Castile."

"Well, be it so; and why should a Bobadilla be proscribed by even a Queen of Castile?"

Luis then had recourse to his most persuasive powers, and, improving the little advantage he had gained, by dint of coaxing and teasing he so far prevailed on Doña Beatriz as to obtain a promise that she would apply to the queen for permission to grant him one private interview with Mercedes. We say the queen, since Isabella, distrusting the influence of blood, had cautioned the Marchioness on this subject; and the prudence of letting the young people see each other as little as possible, had been fully settled between them. It was in redeeming this promise, that the aunt related the substance of the conversation that has just been given, and mentioned to her royal mistress the state of her nephew's feelings as respected herself. The effect of such information was necessarily favorable to the young man's views, and one of its first fruits was the desired permission to have the interview he sought.

"They are not sovereigns," remarked the queen, with a smile that the favorite could see was melancholy, though it surpassed her means of penetration to say whether it proceeded from a really saddened feeling, or whether it were merely the manner in which the mind is apt to glance backward at emotions that it is known can never be again awakened in our bosoms;—"they are not sovereigns, Daughter-Marchioness, to woo by proxy, and wed as strangers. It may not be wise to suffer the intercourse to become too common, but it were cruel to deny the youth, as he is about to depart on an enterprise of so doubtful issue, one opportunity to declare his passion and to make his protestations of constancy. If thy ward hath, in truth, any tenderness for him, the recollection of this interview will soothe many a weary hour while Don Luis is away."

"And add fuel to the flame," returned Doña Beatriz, pointedly.

"We know not that, my good Beatriz, since, the heart being softened by the power of God to a sense of its religious duties, may not the same kind hand direct it and shield it in the indulgence of its more worldly feelings? Mercedes will never forget her duty, and, the imagination feeding itself, it may not be the wisest course to leave that of an enthusiast like our young charge, so entirely to its own pictures. Realities are often less hazardous than the creatures of the fancy. Then, thy nephew will not be a loser by the occasion, for, by keeping constantly in view the object he now seemeth to pursue so earnestly, he will the more endeavor to deserve success."

"I much fear, Señora, that the best conclusions are not to be depended on in an affair that touches the waywardness of the feelings."

"Perhaps not, Beatriz; and yet I do not see that we can well deny this interview, now that Don Luis is so near departure. Tell him I accord him that which he so desireth, and let him bear in mind that a grandee should never quit Castile without presenting himself before his sovereign."

"I fear, Your Highness," returned the Marchioness, laughing, "that Don Luis will feel this last command, however gracious and kind in fact, as a strong rebuke, since he hath more than once done this already, without even presenting himself before his own aunt!"

"On those occasions he went idly, and without consideration; but he is now engaged in an honorable and noble enterprise, and we will make it apparent to him that all feel the difference."

The conversation now changed, it being understood that the request of the young man was to be granted. Isabella had, in this instance, departed from a law she had laid down for her own government, under the influence of her womanly feelings, which often caused her to forget that she was a queen, when no very grave duties existed to keep alive the recollection; for it would have been difficult to decide in which light this pure-minded and excellent female most merited the esteem of mankind—in her high character as a just and conscientious sovereign, or when she acted more directly under the gentler impulses of her sex. As for her friend, she was perhaps more tenacious of doing what she conceived to be her duty, by her ward, than the queen herself; since, with a greater responsibility, she was exposed to the suspicion of acting with a design to increase the wealth and to strengthen the connections of her own family. Still, the wishes of Isabella were laws to the Marchioness of Moya, and she sought an early opportunity to acquaint her ward with her intention to allow Don Luis, for once, to plead his own cause with his mistress, before he departed on his perilous and mysterious enterprise.

Our heroine received this intelligence with the mingled sensations of apprehension, delight, misgivings, and joy, that are so apt to beset the female heart, in the freshness of its affections, when once brought in subjection to the master-passion. She had never thought it possible Luis would sail on an expedition like that in which he was engaged, without endeavoring to see her alone; but, now she was assured that both the queen and her guardian acquiesced in his being admitted, she almost regretted their compliance. These contradictory emotions, however, soon subsided in the tender melancholy that gradually drew around her manner, as the hour for the departure approached. Nor were her feelings on the subject of Luis' ready enlistment in the expedition, more consistent. At times she exulted in her lover's resolution, and in his manly devotion to glory and the good of the church; remembering with pride that, of all the high nobility of Castile, he alone ventured life and credit with the Genoese; and then, again, tormenting doubts came over her, as she feared that the love of roving, and of adventure, was quite as active in his heart, as love of herself. But in all this there was nothing new. The more pure and ingenuous the feelings of those who truly submit to the influence of this passion, the more keenly alive are their distrusts apt to be, and the more tormenting their misgivings of themselves.

Her mind made up, Doña Beatriz acted fairly by the young people. As soon as Luis was admitted to her own presence, on the appointed morning, she told him that he was expected by Mercedes, who was waiting his appearance in the usual reception-room. Scarce giving himself time to kiss the hand of his aunt, and to make those other demonstrations of respect that the customs of the age required from the young to their seniors— more especially when there existed between them a tie of blood as close as that which united the Marchioness of Moya with the Conde de Llera—the young man bounded away, and was soon in the presence of his mistress. As Mercedes was prepared for the interview, she betrayed the feeling of the moment merely by a heightened color, and the greater lustre of eyes that were always bright, though often so soft and melancholy.

"Luis!" escaped from her, and then, as if ashamed of the emotion betrayed in the very tones of her voice, she withdrew the foot that had involuntarily advanced to meet him, even while she kept a hand extended in friendly confidence.

"Mercedes!" and the hand was withdrawn to put a stop to the kisses with which it was covered. "Thou art harder to be seen, of late, than it will be to discover this Cathay of the Genoese; for, between the Doña Isabella and Doña Beatriz, never was paradise watched more closely by guardian angels, than thy person is watched by thy protectors."

"And can it be necessary, Luis, when thou art the danger apprehended?"

"Do they think I shall carry thee off, like some Moorish girl borne away on the crupper of a Christian knight's saddle, and place thee in the caravel of Colon, that we may go in search of Prestor John and the Great Khan, in company?"

"They may think *thee* capable of this act of madness, dear Luis, but they will hardly suspect *me*."

"No, thou art truly a model of prudence in all matters that require feeling for thy lover."

"Luis!" exclaimed the girl, again; and this time unbidden tears started to her eyes.

"Forgive me, Mercedes—dearest, dearest Mercedes; but this delay and all these coldly cruel precautions make me forget myself. Am I a needy and unknown adventurer, that they treat me thus, instead of being a noble Castilian knight!"

"Thou forgettest, Luis, that noble Castilian maidens are not wont to see even noble Castilian cavaliers alone, and, but for the gracious condescension of Her Highness, and the indulgence of my guardian, who happeneth to be thy aunt, this interview could not take place."

"Alone! And dost thou call this being alone, or any excessive favor, on the part of Her Highness, when thou seest that we are watched by the eye, if not by the ear! I fear to speak above my breath, lest the sounds should disturb that venerable lady's meditations!"

As Luis de Bobadilla uttered this, he glanced his eye at the figure of the dueña of his mistress, whose person was visible through an open door, in an adjoining room, where the good woman sat, intently occupied in reading certain homilies.

"Dost mean my poor Pepita," answered Mercedes, laughing; for the presence of her attendant, to whom she had been accustomed from infancy, was no more restraint on her own innocent thoughts and words, than would have proved a reduplication of herself, had such a thing been possible. "Many have been her protestations against this meeting, which she insists is contrary to all rule among noble ladies, and which, she says, would never have been accorded by my poor, sainted mother, were she still living."

"Ay, she hath a look that is sufficient of itself to set every generous mind a-tilting with her. One can see envy of thy beauty and youth, in every wrinkle of her unamiable face."

"Then little dost thou know my excellent Pepita, who envieth nothing, and who hath but one marked weakness, and that is, too much affection, and too much indulgence, for myself."

"I detest a dueña; ay, as I detest an Infidel!"

"Señor," said Pepita, whose vigilant ears, notwithstanding her book and the homilies, heard all that passed, "this is a common feeling among youthful cavaliers, I fear; but they tell me that the very dueña who is so displeasing to the lover, getteth to be a grateful object, in time, with the husband. As my features and wrinkles, however, are so disagreeable to you, and no doubt cause you pain, by closing this door the sight will be shut out, as, indeed, will be the sound of my unpleasant cough, and of your own protestations of love, Señor Knight."

This was said in much better language than was commonly used by women of the dueña's class, and with a good-nature that seemed indomitable, it being completely undisturbed by Luis' petulant remarks.

"Thou shalt not close the door, Pepita," cried Mercedes, blushing rosy red, and springing forward to interpose her own hand against the act. "What is there that the Conde de Llera can have to say to one like me, that *thou* mayest not hear?"

"Nay, dear child, the noble cavalier is about to talk of love!"

"And is it thou, with whom the language of affection is so uncommon, that it frighteneth thee! Hath thy discourse been of aught but love, since thou hast known and cared for me?"

"It augureth badly for thy suit, Señor," said Pepita, smiling, while she suspended the movement of the hand that was about to close the door, "if Doña Mercedes thinketh of your love as she thinketh of mine. Surely, child, thou dost not fancy me a gay, gallant young noble, come to pour out his soul at thy feet, and mistakest my simple words of affection for such as will be likely to flow from the honeyed tongue of a Bobadilla, bent on gaining his suit with the fairest maiden of Castile?"

Mercedes shrunk back, for, though innocent as purity itself, her heart taught her the difference between the language of her lover and the language of her nurse, even when each most expressed affection. Her hand released its hold of the wood, and unconsciously was laid, with its pretty fellow, on her crimsoned face. Pepita profited by her advantage, and closed the door. A smile of triumph gleamed on the handsome features of Luis, and, after he had forced his mistress, by a gentle compulsion, to resume the seat from which she had risen to meet him, he threw himself on a stool at her feet, and stretching out his well-turned limbs in an easy attitude, so as to allow himself to gaze into the beautiful face that he had set up, like an idol, before him, he renewed the discourse.

"This is a paragon of dueñas," he cried, "and I might have known that none of the ill-tempered, unreasonable school of such beings, would be tolerated near thy person. This Pepita is a jewel, and she may consider herself established in her office for life, if, by the cunning of this Genoese, mine own resolution, the queen's repentance, and thy gentle favor, I ever prove so lucky as to become thy husband."

"Thou forgettest, Luis," answered Mercedes, trembling even while she laughed at her own conceit, "that if the husband esteemeth the dueña the lover could not endure, that the lover may esteem the dueña that the husband may be unwilling to abide."

"*Peste!* these are crooked matters, and ill-suited to the straight-forward philosophy of Luis de Bobadilla. There is one thing only, which I can, or do, pretend to know, out of any controversy, and that I am ready to maintain in the face of all the doctors of Salamanca, or all the chivalry of Christendom, that of the Infidel included; which is, that thou art the fairest, sweetest, best, most virtuous, and in all things the most winning maiden of Spain, and that no other living knight so loveth and honoreth his mistress as I love and honor thee!"

The language of admiration is ever soothing to female ears, and Mercedes, giving to the words of the youth an impression of sincerity that his manner fully warranted, forgot the dueña and her little interruption, in the delight of listening to declarations that were so grateful to her affections. Still, the coyness of her sex, and the recent date of their mutual confidence, rendered her answer less open than it might otherwise have been.

"I am told," she said, "that you young cavaliers, who pant for occasions to show your skill and courage with the lance and in the tourney, are ever making some such protestations in favor of this or that noble maiden, in order to provoke others like themselves to make counter assertions, that they may show their prowess as knights, and gain high names for gallantry."

"This cometh of being so much shut up in Doña Beatriz's private rooms, lest some bold Spanish eyes should look profanely on thy beauty, Mercedes. We are not in the age of the errants and the troubadours, when men committed a thousand follies that they might be thought weaker even than nature had made them. In that age, your knights *discoursed* largely of love, but in our own they *feel* it. In sooth, I think this savoreth of some of the profound morality of Pepita!"

"Say naught against Pepita, Luis, who hath much befriended thee to-day, else would thy tongue, and thine eyes too, be under the restraint of her presence. But that which thou termest the morality of the good dueña, is, in truth, the morality of the excellent and most noble Doña Beatriz de Cabrera, Marchioness of Moya, who was born a lady of the House of Bobadilla, I believe."

"Well, well, I dare to say there is no great difference between the lessons of a duchess and the lessons of a dueña in the privacy of the closet, when there is one like thee, beautiful, and rich, and virtuous, to guard. They say you young maidens are told that we cavaliers are so many ogres, and that the only way to reach paradise is to think naught of us but evil, and then, when some suitable marriage hath been decided on, the poor young creature is suddenly alarmed by an order to come forth and be wedded to one of these very monsters."

"And, in this mode, hast thou been treated! It would seem that much pains are taken to make the young of the two sexes think ill of each other. But, Luis, this is pure idleness, and we waste in it most precious moments; moments that may never return. How go matters with Colon—and when is he like to quit the court?"

"He hath already departed; for, having obtained all he hath sought of the queen, he quitted Santa Fé, with the royal authority to sustain him in the fullest manner. If thou hearest aught of one Pedro de Muños, or Pero Gutierrez, at the court of Cathay, thou wilt know on whose shoulders to lay his follies."

"I would rather that thou shouldst undertake this voyage in thine own name, Luis, than under a feigned appellation. Concealments of this nature are seldom wise, and surely thou dost not undertake the enterprise"—the tell-tale blood stole to the cheeks of Mercedes as she proceeded—"with a motive that need bring shame."

"'Tis the wish of my aunt; as for myself, I would put thy favor in my casque, thy emblem on my shield, and let it be known, far and near, that Luis of Llera sought the court of Cathay, with the intent to defy its chivalry to produce as fair or as virtuous a maiden as thyself."

"We are not in the age of errants, sir knight, but in one of reason and truth," returned Mercedes, laughing, though every syllable that proved the earnest and entire devotion of the young man went directly to her heart, strengthening his hold on it, and increasing the flame that burnt within, by adding the fuel that was most adapted to that purpose—"we are not in the age of knights-errant, Don Luis de Bobadilla, as thou thyself hast just affirmed; but one in which even the lover is reflecting, and as apt to discover the faults of his lady-love as to dwell upon her perfections. I look for better things from thee, than to hear that thou hast ridden through the highways of

Cathay, defying to combat and seeking giants, in order to exalt my beauty, and tempting others to decry it, if it were only out of pure opposition to thy idle boastings. Ah! Luis, thou art now engaged in a most truly noble enterprise, one that will join thy name to those of the applauded of men, and which will form thy pride and exultation in after-life, when the eyes of us both shall be dimmed by age, and we shall look back with longings to discover aught of which to be proud."

It was thrice, pleasant to the youth to hear his mistress, in the innocence of her heart, and in the fulness of her feelings, thus uniting his fate with her own; and when she ceased speaking, all unconscious how much might be indirectly implied from her words, he still listened intently, as if he would fain hear the sounds after they had died on his ear.

"What enterprise can be nobler, more worthy to awaken all my resolution, than to win thy hand!" he exclaimed, after a short pause. "I follow Colon with no other object; share his chances, to remove the objections of Doña Isabella; and will accompany him to the earth's end, rather than that thy choice should be dishonored. *Thou* art *my* Great Khan, beloved Mercedes, and thy smiles and affection are the only Cathay I seek."

"Say not so, dear Luis, for thou knowest not the nobility of thine own soul, nor the generosity of thine own intentions. This is a stupendous project of Colon's, and much as I rejoice that he hath had the imagination to conceive it, and the heart to undertake it in his own person, on account of the good it must produce to the heathen, and the manner in which it will necessarily redound to the glory of God, still I fear that I am equally gladdened with the recollection that thy name will be forever associated with the great achievement, and thy detractors put to shame with the resolution and spirit with which so noble an end will have been attained."

"This is nothing but truth, Mercedes, should we reach the Indies; but, should the saints desert us, and our project fail, I fear that even thou wouldst be ashamed to confess an interest in an unfortunate adventurer who hath returned without success, and thereby made himself the subject of sneers and derision, instead of wearing the honorable distinction that thou seemest so confidently to expect."

"Then, Luis de Bobadilla, thou knowest me not," answered Mercedes, hastily, and speaking with a tender earnestness that brought the blood into her cheeks, gradually brightening the brilliancy of her eyes, until they shone with a lustre that seemed almost supernatural—"then, Luis de Bobadilla, thou knowest me not. I wish thee to share in the glory of this enterprise, because calumny and censure have not been altogether idle with thy youth, and because I feel that Her Highness' favor is most easily obtained by it; but, if thou believest that the spirit to engage with Colon was necessary to incline me to think kindly of my guardian's nephew, thou neither understandest the sentiments that draw me toward thee, nor hast a just appreciation of the hours of sorrow I have suffered on thy account."

"Dearest, most generous, noble-hearted girl, I am unworthy of thy truth, of thy pure sincerity, and of all thy devoted feelings! Drive me from thee at once, that I may ne'er again cause thee a moment's grief."

"Nay, Luis, thy remedy, I fear me, would prove worse than the disease that thou wouldst cure," returned the beautiful girl, smiling and blushing as she spoke, and turning her eloquent eyes on the youth in a way to avow volumes of tenderness. "With thee must I be happy, or unhappy, as Providence may will it; or miserable without thee."

The conversation now took that unconnected, and yet comprehensive cast, which is apt to characterize the discourse of those who feel as much as they reason, and it covered more interests, sentiments, and events, than our limits will allow us to record. As usual, Luis was inconsistent, jealous, repentant, full of passion and protestations, fancying a thousand evils at one instant, and figuring in his imagination a terrestrial paradise at the next; while Mercedes was enthusiastic, generous, devoted, and yet high-principled, self-denying, and womanly; meeting her ardent suitor's vows with a tenderness that seemed to lose all other considerations in her love, and repelling with maiden coyness, and with the dignity of her sex, his rhapsodies, whenever they touched upon the exaggerated and indiscreet.

The interview lasted an hour, and it is scarce necessary to say that vows of constancy, and pledges never to marry another, were given, again and again. As the time for separating approached, Mercedes opened a small casket that contained her jewels, and drew forth one which she offered to her lover as a gage of her truth.

"I will not give thee a glove to wear in thy casque at tourneys, Luis," she said, "but I offer this holy symbol, which may remind thee, at the same moment, of the great pursuit thou hast before thee, and of her who will wait its issue with doubts and fears little less active than those of Colon himself. Thou needst no other crucifix to say thy paters before, and these stones are sapphires, which thou knowest are the tokens of fidelity—a feeling that thou mayst encourage as respects thy lasting welfare, and which it would not grieve me to know thou kept'st ever active in thy bosom when thinking of the unworthy giver of the trifle."

This was said half in melancholy, and half in lightness of heart, for Mercedes felt, at parting, both a weight of sorrow that was hard to be borne, and a buoyancy of the very feeling to which she had just alluded, that much disposed her to smile; and it was said with those winning accents with which the youthful and tender avow their emotions, when the heart is subdued by the thoughts of absence and dangers. The gift was a small cross, formed of the stones she had named, and of great intrinsic value, as well as precious from the motives and character of her who offered it.

"Thou hast had a care of my soul, in this, Mercedes," said Luis, smiling, when he had kissed the jewelled cross again and again—"and art resolved if the sovereign of Cathay should refuse to be converted to our faith, that we shall not be converted to his. I fear that my offering will appear tame and valueless in thine eyes, after so precious a boon."

"One lock of thy hair, Luis, is all I desire. Thou knowest that I have no need of jewels."

"If I thought the sight of my bushy head would give thee pleasure, every hair should quit it. and I would sail from Spain with a poll as naked as a priest's, or even an Infidel's; but the Bobadillas have their jewels, and a Bobadilla's bride shall wear them: this necklace was my mother's, Mercedes; it is said to have once been the property of a queen, though none have ever worn it who will so honor it as thou."

"I take it, Luis, for it is thy offering and may not be refused; and yet I take it tremblingly, for I see signs of our different natures in these gifts. Thou hast chosen the gorgeous and the brilliant, which pall in time, and seldom lead to contentment; while my woman's heart hath led me to constancy. I fear some brilliant beauty of the East would better gain thy lasting admiration than a poor Castilian maid who hath little but her faith and love to recommend her!"

Protestations on the part of the young man followed, and Mercedes permitted one fond and long embrace ere they separated. She wept on the bosom of Don Luis, and at the final moment of parting, as ever happens with woman, feeling got the better of form, and her whole soul confessed its weakness. At length Luis tore himself away from her presence, and that night he was on his way to the coast, under an assumed name, and in simple guise; whither Columbus had already preceded.

CHAPTER XI

"But where is Harold? Shall I then forget
To urge the gloomy wanderer o'er the wave?
Little reck'd he of all that men regret;
No loved one now in feign'd lament could rave;
No friend the parting hand extended gave
Ere the cold stranger pass'd to other climes."

Byron.

The reader is not to suppose that the eyes of Europe were on our adventurers. Truth and falsehood, inseparable companions, it would seem, throughout all time, were not then diffused over the land by means of newspapers, with mercenary diligence; and it was only the favored few who got early intelligence of enterprises like that in which Columbus was engaged. Luis de Bobadilla had, therefore, stolen from court unnoticed, and they who came in time to miss his presence, either supposed him to be on a visit to one of his castles, or to have gone forth on another of those wandering tours which were supposed to be blemishes on his chivalry and unworthy of his birth. As for the Genoese himself, his absence was scarcely heeded, though it was understood among the courtiers generally that Isabella had entered into some arrangement with him, which gave the adventurer higher rank and greater advantages than his future services would probably ever justify. The other principal adventurers were too insignificant to attract much attention, and they had severally departed for the coast without the knowledge of their movements extending far beyond the narrow circles of their own acquaintances. Neither was this expedition, so bold in its conception and so momentous in its consequences, destined to sail from one of the more important ports of Spain; but orders to furnish the necessary means had been sent to a haven of altogether inferior rank, and which would seem to have possessed no other recommendations for this particular service, than hardy mariners, and a position without the pass of Gibraltar, which was sometimes rendered hazardous by the rovers of Africa. The order, however, is said to have been issued to the place selected, in consequence of its having incurred some legal penalty, by which it had been condemned to serve the crown for a twelvemonth with two armed caravels. Such punishments, it would seem, were part of the policy of an age in which navies were little more than levies on sea-ports, and when fleets were usually manned by soldiers from the land.

Palos de Moguer, the place ordered to pay this tribute for its transgression, was a town of little importance, even at the close of the fifteenth century, and it has since dwindled to an insignificant fishing village. Like most places that are little favored by nature, its population was hardy and adventurous, as adventure was then limited by ignorance. It possessed no stately caracks, its business and want of opulence confining all its efforts to the lighter caravel and the still more diminutive felucca. All the succor, indeed, that Columbus had been able to procure from the two crowns, by his protracted solicitations, was the order for the equipment of the two caravels mentioned, with the additional officers and men that always accompanied a royal expedition. The reader, however, is not to infer from this fact any niggardliness of spirit, or any want of faith, on the part of Isabella. It was partly owing to the exhausted condition of her treasury, a consequence of the late war with the Moor, and more, perhaps, to the experience and discretion of the great navigator himself, who well understood that, for the purposes of discovery, vessels of this size would be more useful and secure than those that were larger.

On a rocky promontory, at a distance of less than a league from the village of Palos, stood the convent of La Rabida, since rendered so celebrated by its hospitality to Columbus. At the gate of this building, seven years before, the navigator, leading his youthful son by the hand, had presented himself, a solicitor for food in behalf of the wearied boy. The story is too well known to need repetition here, and we will merely add that his long residence in this convent, and the firm friends he had made of the holy Franciscans who occupied it, as well as among others in their vicinity, were also probably motives that influenced him in directing the choice of the crown to this particular place. Columbus had not only circulated his opinions with the monks, but with the more intelligent of the neighborhood, and the first converts he made in Spain were at this place.

Notwithstanding all the circumstances named, the order of the crown to prepare the caravels in question, spread consternation among the mariners of Palos. In that age, it was thought a wonderful achievement to follow the land, along the coast of Africa, and to approach the equator. The vaguest notions existed in the popular mind, concerning those unknown regions, and many even believed that by journeying south it was possible to reach a portion of the earth where animal and vegetable life must cease on account of the intense heat of the sun. The revolution of the planets, the diurnal motion of the earth, and the causes of the changes in the seasons, were then profound mysteries even to the learned; or, if glimmerings of the truth did exist, they existed as the first rays of the dawn dimly and hesitatingly announce the approach of day. It is not surprising, therefore, that the simple-minded and unlettered mariners of Palos viewed the order of the crown as a sentence of destruction on all who might be fated to obey it. The ocean, when certain limits were passed, was thought to be, like the firmament, a sort of chaotic void; and the imaginations of the ignorant had conjured up currents and whirlpools that were believed to lead to fiery climates and frightful scenes of natural destruction. Some even fancied it possible to reach the uttermost boundaries of the earth, and to slide off into vacuum, by means of swift but imperceptible currents.

Such was the state of things, in the middle of the month of July. Columbus was still in the convent of Rabida, in the company of his constant friend and adherent, Fray Juan Perez, when a lay brother came to announce that a stranger had arrived at the gate, asking earnestly for the Señor Christoval Colon.

"Hath he the aspect of a messenger from the court?" demanded the navigator; "for, since the failure of the mission of Juan de Peñalosa, there is need of further orders from their Highnesses to enforce their gracious intentions."

"I think not, Señor," answered the lay brother; "these hard-riding couriers of the queen generally appearing with their steeds in a foam, and with hurried air and blustering voices; whereas this young cavalier behaveth modestly, and rideth a stout Andalusian mule."

"Did he give thee his name, good Sancho?"

"He gave me two, Señor, styling himself Pedro de Muños, or Pedro Gutierrez, without the Don."

"This is well," exclaimed Columbus, turning a little quickly toward the door, but otherwise maintaining a perfect self-command; "I expect the youth, and he is right welcome. Let him come in at once, good Sancho, and that without any useless ceremony."

"An acquaintance of the court, Señor?" observed the prior, in the way one indirectly asks a question.

"A youth that hath the spirit, father, to adventure life and character for the glory of God, through the advancement of his church, by embarking in our enterprise. He cometh of a reputable lineage, and is not without the gifts of fortune. But for the care of guardians, and his own youth, gold would not have been wanting in our need. As it is, he ventureth his own person, if one can be said to risk aught in an expedition that seemeth truly to set even the orders of their Highnesses at defiance."

As Columbus ceased speaking, the door opened and Luis de Bobadilla entered. The young grandee had laid aside all the outward evidences of his high rank, and now appeared in the modest guise of a traveller belonging to a class more likely to furnish a recruit for the voyage, than one of the rank he really was. Saluting Columbus with cordial and sincere respect, and the Franciscan with humble deference, the first at once perceived that this gallant and reckless spirit had truly engaged in the enterprise with a determination to use all the means that would enable him to go through with it.

"Thou art welcome, Pedro," Columbus observed, as soon as Luis had made his salutations; "thou hast reached the coast at a moment when thy presence and support may be exceedingly useful. The first order of Her Highness, by which I should have received the services of the two caravels to which the state is entitled, hath been utterly disregarded; and a second mandate, empowering me to seize upon any vessel that may suit our necessities, hath fared but little better, notwithstanding the Señor de Peñalosa was sent directly from court to enforce its conditions, under a penalty, to the port, of paying a daily tax of two hundred maravedis, until the order should be fulfilled. The idiots have conjured all sorts of ills with which to terrify themselves and their neighbors, and I seem to be as far from the completion of my hopes as I was before I procured the friendship of this holy friar and the royal protection of Doña Isabella. It is a weary thing, my good Pedro, to waste a life in hopes defeated, with such an object in view as the spread of knowledge and the extension of the church!"

"I am the bearer of good tidings, Señor," answered the young noble. "In coming hither from the town of Moguer, I journeyed with one Martin Alonzo Pinzon, a mariner with whom I have formerly voyaged, and we have had much discourse concerning your commission and difficulties. He tells me that he is known to you, Señor Colon, and I should judge from his discourse that he thinketh favorably of the chances."

"He doth—he doth, indeed, good Pedro, and hath often listened to my reasoning like a discreet and skilful navigator, as I make no question he really is. But didst thou say that thou wast *known* to him?"

"Señor, I did. We have voyaged together as far as Cyprus, on one occasion, and, again, to the island of the English. In such long voyages, men get to some knowledge of each other's temperament and disposition, and, of a sooth, I think well of both, in this Señor Pinzon."

"Thou art young to pass an opinion on a mariner of Martin Alonzo's years and experience, son," put in the friar; "a man of much repute in this vicinity, and of no little wealth. Nevertheless, I am rejoiced to hear that he continueth of the same mind as formerly, in relation to the great voyage; for, of late, I did think even he had begun to waver."

Don Luis had expressed himself of the great man of the vicinity, more like a Bobadilla than became his assumed name of Muños, and a glance from the eye of Columbus told him to forget his rank and to remember the disguise he had assumed.

"This is truly encouraging," observed the navigator, "and openeth a brighter view of Cathay. Thou wast journeying between Moguer and Palos, I think thou saidst, when this discourse was had with our acquaintance, the good Martin Alonzo?"

"I was, Señor, and it was he who sent me hither in quest of the admiral. He gave you the title that the queen's favor hath bestowed, and I consider that no small sign of friendship, as most others with whom I have conversed in this vicinity seem disposed to call you by any other name."

"None need embark in this enterprise," returned the navigator, gravely, as if he would admonish the youth that this was an occasion on which he might withdraw from the adventure, if he saw fit, "who feel disposed to act differently, or who distrust my knowledge."

"By San Pedro, my patron! they tell another tale at Palos, and at Moguer, Señor Amirale," returned Luis, laughing; "at which places, I hear, that no man whose skin hath been a little warmed by the sun of the ocean, dare show himself in the highways, lest he be sent to Cathay by a road that no one ever yet travelled, except in fancy! There is, notwithstanding, one free and willing volunteer, Señor Colon, who is disposed to follow you to the edge of the earth, if it be flat, and to follow you quite around it, should it prove to be a sphere; and that is one Pedro de Muños, who engageth with you from no sordid love of gold, or love of aught else that men usually prize; but from the pure love of adventure, somewhat excited and magnified, perhaps, by love of the purest and fairest maid of Castile."

Fray Juan Perez gazed at the speaker, whose free manner and open speech a good deal surprised him; for Columbus had succeeded in awakening so much respect that few presumed to use any levity in his presence, even before he was dignified by the high rank so recently conferred by the commission of Isabella. Little did the good monk suspect that one of a still higher personal rank, though entirely without official station, stood before him, in the guise of Pedro de Muños; and he could not refrain from again expressing the little relish he felt for such freedom of speech and deportment toward those whom he himself habitually regarded with so much respect.

"It would seem, Señor Pedro de Muños," he said, "if that be thy name—though duke, or marquis, or count, would be a title better becoming thy bearing—that thou treatest His Excellency the Admiral with quite as much freedom of thought, at least, as thou treatest the worthy Martin Alonzo of our own neighborhood: a follower should be more humble, and not pass his jokes on the opinions of his leader, in this loose style of expression."

"I crave your pardon, holy father, and that of the admiral, too, who better understandeth me I trust, if there be any just grounds of offence. All I wish to express is, that I know this Martin Alonzo of your neighborhood, as an old fellow-voyager; that we have ridden some leagues in company this very day, and that, after close discourse, he hath manifested a friendly desire to put his shoulder to the wheel, in order to lift the expedition, if not from a slough of mud, at least from the sands of the river; and that he hath promised to come also to this good convent of La Rabida, for that same purpose and no other. As for myself, I can only add, that here I am, ready to follow wheresoever the honorable Señor Colon may see fit to lead."

"'Tis well, good Pedro—'tis well," rejoined the admiral. "I give thee full credit for sincerity and spirit, and that must content thee until an opportunity offereth to convince others. I like these tidings concerning Martin Alonzo, father, since he might truly do us much good service, and his zeal had assuredly begun to flag."

"That might he, and that will he, if he engageth seriously in the affair. Martin is the greatest navigator on all this coast, for, though I did not know that he had ever been even to Cyprus, as would appear by the account of this youth, I was well aware that he had frequently sailed as far north as France, and as far south as the Canaries. Dost think Cathay much more remote than Cyprus, Señor Almirante?"

Columbus smiled at this question, and shook his head in the manner of one who would prepare a friend for some sore disappointment.

"Although Cyprus be not distant from the Holy Land and the seat of the Infidel's power," he answered, "Cathay must lie much more remote. I flatter not myself, nor those who are disposed to follow me, with the hope of reaching the Indies short of a voyage that shall extend to some eight hundred or a thousand leagues."

"'Tis a fearful and a weary distance!" exclaimed the Franciscan; while Luis stood in smiling unconcern, equally indifferent whether he had to traverse one-thousand or ten thousand leagues of ocean, so that the journey led to Mercedes and was productive of adventure. "A fearful and weary distance, and yet I doubt not, Señor Almirante, that you are the very man designed by Providence to overcome it, and to open the way for those who will succeed you, bearing on high the cross of Christ and the promises of his redemption!"

"Let us hope this," returned Columbus, reverently making the usual sign of the sacred emblem to which his friend alluded; "as a proof that we have some worldly foundation for the expectation, here cometh the Señor Pinzon himself, apparently hot with haste to see us."

Martin Alonzo Pinzon, whose name is so familiar to the reader, as one who greatly aided the Genoese in his vast undertaking, now entered the room, seemingly earnest and bent on some fixed purpose, as Columbus' observant eye had instantly detected. Fray Juan Perez was not a little surprised to see that the first salutation of Martin Alonzo, the great man of the neighborhood, was directed to Pedro, the second to the admiral, and the third to himself. There was not time, however, for the worthy Franciscan, who was a little apt to rebuke any dereliction of decency on the spot, to express what he felt on this occasion, ere Martin Alonzo opened his errand with an eagerness that showed he had not come on a mere visit of friendship, or of ceremony.

"I am sorely vexed, Señor Almirante," he commenced, "at learning the obstinacy, and the disobedience to the orders of the queen, that have been shown among our mariners of Palos. Although a dweller of the port itself, and one who hath always viewed your opinions of this western voyage with respect, if not with absolute faith, I did not know the full extent of this insubordination until I met, by accident, an old acquaintance on the highway, in the person of Don Pedro—I ought to say the *Señor* Pedro de Muños, here, who, coming from a distance as he doth, hath discovered more of our backslidings than I had learned myself, on the spot. But, Señor, you are not now to hear for the first time, of what sort of stuff men are made. They are reasoning beings, we are told; notwithstanding which undeniable truth, as there is not one in a hundred who is at the trouble to do his own thinking, means may be found to change the opinions of a sufficient number for all your wants, without their even suspecting it."

"This is very true, neighbor Martin Alonzo," put in the friar—"so true, that it might go into a homily and do no disservice to religion. Man *is* a rational animal, and an accountable animal, but it is not meet that he should be a *thinking* animal. In matters of the church, now, its interests being entrusted to a ministry, what have the unlearned and ignorant to say of its affairs? In matters of navigation, it doth, indeed, seem as if one steersman were better than a hundred! Although man be a reasoning animal, there are quite as many occasions when he is bound to obey without reasoning, and few when he should be permitted to reason without obeying."

"All true, holy friar and most excellent neighbor; so true that you will find no one in Palos to deny that, at least. And now we are on the subject, I may as well add that it is the church that hath thrown more obstacles in the way of the Señor Almirante's success, than any other cause. All the old women of the port declare that the notion of the earth's being round is a heresy, and contrary to the Bible; and, if the truth must be said, there are not a few underlings of this very convent, who uphold them in the opinion. It doth appear unnatural to tell one who hath never quitted the land, and who seeth himself much oftener in a valley than on an eminence, that the globe is round, and, though I have had many occasions to see the ocean, it would not easily find credit with me, were it not for the fact that we see the upper and smaller sails of a ship first, when approaching her, as well as the vanes and crosses of towns, albeit they are the smaller objects about vessels and churches. We mariners have one way to inspirit our followers, and you churchmen have another; and, now that I intend to use my means to put wiser thoughts into the heads of the seamen of Palos, reverend friar, I look to you to set the church's engines at work, so as to silence the women, and to quell the doubts of the most zealous among your own brotherhood."

"Am I to understand by this, Señor Pinzon," demanded Columbus, "that you intend to take a direct and more earnest interest than before in the success of my enterprise?"

"Señor, you may. That is my intention, if we can come to as favorable an understanding about the terms, as your worship would seem to have entered into with our most honored mistress, Doña Isabella de Trastamara. I have had some discourse with Señor Don—I would say with the Señor Pedro de Muños, here—odd's folly, an excess of courtesy is getting to be a vice with me of late—but as he is a youth of prudence, and manifests a desire to embark with you, it hath stirred my fancy so far, that I would gladly be of the party. Señor de Muños and I have voyaged so much together, that I would fain see his worthy countenance once more upon the ocean."

"These are cheerful tidings, Martin Alonzo"—eagerly put in the friar, "and thy soul, and the souls of all who belong to you, will reap the benefits of this manly and pious resolution. It is one thing, Señor Almirante, to have their Highnesses of your side, in a place like Palos, and another to have our worthy neighbor Pinzon, here; for, if they are sovereigns in law, he is an emperor in opinion. I doubt not that the caravels will now be speedily forthcoming."

"Since thou seemest to have truly resolved to enter into our enterprise, Señor Martin Alonzo," added Columbus, with his dignified gravity, "out of doubt, thou hast well bethought thee of the conditions, and art come prepared to let them be known. Do they savor of the terms that have already been in discussion between us?"

"Señor Admiral, they do; though gold is not, just now, as abundant in our purses, as when we last discoursed on this subject. On that head, some obstacles may exist, but on all others, I doubt not, a brief explanation between us will leave the matter free from doubt."

"As to the eighth, for which I stand committed with their Highnesses, Señor Pinzon, there will be less reason, now, to raise that point between us, than when we last met, as other means may offer to redeem that pledge" — as Columbus spoke, his eyes involuntarily turned toward the pretended Pedro, whither those of Martin Alonzo Pinzon significantly followed; "but there will be many difficulties to overcome with these terrified and silly mariners, which may yield to thy influence. If thou wilt come with me into this chamber, we will at once discuss the heads of our treaty, leaving this youth, the while, to the hospitality of our reverend friend."

The prior raising no objection to this proposition, it was immediately put in execution, Columbus and Pinzon withdrawing to a more private apartment, leaving Fray Juan Perez alone with our hero.

"Then thou thinkest seriously, son, of making one in this great enterprise of the admiral's," said the Franciscan, as soon as the door was closed on those who had just left them, eyeing Luis, for the first time, with a more strict scrutiny than hitherto he had leisure to exercise. "Thou carriest thyself much like the young lords of the court, and wilt have occasion to acquire a less towering air in the narrow limits of one of our Palos caravels."

"I am no stranger to Nao, Carraca, Fusta, Pinaza, Carabelon, or Felucca, holy prior, and shall carry myself with the admiral, as I should carry myself before Don Fernando of Aragon, were he my fellow-voyager, or in the presence of Boabdil of Grenada, were that unhappy monarch again seated on the throne from which he hath been so lately hurled, urging his chivalry to charge the knights of Christian Spain."

"These are fine words, son, ay, and uttered with a tilting air, if truth must be said; but they will avail thee nothing with this Genoese, who hath that in him, that would leave him unabashed even in the presence of our gracious lady, Doña Isabella, herself."

"Thou knowest the queen, holy monk?" inquired Luis, forgetting his assumed character, in the freedom of his address.

"I ought to know her inmost heart, son, for often have I listened to her pure and meek spirit, in the secrets of the confessional. Much as she is beloved by us Castilians, no one can know the true, spiritual elevation of that pious princess, and most excellent woman, but they who have had occasion to shrive her."

Don Luis hemmed, played with the handle of his rapier, and then gave utterance to the uppermost thought, as usual.

"Didst thou, by any chance of thy priestly office, father, ever find it necessary to confess a maiden of the court, who is much esteemed by the queen?" he inquired, "and whose spirit, I'll answer for it, is as pure as that of Doña Isabella's itself."

"Son, thy question denoteth greater necessity for repairing to Salamanca, in order to be instructed in the history, and practices, and faith of the church, than to be entering into an enterprise, even as commendable as this of Colon's! Dost thou not know that we churchmen are not permitted to betray the secrets of the confessional, or to draw comparisons between penitents? and, moreover, that we do not take even Doña Isabella, the blessed Maria keep her ever in mind, as the standard of holiness to which all Christians are expected to aim? The maiden of whom thou speakest may be virtuous, according to worldly notions, and yet a grievous sinner in the eyes of mother church."

"I should like, before I quit Spain, to hear a Mendoza, or a Guzman, who hath not a shaven crown, venture to hint as much, most reverend prior!"

"Thou art hot and restive, and talkest idly, son; what would one like thee find to say to a Guzman, or a Mendoza, or a Bobadilla, even, did he affirm what thou wishest? But, who is the maid, in whom thy feelings seem to take so deep, although I question if it be not an unrequited, interest?"

"Nay, I did but speak in idleness. Our stations have made such a chasm between us, that it is little likely we should ever come to speech; nor is my merit such as would be apt to cause her to forget her high advantages."

"Still, she hath a name?"

"She hath, truly, prior, and a right noble one it is. I had the Doña Maria de las Mercedes de Valverde in my thoughts, when the light remark found utterance. Haply, thou may'st know that illustrious heiress?"

Fray Juan Perez, a truly guileless priest, started at the name; then he gazed intently, and with a sort of pity, at the youth; after which he bent his head toward the tiles beneath his feet, smiled, and shook his head like one whose thoughts were very active.

"I do, indeed, know the lady," he said, "and even when last at court, on this errand of Colon's, their own confessor being ill, I shrived her, as well as my royal mistress. That she is worthy of Doña Isabella's esteem is true; but thy admiration for this noble maiden, which must be something like the distant reverence we feel for the clouds that sail above our heads, can scarce be founded on any rational hopes."

"Thou canst not know that, father. If this expedition end as we trust, all who engage in it will be honored and advanced; and why not I, as well as another?"

"In this, thou may'st utter truth, but as for the Doña—" The Franciscan checked himself, for he was about to betray the secret of the confessional. He had, in truth, listened to the contrition of Mercedes, of which her passion for Luis was the principal cause; and it was he who, with a species of pious fraud of which he was himself unconscious, had first pointed out the means by which the truant noble might be made to turn his propensity to rove to the profit of his love; and his mind was full of her beautiful exhibition of purity and natural feeling, nearly even to overflowing. But habit and duty interfered in time, and he did not utter the name that had been trembling on his lips. Still, his thoughts continued in this current, and his tongue gave utterance to that portion of them which he believed to be harmless. "Thou hast been much about the world, it would seem, by Master Alonzo's greeting," he continued, after a short pause; "didst ever meet, son, with a certain cavalier of Castile, named Don Luis de Bobadilla—a grandee, who also bears the title of Conde de Llera?"

"I know little of his hopes, and care less for his titles," returned Luis, calmly, who thought he would manifest a magnanimous indifference to the Franciscan's opinions—"but I have seen the cavalier, and a roving, mad-brained, graceless youth it is, of whom no good can be expected."

"I fear this is but too true," rejoined Fray Juan Perez, shaking his head in a melancholy manner—"and yet they say he is a gallant knight, and the very best lance in all Spain."

"Ay, he may be that," answered Luis, hemming a little louder than was decorous, for his throat began to grow husky—"Ay, he may be that;

but of what avail is a good lance without a good character. I hear little commendable of this young Conde de Llera."

"I trust he is not the man he generally passeth for,"—answered the simple-hearted monk, without in the least suspecting his companion's disguise; "and I do know that there are some who think well of him—nay, whose existence, I might say whose very souls, are wrapped up in him!"

"Holy Franciscan!—why wilt thou not mention the names of one or two of these?" demanded Luis, with an impetuosity that caused the prior to start.

"And why should I give this information to thee, young man, more than to another?"

"Why, father—why, for several most excellent and unanswerable reasons. In the first place, I am a youth myself, as thou seest; and example, they say, is better than precept. Then, too, I am somewhat given to roving, and it may profit me to know how others of the same propensity have sped. Moreover, it would gladden my inmost heart to hear that—but two sufficient reasons are better than three, and thou hast the first number already."

Fray Juan Perez, a devout Christian, a learned churchman, and a liberal scholar, was as simple as a child in matters that related to the world and its passions. Nevertheless, he was not so dull as to overlook the strange deportment and stranger language of his companion. A direction had been given to his thoughts by the mention of the name of our heroine; and, as he himself had devised the very course taken by our hero, the truth began to dawn on his imagination.

"Young cavalier," he exclaimed, "thou art Don Luis de Bobadilla!"

"I shall never deny the prophetic knowledge of a churchman, worthy father, after this detection! I *am* he thou sayest, entered on this expedition to win the love of Mercedes de Valverde."

"'Tis as I thought—and yet, Señor, you might have taken our poor convent less at an advantage. Suffer that I command the lay brothers to place refreshments before you!"

"Thy pardon, excellent prior—Pedro de Muños, or even Pero Gutierrez, hath no need of food; but, now that thou knowest me, there can be less reason for not conversing of the Doña Mercedes?"

"Now that I know thee, Señor Conde, there is greater reason for silence on that head," returned Fray Juan Perez, smiling. "Thine aunt, the most esteemed and virtuous lady of Moya, can give thee all occasion to urge thy suit with this charming maiden, and it would ill become a churchman to temper her prudence by any indiscreet interference."

This explanation was the commencement of a long and confidential dialogue, in which the worthy prior, now that he was on his guard, succeeded in preserving his main secret, though he much encouraged the young man in the leading hope of his existence, as well as in his project to adhere to the fortunes of Columbus. In the mean while, the great navigator himself continued closeted with his new counsellor; and when the two reappeared, it was announced to those without that the latter had engaged in the enterprise with so much zeal, that he actually entertained the intention of embarking on board of one of the caravels in person.

CHAPTER XII

"Yet he to whom each danger hath become
A dark delight, and every wild a home,
Still urges onward—undismayed to tread
Where life's fond lovers would recoil with dread."

The Abencerrage.

The intelligence that Martin Alonzo Pinzon was to make one of the followers of Colon, spread through the village of Palos like wild-fire. Volunteers were no longer wanting; the example of one known and respected in the vicinity, operating far more efficiently on the minds of the mariners, than the orders of the queen or the philosophy of Columbus. Martin Alonzo they knew; they were accustomed to submit to his influence; they could follow in his footsteps, and had confidence in his judgment; whereas, the naked orders of an unseen sovereign, however much beloved, had more of the character of a severe judgment than of a generous enterprise; and as for Columbus, though most men were awed by his dignified appearance and grave manner, when out of sight he was as much regarded as an adventurer at Palos, as he had been at Santa Fé.

The Pinzons set about their share of the expedition after the manner of those who were more accustomed to execute than to plan. Several of the family entered cordially into the work; and a brother of Martin Alonzo's, whose name was Vincente Yañez, also a mariner by profession, joined the adventurers as commander of one of the vessels, while another took service as a pilot. In short, the month that succeeded the incidents just mentioned, was actively employed, and more was done in that short space of time toward bringing about a solution of the great problem of Columbus, than had been accomplished, in a practical way, during the seventeen long years that the subject had occupied his time and engrossed his thoughts.

Notwithstanding the local influence of the Pinzons, a vigorous opposition to the project still existed in the heart of the little community that had been chosen for the place of equipment of the different vessels required. This family had its enemies as well as its friends, and, as is usual with most human undertakings, two parties sprang up, one of which was quite as busily occupied in thwarting the plans of the navigator, as the other was engaged in promoting them. One vessel had been seized for the service, under the order of the court, and her owners became leaders of the dissatisfied faction. Many seamen, according to the usage of that day, had been impressed for duty on this extraordinary and mysterious voyage; and, as a matter of course, they and their friends were not slow to join the ranks of the disaffected. Much of the necessary work was found to be imperfectly done; and when the mechanics were called on to repair these omissions, they absconded in a body. As the time for sailing approached, the contention grew more and more violent, and even the Pinzons had the mortification of discovering that many of those who had volunteered to follow their fortunes, began to waver, and that some had unequivocally deserted.

Such was the state of things, toward the close of the month of July, when Martin Alonzo Pinzon again repaired to the convent of Santa Maria de Rabida, where Columbus continued to pass most of the time that was not given to a direct personal superintendence of the preparations, and where Luis de Bobadilla, who was altogether useless in the actual condition of affairs, also passed many a weary hour, chafing for active duty, and musing on the loveliness, truth, and virtues of Mercedes de Valverde. Fray Juan Perez was earnest in his endeavors to facilitate the execution of the objects of his friends, and he had actually succeeded, if not in absolutely suppressing the expression of all injurious opinion on the part of the less enlightened of the brotherhood, at least in rendering the promulgation of them more cautious and private.

When Columbus and the prior were told that the Señor Pinzon sought an interview, neither was slow in granting the favor. As the hour of departure drew nigh, the importance of this man's exertions became more and more apparent, and both well knew that the royal protection of Isabella herself, just at that moment and in that place, was of less account than that of this active mariner. The Señor Pinzon, therefore, had not long to wait for his audience, having been ushered into the room that was commonly occupied by the zealous Franciscan, almost as soon as his request was preferred.

"Thou art right welcome, worthy Martin Alonzo!" exclaimed the prior, the moment he caught a glimpse of the features of his old acquaintance— "How get on matters at Palos, and when shall we have this holy undertaking in a fair direction for success?"

"By San Francisco, reverend prior, that is more than it will be safe for any man to answer. I have thought we were in a fair way to make sail, a score of times, when some unforeseen difficulty hath arisen. The Santa Maria, on board which the admiral and the Señor Gutierrez, or de Muños, if he will have it so, will embark, is already fitted. She may be set down as a tight craft, and somewhat exceedeth a hundred tons in burthen, so that I trust his excellency, and all the gallant cavaliers who may accompany him, will be as comfortable as the holy monks of Rabica—more especially as the good caravel hath a deck."

"These are, truly, glad tidings," returned the prior, rubbing his hands with delight—"and the excellent craft hath really a deck! Señor Almirante, thou mayst not be in a vessel that is altogether worthy of thy high aim, but, on the whole, thou wilt be both safe and comfortable, keeping in view, in particular, this convenient and sheltering deck."

"Neither my safety nor my convenience is a consideration to be mentioned, friend Juan Perez, when there is question of so much graver matters. I rejoice that thou hast come to the convent this morning, Señor Martin Alonzo, as, being about to address letters to the court, by means of an especial courier, I desire to know the actual condition of things. Thou thinkest the Santa Maria will be in a state for service by the end of the month?"

"Señor, I do The ship hath been prepared with due diligence, and will conveniently hold some three score, should the panic that hath seized on so many of the besotted fools of Palos, leave us that number, who may still be disposed to embark. I trust that the saints look upon our many efforts, and will remember our zeal when we shall come to a joint division of the benefits of this undertaking, which hath had no equal in the history of navigation!"

"The benefits, honest Martin Alonzo, will be found in the spread of the church's dominion, and the increased glory of God!" put in the prior, significantly.

"Out of all question, holy Fray Juan Perez—this is the common aim; though I trust it is permitted to a pains-taking mariner to bethink him of his wife and children, in discreet subordination to those greater ends. I have much mistaken the Señor Colon, if he do not look for some little advantage, in the way of gold, from this visit to Cathay."

"Thou hast not mistaken me, honest Martin Alonzo," returned Columbus, gravely. "I do, indeed, expect to see the wealth of the Indies pouring into the coffers of Castile, in consequence of this voyage. In sooth, excellent prior, in my view, the recovery of the holy sepulchre is dependent mainly on the success of our present undertaking, in the way of a substantial worldly success."

"This is well. Señor Admiral," put in Martin Alonzo, a little hastily, "and ought to gain us great favor in the eyes of all good Christians—more especially with the monks of la Rabida. But it is hard enough to persuade the mariners of the port to obey the queen, in this matter, and to fulfil their engagements with ourselves, without preaching a crusade, as the best means of throwing away the few maravedis they may happen to gain by their hardships and courage. The worthy pilots, Francisco Martin Pinzon, mine own brother, Sancho Ruiz, Pedro Alonzo Niño, and Bartolemeo Roldan, are all now firmly tied to us by the ropes of the law; but should they happen to find a crusade at their end, all the saints in the calendar would scarce have influence to make them hesitate about loosening themselves from the agreement."

"I hold no one but myself bound to this object," returned Columbus, calmly. "Each man, friend Martin Alonzo, will be judged by his own deeds, and called on to fulfil his own vows. Of those who pledge naught, naught will be exacted, and naught given at the great final account of the human race. But what are the tidings of the Pinta, thine own vessel? Hath she been finally put into a condition to buffet the Atlantic?"

"As ever happeneth with a vessel pressed into the royal service, Señor, work hath gone on heavily, and things in general have not borne that merry activity which accompanieth the labor of those who toil of a free will, and for their own benefit."

"The silly mariners have toiled in their own behalf, without knowing it," observed Columbus. "It is the duty of the ignorant to submit to be led by the more enlightened, and to be grateful for the advantages they derive from a borrowed knowledge, albeit it is obtained contrary to their own wishes."

"That is it, truly," added the prior; "else would the office of us churchmen be reduced to very narrow limits. Faith—faith in the church—is the Christian's earliest and latest duty."

"This seemeth reasonable, excellent sirs," returned Master Alonzo, "though the ignorant find it difficult to comprehend matters that they do not understand. When a man fancieth himself condemned to an unheard-of death, he is little apt to see the benefit that lieth beyond the grave. Nevertheless, the Pinta is more nearly ready for the voyage, than any other of our craft, and hath her crew engaged to a man, and that under contracts that will not permit much dispute before a notary."

"There remaineth only the Niña, then," added Columbus; "with her prepared, and our religious duties observed, we may hope finally to commence the enterprise!"

"Señor, you may. My brother, Vicente Yañez, hath finally consented to take charge of this little craft; and that which a Pinzon promiseth, a Pinzon performeth. She will be ready to depart with the Santa Maria and the Pinta, and Cathay must be distant, indeed, if we do not reach it with one or the other of our vessels."

"This is right encouraging, neighbor Martin Alonzo," returned the friar, rubbing his hands with delight; "and I make no question all will come round in the end. What say the crones and loose talkers of Moguer, and of the other ports, touching the shape of the earth, and the chances of the admiral's reaching the Indies, now-a-days?"

"They discourse much as they did, Fray Juan Perez, idly and without knowledge. Although there is not a mariner in any of the havens who doth not admit that the upper sails, though so much the smallest, are the first seen on the ocean, yet do they deny that this cometh of the shape of the earth, but, as they affirm, of the movements of the waters."

"Have none of them ever observed the shadows cast by the earth, in the eclipses of the moon?" asked Columbus, in his calm manner, though he smiled, even in putting the question, as one smiles who, having dipped deeply into a natural problem himself, carelessly lays one of its more popular proofs before those who are less disposed to go beneath the surface. "Do they not see that these shadows are round, and do they not know that a shadow which is round can only be cast by a body that is round?"

"This is conclusive, good Martin Alonzo," put in the prior, "and it ought to remove the doubts of the silliest gossip on the coast. Tell them to encircle their dwellings, beginning to the right, and see if, by following the walls, they do not return to the spot from which they started, coming in from the left."

"Ay, reverend prior, if we could bring our distant voyage down to these familiar examples, there is not a crone in Moguer, or a courtier at Seville, that might not be made to comprehend the mystery. But it is one thing to state a problem fairly, and another to find those who can understand it. Now, I did give some such reasoning to the Alguiazil, in Palos here, and the worthy Señor asked me if I expected to return from this voyage by the way of the lately captured town of Granada. I fancy that the easiest method of persuading these good people to believe that Cathay can be reached by the western voyage, will be by going there and returning."

"Which we will shortly do, Master Martin Alonzo," observed Columbus, cheerfully—"But the time of our departure draweth near, and it is meet that none of us neglect the duties of religion. I commend thee to thy confessor, Señor Pinzon, and expect that all who sail with me, in this great enterprise, will receive the holy communion in my company, before we quit the haven.

This excellent prior will shrive Pedro de Muños and myself, and let each man seek such other holy counsellor and monitor as hath been his practice."

With this intimation of his intention to pay a due regard to the rites of the church before he departed—rites that were seldom neglected in that day—the conversation turned, for the moment, on the details of the preparations. After this the parties separated, and a few more days passed away in active exertions.

On the morning of Thursday, August the second, 1492, Columbus entered the private apartment of Fray Juan Perez, habited like a penitent, and with an air so devout, and yet so calm, that it was evident his thoughts were altogether bent on his own transgressions and on the goodness of God. The zealous priest was in waiting, and the great navigator knelt at the feet of him, before whom Isabella had often knelt, in the fulfilment of the same solemnity. The religion of this extraordinary man was colored by the habits and opinions of his age, as, indeed, in a greater or less degree, must be the religion of every man; his confession, consequently, had that admixture of deep piety with inconsistent error, that so often meets the moralist in his investigations into the philosophy of the human mind. The truth of this peculiarity will be seen, by adverting to one or two of the admissions of the great navigator, as he laid before his ghostly counsellor the catalogue of his sins.

"Then, I fear, holy father," Columbus continued, after having made most of the usual confessions touching the more familiar weaknesses of the human race, "that my mind hath become too much exalted in this matter of the voyage, and that I may have thought myself more directly set apart by God, for some good end, than it might please his infinite knowledge and wisdom to grant."

"That would be a dangerous error, my son, and I carefully admonish thee against the evils of self-righteousness. That God selecteth his agents, is beyond dispute; but it is a fearful error to mistake the impulses of self-love, for the movements of his Divine Spirit! It is hardly safe for any who have not received the church's ordination, to deem themselves chosen vessels."

"I endeavor so to consider it, holy friar," answered Columbus, meekly; "and, yet, there is that within, which constantly urgeth to this belief, be it a delusion, or come it directly from heaven. I strive, father, to keep the feeling in subjection, and most of all do I endeavor to see that it taketh a direction that may glorify the name of God and serve the interests of his visible church."

"This is well, and yet do I feel it a duty to admonish thee against too much credence in these inward impulses. So long as they tend, solely, to increase thy love for the Supreme Father of all, to magnify his holiness, and glorify his nature, thou may'st be certain it is the offspring of good; but when self-exaltation seemeth to be its aim, beware the impulse, as thou wouldst eschew the dictation of the great father of evil!"

"I so consider it; and now having truly and sincerely disburdened my conscience, father, so far as in me lieth, may I hope for the church's consolation, with its absolution?"

"Canst thou think of naught else, son, that should not lie hid from before the keeper of all consciences?"

"My sins are many, holy prior, and cannot be too often or too keenly rebuked; but I do think that they may be fairly included in the general heads that I have endeavored to recall."

"Hast thou nothing to charge thyself with, in connection with that sex that the devil as often useth as his tempters to evil, as the angels would fain employ them as the ministers of grace?"

"I have erred as a man, father; but do not my confessions already meet those sins?"

"Hast thou bethought thee of Doña Beatriz Enriquez? of thy son Fernando, who tarrieth, at this moment, in our convent of la Rabida?"

Columbus bowed his head in submission, and the heavy sigh, amounting almost to a groan, that broke out of his bosom, betrayed the weight of his momentary contrition.

"Thou say'st true, father; that is an offence which should never be forgotten, though so often shrived since its commission. Heap on me the penance that I feel is due, and thou shalt see how a Christian can bend and kiss the rod that he is conscious of having merited."

"The spirit thus to do is all that the church requireth; and thou art now bent on a service too important to her interests to be drawn aside from thy great intentions, for any minor considerations. Still may not a minister of the altar overlook the offence. Thou wilt say a pater, daily, on account of this great sin, for the next twenty days, all of which will be for the good of thy soul; after which the church releaseth thee from this especial duty, as thou wilt, then, be drawing near to the land of Cathay, and may have occasion for all thy thoughts and efforts to effect thy object."

The worthy prior then proceeded to prescribe several light penances, most of which were confined to moderate increases of the daily duties of religion; after which he shrived the navigator. The turn of Luis came next, and more than once the prior smiled involuntarily, as he listened to this hot-blooded and impetuous youth, whose language irresistibly carried back his thoughts to the more meek, natural, and the more gentle admissions of the pure-minded Mercedes. The penance prescribed to Luis was not entirely free from severity, though, on the whole, the young man, who was not much addicted to the duties of the confessional, fancied himself well quit of the affair, considering the length of the account he was obliged to render, and the weight of the balance against him.

These duties performed in the persons of the two principal adventurers, Martin Alonzo Pinzon and the ruder mariners of the expedition appeared before different priests and gave in the usual reckoning of their sins. After this came a scene that was strictly characteristic of the age, and which would be impressive and proper, in all times and seasons, for men about to embark in an undertaking of a result so questionable.

High mass was said in the chapel of the convent, and Columbus received the consecrated bread from the hands of Fray Juan Perez, in humble reliance on the all-seeing providence of God, and with a devout dependence on his fostering protection. All who were about to embark with the admiral imitated his example, communing in his company; for that was a period when the wire-drawn conclusions of man had not yet begun so far to supplant the faith and practices of the earlier church as to consider its rites as the end of religion, but he was still content to regard them as its means. Many a rude sailor, whose ordinary life might not have been either saintly or even free from severe censure, knelt that day at the altar, in devout dependence on God, with feelings, for the moment, that at least placed him on the highway to grace; and it would be presumptuous to suppose that the omniscient Being to whom his offerings were made, did not regard his ignorance with commiseration, and even look upon his superstition with pity. We scoff at the prayers of those who are in danger, without reflecting that they are a homage to the power of God, and are apt to fancy that these passages in devotion are mere mockery, because the daily mind and the ordinary life are not always elevated to the same standard of godliness and purity. It would be more humble to remember the general infirmities of the race; to recollect, that as none are perfect, the question is reduced to one of degree; and to bear in mind, that the Being who reads the heart, may accept of any devout petitions, even though they come from those who are not disposed habitually to walk in his laws. These passing but pious emotions are the workings of the Spirit, since good can come from no other source; and it is as unreasonable as it is irreverent to imagine that the Deity will disregard, altogether, the effects of his own grace, however humble.

Whatever may have been the general disposition of most of the communicants on this occasion, there is little doubt that there knelt at the altar of la Rabida, that day, one in the person of the great navigator himself, who, as far as the eye could perceive, lived habitually in profound deference to the dogmas of religion, and who paid an undeviating respect to all its rites. Columbus was not strictly a devotee; but a quiet, deeply seated enthusiasm, which had taken the direction of Christianity, pervaded his moral system, and at all times disposed him to look up to the protecting hand of the Deity and to expect its aid. The high aims that he entertained for the future have already been mentioned, and there is little doubt of his having persuaded himself that he had been set apart by Providence as the instrument it designed to employ in making the great discovery on which his mind was so intently engaged, as well as in accomplishing other and ulterior purposes. If, indeed, an overruling Power directs all the events of this world, who will presume to say that this conviction of Columbus was erroneous, now that it has been justified by the result? That he felt this sentiment sustaining his courage and constantly urging him onward, is so much additional evidence in favor of his impression, since, under such circumstances, nothing is more probable than that an earnest belief in his destiny would be one of the means most likely to be employed by a supernatural power in inducing its human agent to accomplish the work for which he had actually been selected.

Let this be as it might, there is no doubt that Colon observed the rites of the church, on the occasion named, with a most devout reliance on the truth of his mission, and with the brightest hopes as to its successful termination. Not so, however, with all of his intended followers. Their minds had wavered, from time to time, as the preparations advanced; and the last month had seen them eager to depart, and dejected with misgivings and doubts. Although there were days of hope and brightness, despondency perhaps prevailed, and this so much the more because the apprehensions of mothers, wives, and of those who felt an equally tender interest in the mariners, though less inclined to avow it openly, were thrown into the scale by the side of their own distrust. Gold, unquestionably, was the great aim of their wishes, and there were moments when visions of inexhaustible mines and of oriental treasures floated before their imaginations; at which times none could be more eager to engage in the mysterious undertaking, or more ready to risk their lives and hopes on its success. But these were fleeting impressions, and, as has just been said, despondency was the prevalent feeling among those who were about to embark. It heightened the devotion of the communicants, and threw a gloom over the chastened sobriety of the altar, that weighed heavily on the hearts of most assembled there.

"Our people seem none of the most cheerful, Señor Almirante," said Luis, as they left the convent-chapel in company; "and, if truth must be spoken, one could wish to set forth on an expedition of this magnitude, better sustained by merry hearts and smiling countenances."

"Dost thou imagine, young count, that he hath the firmest mind who weareth the most smiling visage, or that the heart is weak because the countenance is sobered? These honest mariners bethink them of their sins, and no doubt are desirous that so holy an enterprise be not tainted by the corruption of their own hearts, but rather purified and rendered fitting, by their longings to obey the will of God. I trust, Luis"—intercourse had given Columbus a sort of paternal interest in the welfare of the young grandee, that lessened the distance made by rank between them—"I trust, Luis, thou art not, altogether, without these pious longings in thine own person."

"By San Pedro, my new patron! Señor Almirante, I think more of Mercedes de Valverde, than of aught else, in this great affair. She is my polar star, my religion, my Cathay. Go on, in Heaven's name, and discover what thou wilt, whether it be Cipango or the furthest Indies; beard the great Khan on his throne, and I will follow in thy train, with a poor lance and an indifferent sword, swearing that the maid of Castile hath no equal, and ransacking the east, merely to prove in the face of the universe that she is peerless, let her rivals come from what part of the earth they may."

Although Columbus permitted his grave countenance slightly to relax at this rhapsody, he did not the less deem it prudent to rebuke the spirit in which it was uttered.

"I grieve, my young friend," he said, "to find that thou hast not the feelings proper for one who is engaged, as it might be, in a work of Heaven's own ordering. Canst thou not foresee the long train of mighty and wonderful events that are likely to follow from this voyage—the spread of religion, through the holy church; the conquest of distant empires, with their submission to the sway of Castile; the settling of disputed points in science and philosophy, and the attainment of inexhaustible wealth; with the last and most honorable consequence of all, the recovery of the sepulchre of the Son of God, from the hands of the Infidels!"

"No doubt, Señor Colon—no doubt, I see them all, but I see the Doña Mercedes at their end. What care I for gold, who already possess—or shall so soon possess—more than I need? what is the extension of the sway of Castile to me, who can never be its king? and as for the Holy Sepulchre, give me but Mercedes, and, like my ancestors that are gone, I am ready to break a lance with the stoutest Infidel who ever wore a turban, be it in that, or in any other quarrel. In short, Señor Almirante, lead on; and though we go forth with different objects and different hopes, doubt not that they will lead us to the same goal. I feel that you ought to be supported in this great and noble design, and it matters not what may bring me in your train."

"Thou art a mad-brained youth, Luis, and must be humored, if it were only for the sake of the sweet and pious young maiden who seemeth to engross all thy thoughts."

"You have seen her, Señor, and can say whether she be not worthy to occupy the minds of all the youth of Spain?"

"She is fair, and virtuous, and noble, and a zealous friend of the voyage. These are all rare merits, and thou may'st be pardoned for thy enthusiasm in her behalf. But forget not, that, to win her, thou must first win a sight of Cathay."

"In the reality, you must mean, Señor Almirante; for, with the mind's eye, I see it keenly, constantly, and see little else with Mercedes standing on its shores, smiling a welcome, and, by St. Paul! sometimes beckoning me on, with that smile that fires the soul with its witchery, even while it subdues the temper with its modesty. The blessed Maria send us a wind, right speedily, that we may quit this irksome river and wearying convent!"

Columbus made no answer; for, while he had all consideration for a lover's impatience, his thoughts turned to subjects too grave, to be long amused even by a lover's follies.

CHAPTER XIII

"Nor Zayda weeps him only,
But all that dwell between
The great Alhambra's palace walls
And springs of Albalein."

Bryant's Translations.

The instant of departure at length arrived. The moment so long desired by the Genoese was at hand, and years of poverty, neglect, and of procrastination, were all forgotten at that blessed hour; or, if they returned in any manner to the constant memory, it was no longer with the bitterness of hope deferred. The navigator, at last, saw himself in the possession of the means of achieving the first great object for which he had lived the last fifteen years, with the hope, in perspective, of making the success of his present adventure the stepping-stone toward effecting the conquest of the Holy Sepulchre. While those around him were looking with astonishment at the limited means with which ends so great were to be attained, or were struck aghast at the apparent temerity of an undertaking that seemed to defy the laws of nature, and to set at naught the rules of Providence, he had grown more tranquil as the time for sailing drew nearer, and his mind was oppressed merely by a feeling of intense, but of sobered, delight. Fray Juan Perez whispered to Luis, that he could best liken the joy of the admiral to the chastened rapture of a Christian who was about to quit a world of woe, to enter on the untasted, but certain, fruition of blessed immortality.

This, however, was far from being the state of mind of all in Palos. The embarkation took place in the course of the afternoon of the 2d of August, it being the intention of the pilots to carry the vessels that day to a point off the town of Huelvas, where the position was more favorable to making sail than when anchored in front of Palos. The distance was trifling, but it was the commencement of the voyage, and, to many, it was like snapping the cords of life, to make even this brief movement. Columbus, himself, was one of the last to embark, having a letter to send to the court, and other important duties to discharge. At length he quitted the convent, and, accompanied by Luis and the prior, he, too, took his way to the beach. The short journey was silent, for each of the party was deeply plunged in meditation. Never before this hour, did the enterprise seem so perilous and uncertain to the excellent Franciscan. Columbus was carefully recalling the details of his preparations, while Luis was thinking of the maid of Castile, as he was wont to term Mercedes, and of the many weary days that must elapse before he could hope to see her again.

The party stopped on the shore, in waiting for a boat to arrive, at a place where they were removed from any houses. There Fray Juan Perez took his leave of the two adventurers. The long silence that all three had maintained, was more impressive than any ordinary discourse could have been; but it was now necessary to break it. The prior was deeply affected, and it was some little time before he could even trust his voice to speak.

"Señor Christoval," he at length commenced, "it is now many years since thou first appeared at the gate of Santa Maria de Rabida—years of friendship and pleasure have they proved to me."

"It is full seven, Fray Juan Perez," returned Columbus—"seven weary years have they proved to me, as a solicitor for employment—years of satisfaction, father, in all that concerneth thee. Think not that I can ever forget the hour, when, leading Diego, houseless, impoverished, wanderers, journeying on foot, I stopped to tax the convent's charity for refreshment! The future is in the hands of God, but the past is imprinted here"—laying his hand on his heart—"and can never be forgotten. Thou hast been my constant friend, holy prior, and that, too, when it was no credit to favor the nameless Genoese. Should my estimation ever change in men's opinions"—

"Nay, Señor Almirante, it hath changed already," eagerly interrupted the prior. "Hast thou not the commission of the queen—the support of Don Fernando—the presence of this young noble, though still as an incognito—the wishes of all the learned? Dost thou not go forth, on this great voyage, carrying with thee more of our hopes than of our fears?"

"So far as thou art concerned, dear Juan Perez, this may be so. I feel that I have all thy best wishes for success; I know that I shall have thy prayers. Few in Spain, notwithstanding, will think of Colon with respect, or hope, while we are wandering on the great desert of the ocean, beyond a very narrow circle. I fear me, that, even at this moment, when the means of learning the truth of our theories is in actual possession—when we stand, as it might be, on the very threshold of the great portal which opens upon the Indies—that few believe in our chances of success."

"Thou hast Doña Isabella of thy side, Señor!"

"And Doña Mercedes!" put in Luis; "not to speak of my decided and true-hearted aunt!"

"I ask but a few brief months, Señores," returned Columbus, his face turned to heaven with uncovered head, his gray hair floating in the wind, and his eye kindling with the light of enthusiasm—"a few short months, that will pass away untold with the happy—that even the miserable may find supportable, but which to us will seem ages, must now dispose of this question. Prior, I have often quitted the shore feeling that I carried my life in my hand, conscious of all the dangers of the ocean, and as much expecting death as a happy return; but at this glorious moment no doubts beset me; as for life, I know it is in the keeping of God's care; as for success, I feel it is in God's wisdom!"

"These are comfortable sentiments, at so serious a moment, Señor, and I devoutly hope the end will justify them. But, yonder is thy boat, and we must now part. Señor, my son, thou knowest that my spirit will be with thee in this mighty undertaking."

"Holy prior, remember me in thy prayers. I am weak, and have need of this support. I trust much to the efficacy of thy intercessions, aided by those of thy pious brotherhood. Thou wilt bestow on us a few masses?"

"Doubt us not, my friend; all that la Rabida can do with the blessed Virgin, or the saints, shall be exercised, without ceasing, in thy behalf. It is not given to man to foresee the events that are controlled by Providence; and, though we deem this enterprise of thine so certain, and so reasonable, it may nevertheless fail."

"It may *not* fail, father; God hath thus far directed it, and he will not permit it to fail."

"We know not, Señor Colon; our wisdom is but as a grain of mustard seed among the sands of this shore, as compared with his inscrutable designs. I was about to say, as it is possible thou may'st return a disappointed, a defeated man, that thou wilt still find the gate of Santa Maria open to thee; since, in our eyes, it is as meritorious to attempt nobly, as it is often, in the eyes of others, to achieve successfully."

"I understand thee, holy prior; and the cup and the morsel bestowed on the young Diego, were not more grateful than this proof of thy friendship! I would not depart without thy blessing."

"Kneel, then, Señor; for, in this act it will not be Juan Perez de Marchena that will speak, and pronounce, but the minister of God and the church. Even these sands will be no unworthy spot to receive such an advantage."

The eyes of both Columbus and the prior were suffused with tears, for at that moment the heart of each was touched with the emotions natural to a moment so solemn. The first loved the last, because he had proved himself a friend when friends were few and timid; and the worthy monk had some such attachment for the great navigator as men are apt to feel for those they have cherished. Each, also, respected and appreciated the other's motives, and there was a bond of union in their common reverence for the Christian religion. Columbus kneeled on the sands, and received the benediction of his friend, with the meek submission of faith, and with some such feelings of reverence as those with which a pious son would have listened to a blessing pronounced by a natural father.

"Columbus kneeled on the sands, and received the benediction."

"And thou, young lord," resumed Fray Juan Perez, with a husky voice—"thou, too, wilt be none the worse for the prayers of an aged churchman."

Like most of that age, Luis, in the midst of his impetuous feelings, and youthful propensities, had enshrined in his heart an image of the Son of God, and entertained an habitual respect for holy things. He knelt without hesitation, and listened to the trembling words of the priest with thankfulness and respect.

"Adieu, holy prior," said Columbus, squeezing his friend's hand. "Thou hast befriended me when others held aloof: but I trust in God that the day is not now distant, when those who have ever shown confidence in my predictions will cease to feel uneasiness at the mention of my name. Forget us in all things but thy prayers, for a few short months, and then expect tidings that, of a verity, shall exalt Castile to a point of renown which will render this Conquest of Granada but an incident of passing interest amid the glory of the reign of Ferdinand and Isabella!"

This was not said boastfully, but with the quiet earnestness of one who saw a truth that was concealed from most eyes, and this with an intensity so great, that the effect on his moral vision produced a confidence equalling that which is the fruit of the evidence of the senses in ordinary men. The prior understood him, and the assurance thus given cheered the mind of the worthy Franciscan long after the departure of his friend. They embraced and separated.

By this time the boat of Columbus had reached the shore. As the navigator moved slowly toward it, a youthful female rushed wildly past him and Luis, and, regardless of their presence, she threw her arms around a young mariner who had quitted the boat to meet her, and sobbed for a minute on his bosom, in uncontrollable agony, or as women weep in the first outbreak of their emotions.

"Come, then, Pepe," the young wife at length said, hurriedly, and with low earnestness, as one speaks who would fain persuade herself that denial was impossible—"come, Pepe; thy boy hath wept for thee, and thou hast pushed this matter, already, much too far."

"Nay, Monica," returned the husband, glancing his eye at Columbus, who was already near enough to hear his words—"thou knowest it is by no wish of mine that I am to sail on this unknown voyage. Gladly would I abandon it, but the orders of the queen are too strong for a poor mariner like me, and they must be obeyed."

"This is foolish, Pepe," returned the woman, pulling at her husband's doublet to drag him from the water-side—"I have had enough of this; sufficient to break my heart. Come, then, and look again upon thy boy."

"Thou dost not see that the admiral is near, Monica, and we are showing him disrespect."

The habitual deference that was paid by the low to the high, induced the woman, for a moment, to pause. She looked imploringly at Columbus, her fine dark eyes became eloquent with the feelings of a wife and mother, and then she addressed the great navigator, himself.

"Señor," she said, eagerly, "you can have no further need of Pepe. He hath helped to carry your vessels to Huelva, and now his wife and boy call for him at home."

Columbus was touched with the manner of the woman, which was not entirely without a show of that wavering of reason which is apt to accompany excessive grief, and he answered her less strongly than, at a moment so critical, he might otherwise have been disposed to do to one who was inciting to disobedience.

"Thy husband is honored in being chosen to be my companion in the great voyage," he said. "Instead of bewailing his fate, thou wouldst act more like a brave mariner's wife, in exulting in his good fortune."

"Believe him not, Pepe. He speaketh under the Evil One's advice to tempt thee to destruction. He hath talked blasphemy, and belied the word of God, by saying that the world is round, and that one may sail east by steering west, that he might ruin thee and others, by tempting ye all to follow him!"

"And why should I do this, good woman?" demanded the admiral. "What have I to gain by the destruction of thy husband, or by the destruction of any of his comrades?"

"I know not—I care not—Pepe is all to me, and he shall not go with you on this mad and wicked voyage. No good can come of a journey that is begun by belying the truths of God!"

"And what particular evil dost thou dread, in this, more than in another voyage, that thou thus hang'st upon thy husband, and usest such discourse to one who beareth their Highnesses' authority for that he doeth? Thou knewest he was a mariner when thou wert wedded, and yet thou wouldst fain prevent him from serving the queen, as becometh his station and duty."

"He may go against the Moor, or the Portuguese, or the people of Inghleterra, but I would not that he voyage in the service of the Prince of Darkness. Why tell us that the earth is round, Señor, when our eyes show that it is flat? And if round, how can a vessel that hath descended the side of the earth for days, ever return? The sea doth not flow upward, neither can a caravel mount the waterfall. And when thou hast wandered about for months in the vacant ocean, in what manner wilt thou, and those with thee, ever discover the direction that must be taken to return whence ye all sailed? Oh! Señor, Palos is but a little town, and once lost sight of in such a confusion of ideas, it will never be regained."

"Idle and childish as this may seem," observed Columbus, turning quietly to Luis, "it is as reasonable as much that I have been doomed to hear from the learned, during the last sixteen years. When the night of ignorance obscures the mind, the thoughts conjure arguments a thousand times more vain and frivolous than the phenomena of nature that it fancies so unreasonable. I will try the effect of religion on this woman, converting her present feelings on that head, from an enemy into an ally. Monica," calling her kindly and familiarly by name, "art thou a Christian?"

"Blessed Maria! Señor Almirante, what else should I be? Dost think Pepe would have married a Moorish girl?"

"Listen, then, to me, and learn how unlike a believer thou conductest. The Moor is not the only infidel, but this earth groaneth with the burden of their numbers, and of their sins. The sands on this shore are not as numerous as the unbelievers in the single kingdom of Cathay; for, as yet, God hath allotted but a small portion of the earth to those who have faith in the mediation of his Son. Even the sepulchre of Christ is yet retained by infidel hands."

"This have I heard, Señor; and 'tis a thousand pities the faith is so weak in those who have vowed to obey the law, that so crying an evil hath never been cured!"

"Hast thou not been told that such is to be the fate of the world, for a time, but that light will dawn when the word shall pass, like the sound of trumpets, into the ears of infidels, and when the earth, itself, shall be but one vast temple, filled with the praises of God, the love of his name, and obedience to his will?"

"Señor, the good fathers of la Rabida, and our own parish priests, often comfort us with these hopes."

"And hast thou seen naught of late to encourage that hope—to cause thee to think that God is mindful of his people, and that new light is beginning to burst on the darkness of Spain?"

"Pepe, his excellency must mean the late miracle at the convent, where they say that real tears were seen to fall from the eyes of the image of the holy Maria, as she gazed at the child that lay on her bosom."

"I mean not that," interrupted Columbus, a little sternly, though he crossed himself, even while he betrayed dissatisfaction at the allusion to a miracle that was much too vulgar for his manly understanding—"I mean no such questionable wonder, which it is permitted us to believe, or not, as it may be supported by the church's authority. Can thy faith and zeal point to no success of the two sovereigns, in which the power of God, as exercised to the advancement of the faith, hath been made signally apparent to believers?"

"He meaneth the expulsion of the Moor, Pepe!" the woman exclaimed, glancing quickly toward her husband, with a look of pleasure, "that hath happened of late, they say, by conquering the city of Granada; into which place, they tell me, Doña Isabella hath marched in triumph."

"In that conquest, thou seest the commencement of the great acts of our time. Granada hath now its churches; and the distant land of Cathay will shortly follow her example. These are the doings of the Lord, foolish woman; and in holding back thy husband from this great undertaking, thou hinderest him from purchasing a signal reward in heaven, and may unwittingly be the instrument of casting a curse, instead of a blessing, on that very boy, whose image now filleth thy thoughts more than that of his Maker and Redeemer."

The woman appeared bewildered, first looking at the admiral, and then at her husband, after which she bowed her head low, and devoutly crossed herself. Recovering from this self-abasement, she again turned toward Columbus, demanding earnestly—

"And you, Señor—do you sail with the wish and hope of serving God?"

"Such is my principal aim, good woman. I call on Heaven itself, to witness the truth of what I say. May my voyage prosper, only, as I tell thee naught but truth!"

"And you, too, Señor?" turning quickly to Luis de Bobadilla; "is it to serve God that you also go on this unusual voyage?"

"If not at the orders of God, himself, my good woman, it is, at least, at the bidding of an angel!"

"Dost thou think it is so, Pepe? Have we been thus deceived, and has so much evil been said of the admiral and his motives, wrongfully?"

"What hath been said?" quietly demanded Columbus. "Speak freely; thou hast naught to dread from my displeasure."

"Señor, you have your enemies, as well as another, and the wives, and mothers, and the betrothed of Palos, have not been slow to give vent to their feelings. In the first place, they say that you are poor."

"That is so true and manifest, good woman, it would be idle to deny it. Is poverty a crime at Palos?"

"The poor are little respected, Señor, in all this region. I know not why, for to me we seem to be as the rest, but few respect us. Then they say, Señor, that you are not a Castilian, but a Genoese."

"This is also true; is that, too, a crime among the mariners of Moguer, who ought to prize a people as much renowned for their deeds on the sea, as those of the superb republic?"

"I know not, Señor; but many hold it to be a disadvantage not to belong to Spain, and particularly to Castile, which is the country of Doña Isabella, herself; and how can it be as honorable to be a Genoese as to be a Spaniard? I should like it better were Pepe to sail with one who is a Spaniard, and that, too, of Palos or Moguer."

"Thy argument is ingenious, if not conclusive," returned Columbus, smiling, the only outward exhibition of feeling he betrayed—"but cannot one who is both poor and a Genoese serve God?"

"No doubt, Señor; and I think better of this voyage since I know your motive, and since I have seen you and spoken with you. Still, it is a great sacrifice for a young wife to let her husband sail on an expedition so distrusted, and he the father of her only boy!"

"Here is a young noble, an only son, a lover, and that, too, of impetuous feelings, an only child withal, rich, honored, and able to go whither he will, who not only embarketh with me, but embarketh by the consent—nay, I had better say, by the orders of his mistress!"

"Is this so, Señor?" the wife asked, eagerly.

"So true, my good woman, that my greatest hopes depend on this voyage. Did I not tell thee that I went at the bidding of an angel?"

"Ah! these young lords have seductive tongues! But, Señor Almirante, since such is your quality, they say, moreover, that to you this voyage can only bring honors and good, while it may bring misery and death on your followers. Poor and unknown, it maketh you a high officer of the queen; and some think that the Venetian galleys will be none the more heavily freighted, should you need them on the high seas."

"And in what can all this harm thy husband? I go whithersoever he goeth, share his dangers, and expose life for life with him. If there is gold gained by the adventure, he will not be forgotten; and if heaven is made any nearer to us, by our dangers and hardships, Pepe will not be a loser. At the last great reckoning, woman, we shall not be asked who is poor, or who is a Genoese."

"This is true, Señor; and yet it is hard for a young wife to part from her husband. Dost thou wish, in truth, to sail with the admiral, Pepe?"

"It matters little with me, Monica; I am commanded to serve the queen, and we mariners have no right to question her authority. Now I have heard his excellency's discourse, I think less of the affair than before."

"If God is really to be served in this voyage," continued the woman, with dignity, "thou shouldst not be backward, more than another, my husband. Señor, will you suffer Pepe to pass the night with his family, on condition that he goeth on board the Santa Maria in the morning?"

"What certainty have I that this condition will be respected?"

"Señor, we are both Christians, and serve the same God—have been redeemed by the same Saviour."

"This is true, and I will confide in it. Pepe, thou canst remain until the morning, when I shall expect thee at thy station. There will be oarsmen enough, without thee."

The woman looked her thanks, and Columbus thought he read an assurance of good faith in her noble Spanish manner, and lofty look. As some trifling preparations were to be made before the boat could quit the shore, the admiral and Luis paced the sands the while, engaged in deep discourse.

"This hath been a specimen of what I have had to overcome and endure, in order to obtain even yonder humble means for effecting the good designs of Providence," observed Columbus, mournfully, though he spoke without acrimony. "It is a crime to be poor—to be a Genoese—to be aught else than the very thing that one's judges and masters fancy themselves to be! The day will come, Conde de Llera, when Genoa shall think herself in no manner disgraced, in having given birth to Christofero Colombo, and when your proud Castile will be willing to share with her in the dishonor! Thou little know'st, young lord, how far thou art on the road to renown, and toward high deeds, in having been born noble, and the master of large possessions. Thou seest me, here, a man already stricken in years, with a head whitened by time and sufferings, and yet am I only on the threshold of the undertaking that is to give my name a place among those of the men who have served God, and advanced the welfare of their fellow-creatures."

"Is not this the course of things, Señor, throughout the earth? Do not those who find themselves placed beneath the level of their merits, struggle to rise to the condition to which nature intended them to belong, while those whom fortune hath favored through their ancestors, are too often content to live on honors that they have not themselves won? I see naught in this but the nature of man, and the course of the world."

"Thou art right, Luis, but philosophy and fact are different matters. We may reason calmly on principles, when their application in practice causeth much pain. Thou hast a frank and manly nature, young man; one that dreadeth neither the gibe of the Christian, nor the lance of the Moor, and wilt answer to any, in fearlessness and truth. A Castilian thyself, dost *thou*, too, really think one of thy kingdom better than one of Genoa?"

"Not when he of Genoa is Christoval Colon, Señor, and he of Castile is only Luis de Bobadilla," answered the young man, laughing.

"Nay, I will not be denied—hast thou any such notion as this, which the wife of Pepe hath so plainly avowed?"

"What will you, Señor Christoval? Man is the same in Spain, that he is among the Italians, or the English. Is it not his besetting sin to think good of himself, and evil of his neighbor?"

"A plain question that is loyally put, may not be answered with a truism, Luis."

"Nor a civil, honest reply confounded with one that is evasive. We of Castile are humble and most devout Christians, by the same reason that we think ourselves faultless, and the rest of mankind notable sinners. By San Iago, of blessed faith and holy memory! it is enough to make a people vain, to have produced such a queen as Doña Isabella, and such a maiden as Mercedes de Valverde!"

"This is double loyalty, for it is being true to the queen and to thy mistress. With this must I satisfy myself, even though it be no answer. But, Castilian though I am not, even the Guzmans have not ventured on the voyage to Cathay, and the House of Trastamara may yet be glad to acknowledge its indebtedness to a Genoese. God hath no respect to worldly condition, or worldly boundaries, in choosing his agents, for most of the saints were despised Hebrews, while Jesus, himself, came of Nazareth. We shall see, we shall see, young lord, what three months will reveal to the admiration of mankind."

"Señor Almirante, I hope and pray it may be the island of Cipango and the realms of the great Khan; should it not be so, we are men who can not only bear our toils, but who can bear our disappointments."

"Of disappointments in this matter, Don Luis, I look for none—now that I have the royal faith of Isabella, and these good caravels to back me; the drudge who saileth from Madeira to Lisbon, is not more certain of gaining his port than I am certain of gaining Cathay."

"No doubt, Señor Colon, that what any navigator can do, you can do and will perform; nevertheless, disappointment would seem to be the lot of man, and it might be well for all of us to be prepared to meet it."

"The sun that is just sinking beyond yon hill, Luis, is not plainer before my eyes than this route to the Indies. I have seen it, these seventeen years, distinct as the vessels in the river, bright as the polar star, and, I make little doubt, as faithfully. It is well to talk of disappointments, since they are the lot of man; and who can know this better than one that hath been led on by false hopes during all the better years of his life; now encouraged by princes, statesmen, and churchmen; and now derided and scoffed at as a vain projector, that hath neither reason nor fact to sustain him!"

"By my new patron, San Pedro! Señor Almirante, but you have led a most grievous life, for this last age, or so. The next three months will, indeed, be months of moment to you."

"Thou little know'st the calmness of conviction and confidence, Luis," returned Columbus, "if thou fanciest any doubts beset me as the hour of trial approacheth. This day is the happiest I have known, for many a weary year; for, though the preparations are not great, and our barks are but slight and of trifling bulk, yonder lie the means through which a light, that hath long been hid, is about to break upon the world, and to raise Castile to an elevation surpassing that of any other Christian nation."

"Thou must regret, Señor Colon, that it hath not been Genoa, thy native land, that is now about to receive this great boon, after having merited it by generous and free gifts, in behalf of this great voyage."

"This hath not been the least of my sorrows, Luis. It is hard to desert one's own country, and to seek new connections, as life draweth to a close, though we mariners, perhaps, feel the tie less than those who never quit the land. But Genoa would have none of me; and if the child is bound to love and honor the parent, so is the parent equally bound to protect and foster the child. When the last forgets its duty, the first is not to be blamed if it seek support wherever it may be found. There are limits to every human duty; those we owe to God alone, never ceasing to require their fulfilment, and our unceasing attention. Genoa hath proved but a stern mother to me; and though naught could induce me to raise a hand against her, she hath no longer any claims on my service. Besides, when the object in view is the service of God, it mattereth little with which of his creatures we league as instruments. One cannot easily hate the land of his birth, but injustice may lead him to cease to love it. The tie is mutual, and when the country ceaseth to protect person, character, property, or rights, the subject is liberated from all his duties. If allegiance goeth with protection, so should protection go with allegiance. Doña Isabella is now my mistress, and, next to God, her will I serve, and serve only. Castile is henceforth my country."

At this moment it was announced that the pinnace waited, and the two adventurers immediately embarked.

It must have required all the deep and fixed convictions of an ardent temperament, to induce Columbus to rejoice that he had, at length, obtained the means of satisfying his longings for discovery, when he came coolly to consider what those means were. The names of his vessels, the Santa Maria, the Pinta, and the Niña, have already been mentioned, and some allusions have been made to their size and construction. Still, it may aid the reader in forming his opinions of the character of this great enterprise, if we give a short sketch of the vessels, more especially that in which Columbus and Luis de Bobadilla were now received. She was, of course, the Santa Maria, a ship of nearly twice the burden of the craft next her in size. This vessel had been prepared with more care than the others, and some attention had been paid to the dignity and comfort of the Admiral she was destined to carry. Not only was she decked in, but a poop, or round-house, was constructed on her quarter-deck, in which he had his berth. No proper notion can be obtained of the appearance of the Santa Maria, from the taunt-rigged, symmetrical, and low-sterned ships of the present time; for, though the Santa Maria had both a poop and top-gallant-forecastle, as they would be termed to-day, neither was constructed in the snug and unobtrusive manner that is now used. The poop, or round-house, was called a castle, to which it had some fancied resemblance, while the top-gallant-forecastle, in which most of the people lived, was out of proportion large, rose like a separate structure on the bows of the vessel, and occupied about a third of the deck, from forward aft. To those who never saw the shipping that was used throughout Europe, a century since, it will not be very obvious how vessels so small could rise so far above the water, in safety; but this difficulty may be explained; many very old ships, that had some of the peculiarities of this construction, existing within the memory of man, and a few having fallen under our own immediate inspection. The bearings of these vessels were at the loaded water-lines, or very little above them, and they tumbled home, in a way to reduce their beams on their poop decks nearly, if not quite, a fourth. By these precautions, their great height out of the water was less dangerous than might otherwise have been the case; and as they were uniformly short ships, possessing the advantages of lifting easily forward, and were, moreover, low-waisted, they might be considered safe in a sea, rather than the reverse. Being so short, too, they had great beam for their tonnage, which, if not an element of speed, was at least one of security. Although termed ships, these vessels were not rigged in the manner of the ships of the present day, their standing spars being relatively longer than those now in use, while their upper, or shifting spars, were much less numerous, and much less important than those which now point upward, like needles, toward the clouds. Neither had a ship necessarily the same number of spars, in the fifteenth century, as belong to a ship in the nineteenth. The term itself, as it was used in all the southern countries of Europe, being directly derived from the Latin word *navis*, was applied rather as a generic than as a distinctive term, and by no means inferred any particular construction, or particular rig. The caravel was a ship, in this sense, though not strictly so, perhaps, when we descend to the more minute classification of seamen.

Much stress has been justly laid on the fact, that two of the vessels in this extraordinary enterprise were undecked. In that day, when most sea voyages were made in a direction parallel to the main coasts, and when even those that extended to the islands occupied but a very few days, vessels were seldom far from the land; and it was the custom of the mariners, a practice that has extended to our own times, in the southern seas of Europe, to seek a port at the approach of bad weather. Under such circumstances, decks were by no means as essential, either for the security of the craft, the protection of the cargo, or the comfort of the people, as in those cases in which the full fury of the elements must be encountered. Nevertheless, the reader is not to suppose a vessel entirely without any upper covering, because she was not classed among those that were decked; even such caravels, when used on the high seas, usually possessing quarter-decks and forecastles, with connecting gangways; depending on tarpaulings, and other similar preventives, to exclude the wash of the sea from injuring their cargoes.

After all these explanations, however, it must be conceded, that the preparations for the great undertaking of Columbus, while the imaginations of landsmen probably aggravate their incompleteness, strike the experienced seaman as altogether inadequate to its magnitude and risks. That the mariners of the day deemed them positively insufficient is improbable, for men as accustomed to the ocean as the Pinzons, would not have volunteered to risk their vessel, their money, and their persons, in an expedition that did not possess the ordinary means of security.

CHAPTER XIV

"O'er the glad waters of the dark blue sea,
Our thoughts as boundless, and our souls as free,
Far as the breeze can bear, the billows foam,
Survey our empire, and behold our home."

Byron.

As Columbus sought his apartment, soon after he reached the deck of the Holy Maria, Luis had no farther opportunity to converse with him that night. He occupied a part of the same room, it is true, under the assumed appellation of the admiral's secretary; but the great navigator was so much engaged with duties necessary to be discharged previously to sailing, that he could not be interrupted, and the young man paced the narrow limits of the deck until near midnight, thinking, as usual, of Mercedes, and of his return, when, seeking his mattress, he found Columbus already buried in a deep sleep.

The following day was Friday; and it is worthy of remark, that the greatest and most successful voyage that has ever occurred on this globe, was commenced on a day of the week that seamen have long deemed to be so inauspicious to nautical enterprises, that they have often deferred sailing, in order to avoid the unknown, but dreaded consequences. Luis was among the first who appeared again on deck, and casting his eyes upward, he perceived that the admiral was already afoot, and in possession of the summit of the high poop, or castle, whose narrow limits, indeed, were deemed sacred to the uses of the privileged, answering, in this particular, to the more extended promenade of the modern quarter-deck. Here it was that he who directed the movements of a squadron, overlooked its evolutions, threw out his signals, made his astronomical observations, and sought his recreation in the open air. The whole space on board the Santa Maria might have been some fifteen feet in one direction, and not quite as much in the other, making a convenient look-out, more from its exclusion and retirement, than from its dimensions.

As soon as the admiral—or Don Christoval, as he was now termed by the Spaniards, since his appointment to his present high rank, which gave him the rights and condition of a noble—as soon as Don Christoval caught a glance of Luis' eye, he made a sign for the young man to ascend and take a position at his side. Although the expedition was so insignificant in numbers and force, not equalling, in the latter particular, the power of a single modern sloop of war, the authority of the queen, the gravity and mien of Columbus himself, and, most of all, its own mysterious and unwonted object, had, from the first, thrown around it a dignity that was disproportioned to its visible means. Accustomed to control the passions of turbulent men, and aware of the great importance of impressing his followers with a sense of his high station and influence with the court, Columbus had kept much aloof from familiar intercourse with his subordinates, acting principally through the Pinzons and the other commanders, lest he might lose some portion of that respect which he foresaw would be necessary to his objects. It needed not his long experience to warn him that men, crowded together in so small a space, could only be kept in their social and professional stations, by the most rigid observance of forms and decorum, and he had observed a due attention to these great requisites, in prescribing the manner in which his own personal service should be attended to, and his personal dignity supported. This is one of the great secrets of the discipline of a ship, for they who are incapable of reasoning, can be made to feel, and no man is apt to despise him who is well entrenched behind the usages of deference and reserve. We see, daily, the influence of an appellation, or a commission, even the turbulent submitting to its authority, when they might resist the same lawful commands issuing from an apparently less elevated source.

"Thou wilt keep much near my person, Señor Gutierrez," said the admiral, using the feigned name which Luis affected to conceal under that of Pedro de Muños, as he knew a ship was never safe from eaves-droppers, and was willing that the young noble should pass as the gentleman of the king's bedchamber, "this is our station, and here we must remain much of our time, until God, in his holy and wise providence, shall have opened the way for us to Cathay, and brought us near the throne of the Great Khan. Here is our course, and along this track of pathless ocean it is my intention to steer."

As Columbus spoke, he pointed to a chart that lay spread before him on an arm-chest, passing a finger calmly along the line he intended to pursue. The coast of Europe, in its general outlines, was laid down on this chart, with as much accuracy as the geographical knowledge of the day would furnish, and a range of land extended southward as far as Guinea, all beyond which region was *terra incognita* to the learned world at that time. The Canaries and the Azores, which had been discovered some generations earlier, occupied their proper places, while the western side of the Atlantic was bounded by a fancied delineation of the eastern coast of India, or of Cathay, buttressed by the island of Cipango, or Japan, and an Archipelago, that had been represented principally after the accounts of Marco Polo and his relatives. By a fortunate misconception, Cipango had been placed in a longitude that corresponded very nearly with that of Washington, or some two thousand leagues east of the position in which it is actually to be found. This error of Columbus, in relation to the extent of the circumference of the globe, in the end, most probably saved his hardy enterprise from becoming a failure.

Luis, for the first time since he had been engaged in the expedition, cast his eyes over this chart, with some curiosity, and he felt a noble desire to solve the great problem rising within him, as he thus saw, at a glance, all the vast results, as well as the interesting natural phenomena, that were dependent on the issue.

"By San Gennaro of Napoli!" he exclaimed—The only affectation the young noble had, was a habit of invoking the saints of the different countries he had visited, and of using the little oaths and exclamations of distant lands, a summary mode of both letting the world know how far he had journeyed, as well as a portion of the improvement he had derived from his travels—"By San Gennaro, Señor Don Christoval, but this voyage will be one of exceeding merit, if we ever find our way across this great belt of water; and greater still, should we ever manage to return!"

"The last difficulty is the one, at this moment, uppermost in the minds of most in this vessel," answered Columbus. "Dost thou not perceive, Don Luis, the grave and dejected countenances of the mariners, and hearest thou the wailings that are rising from the shore?"

This remark caused the young man to raise his eyes from the chart, and to take a survey of the scene around him. The Niña, a light felucca, in fact, was already under way, and brushing past them under a latine foresail, her sides thronged with boats filled with people, no small portion of whom were females and children, and most of whom were wringing their hands and raising piteous cries of despair. The Pinta was in the act of being cast; and, although the authority of Martin Alonzo Pinzon had the effect to render their grief less clamorous, her sides were surrounded by a similar crowd, while numberless boats plied around the Santa Maria herself; the authority and dignity of the admiral alone keeping them at a distance. It was evident that most of those who remained, fancied that they now saw their departing relations for the last time, while no small portion of those who were on the eve of sailing, believed they were on the point of quitting Spain forever.

"Hast looked for Pepe, this morning, among our people?" demanded Columbus, the incident of the young sailor recurring to his thoughts, for the first time that morning: "if he prove false to his word, we may regard it as an evil omen, and have an eye on all our followers, while there is a chance of escape."

"If his absence would be an omen of evil, Señor Almirante, his presence ought to be received as an omen of good. The noble fellow is on this yard, above our heads, loosening the sail."

Columbus turned his eyes upward, and there, indeed, was the young mariner in question, poised on the extreme and attenuated end of the latine yard, that ships even then carried on their after-masts, swinging in the wind while he loosened the gasket that kept the canvas in its folds. Occasionally he looked beneath him, anxious to discover if his return had been noted; and, once or twice, his hands, usually so nimble, lingered in their employment, as he cast glances over the stern of the vessel, as if one also drew his attention in that quarter. Columbus made a sign of recognition to the gratified young mariner, who instantly permitted the canvas to fall; and then he walked to the taffrail, accompanied by Luis, in order to ascertain if any boat was near the ship. There, indeed, close to the vessel, lay a skiff, rowed by Monica alone, and which had been permitted to approach so near on account of the sex of its occupant. The moment the wife of Pepe observed the form of the admiral, she arose from her seat, and clasped her hands toward him, desirous, but afraid, to speak. Perceiving that the woman was awed by the bustle, the crowd of persons, and the appearance of the ship, which she was almost near enough to touch with her hand, Columbus addressed her. He spoke mildly, and his looks, usually so grave, and sometimes even stern, were softened to an expression of gentleness that Luis had never before witnessed.

"I see that thy husband hath been true to his promise, good woman," he said; "and I doubt not that thou hast told him it is wiser and better manfully to serve the queen, than to live under the disgrace of a runaway."

"Señor, I have. I give Doña Isabella my husband, without a murmur, if not cheerfully, now I know that you go forth to serve God. I see the wickedness of my repinings, and shall pray that he may be foremost, on all occasions, until the ears of the Infidel shall be opened to the words of the true faith."

"This is said like a Spanish wife, and a Christian woman! Our lives are in the care of Providence, and doubt not of seeing Pepe, in health and safety, after he hath visited Cathay, and done his share in its discovery."

"Ah! Señor—when?" exclaimed the wife, unable, in spite of her assumed fortitude, and the strong feelings of religious duty, to suppress the impulses of a woman.

"In God's time, my good—how art thou named?"

"Monica, Señor Almirante, and my husband is called Pepe; and the boy, the poor, fatherless child, hath been christened Juan. We have no Moorish blood, but are pure Spaniards, and I pray your Excellency to remember it, on such occasions as may call for more dangerous duty than common."

"Thou may'st depend on my care of the father of Juan," returned the admiral, smiling, though a tear glistened in his eye. "I, too, leave behind those that are dear to me as my own soul, and among others a motherless son. Should aught serious befall our vessel, Diego would be an orphan; whereas thy Juan would at least enjoy the care and affection of her who brought him into the world."

"Señor, a thousand pardons!" said the woman, much touched by the feeling that was betrayed by the admiral in his voice. "We are selfish, and forget that others have sorrows, when we feel our own too keenly. Go forth, in God's name, and do his holy will—take my husband with you; I only wish that little Juan was old enough to be his companion."

Monica could utter no more, but dashing the tears from her eyes, she resumed the oars, and pulled the little skiff slowly, as if the inanimate machine felt the reluctance of the hands that propelled it, toward the land. The short dialogue just related, had been carried on in voices so loud as to be heard by all near the speakers; and when Columbus turned from the boat, he saw that many of his crew had been hanging suspended in the rigging, or on the yards, eagerly listening to what had been said. At this precise instant the anchor of the Santa Maria was raised from the bottom, and the ship's head began to incline from the direction of the wind. At the next moment, the flap of the large square foresail that crafts of her rig then carried, was heard, and in the course of the next five minutes, the three vessels were standing slowly but steadily down the current of the Odiel, in one of the arms of which river they had been anchored, holding their course toward a bar near its mouth. The sun had not yet risen, or rather it rose over the hills of Spain, a fiery ball, just as the sails were set, gilding with a melancholy glory, a coast that not a few in the different vessels apprehended they were looking upon for the last time. Many of the boats clung to the two smaller craft until they reached the bar of Saltes, an hour or two later, and some still persevered until they began to toss in the long waves of the breathing ocean, when, the wind being fresh at the west, they reluctantly cast off, one by one, amid sighs and groans. The liberated ships, in the meanwhile, moved steadily into the blue waters of the shoreless Atlantic, like human beings silently impelled by their destinies toward fates that they can neither foresee, control, nor avoid.

The day was fine, and the wind both brisk and fair. Thus far the omens were propitious; but the unknown future threw a cloud over the feelings of a large portion of those who were thus quitting, in gloomy uncertainty, all that was most dear to them. It was known that the admiral intended making the best of his way toward the Canaries, thence to enter on the unknown and hitherto untrodden paths of the desert ocean that lay beyond. Those who doubted, therefore, fixed upon those islands as the points where their real dangers were to commence, and already looked forward to their appearance in the horizon, with feelings akin to those with which the guilty regard the day of trial, the condemned the morning of execution, or the sinner the bed of death. Many, however, were superior to this weakness, having steeled their nerves and prepared their minds for any hazards, though the feelings of nearly all fluctuated: there being hours when hope, and anticipations of success, seemed to cheer the entire crews; and then, moments would occur, in which the disposition was to common doubts, and a despondency that was nearly general.

A voyage to the Canaries or the Azores, in that age, was most probably to be classed among the hardiest exploits of seamen. The distance was not as great, certainly, as many of their more ordinary excursions, for vessels frequently went, even in the same direction, as far as the Cape de Verdes; but all the other European passages lay along the land, and in the Mediterranean the seaman felt that he was navigating within known limits, and was apt to consider himself as embayed within the boundaries of human knowledge. On the contrary, while sailing on the broad Atlantic, he was, in some respects, placed in a situation resembling that of the æronaut, who, while floating in the higher currents of the atmosphere, sees beneath him the earth as his only alighting place, the blue void of untravelled space stretching in all other directions about him.

The Canary Isles were known to the ancients. Juba, the king of Mauritania, who was a contemporary of Cæsar. is said to have described them with tolerable accuracy, under the general name of the Fortunate Isles. The work itself has been lost, but the fact is known through the evidence of other writers; and by the same means it is known that they possessed, even in that remote age, a population that had made some respectable advances toward civilization. But in the process of time, and during the dark period that succeeded the brightness of the Roman sway, even the position of these islands was lost to the Europeans; nor was it again ascertained until the first half of the fourteenth century, when they were discovered by certain fugitive Spaniards who were hard pressed by the Moors. After this, the Portuguese, then the most hardy navigators of the known world, got possession of one or two of them, and made them the starting points for their voyages of discovery along the coast of Guinea. As the Spaniards reduced the power of the Mussulmans, and regained their ancient sway in the peninsula, they once more turned their attention in this direction, conquering the natives of several of the other islands, the group belonging equally to those two Christian nations, at the time of our narrative.

Luis de Bobadilla, who had navigated extensively in the more northern seas, and who had passed and repassed the Mediterranean in various directions, knew nothing of these islands except by report; and as they stood on the poop, Columbus pointed out to him their position, and explained their different characters; relating his intentions in connection with them, dwelling on the supplies they afforded, and on their facilities as a point of departure.

"The Portuguese have profited much by their use of these islands," said Columbus, "as a place for victualling, and wooding, and watering, and I see no reason why Castile may not, now, imitate their example, and receive her share of the benefits. Thou seest how far south our neighbors have penetrated, and what a trade and how much riches are flowing into Lisbon through these noble enterprises, which, notwithstanding, are but as a bucket of water in the ocean, when compared with the wealth of Cathay and all the mighty consequences that are to follow from this western voyage of ours."

"Dost thou expect to reach the territories of the Great Khan, Don Christoval," demanded Luis, "within a distance as small as that to which the Portuguese hath gone southwardly?"

The navigator looked warily around, to ascertain who might hear his words, and finding that no one was within reach of the sound of his voice while he used a proper caution, he lowered its tones, and answered in a manner which greatly flattered his young companion, as it proved that the admiral was disposed to treat him with the frankness and confidence of a friend.

"Thou know'st, Don Luis," the navigator resumed, "the nature of the spirits with whom we have to deal. I shall not even be certain of their services, so long as we continue near the coast of Europe; for naught is easier than for one of yonder craft to abandon me in the night, and to seek a haven on some known coast, seeking his justification in some fancied necessity."

"Martin Alonzo is not a man to do that ignoble and unworthy act!" interrupted Luis.

"He is not, my young friend, for a motive as base as fear," returned Columbus, with a sort of thoughtful smile, which showed how truly and early he had dived into the real characters of those with whom he was associated. "Martin Alonzo is a bold and intelligent navigator, and we may look for good service at his hands, in all that toucheth resolution and perseverance. But the eyes of the Pinzons cannot be always open, and the knowledge of all the philosophers of the earth could make no resistance against the headlong impetuosity of a crew of alarmed mutineers. I do not feel certain of our own people while there is a hope of easy return; much less of men who are not directly under my own eye and command. The question thou hast asked, Luis, may not, therefore, be publicly answered, since the distance we are about to sail over would frighten our easily alarmed mariners. Thou art a cavalier; a knight of known courage, and may be depended on; and I may tell thee, without fear of arousing any unworthy feeling, that the voyage on which we are now fairly embarked, hath never had a precedent on this earth, for its length, or for the loneliness of its way."

"And yet, Señor, thou enterest on it with the confidence of a man certain of reaching his haven?"

"Luis, thou hast well judged my feelings. As to all those common dreads of descents, and ascents, of the difficulties of a return, and of reaching the margin of the world, whence we may glide off into space, neither thou, nor I, shall be much subjected."

"By San Iago! Señor Don Christoval, I have no very settled notions about these things. I have never known of any one who hath slidden off the earth into the air, it is true, nor do I much think that such a slide is likely to befall us and our good ships; but, on the other hand, we have as yet only doctrine to prove that the earth is round, and that it is possible to journey east, by sailing west. On these subjects, then, I hold myself neuter; while, at the same time, thou may'st steer direct for the moon, and Luis de Bobadilla will be found at thy side."

"Thou makest thyself less expert in science, mad-brained young noble, than is either true or necessary; but we will say no more of this, at present. There will be sufficient leisure to make thee familiar with all my intricate reasons and familiar motives. And is not this, Don Luis, a most heavenly sight? Here am I in the open ocean, honored by the two sovereigns with the dignity of their viceroy and admiral; with a fleet that is commissioned by their Highnesses to carry the knowledge of their power and authority to the uttermost parts of the earth; and, most of all, to raise the cross of our blessed Redeemer before the eyes of Infidels, who have never yet even heard his name, or, if they have, reverence it as little as a Christian would reverence the idols of the heathens!"

This was said with the calm but deep enthusiasm that colored the entire character of the great navigator, rendering him, at times, equally the subject of distrust and of profound respect. On Luis, as, indeed, on most others who lived in sufficient familiarity with the man to enable them to appreciate his motives, and to judge correctly of the uprightness of his views, the effect, however, was always favorable, and probably would have been so had Mercedes never existed. The young man, himself, was not entirely without a tinge of enthusiasm, and, as is ever the case with the single-minded and generous, he best knew how to regard the impulses of those who were influenced by similar qualities. This answer was consequently in accordance with the feelings of the admiral, and they remained on the poop several hours, discoursing of the future, with the ardor of those who hoped for every thing, but in a manner too discursive and general to render a record of the dialogue easy or necessary.

It was eight o'clock in the morning when the vessels passed the bar of Saltes, and the day had far advanced before the navigators had lost sight of the familiar eminences that lay around Palos, and the other well-known land-marks of the coast. The course was due south, and, as the vessels of that day were lightly sparred, and spread comparatively very little canvas, when considered in connection with the more dashing navigation of our own times, the rate of sailing was slow, and far from promising a speedy termination to a voyage that all knew must be long without a precedent, and which so many feared could never have an end. Two marine leagues, of three English miles, an hour, was good progress for a vessel at that day, even with a fresh and favorable wind; though there are a few memorable days' works set down by Columbus himself, which approach to a hundred and sixty miles in the twenty-four hours, and which are evidently noted as a speed of which a mariner might well be proud. In these days of locomotion and travelling, it is scarcely necessary to tell the intelligent reader this is but a little more than half the distance that is sailed over by a fast ship, under similar circumstances, and in our own time.

Thus the sun set upon the adventurers, in this celebrated voyage, when they had sailed with a strong breeze, to use the words of Columbus' own record, some eleven hours, after quitting the bar. By this time, they had made good less than fifty miles, in a due south course from the place of their departure. The land in the neighborhood of Palos had entirely sunk behind the watery margin of the ocean, in that direction, and the coast trending eastward, it was only here and there that the misty summits of a few of the mountains of Seville could just be discovered by the experienced eyes of the older mariners, as the glowing ball of the sun sunk into the watery bed of the western horizon, and disappeared from view. At this precise moment, Columbus and Luis were again on the poop, watching, with melancholy interest, the last shadows cast by Spanish land. while two seamen were at work near them, splicing a rope that had been chafed asunder. The latter were seated on the deck, and as, out of respect to the admiral, they had taken their places a little on one side, their presence was not at first noted.

"There setteth the sun beneath the waves of the wide Atlantic, Señor Gutierrez," observed the admiral, who was ever cautious to use one or the other of Luis' feigned appellations, whenever any person was near. "There the sun quitteth us, Pero, and in his daily course I see a proof of the globular form of the earth; and of the truth of a theory which teacheth us that Cathay may be reached by the western voyage."

"I am ever ready to admit the wisdom of all your plans, expectations, and thoughts, Señor Don Christoval," returned the young man, punctiliously observant of respect, both in speech and manner; "but I confess I cannot see what the daily course of the sun has to do with the position of Cathay, or with the road that leads to it. We know that the great luminary travelleth the heavens without ceasing, that it cometh up out of the sea in the morning, and goeth down to its watery bed at night; but this it doth on the coast of Castile, as well as on that of Cathay; and, therefore, to me it doth appear, that no particular inference, for or against our success, is to be drawn from the circumstance."

As this was said, the two sailors ceased working, looking curiously up into the face of the admiral, anxious to hear his reply. By this movement Luis perceived that one was Pepe, to whom he gave a nod of recognition, while the other was a stranger. The last had every appearance of a thorough-bred seaman of that period, or of being, what would have been termed in English, and the more northern languages of Europe, a regular "sea-dog;" a term that expresses the idea of a man so completely identified with the ocean by habit, as to have had his exterior, his thoughts, his language, and even his morality, colored by the association. This sailor was approaching fifty, was short, square, athletic, and still active, but there was a mixture of the animal with the intellectual creature about his coarse, heavy features, that is very usual in the countenances of men of native humor and strong sense, whose habits have been coarse and sensual. That he was a prime seaman, Columbus knew at a glance, not only from his general appearance, but from his occupation, which was such as only fell to the lot of the most skilful men of every crew.

"I reason after this fashion, Señor," answered the admiral, as soon as his eye turned from the glance that he, too, had thrown upon the men; "the sun is not made to journey thus around the earth without a sufficient motive, the providence of God being ruled by infinite wisdom. It is not probable that a luminary so generous and useful should be intended to waste any of its benefits; and we are certain already that day and night journey westward over this earth as far as it is known to us, whence I infer that the system is harmonious, and the benefits of the great orb are unceasingly bestowed on man, reaching one spot on the earth as it quits another. The sun that hath just left us is still visible in the Azores, and will be seen again at Smyrna, and among the Grecian Islands, an hour, or more, before it again meets our eyes. Nature hath designed naught for uselessness; and I believe that Cathay will be enlightened by that ball which hath just left us, while we shall be in the deepest hour of the night, to return by its eastern path, across the great continent of Asia, and to greet us again in the morning. In a word, friend Pedro, that which Sol is now doing with such nimble speed in the heavens, we are more humbly imitating in our own caravels; give us sufficient time, and we, too, might traverse the earth, coming in from our journey by the land of the Tartars and the Persians."

"From all of which you infer that the world is round, wherein we are to find the certainty of our success?"

"This is so true, Señor de Muños, that I should be sorry to think any man who now saileth under my command did not admit it. Here are two seamen who have been listening to our discourse, and we will question them, that we may know the opinions of men accustomed to the ocean. Thou art the husband with whom I held discourse on the sands, the past evening, and thy name is Pepe?"

"Señor Almirante, your Excellency's memory doth me too much honor, in not forgetting a face that is altogether unworthy of being noticed and remembered."

"It is an honest face, friend, and no doubt speaketh for a true heart. I shall count on thee as a sure support, let things go as they may."

"His Excellency hath not only a right to command me, as her Highness' admiral, but he hath now the good-will of Monica, and that is much the same as having gained her husband."

"I thank thee, honest Pepe, and shall count on thee, with certainty, in future," answered Columbus, turning toward the other seaman—"And thou, shipmate—thou hast the air of one that the sight of troubled water will not alarm—thou hast a name?"

"That I have, noble admiral," returned the fellow, looking up with a freedom that denoted one used to have his say; "though it hath neither a Don, nor a Señor, to take it in tow. My intimates commonly call out Sancho, when pressed for time, and when civility gets the better of haste, they add Mundo, making Sancho Mundo for the whole name of a very poor man."

"Mundo is a large name for so small a person," said the admiral, smiling, for he foresaw the expediency of having friends among his crew, and knew men sufficiently to understand that, while undue familiarity undermined respect, a little unbending had a tendency to win hearts. "I wonder that thou shouldst venture to wear a sound so lofty!"

"I tell my fellows, your Excellency, that Mundo is my title, and not my name; but that I am greater than kings, even, who are content to take their titles from a part of that, of which I bear all."

"And were thy father and thy mother called Mundo, also? Or, is this name taken in order to give thee an occasion to show thy smartness, when questioned by thy officers?"

"As for the good people you deign to mention, Señor Don Almirante, I shall leave them to answer for themselves, and that for the simple reason that I do not know how they were called, or whether they had any names at all. They tell me I was found, when a few hours old, under a worn-out basket at the ship-yard gate of old" —

"Never mind the precise spot, friend Sancho—thou wert found with a basket for a cradle, and that maketh a volume in thy history, at once."

"Nay, Excellency, I would not leave the spot a place of dispute hereafter— but it shall be as you please. They say no one here knoweth exactly where we are going, and it will be more suitable that the like ignorance should rest over the places whence we came. But having the world before me, they that christened me gave me as much of it as was to be got by a name."

"Thou hast been long a mariner, Sancho Mundo—if Mundo thou wilt be."

"So long, Señor, that it sickeneth me, and taketh away the appetite to walk on solid ground. Being so near the gate, it was no great matter to put me into the ship-yard, and I was launched one day in a caravel, and got to sea in her, no one knows how. From that time I have submitted to fate, and go out again, as soon as possible, after I come into port."

"And by what lucky chance have I obtained thy services, good Sancho, in this great expedition?"

"The authorities of Moguer took me under the queen's order, your Excellency, thinking that this Voyage would be more to my mind than another, as it was likely never to have an end."

"Art thou a compelled adventurer, on this service?"

"Not I, Señor Don Almirante, although they who sent me here fancy as much. It is natural for a man to wish to see his estates, once in his life, and I am told that we are bound on a voyage to the other side of the world. God forbid that I should hold aloof, on such an occasion."

"Thou art a Christian, Sancho, and hast a desire to aid in carrying the cross among the heathen?"

"Señor, your Excellency, Don Almirante, it matters little to Sancho with what the barque is laden, so that she do not need much pumping, and that the garlic is good. If I am not a very devout Christian, it is the fault of them that found me near the ship-yard gate, since the church and the font are both within call from that very spot. I know that Pepe, here, is a Christian, Señor, for I saw him in the arms of the priest, and I doubt not that there are old men at Moguer who can testify to as much in my behalf. At all hazards, noble Admiral, I will take on myself to say that I am neither Jew, nor Mussulman."

"Sancho, thou hast that about thee, that bespeakest a skilful and bold mariner."

"For both of these qualities, Señor Don Colon, let others speak. When the gale cometh, your own eyes may judge of the first; and when the caravel shall reach the edge of the earth, whither some think it is bound, there will be a good occasion to see who can, and who cannot, look off without trembling."

"It is enough: I count both thee and Pepe as among my truest followers." As Columbus said this, he walked away, resuming the dignified gravity that usually was seated in his countenance, and which so much aided his authority, by impressing the minds of others with respect. In a few minutes he and Luis descended to their cabin.

"I marvel, Sancho," said Pepe, as soon as he and his messmate were left alone on the poop, "that thou wilt venture to use thy tongue so freely, even in the presence of one that beareth about with him the queen's authority! Dost thou not fear to offend the admiral?"

"So much for having a wife and a child! Canst thou not make any difference between them that have had ancestors and who have descendants, and one that hath no other tie in the world than his name? The Señor Don Almirante is either an exceeding great man, and chosen by Providence to open the way into the unknown seas of which he speaketh; or he is but a hungry Genoese, that is leading us he knoweth not whither, that he may eat, and drink, and sleep, in honor, while we are toiling at his heels, like patient mules dragging the load that the horse despiseth. In the one case, he is too great and exalted to heed idle words; and in the other, what is there too bad for a Castilian to tell him?"

"Ay, thou art fond of calling thyself a Castilian, in spite of the ship-yard and the basket, and notwithstanding Moguer is in Seville."

"Harkee, Pepe; is not the queen of Castile our mistress? And are not subjects—true and lawful subjects, I mean, like thee and me—are not such subjects worthy of being the queen's countrymen? Never disparage thyself, good Pepe, for thou wilt ever find the world ready enough to do that favor for thee. As to this Genoese, he shall be either friend or enemy to Sancho; if the first, I expect much consolation from it; if the last, let him hunt for his Cathay till doomsday, he shall be never the wiser."

"Well, Sancho, if words can mar a voyage, or make a voyage, thou art a ready mariner; none know how to discourse better than thou."

Here the men both rose, having completed their work, and they left the poop, descending among the rest of the crew. Columbus had not miscalculated his aim, his words and condescension having produced a most favorable effect on the mind of Sancho Mundo, for so the man was actually called; and in gaining one of as ready a wit and loose a tongue for a friend, he obtained an ally who was not to be despised. Of such materials, and with the support of such instruments as this, is success too often composed; it being possible for the discovery of a world, even, to depend on the good word of one less qualified to influence opinions than Sancho Mundo.

CHAPTER XV

"While you here do snoring lie,
Open-ey'd conspiracy
His time doth take:
If of life you keep a care,
Shake off slumber, and beware;
Awake! Awake!"

Ariel.

The wind continuing fair, the three vessels made good progress in the direction of the Canaries; Sunday, in particular, proving a propitious day, the expedition making more than one hundred and twenty miles in the course of the twenty-four hours. The wind still continued favorable, and on the morning of Monday, the 6th of August, Columbus was cheerfully conversing with Luis, and one or two other companions who were standing near him on the poop, when the Pinta was seen suddenly to take in her forward sails, and to come up briskly, not to say awkwardly, to the wind. This manœuvre denoted some accident, and the Santa Maria fortunately having the advantage of the wind, immediately edged away to speak her consort.

"How now, Señor Martin Alonzo," hailed the admiral, as the two caravels came near enough together to speak each other. "For what reason hast thou so suddenly paused in thy course?"

"Fortune would have it so, Señor Don Christoval, seeing that the rudder of the good caravel hath broken loose, and we must fain secure it ere we may again trust ourselves to the breeze."

A severe frown came over the grave countenance of the great navigator, and after bidding Martin Alonzo do his best to repair the damage, he paced the deck, greatly disturbed, for several minutes. Observing how much the admiral took this accident to heart, the rest descended to the deck below, leaving Columbus alone with the pretended groom of the king's chamber.

"I trust, Señor, this is no serious injury, or one in any way likely to retard our advance," said Luis, after manifesting that respect which all near him felt for the admiral, by a pause. "I know honest Martin Alonzo to be a ready seaman, and should think his expedients might easily serve to get us as far as the Canaries, where greater damages can meet with their remedies."

"Thou say'st true, Luis, and we will hope for the best. I feel regret the sea is so high that we can offer no assistance to the Pinta, but Martin Alonzo is, indeed, an expert mariner, and on his ingenuity we must rely. My concern, however, hath another and a deeper source than the unloosing of this rudder, serious as such an injury ever is to a vessel at sea. Thou know'st that the Pinta hath been furnished to the service of the queen, under the order claiming the forfeited duty from the delinquents of Palos, and sorely against the will of the caravel's owners hath the vessel been taken. Now these persons, Gomez Rascon and Christoval Quintero, are on board her, and, I question not, have designed this accident. Their artifices were practised long, to our delay, before quitting the haven, and, it would seem, are to be continued to our prejudice here on the open ocean."

"By the allegiance I owe the Doña Isabella! Señor Don Christoval, but I would find a speedy cure for such a treason, if the office of punishment rested with me. Let me jump into the skiff and repair to the Pinta, where I will tell these Masters Rascon and Quintero, that should their rudder ever dare to break loose again, or should any other similar and untoward accident chance to arrive, the first shall be hanged at the yard of his own caravel, and the last be cast into the sea to examine into the state of her bottom, the rudder included."

"We may not practice such high authority without great occasion and perfect certainty of guilt. I hold it to be wiser to seek another caravel at the Canaries, for, by this accident, I well see we shall not be rid of the artifices of the two owners, until we are rid of their vessel. It will be hazardous to launch the skiff in this sea, or I would proceed to the Pinta myself; but as it is, let us have confidence in Martin Alonzo and his skill."

Columbus thus encouraged the people of the Pinta to exert themselves, and in about an hour or two, the three vessels were again making the best of their way toward the Canaries. Notwithstanding the delay, nearly ninety miles were made good in the course of the day and night. But the following morning the rudder again broke loose, and, as the damage was more serious than in the former instance, it was still more difficult to repair. These repeated accidents gave the admiral great concern, for he took them to be so many indications of the disaffection of his followers. He fully determined, in consequence, to get rid of the Pinta, if it were possible to find another suitable vessel among the islands. As the progress of the vessels was much retarded by the accident, although the wind continued favorable, the expedition only got some sixty miles, this day, nearer to its place of destination.

On the following morning, the three vessels came within hail of each other; and a comparison of the nautical skill of the different navigators, or pilots, as it was then the custom to style them, took place, each offering his opinion as to the position of the vessels.

It was not the least of the merits of Columbus, that he succeeded in his great experiment with the imperfect aid of the instruments then in use. The mariner's compass, it is true, had been in common service quite a century, if not longer, though its variations—a knowledge of which is scarcely less important in long voyages than a knowledge of the instrument itself—were then unknown to seamen, who seldom ventured far enough from the land to note these mysteries of nature, and who, as a class, still relied almost as much on the ordinary position of the heavenly bodies to ascertain their routes, as on the nicer results of calculation. Columbus, however, was a striking exception to this little-instructed class, having made himself thoroughly acquainted with all the learning of the period that could be applied in his profession, or which might aid him in effecting the great purpose for which alone he now seemed to live.

As might be expected, the comparison resulted altogether in the admiral's favor, the pilots in general being soon convinced that he alone knew the true position of the vessels, a fact that was soon unanswerably determined by the appearance of the summits of the Canaries, which hove up out of the ocean, in a south-easterly direction, resembling well-defined dark clouds clustering in the horizon. As objects like these are seen at a great distance at sea, more especially in a transparent atmosphere, and the wind became light and variable, the vessels, notwithstanding, were unable to reach Grand Canary until Thursday, the 8th of August, or nearly a week after they had left Palos. There they all ran in, and anchored in the usual haven. Columbus immediately set about making an inquiry for another caravel, but, proving unsuccessful, he sailed for Gomera, where he believed it might be easier to obtain the craft he wanted. While the admiral was thus employed with the Santa Maria and the Niña, Martin Alonzo remained in port, being unable to keep company in the crippled condition of the Pinta. But no suitable vessel being found, Columbus reluctantly returned to Grand Canary, and, after repairing the Pinta, which vessel was badly caulked, among the other devices that had been adopted to get her freed from the service, he sailed again for Gomera, from which island he was to take his final departure.

During these several changes, a brooding discontent began to increase among most of the common mariners, while some even of a higher class, were not altogether free from the most melancholy apprehensions for the future. While passing from Grand Canary to Gomera, with all his vessels, Columbus was again at his post, with Luis and his usual companions near him, when the admiral's attention was drawn to a conversation that took place between a group of the men, who had collected near the main-mast. It was night, and there being little wind, the voices of the excited disputants reached further than they themselves were aware.

"I tell thee, Pepe," said the most vociferous and most earnest of the speakers, "that the night is not darker than the future of this crew. Look to the west, and what dost see there? Who hath ever heard of land, after he hath quitted the Azores; and who is so ignorant as not to know that Providence hath placed water around all the continents, with a few islands as stopping-places for mariners, and spread the broad ocean beyond, with an intention to rebuke an over-eager curiosity to pry into matters that savor more of miracles than of common worldly things?"

"This is well, Pero," answered Pepe; "but I know that Monica thinks the admiral is sent of God, and that we may look forward to great discoveries, through his means; and most especially to the spreading of religion among the heathens."

"Ay, thy Monica should have been in Doña Isabella's seat, so learned and positive is she in all matters, whether touching her own woman's duties, or thine own. She is *thy* queen, Pepe, as all in Moguer will swear; and there are some who say she would gladly govern the port, as she governeth thee."

"Say naught against the mother of my child, Pero," interrupted Pepe, angrily. "I can bear thy idle words against myself, but he that speaketh ill of Monica will have a dangerous enemy."

"Thou art bold of speech, Pero, when away a hundred leagues from thine own better nine-tenths," put in a voice that Columbus and Luis both knew, on the instant, to belong to Sancho Mundo, "and art bold enough to jeer Pepe touching Monica, when we all well know who commandeth in a certain cabin, where thou art as meek as a hooked dolphin, whatever thou may'st be here. But, enough of thy folly about women; let us reason upon our knowledge as mariners, if thou wilt; instead of asking questions of one like Pepe, who is too young to have had much experience, I offer myself as thy catechist."

"What hast *thou*, then, to say about this unknown land that lieth beyond the great ocean, where man hath never been, or is at all likely to go, with followers such as these?"

"I have this to say, silly and idle-tongued Pero—that the time was when even the Canaries were unknown; when mariners did not dare to pass the straits, and when the Portuguese knew nothing of their mines and Guinea, lands that I myself have visited, and where the noble Don Christoval hath also been, as I know on the testimony of mine own eyes."

"And what hath Guinea, or what have the mines of the Portuguese to do with this western voyage? All know that there is a country called Africa; and what is there surprising that mariners should reach a land that is known to exist; but who knoweth that the ocean hath other continents, any more than that the heavens have other earths?"

"This is well, Pero," observed an attentive by-stander; "and Sancho will have to drain his wits to answer it."

"It is well for those who wag their tongues, like women, without thought of what they say," coolly returned Sancho, "but will have little weight with Doña Isabella, or Don Almirante. Harkee, Pero, thou art like one that hath trodden the path between Palos and Moguer so often, that thou fanciest there is no road to Seville or Granada. There must be a beginning to all things; and this voyage is, out of doubt, the beginning of voyages to Cathay. We go west, instead of east, because it is the shorter way; and because, moreover, it is the *only* way for a caravel. Now, answer me, messmate; is it possible for a craft, let her size or rig be what it may, to pass over the hills and valleys of a continent—I mean under her canvas, and by fair sailing?"

Sancho waited for a reply, and received a common and complete admission of the impossibility of the thing.

"Then cast your eyes at the admiral's chart, in the morning, as he keepeth it spread before him on the poop, yonder, and you will see that there is land from one pole to the other, on each side of the Atlantic, thereby rendering navigation impossible, in any other direction than this we are now taking. The notion of Pero, therefore, runs in the teeth of nature."

"This is so true, Pero," exclaimed another, the rest assenting, "that thy mouth ought to be shut."

But Pero had a mouth that was not very easily closed; and it is probable that his answer would have been to the full as acute and irrefutable as that of Sancho, had not a common exclamation of alarm and horror burst from all around him. The night was sufficiently clear to permit the gloomy outlines of the Peak of Teneriffe to be distinctly visible, even at some distance; and, just at that moment, flashes of flame shot upward from its pointed summit, illuminating, at instants, the huge pile, and then leaving it in shadowy darkness, an object of mystery and terror. Many of the seamen dropped on their knees and began to tell their beads, while all, as it might be instinctively, crossed themselves. Next arose a general murmur; and in a few minutes, the men who slept were awoke, and appeared among their fellows, awe-struck and astounded spectators of the phenomenon. It was soon settled that the attention of the admiral should be drawn to this strange event, and Pero was selected for the spokesman.

All this time, Columbus and his companions remained on the poop, and, as might have been expected, this unlooked-for change in the appearance of the Peak had not escaped their attention. Too enlightened to be alarmed by it, they were watching the workings of the mountain, when Pero, accompanied by nearly every sailor in the vessel, appeared on the quarter-deck. Silence having been obtained, Pero opened the subject of his mission with a zeal that was not a little stimulated by his fears.

"Señor Almirante," he commenced, "we have come to pray your Excellency to look at the summit of the Island of Teneriffe, where we all think we see a solemn warning against persevering in sailing into the unknown Atlantic. It is truly time for men to remember their weakness, and how much they owe to the goodness of God, when even the mountains vomit flames and smoke!'"

"Have any here ever navigated the Mediterranean, or visited the island of which Don Ferdinand, the honored consort of our lady the queen, is master?" demanded Columbus, calmly.

"Señor Don Almirante," hastily answered Sancho, "I have done so, unworthy as I may seem to have enjoyed that advantage. And I have seen Cyprus, and Alexandria, and even Stamboul, the residence of the Great Turk."

"Well, then, thou may'st have also seen Ætna, another mountain which continueth to throw up those flames, in the midst of a nature and a scene on which Providence would seem to have smiled with unusual benignity, instead of angrily frowning, as ye seem to imagine."

Columbus then proceeded to give his people an explanation of the causes of volcanoes, referring to the gentlemen around him to corroborate the fidelity of his statements. He told them that he looked upon this little eruption as merely a natural occurrence; or, if he saw any omen at all in the event, it was propitious rather than otherwise; Providence seeming disposed to light them on their way. Luis and the rest next descended among the crew, where they used their reasoning powers in quieting an alarm that, at first, had threatened to be serious. For the moment they were successful, or perhaps it would be better to say that they succeeded completely, so far as the phenomenon of the volcano was concerned, and this less by the arguments of the more intelligent of the officers, than by means of the testimony of Sancho, and one or two others of the common men, who had seen similar scenes elsewhere. With difficulties like these had the great navigator to contend, even after he had passed years in solicitations to obtain the limited means which had been finally granted, in order to effect one of the sublimest achievements that had yet crowned the enterprise of man!

The vessels reached Gomera on the 2d of September, where they remained several days, in order to complete their repairs, and to finish taking in their supplies, ere they finally left the civilized abodes of man, and what might then be deemed the limits of the known earth. The arrival of such an expedition, in an age when the means of communication were so few that events were generally their own announcers, had produced a strong sensation among the inhabitants of the different islands visited by the adventurers. Columbus was held in high honor among them, not only on account of the commission he had received from the two sovereigns, but on account of the magnitude and the romantic character of his undertaking.

There existed a common belief among all the adjacent islands, including Madeira, the Azores, and the Canaries, that land lay to the westward; their inhabitants living under a singular delusion in this particular, which the admiral had an occasion to detect, during his second visit to Gomera. Among the most distinguished persons who were then on the island, was Doña Inez Peraza, the mother of the Count of Gomera. She was attended by a crowd of persons, not only belonging to her own, but who had come from other islands to do her honor. She entertained the admiral in a manner suited to his high rank, admitting to her society such of the adventurers as Columbus saw fit to point out as worthy of the honor. Of course the pretended Pedro de Muños, or Pero Gutierrez, as he was now indifferently termed, was of the number; as, indeed, were most of those who might be deemed any way suited to so high and polished a society.

"I rejoice, Don Christopher," said Doña Inez Peraza, on this occasion, "that their Highnesses have at length yielded to your desire to solve this great problem, not only on account of our Holy Church, which, as you say, hath so deep an interest in your success, and the honor of the two sovereigns, and the welfare of Spain, and all the other great considerations that we have so freely touched upon in our discourse already, but on account of the worthy inhabitants of the Fortunate Islands, who have not only many traditions touching land in the west, but most of whom believe that they have more than once seen it, in that quarter, in the course of their lives."

"I have heard of this, noble lady, and would be grateful to have the account from the mouths of eye-witnesses, now we are here, together, conversing freely concerning that which is of so much interest to us all."

"Then, Señor, I will entreat this worthy cavalier, who is every way capable of doing the subject justice, to be spokesman for us, and to let you know what we all believe in these islands, and what so many of us fancy we have seen. Acquaint the admiral, Señor Dama, I pray thee, of the singular yearly view that we get of unknown land lying afar off, in the Atlantic."

"Most readily, Doña Inez, and all the more so at your gracious bidding," returned the person addressed, who disposed himself to tell the story, with a readiness that the lovers of the wonderful are apt to betray when a fitting opportunity offers to indulge a favorite propensity. "The illustrious admiral hath probably heard of the island of St. Brandan, that lieth some eighty or a hundred leagues to the westward of Ferro, and which hath been so often seen, but which no navigator hath yet been able to reach, in our days at least?"

"I have often heard of this fabled spot, Señor," the admiral gravely replied; "but pardon me if I say that the land never yet existed, which a mariner hath seen and yet a mariner hath not reached."

"Nay, noble admiral," interrupted a dozen eager voices, among which that of the lady, herself, was very distinctly audible, "that it hath been seen most here know: and that it hath never been reached, is a fact to which more than one disappointed pilot can testify."

"That which we have seen, we know; and that which we know, we can describe," returned Columbus, steadily. "Let any man tell me in what meridian, or on what parallel this St. Brandan, or St. Barandon, lieth, and a week shall make *me* also certain of its existence."

"I know little of meridians or parallels, Don Christopher," said the Señor Dama, "but I have some ideas of visible things. This island have I often seen, more or less plainly at different times; and that, too, under the serenest skies, and at occasions when it was not possible greatly to mistake either its form or its dimensions. Once I remember to have seen the sun set behind one of its heights."

"This is plain evidence, and such as a navigator should respect; and yet do I take what you imagine yourself to have seen, Señor, to be some illusion of the atmosphere."

"Impossible!—impossible!" was said, or echoed, by a dozen voices. "Hundreds yearly witness the appearance of St. Brandan, and its equally sudden and mysterious disappearance."

"Therein, noble lady and generous cavalier, lieth the error into which ye have fallen. Ye see the Peak the year round; and he who will cruise a hundred miles, north or south, east or west, of it, will continue to see it, the year round, except on such days as the state of the atmosphere may forbid. The land which God hath created stationary, will be certain to remain stationary, until disturbed by some great convulsion that cometh equally of his providence and his laws."

"All this may be true, Señor; doubtless it *is* true; but every rule hath its exceptions. You will not deny that God ruleth the world mysteriously, and that his ends are not always visible to human eyes. Else, why hath the Moor so long been permitted to rule in Spain? why hath the Infidel, at this moment, possession of the Holy Sepulchre? why have the sovereigns been so long deaf to your own well-grounded wishes and entreaties to be permitted to carry their banners, in company with the cross, to Cathay, whither you are now bound? Who knoweth that these appearances of St. Brandan may not be given as signs to encourage one like yourself, bent on still greater ends than even reaching its shores?"

Columbus was an enthusiast; but his was an enthusiasm that was seated in his reverence for the acknowledged mysteries of religion, which sought no other support from things incomprehensible, than might reasonably be thought to belong to the exercise of infallible wisdom, and which manifested a proper reverence for a Divine Power. Like most of that period, he believed in modern miracles; and his dependence on the direct worldly efficacy of votive offerings, penances, and prayers, was such as marked the age in general, and his calling in particular. Still, his masculine understanding rejected the belief of vulgar prodigies; and while he implicitly thought himself set apart and selected for the great work before him, he was not disposed to credit that an airy exhibition of an island was placed in the west to tempt mariners to follow its shadowy outline to the more distant regions of Cathay.

"That I feel the assurance of the Providence of God having selected me as the humble instrument of connecting Europe with Asia, by means of a direct voyage by sea, is certain," returned the navigator, gravely, though his eye lighted with its latent enthusiasm; "but I am far from indulging in the weakness of thinking that direct miraculous agencies are to be used to guide me on my way. It is more in conformity to the practice of divine wisdom, and certainly more grateful to my own self-love, that the means employed are such as a discreet pilot, and the most experienced philosophers, might feel proud in finding themselves selected to display. My thoughts have first been turned to the contemplation of this subject; then hath my reason been enlightened by a due course of study and reflection, and science hath aided in producing the conviction necessary to impel myself to proceed, and to enable me to induce others to join in this enterprise."

"And do all your followers, noble admiral, act under the same guidance?" demanded the Doña Inez, glancing at Luis, whose manly graces, and martial aspect, had found favor in the eyes of most of the ladies of the island. "Is the Señor Gutierrez equally enlightened in this manner? and hath he, too, devoted his nights to study, in order that the cross may be carried to the heathen, and Castile and Cathay may be more closely united?"

"The Señor Gutierrez is a willing adventurer, Señora, but he must be the expounder of his own motives."

"Then we will call on the cavalier, himself, for an answer. These ladies feel a desire to know what may have impelled one who would be certain to succeed at the court of Doña Isabella, and in the Moorish wars, to join in such an expedition."

"The Moorish wars are ended, Señora," replied Luis, smiling; "and Doña Isabella, and all the ladies of her court, most favor the youths who show a manly disposition to serve the interests, and to advance the honor of Castile. I know very little of philosophy, and have still smaller pretensions to the learning of churchmen; but I think I see Cathay before me, shining like a brilliant star in the heavens, and am willing to adventure body and soul in its search."

Many pretty exclamations of admiration broke from the circle of fair listeners; it being most easy for spirit to gain applause, when it is recommended by high personal advantages, and comes from the young and favored. That Columbus, a weather-worn veteran of the ocean, should see fit to risk a life that was already drawing near its close, in a rash attempt to pry into the mysteries of the Atlantic, seemed neither so commendable, nor so daring, but many discovered high qualities in the character of one who was just entering on his career, and that under auspices apparently so flattering, and who threw all his hopes on the uncertain chances of success in a scheme so unusual. Luis was human, and he was in the full enjoyment of the admiration his enterprise had evidently awakened among so many sensitive young creatures, when Doña Inez most inopportunely interposed to interrupt his happiness, and to wound his self-esteem.

"This is having more honorable views than my letters from Seville attribute to one youth, who belongeth to the proudest of our Castilian houses, and whose titles alone should invite him to add new lustre to a name that hath so long been the Spanish boast," resumed the Señora Peraza. "The reports speak of his desire to rove, but in a manner unworthy of his rank; and that, too, in a way to serve neither the sovereigns, his country, nor himself."

"And who may this misguided youth be, Señora?" eagerly inquired Luis, too much elated by the admiration he had just excited to anticipate the answer. "A cavalier thus spoken of, needeth to be warned of his reputation, that he may be stimulated to attempt better things."

"His name is no secret, since the court speaketh openly of his singular and ill-judged career; and it is said that even his love hath been thwarted in consequence. I mean a cavalier of no less lineage and name than Don Luis de Bobadilla, the Count of Llera."

It is said that listeners seldom hear good of themselves, and Luis was now fated to verify the truth of the axiom. He felt the blood rushing to his face, and it required a strong effort at self-command to prevent him from breaking out in exclamations, that would probably have contained invocations of half the patron saints he had ever heard of, had he not happily succeeded in controlling the sudden impulse. Gulping the words he had been on the point of uttering, he looked round, with an air of defiance, as if seeking the countenance of some man who might dare even to smile at what had been said. Luckily, at that moment, Columbus had drawn all of the males present around himself, in warm discussion of the probable existence of the island of St. Brandan; and Luis nowhere met a smile, with which he could conveniently quarrel, that had a setting of beard to render it hostile. Fortunately, the gentle impulses that are apt to influence a youthful female, induced one of Doña Inez's fair companions to speak, and that in a way greatly to relieve the feelings of our hero.

"True, Señora," rejoined the pretty young advocate, the first tones of whose voice had an effect to calm the tempest that was rising in the bosom of the young man; "true Señora, it is said that Don Luis is a wanderer, and one of unsettled tastes and habits, but it is also said he hath a most excellent heart, is generous as the dews of heaven themselves, and carrieth the very best lance of Castile, as he is also like to carry off the fairest maiden."

"It is vain, Señor de Muños, for churchmen to preach, and parents to frown," said Doña Inez, smiling, "while the beautiful and young will prize courage, and deeds in arms, and an open hand, before the more homely virtues commended by our holy religion, and so zealously inculcated by its servants. The unhorsing of a knight or two in the tourneys, and the rallying a broken squadron under a charge of the Infidel, counteth far more than years of sobriety, and weeks of penance and prayer."

"How know we that the cavalier you mention, Señora, may not have his weeks of penance and his hours of prayer?" answered Luis, who had now found his voice. "Should he be so fortunate as to enjoy a conscientious religious adviser, he can scarce escape both, prayer being so often ordered in the way of penance. He seemeth, indeed, to be a miserable dog, and I wonder not that his mistress holdeth him cheap. Is the name of the lady, also, given in your letter?"

"It is. She is the Doña Maria de las Mercedes de Valverde, nearly allied to the Guzmans and the other great houses, and one of the fairest maidens of Spain."

"That is she!" exclaimed Luis; "and one of the most virtuous, as well as fair, and wise as virtuous!"

"How now, Señor, is it possible that you can have sufficient knowledge of one so situated, as to speak thus positively of her qualities, as well as of her appearance?"

"Her beauty I have seen, and of her excellence one may speak by report. But doth your correspondent, Señora, say aught of what hath become of the graceless lover?"

"It is rumored that he hath again quitted Spain, and, as is supposed, under the grave displeasure of the sovereigns, since it hath been remarked that the queen now never nameth him. None know the road he hath taken, but there is little doubt that he is again roaming the seas, as usual, in quest of low adventures among the ports of the east."

The conversation now changed, and soon after the admiral and his attendants repaired to their different vessels.

"Of a verity, Señor Don Christoval," said Luis, as he walked alone with the great navigator toward the shore, "one little knoweth when he is acquiring fame, and when not. Though but an indifferent mariner, and no pilot, I find my exploits on the ocean are well bruited abroad! If your Excellency but gain half the reputation I already enjoy, by this present expedition, you will have reason to believe that your name will not be forgotten by posterity."

"It is a tribute the great pay for their elevation, Luis," returned the admiral, "that all their acts are commented on, and that they can do little that may be concealed from observation, or escape remarks."

"It would be as well, Señor Almirante, to throw into the scales, at once, calumnies, and lies, and uncharitableness, for all these are to be added to the list. Is it not wonderful, that a young man cannot visit a few foreign lands, in order to increase his knowledge and improve his parts, but all the gossips of Castile should fill their letters to the gossips of the Canaries, with passages touching his movements and demerits? By the Martyrs of the East! if I were Queen of Castile, there should be a law against writing of others' movements, and I do not know, but a law against women's writing letters at all!"

"In which case, Señor de Muños, thou wouldst never possess the satisfaction of receiving a missive from the fairest hand in Castile."

"I mean a woman's writing to a woman, Don Christopher. As to letters from noble maidens intended to cheer the hearts and animate the deeds of cavaliers who adore them, they are useful, out of doubt, and the saints be deaf to the miscreant who would forbid or intercept them! No, Señor, I trust that travelling hath at least made me liberal, by raising me above the narrow prejudices of provinces and cities, and I am far from wishing to put an end to letters from mistresses to their knights, or from parents to their children, or even from wives to their husbands; but, as for the letters of a gossip to a gossip, by your leave, Señor Almirante, I detest them just as much as the Father of Sin detests this expedition of ours!"

"An expedition, certainly, that he hath no great reason to love," answered Columbus, smiling; "since it will be followed by the light of revelation and the triumph of the cross. But what is thy will, friend, that thou seemest in waiting for me, to disburden thyself of something? Thy name is Sancho Mundo, if I remember thy countenance?"

"Señor Don Almirante, your memory hath not mistaken," returned the person addressed; "I am Sancho Mundo, as your Excellency saith, sometimes called Sancho of the Ship-Yard Gate. I desire to say a few words concerning the fate of our voyage, whenever it shall suit you, noble Señor, to hear me where there are no ears present that you distrust."

"Thou may'st speak freely now; this cavalier being my confidant and secretary."

"It is not necessary that I should tell a great pilot, like your Excellency, who is King of Portugal, or what the mariners of Lisbon have been about these many years, since you know all better than myself. Therefore I will just add, that they are discovering all the unknown lands they can, for themselves, and preventing others, as much as in them lies, from doing the same thing."

"Don John of Portugal is an enlightened prince, fellow, and thou wouldst do well to respect his character and rank. His Highness is a liberal sovereign, and hath sent many noble expeditions forth from his harbor."

"That he hath, Señor, and this last is not the least in its designs and intentions," answered Sancho, turning a look of irony toward the admiral, that showed the fellow had more in reserve than he cared to divulge without some wheedling. "No one doubts Don John's willingness to send forth expeditions."

"Thou hast heard some intelligence, Sancho, that it is proper I should know! Speak freely, and rely on my repaying any service of this sort to the full extent of its deservings."

"If your Excellency will have patience to hear me, I will give the whole story, with all minuteness and particularity, and that in a way to leave no part untold, and all parts to be as easily understood as heart can wish, or a priest in the confessional could desire."

"Speak; no one will interrupt thee. As thou art frank, so will be thy reward."

"Well, then, Señor Don Almirante, you must know that about eleven years since, I made a voyage from Palos to Sicily, in a caravel belonging to the Pinzons, here; not to Martin Alonzo, who commandeth the Pinta, under your Excellency's order, but to a kinsman of his late father's, who caused better craft to be constructed than we are apt to get in these days of hurry, and rotten cordage, and careless caulking, to say nothing of the manner in which the canvas is" —

"Nay, good Sancho," interrupted the impatient Luis, who was yet smarting under the remarks of Doña Inez's correspondent—"thou forgettest night is near, and that the boat is waiting for the admiral."

"How should I forget that, Señor, when I can see the sun just dipping into the water, and I belong to the boat myself, having left it in order to tell the noble admiral what I have to say?"

"Permit the man to relate his story in his own manner, Señor Pedro, I pray thee," put in Columbus. "Naught is gained by putting a seamen out in his reckoning."

"No, your Excellency, or in kicking with a mule. And so, as I was saying, I went that voyage to Sicily, and had for a messmate one José Gordo, a Portuguese by birth, but a man who liked the wines of Spain better than the puckering liquors of his own country, and so sailed much in Spanish craft. I never well knew, notwithstanding, whether José was, in heart, most of a Portuguese, or a Spaniard, though he was certainly but an indifferent Christian."

"It is to be hoped that his character hath improved," said Columbus, calmly. "As I foresee that something is to follow on the testimony of this José, you will let me say, that an indifferent Christian is but an indifferent witness. Tell me, at once, therefore, what he hath communicated, that I may judge for myself of the value of his words."

"Now, he that doubteth your Excellency will not discover Cathay is a heretic, seeing that you have discovered my secret without having heard it! José has just arrived, in the felucca that is riding near the Santa Maria, and hearing that we were an expedition that had one Sancho Mundo engaged in it, he came speedily on board of us to see his old shipmate."

"All that is so plain, that I wonder thou thinkest it worthy of relating, Sancho; but, now we have him safe on board the good ship, we can come at once to the subject of his communication."

"That may we, Señor; and so, without any unnecessary delay, I will state, that the subject was touching Don Juan of Portugal, Don Ferdinand of Aragon, Doña Isabella of Castile, your Excellency, Señor Don Almirante, the Señor de Muños here, and myself."

"This is a strange company!" exclaimed Luis, laughing, while he slipped a piece of eight into the hand of the sailor; "perhaps that may aid thee in shortening the story of the singular conjunction."

"Another, Señor, would bring the tale to an end at once. To own the truth, José is behind that wall, and as he told me he thought his news worth a dobla, he will be greatly displeased at finding I have received my half of it, while his half still remaineth unpaid."

"This, then, will set his mind at rest," said Columbus, placing an entire dobla in the hand of the cunning fellow, for the admiral perceived by his manner that Sancho had really something of importance to communicate. "Thou canst summon José to thy aid, and deliver thyself, at once, of thy burden."

Sancho did as directed, and in a minute José had appeared, had received the dobla, weighed it deliberately on his finger, pocketed it, and commenced his tale. Unlike the artful Sancho, he told his story at once, beginning at the right end, and ceasing to speak as soon as he had no more to communicate. The substance of the tale is soon related. José had come from Ferro, and had seen three armed caravels, wearing the flag of Portugal, cruising among the islands, under circumstances that left little doubt their object was to intercept the Castilian expedition. As the man referred to a passenger or two, who had landed within the hour, to corroborate his statement, Columbus and Luis immediately sought the lodgings of these persons, in order to hear their report of the matter. The result proved the sailor had stated nothing but what was true.

"Of all our difficulties and embarrassments, Luis," resumed the admiral, as the two finally proceeded to the shore, "this is much the most serious! We may be detained altogether by these treacherous Portuguese, or we may be followed in our voyage, and have our fair laurels seized upon by others, and all the benefits so justly due for our toil and risk usurped, or at least disputed, by men who had not the enterprise and knowledge to accept the boon, when fairly offered to them."

"Don John of Portugal must have sent far better knights than the Moors of Granada to do the feat," answered Luis, who had a Spaniard's distaste for his peninsular neighbors; "he is a bold and learned prince, they say, but the commission and ensigns of the sovereign of Castile are not to be disregarded, and that, too, in the midst of her own islands, here."

"We have no force fit to contend with that which hath most probably been sent against us. The number and size of our vessels are known, and the Portuguese, questionless, have resorted to the means necessary to effect their purposes, whatever those purposes may be. Alas! Luis, my lot hath been hard, though I humbly trust that the end will repay me for all! Years did I sue the Portuguese to enter fairly into this voyage, and to endeavor to do that, in all honor, which our gracious mistress, Doña Isabella, hath now so creditably commenced; he listened to my reasons and entreaties with cold ears—nay, repelled them, with ridicule and disdain; and yet, here am I scarce fairly embarked in the execution of schemes that they have so often derided, than they endeavor to defeat me by violence and treachery."

"Noble Don Christoval, we will die to a Castilian, ere this shall come to pass!"

"Our only hope is in speedy departure. Thanks to the industry and zeal of Martin Alonzo, the Pinta is ready, and we may quit Gomera with the morning's sun. I doubt if they will have the hardihood to follow us into the trackless and unknown Atlantic, without any other guides than their own feeble knowledge; and we will depart with the return of the sun. All now dependeth on quitting the Canaries unseen."

As this was said they reached the boat, and were quickly pulled on board the Santa Maria. By this time the peaks of the islands were towering like gloomy shadows in the atmosphere, and, soon after, the caravels resembled dark, shapeless specks, on the unquiet element that washed their hulls.

CHAPTER XVI

"They little thought how pure a light,
With years, should gather round that day;
How love should keep their memories bright—
How wide a realm their sons should sway."

Bryant.

The night that succeeded was one of very varied feelings among the adventurers. As soon as Sancho secured the reward, he had no further scruples about communicating all he knew, to any who were disposed to listen; and long ere Columbus returned on board the vessel, the intelligence had spread from mouth to mouth, until all in the little squadron were apprised of the intentions of the Portuguese. Many hoped that it was true, and that their pursuers might be successful; any fate being preferable, in their eyes, to that which the voyage promised; but, such is the effect of strife, much the larger portion of the crew were impatient to lift the anchors and to make sail, if it were only to get the mastery in the race. Columbus, himself, experienced the deepest concern, for it really seemed as if a hard fortune was about to snatch the cup from his lips, just as it had been raised there, after all his cruel sufferings and delays. He consequently passed a night of deep anxiety, and was the first to rise in the morning.

Every one was on the alert with the dawn; and as the preparations had been completed the previous night, by the time the sun had risen, the three vessels were under way, the Pinta leading, as usual. The wind was light, and the squadron could barely gather steerage way; but as every moment was deemed precious, the vessels' heads were kept to the westward. When a short time out, a caravel came flapping past them, after having been several hours in sight, and the admiral spoke her. She proved to be from Ferro, the most southern and western island of the group, and had come nearly on the route the expedition intended to steer, until they quitted the known seas.

"Dost thou bring any tidings from Ferro?" inquired Columbus, as the strange ship drifted slowly past the Santa Maria; the progress of each vessel being little more than a mile in the hour. "Is there aught of interest in that quarter?"

"Did I know whether, or not, I am speaking to Don Christopher Columbus, the Genoese that their Highnesses have honored with so important a commission, I should feel more warranty to answer what I have both heard and seen, Señor," was the reply.

"I am Don Christopher himself, their Highnesses' admiral and viceroy, for all seas and lands that we may discover, and, as thou hast said, a Genoese in birth, though a Castilian by duty, and in love to the queen."

"Then, noble admiral, I may tell you that the Portuguese are active, three of their caravels being off Ferro, at this moment, with the hope of intercepting your expedition."

"How is this known, friend, and what reason have I for supposing that the Portuguese will dare to send forth caravels, with orders to molest those who sail as the officers of Isabella the Catholic? They must know that the Holy Father hath lately conferred this title on the two sovereigns, in acknowledgment of their great services in expelling the Moor from Christendom."

"Señor, there hath been a rumor of that among the islands, but little will the Portuguese care for aught of that nature, when he deemeth his gold in danger. As I quitted Ferro, I spoke the caravels, and have good reason to think that rumor doth them no injustice."

"Did they seem warlike, and made they any pretensions to a right to interrupt our voyage?"

"To us they said naught of this sort, except to inquire, tauntingly, if the illustrious Don Christoval Colon, the great viceroy of the east, sailed on board us. As for preparation, Señor, they had many lombardas, and a multitude of men in breast-plates and casques. I doubt if soldiers are as numerous at the Azores, as when they sailed."

"Keep they close in with the island, or stretch they off to seaward?"

"Mostly the latter, Señor, standing far toward the west in the morning, and beating up toward the land as the day closeth. Take the word of an old pilot, Don Christopher, the mongrels are there for no good."

This was barely audible, for, by this time, the caravels had drifted past each other, and were soon altogether beyond the reach of the voice.

"Do you believe that the Castilian name standeth so low, Don Christopher," demanded Luis, "that these dogs of Portuguese dare do this wrong to the flag of the queen?"

"I dread naught from force, beyond detention and frauds, certainly; but these, to me, at this moment, would be little less painful than death.

Most do I apprehend that these caravels, under the pretence of protecting the rights of Don John, are directed to follow us to Cathay, in which case we should have a disputed discovery, and divided honors. We must avoid the Portuguese, if possible; to effect which purpose, I intend to pass to the westward, without nearing the island of Ferro, any closer than may be rendered absolutely indispensable."

Notwithstanding a burning impatience now beset the admiral, and most with him, the elements seemed opposed to his passage from among the Canaries, into the open ocean. The wind gradually failed, until it became so calm that the sails were hauled up, and the three vessels lay, now laying their sides with the brine, and now rising to the summit of the ground-swell, resembling huge animals that were lazily reposing, under the heats of summer, in drowsy indolence.

Many was the secret *pater*, or *ave*, that was mumbled by the mariners, and not a few vows of future prayers were made, in the hope of obtaining a breeze. Occasionally it seemed as if Providence listened to these petitions, for the air would fan the cheek, and the sails would fall, in the vain expectation of getting ahead; but disappointment as often followed, until all on board felt that they were fated to linger under the visitations of a calm. Just at nightfall, however, a light air arose, and, for a few hours, the wash of the parted waters was audible under the bows of the vessels, though their way was barely sufficient to keep them under the command of their helms. About midnight, however, even this scarcely perceptible motion was lost, and the craft were again lazily wallowing in the ground-swells that the gales had sent in from the vast expanse of the Western Ocean.

When the light reappeared, the admiral found himself between Gomera and Teneriffe, the lofty peak of the latter casting its pointed shadow, like that thrown by a planet, far upon the water, until its sharp apex was renewed, in faint mimicry, along the glassy surface of the ocean. Columbus was now fearful that the Portuguese might employ their boats, or impel some light felucca by her sweeps, in order to find out his position; and he wisely directed the sails to be furled, in order to conceal his vessels, as far as possible, from any prying eyes. The season had advanced to the 7th of September, and such was the situation of this renowned expedition, exactly five weeks after it had left Spain; for this inauspicious calm occurred on a Friday, or on that day of the week on which it had originally sailed.

All practice shows that there is no refuge from a calm at sea, except in patience. Columbus was much too experienced a navigator, not to feel this truth, and, after using the precaution mentioned, he, and the pilots under him, turned their attention to the arrangements required to render the future voyage safe and certain. The few mathematical instruments known to the age, were got up, corrected, and exhibited, with the double intention of ascertaining their state, and of making a display before the common men, that would heighten their respect for their leaders, by adding to their confidence in their skill. The admiral, himself, had already obtained a high reputation as a navigator, among his followers, in consequence of his reckonings having proved so much more accurate than those of the pilots, in approaching the Canaries; and as he now exhibited the instruments then used as a quadrant, and examined his compasses, every movement he made was watched by the seamen, with either secret admiration, or jealous vigilance; some openly expressing their confidence in his ability to proceed wherever he wished to go, and others covertly betraying just that degree of critical knowledge which ordinarily accompanies prejudice, ignorance, and malice.

Luis had never been able to comprehend the mysteries of navigation, his noble head appearing to repudiate learning, as a species of accomplishment but little in accordance with its wants or its tastes. Still, he was intelligent; and within the range of knowledge that it was usual for laymen of his rank to attain, few of his age did themselves more credit in the circles of the court. Fortunately, he had the most perfect reliance on the means of the admiral; and being almost totally without personal apprehensions, Columbus had not a more submissive or blind follower, than the young grandee, under his command.

Man, with all his boasted philosophy, intelligence, and reason, exists the dupe of his own imagination and blindness, as much as of the artifices and designs of others. Even while he fancies himself the most vigilant and cautious, he is as often misled by appearances as governed by facts and judgment; and perhaps half of those who were spectators of this calculated care in Columbus, believed that they felt, in their renewed confidence, the assurances of science and logical deductions, when in truth their senses were impressed, without, in the slightest degree, enlightening their understandings.

Thus passed the day of the 7th September, the night arriving and still finding the little squadron, or fleet, as it was termed in the lofty language of the day, floating helplessly between Teneriffe and Gomera. Nor did the ensuing morning bring a change, for a burning sun beat, unrelieved by a breath of air, on the surface of a sea that was glittering like molten silver. When the admiral was certain, however, by having sent men aloft to examine the horizon, that the Portuguese were not in sight, he felt infinitely relieved, little doubting that his pursuers still lay, as inactive as himself, to the westward of Ferro.

"By the seamen's hopes! Señor Don Christopher," said Luis, as he reached the poop, where Columbus had kept an untiring watch for hours, he himself having just risen from a siesta, "the fiends seem to be leagued against us! Here are we in the third day of our calm, with the Peak of Teneriffe as stationary as if it were a mile-stone, set to tell the porpoises and dolphins the rate at which they swim. If one believed in omens, he might fancy that the saints were unwilling to see us depart, even though it be on their own errand."

"We *may not* believe in omens, when they are no more than the fruits of natural laws," gravely returned the admiral. "There will shortly be an end of this calm, for a haze is gathering in the atmosphere that promises air from the east, and the motion of the ship will tell thee, that the winds have been busy far to the westward. Master Pilot," addressing the officer of that title, who had charge of the deck at the moment, "thou wilt do well to unfurl thy canvas, and prepare for a favoring breeze, as we shall soon be overtaken by wind from the north-east."

This prediction was verified about an hour later, when all three of the vessels began, again, to part the waters with their sterns. But the breeze, if any thing, proved more tantalizing to the impatient mariners than the calm itself had been; for a strong head sea had got up, and the air proving light, the different craft struggled with difficulty toward the west.

All this time, a most anxious look-out was kept for the Portuguese caravels, the appearance of which, however, was less dreaded than it had been, as they were now supposed to be a considerable distance to leeward. Columbus, and his skilful assistants, Martin Alonzo and Vicente Yañez, or the brothers Pinzon, who commanded the Pinta and the Niña, practised all the means that their experience could suggest to get ahead. Their progress, however, was not only slow but painful, as every fresh impulse given by the breeze, served to plunge the bows of the vessels into the sea with a violence that threatened injuries to the spars and rigging. So trifling, indeed, was their rate of sailing, that it required all the judgment of Columbus to note the nearly imperceptible manner in which the tall, cone-like summit of the Peak of Teneriffe lowered, as it might be, inch by inch. The superstitious feelings of the common men being more active than usual, even, some among them began to whisper that the elements were admonishing them against proceeding, and that tardy as it might seem, the admiral would do well to attend to omens and signs that nature seldom gave without sufficient reason. These opinions, however, were cautiously uttered—the grave, earnest manner of Columbus having created so much respect, as to suppress them in his presence; and the mariners of the other vessels still followed the movements of their admiral with that species of blind dependence which marks the submission of the inferior to the superior, under such circumstances.

When Columbus retired to his cabin for the night, Luis observed that his countenance was unusually grave, as he ended his calculations of the days' work.

"I trust all goes to your wishes, Don Christopher," the young man gaily observed. "We are now fairly on our journey, and, to my eyes, Cathay is already in sight."

"Thou hast that within thee, Don Luis," returned the admiral, "which rendereth what thou wishest to see distinct, and maketh all colors gay. With me it is a duty to see things as they *are*, and, although Cathay lieth plainly before the vision of my mind—thou, Lord, who hast implanted, for thine own great ends, the desire to reach that distant land, only know'st how plainly!—although Cathay is thus plain to my moral view, I am bound to heed the physical obstacles that may exist to our reaching it."

"And are these obstacles getting to be more serious than we could hope, Señor?"

"My trust is still in God—look here, young lord," laying his finger on the chart; "at this point were we in the morning, and to this point have we advanced by means of all the toil of the day, down to this portion of the night. Thou seest that a line of paper marketh the whole of our progress; and, here again, thou seest that we have to cross this vast desert of ocean, ere we may even hope to draw near the end of our journey. By my calculation, with all our exertions, and at this critical moment—critical not only as regardeth the Portuguese, but critical as regardeth our own people—we have made but nine leagues, which are a small portion of the thousand that lie before us. At this rate we may dread a failure of our provisions and water."

"I have all confidence in your resources, Don Christopher, and in your knowledge and experience."

"And I have all confidence in the protection of God; trusting that he will not desert his servant in the moment that he most needeth his support."

Here Columbus prepared himself to catch a few hours' sleep, though it was in his clothes, the interest he felt in the position of his vessels forbidding him to undress. This celebrated man lived in an age when a spurious philosophy, and a pretending but insufficient exercise of reason, placed few, even in appearance, above the frank admission of their constant reliance on a divine power. We say in appearance, as no man, whatever may be the extent of his delusions on this subject, really believes that he is altogether sufficient for his own protection. This absolute self-reliance is forbidden by a law of nature, each carrying in his own breast a monitor to teach him his real insignificance, demonstrating daily, hourly, at each minute even, that he is but a diminutive agent used by a superior power in carrying out its own great and mysterious ends, for the sublime and beneficent purposes for which the world and all it contains has been created. In compliance with the usage of the times, Columbus knelt, and prayed fervently, ere he slept; nor did Luis de Bobadilla hesitate about imitating an example that few, in that day, thought beneath their intelligence or their manhood. If religion had the taint of superstition in the fifteenth century, and men confided too much in the efficacy of momentary and transient impulses, it is certain that it also possessed an exterior of graceful meekness and submission to God, in losing which, it may be well questioned if the world has been the gainer.

The first appearance of light brought the admiral and Luis to the deck. They both knelt again on the poop, and repeated their paters; and then, yielding to the feelings natural to their situation, they arose, eager to watch for what might be revealed by the lifting of the curtain of day. The approach of dawn, and the rising of the sun at sea, have been so often described, that the repetition here might be superfluous; but we shall state that Luis watched the play of colors that adorned the eastern sky, with a lover's refinement of feeling, fancying that he traced a resemblance to the passage of emotions across the tell-tale countenance of Mercedes, in the soft and transient hues that are known to precede a fine morning in September, more especially in a low latitude. As for the admiral, his more practical gaze was turned in the direction in which the island of Ferro lay, awaiting the increase of the light in order to ascertain what changes had been wrought during the hours he had slept. Several minutes passed in profound attention, when the navigator beckoned Luis to his side.

"Seest thou that dark, gloomy pile, which is heaving up out of the darkness, here at the south and west of us?" he said—"it gaineth form and distinctness at each instant, though distant some eight or ten leagues; that is Ferro, and the Portuguese are there, without question, anxiously expecting our appearance. In this calm, neither can approach the other, and thus far we are safe. It is now necessary to ascertain if the pursuing caravels are between us and the land, or not; after which, should it prove otherwise, we shall be reasonably safe, if we approach no nearer to the island, and we can maintain, as yesterday, the advantage of the wind. Seest thou any sail, Luis, in that quarter of the ocean?"

"None, Señor; and the light is already of sufficient strength to expose the white canvas of a vessel, were any there."

Columbus made an ejaculation of thankfulness, and immediately ordered the look-out aloft to examine the entire horizon. The report was favorable; the dreaded Portuguese caravels being nowhere visible. As the sun arose, however, a breeze sprung up at the southward and westward, bringing Ferro, and consequently any vessels that might be cruising in that quarter, directly to windward of the fleet. Sail was made without the loss of a moment; and the admiral stood to the northward and westward, trusting that his pursuers were looking out for him on the south side of the island, which was the ground where those who did not thoroughly understand his aim, would be most likely to expect him. By this time the westerly swell had, in a great measure, gone down; and though the progress of the vessels was far from rapid, it was steady, and seemed likely to last. The hours went slowly by, and as the day advanced, objects became less and less distinct on the sides of Ferro. Its entire surface next took the hazy appearance of a dim and ill-defined cloud; and then it began slowly to sink into the water. Its summit was still visible, as the admiral, with the more privileged of his companions, assembled on the poop, to take a survey of the ocean and of the weather. The most indifferent observer might now have noted the marked difference in the state of feeling which existed among the adventurers on board the Santa Maria. On the poop, all was cheerfulness and hope, the present escape having induced even the distrustful, momentarily, to forget the uncertain future; the pilots, as usual, were occupied and sustained by a species of marine stoicism; while a melancholy had settled on the crew that was as apparent as if they were crowding around the dead. Nearly every man in the ship was in some one of the groups that had assembled on deck; and every eye seemed riveted, as it might be by enchantment, on the fading and falling heights of Ferro. While things were in this state, Columbus approached Luis, and aroused him from a sort of trance, by laying a finger lightly on his shoulder.

"It cannot be that the Señor de Muños is affected by the feelings of the common men," observed the admiral, with a slight mixture of surprise and reproach; "this, too, at a moment that all of an intelligence sufficient to foresee the glorious consequences, are rejoicing that a heaven-sent breeze is carrying us to a safe distance from the pursuing and envious caravels! Why dost thou thus regard the people beneath, with a steady eye and unwavering look? Is it that thou repentest embarking, or dost thou merely muse on the charms of thy mistress?"

"By San Iago! Don Christopher, this time your sagacity is at fault. I neither repent, nor muse as you would imply; but I gaze at yonder poor fellows with pity for their apprehensions."

"Ignorance is a hard master, Señor Pedro, and one that is now exercising his power over the imaginations of the seamen, with the ruthlessness of a tyrant. They dread the worst merely because they have not the knowledge to foresee the best. Fear is a stronger passion than hope, and is ever the near ally of ignorance. In vulgar eyes that which hath not yet been—nay, which hath not, in some measure, become familiar by use—is deemed impossible; men reasoning in a circle that is abridged by their information. Those fellows are gazing at the island, as it disappears, like men taking a last look at the things of life. Indeed, this concern exceedeth even what I could have anticipated."

"It lieth deep, Señor, and yet it riseth to the eyes; for I have seen tears on cheeks that I could never have supposed wetted in any manner but by the spray of the ocean!"

"There are our two acquaintances, Sancho and Pepe, neither of whom seemeth particularly distressed, though the last hath a cast of melancholy in his face. As for the first, the knave showeth the indifference of a true mariner—one who is never so happy as when furthest from the dangers of rocks and shoals: to such a man, the disappearance of one island, and the appearance of another, are alike matters of indifference. He seeth but the visible horizon around him, and considereth the rest of the world, temporarily, as a blank. I look for loyal service in that Sancho, in despite of his knavery, and count upon him as one of the truest of my followers."

Here the admiral was interrupted by a cry from the deck beneath him, and, looking round, his practised and quick eye was not slow in discovering that the horizon to the southward presented the usual watery blank of the open ocean. Ferro had, in fact, altogether disappeared, some of the most sanguine of the seamen having fancied that they beheld it, even after it had finally sunk behind the barrier of waves. As the circumstance became more and more certain, the lamentations among the people grew less and less equivocal and louder, tears flowed without shame or concealment, hands were wrung in a sort of a senseless despair, and a scene of such clamor ensued, as threatened some serious danger to the expedition from this new quarter. Under such circumstances, Columbus had all the people collected beneath the break of the poop, and standing on the latter, where he could examine every countenance for himself, he addressed them on the subject of their grief. On this occasion the manner of the great navigator was earnest and sincere, leaving no doubt that he fully believed in the truth of his own arguments, and that he uttered nothing with the hope to delude or to mislead.

"When Don Ferdinand and Doña Isabella, our respected and beloved sovereigns, honored me with the commission of admiral and viceroy, in those secret seas toward which we are now steering," he said, "I considered it as the most glorious and joyful event of my life, as I now consider this moment, that seemeth to some among you so painful, as second to it in hope and cause for felicitation. In the disappearance of Ferro, I see also the disappearance of the Portuguese; for, now that we are in the open ocean, without the limits of any known land, I trust that Providence hath placed us beyond the reach and machinations of all our enemies. While we prove true to ourselves, and to the great objects that are before us, there is no longer cause for fear. If any person among you hath a mind to disburden himself, in this matter, let him speak freely; we being much too strong in argument to wish to silence doubts by authority."

"Then, Señor Don Almirante," put in Sancho, whose tongue was ever ready to wag, as occasion offered, "it is just that which maketh your Excellency so joyful that maketh these honest people so sad. Could they always keep the island of Ferro in sight, or any other known land, they would follow you to Cathay with as gentle a pull as the launch followeth the caravel in a light breeze and smooth water; but it is this leaving all behind, as it might be, earth as well as wives and children, that saddens their hearts, and uncorks their tears."

"And thou, Sancho, an old mariner that wast born at sea" —

"Nay, your Excellency, illustrious Señor Don Almirante," interrupted Sancho, looking up with pretended simplicity, "not exactly at sea, though within the scent of its odor; since, having been found at the shipwright's gate, it is not probable they would have made a haven just to land so small a part of the freight."

"Well, born *near* the sea, if thou wilt—but from thee I expect better things than unmanly lamentations because an island hath sunk below the horizon."

"Excellency, you may; it mattereth little to Sancho, if half the islands in the sea were sunk a good deal lower. There are the Cape de Verdes, now, which I never wish to look upon again, and Lampidosa, besides Stromboli and others in that quarter, would be better out of the way, than where they are, as for any good they do us seamen. But, if your Excellency will condescend to tell these honest people whither it is that we are bound, and what you expect to find in port, and, more especially, when we are to come back, it would comfort them in an unspeakable degree."

"As I hold it to be the proper office of men in authority to let their motives be known, when no evil followeth the disclosure, this will I most cheerfully do, requiring the attention of all near me, and chiefly of those who are most uneasy concerning our present position and future movements. The end of our voyage is Cathay, a country that is known to lie in the uttermost eastern extremity of Asia, whither it hath been more than once reached by Christian travellers; and its difference from all other voyages, or journeys, that may have been attempted in order to reach the same country, is in the circumstance that we go west, while former travellers have proceeded east. But this is effecting our purposes by means that belong only to stout-hearted mariners, since none but those who are familiar with the ocean, skilful pilots, and obedient and ready seamen, can traverse the waters, without better guides than the knowledge of the stars, currents, winds, and other phenomena of the Atlantic, and such aids as may be gleaned from science. The reason on which I act, is a conviction that the earth is round, whence it followeth that the Atlantic, which we know to possess an eastern boundary of land, must also have a western; and from certain calculations that leave it almost certain, that this continent, which I hold will prove to be India, cannot lie more than some twenty-five or thirty days' sailing, if as many, from our own Europe. Having thus told when and where I expect to find the country we seek, I will now touch a little on the advantages that we may all expect to derive from the discovery. According to the accounts of a certain Marco Polo, and his relatives, gentlemen of Venice, and men of fair credit and good reputations, the kingdom of Cathay is not only one of the most extensive known, but one that most aboundeth in gold and silver, together with the other metals of value, and precious stones. Of the advantages of the discovery of such a land to yourselves, ye may judge by its advantages to me. Their Highnesses have dignified me with the rank of admiral and viceroy, in anticipation of our success, and, persevering to a successful termination of your efforts, the humblest man among ye may look with confidence to some signal mark of their favor. Rewards will doubtless be rendered in proportion to your merits; he that deserveth much, receiving more than he who hath deserved less. Still will there be sufficient for all. Marco Polo and his relatives dwelt seventeen years in the court of the Great Khan, and were every way qualified to give a true account of the riches and resources of those regions; and well were they—simple Venetian gentlemen, without any other means than could be transported on the backs of beasts of burden—rewarded for their toils and courage. The jewels alone, with which they returned, served long to enrich their race, renovating a decayed but honorable family, while they did their enterprise and veracity credit in the eyes of men.

"As the ocean, for a long distance this side of the continent of Asia and the kingdom of Cathay, is known to abound with islands, we may expect first to meet with them, where, it would be doing nature herself injustice, did we not anticipate fragrant freights of balmy spices, and other valuable commodities with which that favored quarter of the earth, it is certain, is enriched. Indeed, it is scarce possible for the imagination to conceive of the magnitude of the results that await our success, while naught but ridicule and contempt could attend a hasty and inconsiderate return. Going not as invaders, but as Christians and friends, we have no reason to expect other than the most friendly reception; and, no doubt, the presents and gifts, alone, that will naturally be offered to strangers who have come so far, and by a road that hath hitherto been untravelled, will forty-fold repay you for all your toils and troubles.

"I say nothing of the honor of being among those who have first carried the cross to the heathen world," continued the admiral, uncovering himself, and looking around him with solemn gravity; "though our fathers believed it to be no little distinction to have been one in the armies that contended for the possession of the sepulchre. But neither the church, nor its great master, forgetteth the servitor that advanceth its interests, and we may all look for blessings, both here and hereafter."

As he concluded, Columbus devoutly crossed himself, and withdrew from the sight of his people among those who were on the poop. The effect of this address was, for the moment, very salutary, and the men saw the clouds that hung over the land disappear, like the land itself, with less feeling than they had previously manifested. Nevertheless, they remained distrustful and sad, some dreaming that night of the pictures that Columbus had drawn of the glories of the East, and others fancying, in their sleep, that demons were luring them into unknown seas, where they were doomed to wander forever, as a punishment for their sins; conscience asserting its power in all situations, and most vividly in those of distrust and uncertainty.

Shortly before sunset, the admiral caused the three vessels to heave-to, and the two Pinzons to repair on board his own ship. Here he laid before these persons his orders and plans for their government, in the event of a separation.

"Thus you will understand me, Señores," he concluded, after having explained at length his views: "Your first and gravest duty will be to keep near the admiral, in all weather, and under every circumstance, so long as it may be possible; but, failing of the possibility, you will make your way due westward, on this parallel of latitude, until you have gone seven hundred leagues from the Canaries; after which, you are to lie-to at night, as, by that time, it is probable you will be among the islands of Asia; and it will be both prudent, and necessary to our objects, to be more on the alert for discoveries, from that moment. Still, you will proceed westward, relying on seeing me at the court of the Great Khan, should Providence deny us an earlier meeting."

"This is well, Señor Almirante," returned Martin Alonzo, raising his eyes, which had long been riveted on the chart, "but it will be far better for all to keep together, and chiefly so to us, who are little used to the habits of princes, if we wait for your Excellency's protection before we rush unheedingly into the presence of a sovereign as potent as the Grand Khan."

"Thou showest thy usual prudence, good Martin Alonzo, and I much commend thee for it. It were, indeed, better that thou shouldst wait my arrival, since that eastern potentate may conceive himself better treated by receiving the first visit from the viceroy of the sovereigns, who is the bearer of letters directly from his own royal master and mistress, than by receiving it from one of inferior rank. Look thou well to the islands and their products, Señor Pinzon, shouldst thou first gain those seas, and await my appearance, before thou proceedest to aught else. How stand thy people affected on taking leave of the land?"

"Ill enough, Señor; so much so, indeed, as to put me in fear of a mutiny. There are those in the Pinta who need to stand in wholesome dread of the anger of their Highnesses, to prevent their making a sudden and violent return to Palos."

"Thou wouldst do well to look sharply to this spirit, that it may be kept under. Deal kindly and gently with these disaffected spirits as long as may be, encouraging them by all fair and reasonable promises; but beware that the distemper get not the mastery of thy authority. And now, Señores, as the night approacheth, take boat and return to your vessels, that we may profit by the breeze."

When Columbus was again alone with Luis, he sat in his little cabin, with a hand supporting his head, musing like one lost in reflection.

"Thou hast long known this Martin Alonzo, Don Luis de Bobadilla?" he at length asked, betraying the current of his thoughts, by the nature of the question.

"Long, Señor, as youths count time; though it would seem but a day in the calculations of aged men."

"Much dependeth on him; I hope he may prove honest; as yet he hath shown himself liberal, enterprising, and manly."

"He is human, Don Christopher, and therefore liable to err. Yet as men go, I esteem Martin Alonzo far from being among the worst of his race. He hath not embarked in this enterprise under knightly vows, nor with any churchman's zeal; but give him the chance of a fair return for his risks, and you will find him as true as interest ever leaveth a man, when there is any occasion to try his selfishness."

"Then thou, only, will I trust with my secret. Look at this paper, Luis. Here thou seest that I have been calculating our progress since morning, and I find that we have come full nineteen leagues, though it be not in a direct westerly line. Should I let the people know how far we may have truly come, at the end of some great distance, there being no land visible, fear will get the mastery over them, and no man can foresee the consequences. I shall write down publicly, therefore, but fifteen leagues, keeping the true reckoning sacred for thine eye and mine. God will forgive me this deception, in consideration that it is practised in the interest of his own church. By making these small deductions daily, it will enable us to advance a thousand leagues, without awakening alarm sufficient for more than seven or eight hundred."

"This is reducing courage to a scale I little dreamt of, Señor," returned Luis, laughing. "By San Luis, my true patron! we should think ill of the knight who found it necessary to uphold his heart by a measurement of leagues."

"All unknown evils are dreaded evils. Distance hath its terrors for the ignorant, and it may justly have its terrors for the wise, young noble, when it is measured on a trackless ocean; and there ariseth another question touching those great staples of life, food and water."

With this slight reproof of the levity of his young friend, the admiral prepared himself for his hammock by kneeling and repeating the prayers of the hour.

CHAPTER XVII

"Whither, 'midst falling dew,
While glow the heavens with the last steps of day,
Far, through their rosy depths, dost thou pursue
Thy solitary way?"

Bryant.

The slumbers of Columbus were of short duration. While his sleep lasted it was profound, like that of a man who has so much control over his will as to have reduced the animal functions to its domination, for he awoke regularly at short intervals, in order that his watchful eye might take a survey of the state of the weather, and of the condition of his vessels. On this occasion, the admiral was on deck again, a little after one, where he found all things seemingly in that quiet and inspiring calm that ordinarily marks, in fine weather, a middle watch at sea. The men on deck mostly slumbered; the drowsy pilot, and the steersman, with a look-out or two, alone remaining erect and awake. The wind had freshened, and the caravel was ploughing her way ahead, with an untiring industry, leaving Ferro and its dangers, at each instant, more and more remote. The only noises that were audible, were the gentle sighing of the wind among the cordage, the wash of the water, and the occasional creaking of a yard, as the breeze forced it, with a firmer pressure, to distend its tackle and to strain its fittings.

The night was dark, and it required a moment to accustom the eye to objects by a light so feeble: when this was done, however, the admiral discovered that the ship was not close by the wind, as he had ordered that she should be kept. Walking to the helm, he perceived that it was so far borne up, as to cause her head to fall off toward the north-east, which was, in fact, in the direction to Spain.

"Art thou a seaman, and disregardest thy course, in this heedless manner?" sternly demanded the admiral; "or art thou only a muleteer, who fancieth he is merely winding his way along a path of the mountains. Thy heart is in Spain, and thou thinkest that a vain wish to return may meet with some relief in this idle artifice!"

"Alas, Señor Almirante! your Excellency hath judged rightly in believing that my heart is in Spain, where it ought to be, moreover, as I have left behind me at Moguer seven motherless children."

"Dost thou not know, fellow, that I, too, am a father, and that the dearest objects of a father's hopes are left behind me, also? In what, then, dost thou differ from me, my son being also without a mother's care?"

"Excellency, he hath an admiral for a father, while my boys have only a helmsman!"

"And what will it matter to Don Diego"—Columbus was fond of dwelling on the honors he had received from the sovereigns, even though it were a little irregularly—"what will it matter to Don Diego, my son, that his parent perished an admiral, if he perish at all; and in what will he profit more than your children, when he findeth himself altogether without a parent?"

"Señor, it will profit him to be cherished by the king and queen, to be honored as your child, and to be fostered and fed as the offspring of a viceroy, instead of being cast aside as the issue of a nameless mariner."

"Friend, thou hast some reason in this, and in-so-much I respect thy feelings," answered Columbus, who, like our own Washington, appears to have always submitted to a lofty and pure sense of justice; "but thou wouldst do well to remember the influence that thy manly and successful perseverance in this voyage may produce on the welfare of thy children, instead of thus dwelling on weak forebodings of ills that are little likely to come to pass. Neither of us hath much to expect, should we fail of our discoveries, while both may hope every thing should we succeed. Can I trust thee now, to keep the ship on her course, or must I send for another mariner to relieve the helm?"

"It may be better, noble admiral, to do the last. I will bethink me of thy counsel, and strive with my longings for home; but it would be safer to seek another for this day, while we are so near to Spain."

"Dost thou know one Sancho Mundo, a common seaman of this crew?"

"Señor, we all know him; he hath the name of the most skilful of our craft, of all in Moguer."

"Is he of thy watch, or sleepeth he with his fellows of the relief below?"

"Señor, he is of our watch; and sleepeth not with his fellows below, for the reason that he sleepeth on deck. No care, or danger, can unsettle the confidence of Sancho! To him the sight of land is so far an evil, that I doubt if he rejoice should we ever reach those distant countries that your Excellency seemeth to expect we may."

"Go find this Sancho, and bid him come hither; I will discharge thy office the while."

Columbus now took the helm with his own hands, and with a light play of the tiller brought the ship immediately up as near the wind as she would lie. The effect was felt in more quick and sudden plunges into the sea, a deeper heel to leeward, and a fresh creaking aloft, that denoted a renewed and increased strain on all the spars and their tackle. In the course of a few minutes, however, Sancho appeared, rubbing his eyes, and yawning.

"Take thou this duty," said the admiral, as soon as the man was near him, "and discharge it faithfully. Those who have been here already, have proved unfaithful, suffering the vessel to fall off, in the direction of Spain; I expect better things of thee. I think, friend Sancho, I may count on thee as a true and faithful follower, even in extremity?"

"Señor Don Almirante," said Sancho, who took the helm, giving it a little play to feel his command of it, as a skilful coachman brings his team in subjection on first assuming the reins, "I am a servant of the crown's, and your inferior and subordinate; such duty as becometh me, I am ready to discharge."

"Thou hast no fear of this voyage—no childish forebodings of becoming an endless wanderer in an unknown sea, without hope of ever seeing wife or child again?"

"Señor, you seem to know our hearts as well as if your Excellency had made them with your own hands, and then put them into our miserable bodies!"

"Thou hast, then, none of these unsuitable and unseamanlike apprehensions?"

"Not as much, Excellency, as would raise an ave in a parish priest, or a sigh in an old woman. I may have my misgivings, for we all have weaknesses, but none of them incline to any dread of sailing about the ocean, since that is my happiness; nor to any concern about wife and children, not having the first, and wishing not to think I have the last."

"If thou hast misgivings, name them. I could wish to make one firm as thou, wholly my friend."

"I doubt not, Señor, that we shall reach Cathay, or whatever country your Excellency may choose to seek; I make no question of your ability to beard the Great Khan, and, at need, to strip the very jewels from his turban—

as turban he must have, being an Infidel; nor do I feel any misgivings about the magnitude and richness of our discoveries and freights, since I believe, Señor Don Almirante, you are skilful enough to take the caravels in at one end of the earth and out at the other; or, even to load them with carbuncles, should diamonds be wanting."

"If thou hast this faith in thy leader, what other distrust can give thee concern?"

"I distrust the value of the share, whether of honor or of jewels, that will fall to the lot of one Sancho Mundo, a poor, unknown, almost shirtless mariner, that hath more need of both than hath ever crossed the mind of our gracious lady, Doña Isabella, or of her royal consort."

"Sancho, thou art a proof that no man is without his failings, and I fear thou art mercenary. They say all men have their prices; thou seemest clearly to have thine."

"Your Excellency hath not been sailing about the world for nothing, or you could not tell every man his inclinations so easily. I have ever suspected I was mercenary, and so have accepted all sorts of presents to keep the feeling down. Nothing appeases a mercenary longing like gifts and rewards; and as for price, I strive hard to keep mine as high as possible, lest it should bring me into discredit for a mean and grovelling spirit. Give me a high price, and plenty of gifts, and I can be as disinterested as a mendicant friar."

"I understand thee, Sancho; thou art to be bought, but not to be frightened. In thy opinion a single dobla is too little to be divided between thee and thy friend, the Portuguese. I will make a league with thee on thine own terms; here is another piece of gold; see that thou remainest true to me throughout the voyage."

"Count on me, without scruple, Señor Don Almirante, and with scruples, too, should they interfere. Your Excellency hath not a more disinterested friend in the fleet. I only hope that when the share-list shall be written out, the name of Sancho Mundo may have an honorable place, as will become his fidelity. And now, your Excellency, go sleep in peace; the Santa Maria shall lie as near to the route to Cathay, as this south-westerly breeze will suffer."

Columbus complied, though he rose once or twice more, during the night, to ascertain the state of the weather, and that the men did their duties. So long as Sancho remained at the helm, he continued faithful to his compact; but, as he went below with his watch, at the usual hour, successors were put in his place, who betrayed the original treachery of the other helmsman. When Luis left his hammock, Columbus was already at work, ascertaining the distance that had been run in the course of the night. Catching the inquiring glance of the young man, the admiral observed, gravely, and not altogether without melancholy in his manner—

"We have had a good run, though it hath been more northerly than I could have desired. I find that the vessels are thirty leagues further from Ferro than when the sun set, and thou seest, here, that I have written four-and-twenty in the reckoning, that is intended for the eyes of the people. But there hath been great weakness at work this night among the steersmen, if not treachery: they have kept the ship away in a manner to cause her to run a part of the time in a direction nearly parallel to the coast of Europe, so that they have been endeavoring to deceive me, on the deck, while I have thought it necessary to attempt deceiving them in the cabin. It is painful, Don Luis, to find such deceptions resorted to, or such deceptions necessary, when one is engaged in an enterprise that surpasseth all others ever yet attempted by man, and that, too, with a view to the glory of God, the advantage of the human race, and the especial interests of Spain."

"The holy churchmen, themselves, Don Christopher, are obliged to submit to this evil," answered the careless Luis; "and it does not become us laymen to repine at what they endure. I am told that half the miracles they perform are, in truth, miracles of but a very indifferent quality; the doubts and want of faith of us hardened sinners rendering such little inventions necessary for the good of our souls."

"That there are false-minded and treacherous churchmen, as well as false-minded and treacherous laymen, Luis, I little doubt," answered the admiral; "but this cometh of the fall of man, and of his evil nature. There are also righteous and true miracles, that come of the power of God, and which are intended to uphold the faith, and to encourage those who love and honor his holy name. I do not esteem any thing that hath yet befallen us to belong very distinctly to this class; nor do I venture to hope that we are to be favored in this manner by an especial intervention in our behalf; but it exceedeth all the machinations of the devils to persuade me that we shall be deserted while bent on so glorious a design, or that we are not, indirectly and secretly, led, in our voyage, by a spirit and knowledge that both come of Divine grace and infinite wisdom."

"This may be so, Don Christopher, so far as you are concerned; though, for myself, I claim no higher a guide than an angel. An angel's purity, and, I hope I may add, an angel's love, lead me, in my blind path across the ocean!"

"So it seemeth to thee, Luis; but thou canst not know that a higher power doth not use the Doña Mercedes as an instrument in this matter.

Although no miracle rendereth it apparent to the vulgar, a spirit is placed in my breast, in conducting this enterprise, that I should deem it blasphemy to resist. God be praised, my boy, we are at last quit of the Portuguese, and are fairly on our road! At present all our obstacles must arise from the elements, or from our own fears. It gladdeneth my heart to find that the two Pinzons remain true, and that they keep their caravels close to the Santa Maria, like men bent on maintaining their faith, and seeing an end of the adventure."

As Luis was now ready, he and the admiral left the cabin together. The sun had risen, and the broad expanse of the ocean was glittering with his rays. The wind had freshened, and was gradually getting further to the south, so that the vessels headed up nearly to their course; and, there being but little sea, the progress of the fleet was, in proportion, considerable. Every thing appeared propitious; and the first burst of grief, on losing sight of known land, having subsided, the crews were more tranquil, though dread of the future was smothered, like the latent fires of a volcano, rather than extinguished. The aspect of the sea was favorable, offering nothing to view that was unusual to mariners; and, as there is always something grateful in a lively breeze, when unaccompanied with danger, the men were probably encouraged by a state of things to which they were accustomed, and which brought with it cheerfulness and hope. In the course of the day and night, the vessels ran a hundred and eighty miles still further into the trackless waste of the ocean, without awakening half the apprehensions in the bosoms of the mariners that they had experienced on losing sight of land. Columbus, however, acting on the cautious principle he had adopted, when he laid before his people the result of the twenty-four hours' work, reduced the distance to about one hundred and fifty.

Tuesday, the 10th of September, brought a still more favorable change of wind. This day, for the first time since quitting the Canaries, the heads of the vessels were laid fairly to the west; and, with the old world directly behind them, and the unknown ocean in their front, the adventurers proceeded onward with a breeze at south-east. The rate of sailing was about five miles in the hour; compensating for the want of speed, by the steadiness of their progress, and by the directness of their course.

The observations that are usually made at sea, when the sun is in the zenith, were over, and Columbus had just announced to his anxious companions that the vessels were gradually setting south, owing to the drift of some invisible current. when a cry from the mast-head announced the proximity of a whale. As the appearance of one of these monsters of the deep breaks the monotony of a sea life, every one was instantly on the look-out, some leaping into the rigging and others upon the rails, in order to catch a glimpse of his gambols.

"Dost thou see him, Sancho?" demanded the admiral of Mundo, the latter being near him at the moment. "To me the water hath no appearance of any such animals being at hand."

"Your Excellency's eye, Señor Don Almirante, is far truer than that of the babbler's aloft. Sure as this is the Atlantic, and yonder is the foam of the crests of the waves, there is no whale."

"The flukes!—the flukes!" shouted a dozen voices at once, pointing to a spot where a dark object arose above the froth of the sea, showing a pointed summit, with short arms extended on each side. "He playeth with his head beneath the water, and the tail uppermost!"

"Alas!—alas!" exclaimed the practised Sancho, with the melancholy of a true seaman, "what these inexperienced and hasty brawlers call the fluke of a whale, is naught but the mast of some unhappy ship, that hath left her bones, with her freight and her people, in the depths of the ocean!"

"Thou art right, Sancho," returned the admiral. "I now see that thou meanest: it is truly a spar, and doubtless betokeneth a shipwreck."

This fact passed swiftly from mouth to mouth, and the sadness that ever accompanies the evidences of such a disaster, settled on the faces of all the beholders. The pilots alone showed indifference, and they consulted on the expediency of endeavoring to secure the spar, as a resource in time of need; but they abandoned the attempt on acccount of the agitation of the water, and of the fairness of the wind, the latter being an advantage a true mariner seldom likes to lose.

"There is a warning to us!" exclaimed one of the disaffected, as the Santa Maria sailed past the waving summit of the spar; "God hath sent this sign to warn us not to venture where he never intended navigators to go!"

"Say, rather," put in Sancho, who, having taken the fee, had ever since proved a willing advocate, "it is an omen of encouragement sent from heaven. Dost thou not see that the part of the mast that is visible resembleth a cross, which holy sign is intended to lead us on, filled with hopes of success?"

"This is true, Sancho," interrupted Columbus. "A cross hath been reared for our edification, as it might be, in the midst of the ocean, and we are to regard it as a proof that Providence is with us, in our attempt to carry its blessings to the aid and consolation of the heathen of Asia."

As the resemblance to the holy symbol was far from fanciful, this happy hit of Sancho's was not without its effect. The reader will understand the likeness all the better, when he is told that the upper end of a mast has much the appearance of a cross, by means of the trussel-trees; and, as often happens, this particular spar was floating nearly perpendicular, owing to some heavy object being fast to its heel, leaving the summit raised some fifteen or twenty feet above the surface of the sea. In a quarter of an hour this last relic of Europe and of civilization disappeared in the wake of the vessels, gradually diminishing in size and settling toward the water, until its faint outlines vanished in threads, still wearing the well-known shape of the revered symbol of Christianity.

After this little incident, the progress of the vessels was uninterrupted by any event worthy of notice for two days and nights. All this time the wind was favorable, and the adventurers proceeded due west, by compass, which was, in fact, however, going a little north of the real point—a truth that the knowledge of the period had not yet mastered. Between the morning of the 10th September, and the evening of the 13th, the fleet had passed over near ninety leagues of ocean, holding its way in a line but a little deviating from a direct one athwart the great waste of water, and having consequently reached a point as far, if not further west than the position of the Azores, then the most westerly land known to European navigators. On the 13th, the currents proved to be adverse, and, having a south-easterly set, they had a tendency to cause the ships to sheer southwardly, bringing them, each hour, nearer to the northern margin of the trades

The admiral and Luis were at their customary post, on the evening of the 13th—the day last mentioned—as Sancho left the helm, his tour of duty having just ended. Instead of going forward, as usual, among the people, the fellow hesitated, surveyed the poop with a longing eye, and, finding it occupied only by the admiral and his constant companion, he ascended the ladder, as if desirous of making some communication.

"Wouldst thou aught with me, Sancho?" demanded the admiral, waiting for the man to make certain that no one else was on the narrow deck. "Speak freely: thou hast my confidence."

"Señor Don Almirante, your Excellency well knoweth that I am no fresh-water fish, to be frightened at the sight of a shark or a whale, or one that is terrified because a ship headeth west, instead of east; and yet I do come to say that this voyage is not altogether without certain signs and marvels, that it may be well for a mariner to respect, as unusual, if not ominous."

"As thou sayest, Sancho, thou art no driveller to be terrified by the flight of a bird, or at the presage of a drifting spar, and thou awakenest my curiosity to know more The Señor de Muños is my confidential secretary, and nothing need be hid from him. Speak freely, then, and without further delay. If gold is thy aim be certain thou shalt have it."

"No, Señor, my news is not worth a maravedi, or it is far beyond the price of gold; such as it is, your Excellency can take it, and think no more of my reward. You know, Señor, that we old mariners will have our thoughts as we stand at the helm, sometimes fancying the smiles and good looks of some hussy ashore, sometimes remembering the flavor of rich fruits and well-savored mutton; and then, again, for a wonder, bethinking us of our sins."

"Fellow, all this I well know; but it is not matter for an admiral's ear."

"I know not that, Señor; I have known admirals who have relished mutton after a long cruise; ay, and who have bethought them, too, of smiling faces and bright eyes, and who, if they did not, at times, bethink them of their sins, have done what was much worse, help to add to the great account that was heaping up against them. Now, there was" —

"Let me toss this vagabond into the sea, at once, Don Christopher," interrupted the impatient Luis, making a forward movement as if to execute the threat, an act which the hand of Columbus arrested; "we shall never hear a tale the right end first, as long as he remaineth in the ship."

"I thank you, my young Lord of Llera," answered Sancho, with an ironical smile; "if you are as ready at drowning seamen, as you are at unhorsing Christian knights in the tourney, and Infidels in the fray, I would rather that another should be master of my baths."

"Thou know'st me, knave? Thou hast seen me on some earlier voyage."

"A cat may look at a king, Señor Conde; and why not a mariner on his passenger? But spare your threats, and your secret is in safe hands. If we reach Cathay, no one will be ashamed of having made the voyage; and if we miss it, it is little likely that any will go back to relate the precise manner in which your Excellency was drowned, or starved to death, or in what other manner you became a saint in Abraham's bosom."

"Enough of this!" said Columbus, sternly; "relate what thou hast to say, and see that thou art discreet touching this young noble."

"Señor, your word is law. Well, Don Christopher, it is one of the tricks of us mariners, at night, to be watching an old and constant friend, the north star; and while thus occupied an hour since, I noted that this faithful guide and the compass by which I was steering, told different tales."

"Art certain of this?" demanded the admiral, with a quickness and emphasis that betrayed the interest he felt in the communication.

"As certain, Señor, as fifty years' looking at the star, and forty years' watching of the compass can make a man. But there is no occasion, your

Excellency, to depend on my ignorance, since the star is still where God placed it; and there is your private compass at your elbow—one may be compared with the other."

Columbus had already bethought him of making this comparison; and by the time Sancho ceased speaking, he and Luis were examining the instrument with eager curiosity. The first, and the most natural, impression, was a belief that the needle of the instrument below was defective, or, at least, influenced by some foreign cause; but an attentive observation soon convinced the navigator that the remark of Sancho was true. He was both astonished and concerned to find that the habitual care, and professional eye of the fellow had been active, and quick to note a change as unusual as this. It was, indeed, so common with mariners to compare their compasses with the north star—a luminary that was supposed never to vary its position in the heavens, as that position related to man—that no experienced seaman, who happened to be at the helm at nightfall, could well overlook the phenomenon.

After repeated observations with his own compasses, of which he kept two—one on the poop, and another in the cabin, and having recourse also to the two instruments in the binnacle, Columbus was compelled to admit to himself that all four varied, alike, from their usual direction, nearly six degrees. Instead of pointing due north, or, at least, in a direct line toward a point on the horizon immediately beneath the star, they pointed some five or six degrees to the westward of it. This was both a novel and an astounding departure from the laws of nature, as they were then understood, and threatened to render the desired results of the voyage so much the more difficult of attainment, as it at once deprived the adventurers of a sure reliance on the mariner's principal guide, and would render it difficult to sail, with any feeling of certainty as to the course, in cloudy weather, or dark nights. The first thought of the admiral, on this occasion, however, was to prevent the effect which such a discovery would be likely to produce on men already disposed to anticipate the worst.

"Thou wilt say nothing of this, Sancho?" he observed to the man. "Here is another dobla to add to thy store."

"Excellency, pardon a humble seaman's disobedience, if my hand refuse to open to your gift. This matter toucheth of supernatural means; and, as the devil may have an agency in the miracle, in order to prevent our converting them heathen, of whom you so often speak, I prefer to keep my soul as pure as may be, in the matter, since no one knoweth what weapons we may be driven to use, should we come to real blows with the Father of Sin."

"Thou wilt, at least, prove discreet?"

"Trust me for that, Señor Don Almirante; not a word shall pass my lips about this matter, until I have your Excellency's permission to speak."

Columbus dismissed the man, and then he turned toward Luis, who had been a silent but attentive listener to what had passed.

"You seem disturbed at this departure from the usual laws of the compass, Don Christopher," observed the young man, gaily. "To me it would seem better to rely altogether on Providence, which would scarcely lead us out here, into the wide Atlantic, on its own errand, and desert us when we most need its aid."

"God implants in the bosom of his servants a desire to advance his ends, but human agents are compelled to employ natural means, and, in order to use such means advantageously, it is necessary to understand them. I look upon this phenomenon as a proof that our voyage is to result in discoveries of unknown magnitude, among which, perhaps, are to be numbered some clue to the mysteries of the needle. The mineral riches of Spain differ, in certain particulars, from the mineral riches of France; for, though some things are common to all lands, others are peculiar to particular countries. We may find regions where the loadstone abounds, or may, even now, be in the neighborhood of some island that hath an influence on our compasses that we cannot explain."

"Is it known that islands have ever produced this effect on the needle?"

"It is not—nor do I deem such a circumstance very probable, though all things are possible. We will wait patiently for further proofs that this phenomenon is real and permanent, ere we reason further on a matter that is so difficult to be understood."

The subject was now dropped, though the unusual incident gave the great navigator an uneasy and thoughtful night. He slept little, and often was his eye fastened on the compass that was suspended in his cabin as a "tell-tale," for so seamen term the instrument by which the officer overlooks the course that is steered by the helmsman, even when the latter least suspects his supervision. Columbus arose sufficiently early to get a view of the star before its brightness was dimmed by the return of light, and made another deliberate comparison of the position of this familiar heavenly body with the direction of the needles. The examination proved a slight increase of the variation, and tended to corroborate the observations of the previous night. The result of the reckoning showed that the vessels had run nearly a hundred miles in the course of the last twenty-four hours, and Columbus now believed himself to be about six times that distance west of Ferro, though even the pilots fancied themselves by no means as far.

As Sancho kept his secret, and no other eye among the helmsmen was as vigilant, the important circumstance, as yet, escaped general attention. It was only at night, indeed, that the variation could be observed by means of the polar star, and it was yet so slight that no one but a very experienced and quick-eyed mariner would be apt to note it. The whole of the day and night of the 14th consequently passed without the crew's taking the alarm, and this so much the more as the wind had fallen, and the vessels were only some sixty miles further west than when they commenced. Still, Columbus noted the difference, slight as was the change, ascertaining, with the precision of an experienced and able navigator, that the needle was gradually varying more and more to the westward, though it was by steps that were nearly imperceptible.

CHAPTER XVIII

"On thy unaltering blaze
The half-wrecked mariner, his compass lost,
Fixes his steady gaze,
And steers, undoubting, to the friendly coast;
And they who stray in perilous wastes, by night,
Are glad when thou dost shine to guide their footsteps
right."

Hymn to the North Star.

The following day was Saturday, the 15th, when the little fleet was ten days from Gomera; or it was the sixth morning since the adventurers had lost sight of the land. The last week had been one of melancholy forebodings, though habit was beginning to assert its influence, and the men manifested openly less uneasiness than they had done in the three or four previous days. Their apprehensions were getting to be dormant for want of any exciting and apparent stimulus, though they existed as latent impulses, in readiness to be roused at the occurrence of any untoward event. The wind continued fair, though light—the whole twenty-four hours' work showing considerably less than a hundred miles, as the true progress west. All this time Columbus kept his attention fastened on the needles, and he perceived that as the vessels slowly made their westing, the magnets pointed more and more, though by scarcely palpable changes, in the same direction.

The admiral and Luis, by this time, had fallen into such habits of close communication, that they usually rose and slept at the same time. Though far too ignorant of the hazards he ran to feel uneasiness, and constitutionally, as well as morally, superior to idle alarms, the young man had got to feel a sort of sportsman's excitement in the result; and, by this time, had not Mercedes existed, he would have been as reluctant to return without seeing Cathay, as Columbus himself. They conversed together of their progress and their hopes, without ceasing, and Luis took so much interest in his situation as to begin to learn how to discriminate in matters that might be supposed to affect its duration and ends.

On the night of the Saturday just mentioned, Columbus and his reputed secretary were alone on the poop, conversing, as usual, on the signs of the times, and of the events of the day.

"The Niña had something to say to you, last evening, Don Christopher," observed the young man; "I was occupied in the cabin, with my journal, and had no opportunity of knowing what passed."

"Her people had seen a bird or two, that are thought never to go far from the land. It is possible that islands are at no great distance, for man hath nowhere passed over any very great extent of sea without meeting with them. We cannot, however, waste the time necessary for a search, since the glory and profit of ascertaining the situation of a group of islands would be but a poor compensation for the loss of a continent."

"Do you still remark those unaccountable changes in the needles, Señor?"

"In this respect there is no change, except that which goeth to corroborate the phenomenon. My chief apprehension is of the effect on the people, when the circumstance shall be known."

"Are there no means to persuade them that the needle pointeth thus west, as a sign Providence willeth they should pursue that course, by persevering in the voyage?"

"This might do, Luis," answered the admiral, smiling, "had not fear so sharpened their wits, that their first question would be an inquiry why Providence should deprive us of the means of knowing whither we are travelling, when it so much wisheth us to go in any particular direction."

A cry from the watch on deck arrested the discourse, while a sudden brightness broke on the night, illuminating the vessels and the ocean, as if a thousand lamps were shedding their brilliancy upon the surrounding portion of the sphere. A ball of fire was glancing athwart the heavens, and seemed to fall into the sea, at the distance of a few leagues, or at the limits of the visible horizon. Its disappearance was followed by a gloom as profound as the extraordinary and fleeting light had been brilliant. This was only the passage of a meteor; but it was such a meteor as men do not see more than once in their lives—if it is seen as often; and the superstitious mariners did not fail to note the incident among the extraordinary omens that accompanied the voyage; some auguring good, and others evil, from the event.

"By St. Iago!" exclaimed Luis, as soon as the light had vanished, "Señor Don Christopher, this voyage of ours doth not seem fated to pass away unheeded by the elements and other notable powers! Whether these portents speak in our favor, or not, they speak us any thing but men engaged in an every-day occupation."

"Thus it is with the human mind!" returned Columbus. "Let but its owner pass beyond the limits of his ordinary habits and duties, and he sees marvels in the most simple changes of the weather—in a flash of lightning—a blast of air—or the passage of a meteor; little heeding that these miracles exist in his own consciousness, and have no connection with the every-day laws of nature. These sights are by no means uncommon, especially in low latitudes; and they augur neither for nor against our enterprise."

"Except, Señor Almirante, as they may beset the spirits and haunt the imaginations of the men. Sancho telleth me, that a brooding discontent is growing among them; and that, while they seem so tranquil, their disrelish of the voyage is hourly getting to be more and more decided."

Notwithstanding this opinion of the admiral, and some pains that he afterward took to explain the phenomenon to the people on deck, the passage of the meteor had, indeed, not only produced a deep impression on them, but its history went from watch to watch, and was the subject of earnest discourse throughout the night. But the incident produced no open manifestation of discontent; a few deeming it a propitious omen, though most secretly considered it an admonition from heaven against any impious attempts to pry into those mysteries of nature that, according to their notions, God, in his providence, had not seen fit to reveal to man.

All this time the vessels were making a steady progress toward the west. The wind had often varied, both in force and direction, but never in a manner to compel the ships to shorten sail, or to deviate from what the admiral believed to be the proper course. They supposed themselves to be steering due west, but, owing to the variation, were in fact now holding a west-and-by-south course, and were gradually getting nearer to the trades; a movement in which they had also been materially aided by the force of the currents. In the course of the 15th and 16th of the month, the fleet had got about two hundred miles further from Europe, Columbus taking the usual precaution to lessen the distance in the public reckoning. The latter day was a Sunday; and the religious offices, which were then seldom neglected in a Christian ship, produced a deep and sublime effect on the feelings of the adventurers. Hitherto the weather had partaken of the usual character of the season, and a few clouds, with a slight drizzling rain, had relieved the heat; but these soon passed away, and were succeeded by a soft south-east wind, that seemed to come charged with the fragrance of the land. The men united in the evening chants, under these propitious circumstances; the vessels drawing near each other, as if it might be to form one temple in honor of God, amid the vast solitudes of an ocean that had seldom, if ever, been whitened by a sail. Cheerfulness and hope succeeded to this act of devotion, and both were speedily heightened by a cry from the look-out aloft, who pointed ahead and to leeward, as if he beheld some object of peculiar interest in that quarter. The helms were varied a little; and in a few minutes the vessels entered into a field of sea-weed, that covered the ocean for miles. This sign of the vicinity of land was received by the mariners with a shout; and the very beings who had so shortly before been balancing on the verge of despair, now became elate with joy.

These weeds were indeed of a character to awaken hope in the bosom of the most experienced mariner. Although some had lost their freshness, a great proportion of them were still green, and had the appearance of having been quite recently separated from their parent rocks, or the earth that had nourished them. No doubt was now entertained, even by the pilots, of the vicinity of land. Tunny-fish were also seen in numbers, and the people of the Niña were sufficiently fortunate to strike one. The seamen embraced each other, with tears in their eyes, and many a hand was squeezed in friendly congratulation, that the previous day would have been withheld in surly misanthropy.

"And do you partake of all this hope, Don Christopher?" demanded Luis; "are we really to expect the Indies as a consequence of these marine plants, or is the expectation idle?"

"The people deceive themselves in supposing our voyage near an end. Cathay must yet be very distant from us. We have come but three hundred and sixty leagues since losing sight of Ferro, which, according to my computations, cannot be much more than a third of our journey. Aristotle mentioned that certain vessels of Cadiz were forced westward by heavy gales, until they reached a sea covered with weeds, a spot where the tunny-fish abounded. This is the fish, thou must know, Luis, that the ancients fancied could see better with the right eye than with the left, because it hath been noted that, in passing the Bosphorus, they ever take the right shore in proceeding toward the Euxine, and the left in returning" —

"By St. Francis! there can be no wonder if creatures so one-sided in their vision, should have strayed thus far from home," interrupted the light-hearted Luis, laughing. "Doth Aristotle, or the other ancients, tell us how they regarded beauty; or whether their notions of justice were like those of the magistrate who hath been fed by both parties?"

"Aristotle speaketh only of the presence of the fish in the weedy ocean, as we see them before us. The mariners of Cadiz fancied themselves in the neighborhood of sunken islands, and, the wind permitting, made the best of their way back to their own shores. Thia place, in my judgment, we have now reached; but I expect to meet with no land, unless, indeed, we may happen to fall in with some island that lieth off here in the ocean, as a sort of beacon between the shore of Europe and that of Asia. Doubtless land is not distant, whence these weeds have drifted, but I attach little importance to its sight, or discovery. Cathay is my aim, Don Luis, and I am a searcher for continents, not islands."

It is now known that while Columbus was right in his expectations of not finding a continent so early, he was mistaken in supposing land to lie any where in that vicinity. Whether these weeds are collected by the course of the currents, or whether they rise from the bottom, torn from their beds by the action of the water, is not yet absolutely ascertained, though the latter is the most common opinion, extensive shoals existing in this quarter of the ocean. Under the latter supposition, the mariners of Cadiz were nearer the truth than is first apparent, a sunken island having all the characteristics of a shoal, but those which may be supposed to be connected with the mode of formation.

No land was seen. The vessels continued their progress at a rate but little varying from five miles the hour, shoving aside the weeds, which at times accumulated in masses, under their bows, but which could offer no serious obstacle to their progress. As for the admiral, so lofty were his views, so steady his opinions concerning the great geographical problem he was about to solve, and so determined his resolution to persevere to the end, that he rather hoped to miss than to fall in with the islands, that he fancied could be at no great distance. The day and night carried the vessels rather more than one hundred miles to the westward, placing the fleet not far from midway between the meridians that bounded the extreme western and eastern margins of the two continents, though still much nearer to Africa than to America, following the parallel of latitude on which it was sailing. As the wind continued steady, and the sea was as smooth as a river, the three vessels kept close together, the Pinta, the swiftest craft, reducing her canvas for that purpose. During the afternoon's watch of the day that succeeded that of the meeting with the weeds, which was Monday, the 17th September, or the eighth day after losing sight of Ferro, Martin Alonzo Pinzon hailed the Santa Maria, and acquainted the pilot on deck of his intention to get the amplitude of the sun, as soon as the luminary should be low enough, with a view to ascertain how far his needles retained their virtue. This observation, one of no unusual occurrence among mariners, it was thought had better be made in all the caravels simultaneously, that any error of one might be corrected by the greater accuracy of the rest.

Columbus and Luis were in a profound sleep in their cots, taking their siestas, when the former was awakened by such a shake of the shoulder as seamen are wont to give, and are content to receive. It never required more than a minute to arouse the great navigator from his deepest slumbers to the fullest possession of his faculties, and he was awake in an instant.

"Señor Dor Almirante," said Sancho, who was the intruder, "it is time to be stirring: all the pilots are on deck in readiness to measure the amplitude of the sun, as soon as the heavenly bodies are in their right places. The west is already beginning to look like a dying dolphin, and ere many minutes it will be gilded like the helmet of a Moorish Sultan."

"An amplitude measured!" exclaimed Columbus, quitting his cot on the instant. "This is news, indeed! Now we may look for such a stir among the people, as hath not been witnessed since we left Cadiz!"

"So it hath appeared to me, your Excellency, for the mariner hath some such faith in the needle as the churchman bestoweth on the goodness of the Son of God. The people are in a happy humor at this moment, but the saints only know what is to come!"

The admiral awoke Luis, and in five minutes both were at their customary station on the poop. Columbus had gained so high a reputation for skill in navigation, his judgment invariably proving right, even when opposed to those of all the pilots in the fleet, that the latter were not sorry to perceive he had no intention to take an instrument in hand, but seemed disposed to leave the issue to their own skill and practice. The sun slowly settled, the proper time was watched, and then these rude mariners set about their task, in the mode that was practised in their time. Martin Alonzo Pinzon, the most ready and best taught of them all, was soonest through with his task. From his lofty stand, the admiral could overlook the deck of the Pinta, which vessel was sailing but a few hundred yards from the Santa Maria, and it was not long before he observed her commander moving from one compass to another, in the manner of a man who was disturbed. Another minute or two elapsed, when the skiff of the caravel was launched; a sign was made for the admiral's vessel to shorten sail, and Martin Alonzo was soon forcing his way through the weeds that still covered the surface of the ocean, toward the Santa Maria. As he gained the deck of the latter ship, on one of her sides, his kinsman, Vicente Yañez, the commander of the Niña, did the same thing on the other. In the next instant both were at the side of the great navigator, on the poop, whither they had been followed by Sancho Ruiz and Bartolemeo Roldan, the two pilots of the admiral.

"What meaneth this haste, good Martin Alonzo?" calmly asked Columbus: "thou and thy brother, Vicente Yañez, and these honest pilots, hurry toward me as if ye had cheering tidings from Cathay."

"God only knoweth, Señor Almirante, if any of us are ever to be permitted to see that distant land, or any shore that is only to be reached by mariners through the aid of a needle," answered the elder Pinzon, with a haste that almost rendered him breathless. "Here have we all been at the comparison of the instruments, and we find them, without a single exception, varying from the true north, by, at least, a full point!"

"That would be a marvel, truly! Ye have made some oversight in your observations, or have been heedless in the estimates."

"Not so, noble admiral," put in Vicente Yañez, to sustain his brother. "Even the magnets are becoming false to us; and as I mentioned the circumstance to the oldest steersman of my craft, he assures me that the north star did not tally with his instrument throughout the night!"

"Others say the same, here," added Ruiz—"nay, some are ready to swear that the wonder hath been noted ever since we entered the sea of weeds!"

"This may be so, Señores," answered Columbus, with an undisturbed mien, "and yet no evil follow. We all know that the heavenly bodies have their revolutions, some of which no doubt are irregular, while others are more in conformity with certain settled rules. Thus it is with the sun himself, which passeth once around the earth in the short space of twenty-four hours, while no doubt he hath other, and more subtle movements, that are unknown to us, on account of the exceeding distance at which he is placed in the heavens. Many astronomers have thought that they have been able to detect these variations, spots having been seen on the disc of the orb at times, which have disappeared, as if hid behind the body of the luminary. I think it will be found that the north star hath made some slight deviation in its position, and that it will continue thus to move for some short period, after which, no doubt, it will be found returning to its customary position, when it will be seen that its temporary eccentricity hath in no manner disturbed its usual harmony with the needles. Note the star well throughout the night, and in the morning let the amplitude be again taken, when I think the truth of my conjecture will be proved by the regularity of the movement of the heavenly body. So far from being discouraged by this sign, we ought rather to rejoice that we have made a discovery, which, of itself, will entitle the expedition to the credit of having added materially to the stores of science!"

The pilots were fain to be satisfied with this solution of their doubts, in the absence of any other means of accounting for them. They remained long on the poop discoursing of the strange occurrence; and as men, even in their blindest moods, usually reason themselves into either tranquillity or apprehension, they fortunately succeeded in doing the first on this occasion. With the men there was more difficulty, for when it became known to the crews of the three vessels that the needles had begun to deviate from their usual direction, a feeling akin to despair seized on them, almost without exception. Here Sancho was of material service. When the panic was at its height, and the people were on the point of presenting themselves to the admiral, with a demand that the heads of the caravels should be immediately turned toward the north-east, he interposed with his knowledge and influence to calm the tumult. The first means this trusty follower had recourse to, in order to bring his shipmates back to reason, was to swear, without reservation, that he had frequently known the needle and the north star to vary, having witnessed the fact with his own eyes on twenty previous occasions, and no harm to come of it. He invited the elder and more experienced seamen to make an accurate observation of the difference which already existed, which was quite a point of the compass, and then to see, in the morning, if this difference had not increased in the same direction.

"This," he continued, "will be a certain sign, my friends, that the star is in motion, since we can all see that the compasses are just where they have been ever since we left Palos de Moguer. When one of two things is in motion, and it is certain which stands still, there can be no great difficulty in saying which is the uneasy one. Now, look thou here, Martin Martinez," who was one of the most factious of the disaffected; "words are of little use when men can prove their meaning by experiments like this. Thou seest two balls of spun-yarn on this windlass; well, it is wanted to be known which of them remains there, and which is taken away. I remove the smallest ball, thou perceivest, and the largest remains; from which it followeth, as only one can remain, and that one is the larger ball, why the smaller must be taken away. I hold no man fit to steer a caravel, by needle or by star, who will deny a thing that is proven as plainly and as simply as this!"

Martin Martinez, though a singularly disaffected man, was no logician; and, Sancho's oaths backing his demonstrations to the letter, his party soon became the most numerous. As there is nothing so encouraging to the dull-minded and discontented mutineer, as to perceive that he is of the strongest side, so is there nothing so discouraging as to find himself in the minority; and Sancho so far prevailed as to bring most his fellows round to a belief in the expediency of waiting to ascertain the state of things in the morning, before they committed themselves by any act of rashness.

"Thou hast done well, Sancho," said Columbus, an hour later, when the mariner came secretly to make his nightly report of the state of feeling among the people. "Thou hast done well in all but these oaths, taken to prove that thou hast witnessed this phenomenon before. Much as I have navigated the earth, and careful as have been my observations, and ample as have been my means, never before have I known the needle to vary from its direction toward the north star: and I think that which hath escaped my notice would not be apt to attract thine."

"You do me injustice, Señor Don Almirante, and have inflicted a wound touching my honesty, that a dobla only can cure" —

"Thou knowest, Sancho, that no one felt more alarm when the deviation of the needle was first noted, than thyself. So great, in sooth, was thy apprehension, that thou even refused to receive gold, a weakness of which thou art usually exceedingly innocent."

"When the deviation was first noted, your Excellency, this was true enough; for, not to attempt to mislead one who hath more penetration than befalleth ordinary men, I did fancy that our hopes of ever seeing Spain or St. Clara de Moguer again, were so trifling as to make it of no great consequence who was admiral, and who a simple helmsman."

"And yet thou wouldst now brazen it out, and deny thy terror! Didst thou not swear to thy fellows, that thou hadst often seen this deviation before; ay, even on as many as twenty occasions?"

"Well, Excellency, this is a proof that a cavalier may make a very capital viceroy and admiral, and know all about Cathay, without having the clearest notions of history! I told my shipmates, Don Christopher, that I had noted these changes before this night, and if tied to the stake to be burnt as a martyr, as I sometimes think will one day be the fate of all of us superfluously honest men, I would call on yourself, Señor Almirante, as the witness of the truth of what I had sworn to."

"Thou wouldst, then, summon a most unfortunate witness, Sancho, since I neither practise false oaths myself, nor encourage their use in others."

"Don Luis de Bobadilla y Pedro de Muños, here, would then be my reliance," said the imperturbable Sancho; "for proof a man hath a right to, when wrongfully accused, and proof I will have. Your Excellency will please to remember that it was on the night of Saturday, the 15th, that I first notified your worship of this very change, and that we are now at the night of Monday, the 17th. I swore to twenty times noting this phenomenon, as it is called, in those eight-and-forty hours, when it would have been nearer the truth had I said two hundred times. Santa Maria! I did nothing but note it for the first few hours!"

"Go to, Sancho; thy conscience hath its latitude as well as its longitude; but thou hast thy uses. Now, that thou understandest the reason of the variation, however, thou wilt encourage thy fellows, as well as keep up thy spirits."

"I make no question that it is all as your Excellency sayeth about the star's travelling," returned Sancho; "and it hath crossed my mind that it is possible we are nearer Cathay than we have thought; this movement being made by some evil-disposed spirits on purpose to make us lose the way."

"Go to thy hammock, knave, and bethink thee of thy sins; leaving the reasons of these mysteries to those who are better taught. There is thy dobla, and see that thou art discreet."

In the morning every being in the three caravels waited impatiently for the results of the new observations. As the wind continued favorable, though far from fresh, and a current was found setting to the westward, the vessels had made, in the course of twenty-four hours, more than a hundred and fifty miles, which rendered the increase in the variation perceptible, thus corroborating a prophecy of Columbus, that had been ventured on previous observation. So easily are the ignorant the dupes of the plausible, that this solution temporarily satisfied all doubts, and it was generally believed that the star had moved, while the needle remained true.

How far Columbus was misled by his own logic in this affair, is still a matter of doubt. That he resorted to deceptions which might be considered innocent, in order to keep up the courage of his companions, is seen in the fact of the false, or public reckoning; but there is no proof that this was one of the instances in which he had recourse to such means. No person of any science believed, even when the variation of the compass was unknown, that the needle pointed necessarily to the polar star; the coincidence in the direction of the magnetic needle and the position of the heavenly body, being thought accidental; and there is nothing extravagant in supposing that the admiral—who had the instrument in his possession, and was able to ascertain that none of its virtue was visibly lost, while he could only reason from supposed analogy concerning the evolutions of the star—should imagine that a friend he had ever found so faithful, had now deserted him, leaving him disposed to throw the whole mystery of the phenomenon on the more distant dwellers in space. Two opinions have been ventured concerning the belief of the celebrated navigator, in the theory he advanced on this occasion; the one affirming, and the other denying his good faith in urging the doctrine he had laid down. Those who assert the latter, however, would seem to reason a little loosely themselves, their argument mainly resting on the improbability of a man like Columbus uttering so gross a scientific error, at a time when science itself knew no more of the existence of the phenomenon, than is known to-day of its cause. Still it is possible that the admiral may not have had any settled notions on the subject, even while he was half inclined to hope his explanation was correct; for it is certain that, in the midst of the astronomical and geographical ignorance of his age, this extraordinary man had many accurate and sublime glimpses of truths that were still in embryo as respected their development and demonstration by the lights of precise and inductive reasoning.

Fortunately, if the light brought with it the means of ascertaining with certainty the variation of the needle, it also brought the means of perceiving that the sea was still covered with weeds, and other signs that were thought to be encouraging, as connected with the vicinity of land. The current being now in the same direction as the wind, the surface of the ocean was literally as smooth as that of an inland sheet of water, and the vessels were enabled to sail, without danger, within a few fathoms of each other.

"This weed, Señor Almirante," called out the elder Pinzon, "hath the appearance of that which groweth on the banks of streams, and I doubt that we are near to the mouth of some exceeding great river!"

"This may be so," returned Columbus; "than which there can be no more certain sign than may be found in the taste of the water. Let a bucket be drawn, that we may know."

While Pepe was busied in executing this order, waiting until the vessel had passed through a large body of weeds for that purpose, the quick eye of the admiral detected a crab struggling on the surface of the fresh-looking plants, and he called to the helmsman in sufficient season, to enable him so far to vary his course, as to allow the animal to be taken.

"Here is a most precious prize, good Martin Alonzo," said Columbus, holding the crab between a finger and thumb, that the other might see it. "These animals are never known to go further than some eighty leagues from the land; and see, Señor, yonder is one of the white tropic birds, which, it is said, never sleep on the water! Truly, God favoreth us; and what rendereth all these tokens more grateful, is the circumstance of their coming from the west—the hidden, unknown, mysterious west!"

A common shout burst from the crews at the appearance of these signs, and again the beings who lately had been on the verge of despair, were buoyed up with hope, and ready to see propitious omens in even the most common occurrences of the ocean. All the vessels had hauled up buckets of water, and fifty mouths were immediately wet with the brine; and so general was the infatuation, that every man declared the sea far less salt than usual. So complete, indeed, was the delusion created by these cheerful expectations, and so thoroughly had all concern in connection with the moving star been removed by the sophism of Sancho, that even Columbus, habitually so wary, so reasoning, so calm, amid his loftiest views, yielded to his native enthusiasm, and fancied that he was about to discover some vast island, placed midway between Asia and Europe; an honor not to be despised, though it fell so far short of his higher expectations.

"Truly, friend Martin Alonzo," he said, "this water seemeth to have less of the savor of the sea, than is customary at a distance from the outlet of large rivers!"

"My palate telleth the same tale, Señor Almirante. As a further sign, the Niña hath struck another tunny, and her people are at this moment hoisting it in."

Shout succeeded shout, as each new encouraging proof appeared; and the admiral, yielding to the ardor of the crews, ordered sail to be pressed on all the vessels, that each might endeavor to outstrip the others, in the hope of being the first to discover the expected island. This strife soon separated the caravels, the Pinta easily outsailing the other two, while the Santa Maria and the Niña came on more slowly, in her rear. All was gaiety and mirth, the livelong day, on board those isolated vessels, that, unknown to those they held, were navigating the middle of the Atlantic, with horizon extending beyond horizon, without change in the watery boundary, as circle would form without circle, on the same element, were a vast mass of solid matter suddenly dropped into the sea.

CHAPTER XIX

"The sails were filled, and fair the light winds blew,
As glad to waft him from his native home;
And fast the white rocks faded from his view,
And soon were lost in circumambient foam:
And then, it may be, of his wish to roam
Repented he, but in his bosom slept
The silent thought, nor from his lips did come
One word of wail, whilst others sate and wept,
And to the reckless gales unmanly moaning kept."

Childe Harold's Pilgrimage.

As night drew near, the Pinta shortened sail, permitting her consorts to close. All eyes now turned anxiously to the west, where it was hoped that land might at any moment appear. The last tint, however, vanished from the horizon, and darkness enveloped the ocean without bringing any material change. The wind still blew a pleasant breeze from the south-east, and the surface of the ocean offered little more inequality than is usually met on the bosoms of large rivers. The compasses showed a slightly increasing deviation from their old coincidence with the polar star, and no one doubted, any longer, that the fault was in the heavenly body. All this time the vessels were getting to the southward, steering, in fact, west and by south, when they thought they were steering west—a circumstance that alone prevented Columbus from first reaching the coast of Georgia, or that of the Carolinas, since, had he missed the Bermudas, the current of the Gulf Stream meeting him on his weather bow, he would have infallibly been set well to the northward, as he neared the continent.

The night passed as usual, and at noon of the 17th, or at the termination of the nautical day, the fleet had left another long track of ocean between it and the old world. The weeds were disappearing, and with them the tunny fish, which were, in truth, feeding on the products of shoals that mounted several thousands of feet nearer to the surface of the water, than was the case with the general bed of the Atlantic. The vessels usually kept near each other at noon, in order to compare their observations; but the Pinta, which, like a swift steed, was with difficulty restrained, shot ahead, until the middle of the afternoon, when, as usual, she lay-by for the admiral to close. As the Santa Maria came sweeping on, the elder Pinzon stood, cap in hand, ready to speak her, waiting only for her to come within sound of his voice.

"God increaseth the signs of land, and the motives of encouragement, Señor Don Christopher," he called out, cheerfully, while the Pinta filled her sails in order to keep way with the admiral. "We have seen large flights of birds ahead, and the clouds at the north look heavy and dense, as if hovering over some island, or continent, in that quarter."

"Thou art a welcome messenger, worthy Martin Alonzo; though I wish thee to remember, that the most I expect to meet with in this longitude is some cluster of pleasant islands, Asia being yet several days' sail more distant. As the night approacheth, thou wilt see thy clouds take still more of the form of the land, and I doubt that groups may be found on each side of us; but our high destination is Cathay, and men with such an object before them, may not turn aside for any lesser errand."

"Have I your leave, noble admiral, to push ahead in the Pinta, that our eyes may first be greeted with the grateful sight of Asia? I nothing doubt of seeing it ere morning."

"Go, of God's sake, good pilot, if thou thinkest this; though I warn thee that no continent can yet meet thine eyes. Nevertheless, as any land in these distant and unknown seas must be a discovery, and bring credit on Castile, as well as on ourselves, he who first perceiveth it will merit the reward. Thou, or any one else, hath my full permission to discover islands, or continents, in thousands."

The people laughed at this sally, for the light-hearted are easily excited to mirth; and then the Pinta shot ahead. As the sun set, she was seen again lying-to for her companions—a dark speck on the rainbow colors of the glorious sky. The horizon at the north presented masses of clouds, in which it was not difficult to fancy the summits of ragged mountains, receding valleys, with headlands, and promontories, foreshortened by distance.

The following day the wind baffled, for the first time since encountering the trades; and the clouds collected over-head, dispersing drizzling showers on the navigators. The vessels now lay near each other, and conversation flew from one to the other—boats passing and repassing, constantly.

"I have come, Señor Almirante," said the elder Pinzon, as he reached the deck of the Santa Maria, "at the united request of my people, to beg that we may steer to the north, in quest of land, islands and continent, that no doubt lie there, and thus crown this great enterprise with the glory that is due to our illustrious sovereigns, and your own forethought."

"The wish is just, good Martin Alonzo, and fairly expressed, but it may not be granted. That we should make creditable discoveries, by thus steering, is highly probable, but in so doing we should fall far short of our aim. Cathay and the Great Khan still lie west; and we are here, not to add another group, like the Canaries, or the Azores, to the knowledge of man, but to complete the circle of the earth, and to open the way for the setting up of the cross in the regions that have so long been the property of infidels."

"Hast thou nothing to say, Señor de Muños, in support of our petition? Thou hast favor with his Excellency, and may prevail on him to grant us this small behest!"

"To tell thee the truth, good Martin Alonzo," answered Luis, with more of the indifference of manner that might have been expected from the grandee to the pilot, than the respect that would become the secretary to the second person of the expedition—"to tell thee the truth good Martin Alonzo, my heart is so set on the conversion of the Great Khan, that I wish not to turn either to the right or left, until that glorious achievement be sufficiently secure. I have observed that Satan effecteth little against those who keep in the direct path, while his success with those who turn aside is so material, as to people his dominions with errants."

"Is there no hope, noble admiral? and must we quit all these cheering signs, without endeavoring to trace them to some advantageous conclusion?"

"I see no better course, worthy friend. This rain indicateth land; also this calm; and here is a visitor that denoteth more than either—yonder, in the direction of thy Pinta, where it seemeth disposed to rest its wings."

Pinzon, and all near him, turned, and, to their common delight and astonishment, they saw a pelican, with extended wings that spread for ten feet, sailing a few fathoms above the sea, and apparently aiming at the vessel named. The adventurous bird, however, as if disdaining to visit one of inferior rank, passed the Pinta, and, sweeping up grandly toward the admiral, alighted on a yard of the Santa Maria.

"If this be not a certain sign of the vicinity of land," said Columbus gravely, "it is what is far better, a sure omen that God is with us. He is sending these encouraging calls to confirm us in our intention to serve him, and to persevere to the end. Never before, Martin Alonzo, have I seen a bird of this species a day's sail from the shore!"

"Such is my experience, too, noble admiral; and, with you, I look upon this visit as a most propitious omen. May it not be a hint to turn aside, and to look further in this quarter?"

"I accept it not as such, but rather as a motive to proceed. At our return from the Indies, we may examine this part of the ocean with greater security, though I shall think naught accomplished until India be fairly reached, and India is still hundreds of leagues distant. As the time is favorable, however, we will call together our pilots, and see how each man placeth his vessel on the chart."

At this suggestion, all the navigators assembled on board the Santa Maria, and each man made his calculations, sticking a pin in the rude chart—rude as to accuracy, but beautiful as to execution—that the admiral, with the lights he then possessed, had made of the Atlantic ocean. Vicente Yañez, and his companions of the Niña, placed their pin most in advance, after measuring off four hundred and forty marine leagues from Gomera. Martin Alonzo varied a little from this, setting his pin some twenty leagues farther east. When it was the turn of Columbus, he stuck a pin twenty leagues still short of that of Martin Alonzo, his companions having, to all appearance, like less skilful calculators, thus much advanced ahead of their true distance. It was then determined what was to be stated to the crews, and the pilots returned to their respective vessels.

It would seem that Columbus really believed he was then passing between islands, and his historian, Las Casas, affirms that he was actually right in his conjecture; but if islands ever existed in that part of the ocean, they have long since disappeared; a phenomenon which, while it is not impossible, can scarcely be deemed probable. It is said that breakers have been seen, even within the present century, in this vicinity, and it is not unlikely that extensive banks do exist, though Columbus found no bottom with two hundred fathoms of line. The great collection of weeds, is a fact authenticated by some of the oldest records of human investigations, and is most probably owing to some effect of the currents which has a tendency to bring about such an end; while the birds must be considered as stragglers lured from their usual haunts by the food that would be apt to be collected by the union of weeds and fish. Aquatic birds can always rest on the water, and the animal that can wing its way through the air at the rate of thirty, or even fifty miles the hour, needs only sufficient strength, to cross the entire Atlantic in four days and nights.

Notwithstanding all these cheering signs, the different crews soon began to feel again the weight of a renewed despondency. Sancho, who was in constant but secret communication with the admiral, kept the latter properly advised of the state of the people, and reported that more murmurs than usual prevailed, the men having passed again, by the suddenness of the reaction, from the most elastic hope, nearly to the verge of despair. This fact was told Columbus just at sunset on the evening of the 20th, or on that of the eleventh day after the fleet lost sight of land, and while the seaman was affecting to be busy on the poop, where he made most of his communications.

"They complain, your Excellency," continued Sancho, "of the smoothness of the water; and they say that when the winds blow at all, in these seas, they come only from the eastward, having no power to blow from any other quarter. The calms, they think, prove that we are getting into a part of the ocean where there is no wind; and the east winds, they fancy, are sent by Providence to drive those there who have displeased Heaven by a curiosity that it was never intended that any who wear beards should possess."

"Do thou encourage them, Sancho, by reminding the poor fellows that calms prevail, at times, in all seas; and, as for the east winds, is it not well known that they blow from off the African shores, in low latitudes, at all seasons of the year, following the sun in his daily track around the earth? I trust thou hast none of this silly apprehension?"

"I endeavor to keep a stout heart, Señor Don Almirante, having no one before me to disgrace, and leaving no one behind me to mourn over my loss. Still, I should like to hear a little about the riches of those distant lands, as I find the thoughts of their gold and precious stones have a sort of religious charm over my weakness, when I begin to muse upon Moguer and its good cheer."

"Go to, knave; thy appetite for money is insatiable; take yet another dobla, and as thou gazest on it thou mayst fancy what thou wilt of the coin of the Great Khan; resting certain that so great a monarch is not without gold, any more than he is probably without the disposition to part with it, when there is occasion."

Sancho received his fee, and left the poop to Columbus and our hero.

"These ups and downs among the knaves," said Luis, impatiently, "were best quelled, Señor, by an application of the flat of the sword, or, at need, of its edge."

"This may not be, my young friend, without, at least, far more occasion than yet existeth for the severity. Think not that I have passed so many years of my life in soliciting the means to effect so great a purpose, and have got thus far on my way, in unknown seas, with a disposition to be easily turned aside from my purpose. But God hath not created all alike; neither hath he afforded equal chances for knowledge to the peasant and the noble. I have vexed my spirit too often, with arguments on this very subject, with the great and learned, not to bear a little with the ignorance of the vulgar. Fancy how much fear would have quickened the wits of the sages of Salamanca, had our discussion been held in the middle of the Atlantic, where man never had been, and whence no eyes but those of logic and science could discover a safe passage."

"This is most true, Señor Almirante; and yet, methinks the knights that were of your antagonists should not have been wholly unmanned by fear. What danger have we here? this is the wide ocean, it is true, and we are no doubt distant some hundreds of leagues from the known islands, but, we are not the less safe. By San Pedro! I have seen more lives lost in a single onset of the Moors, than these caravels could hold in bodies, and blood enough spilt to float them!"

"The dangers our people dread may be less turbulent than those of a Moorish fray, Don Luis, but they are not the less terrible. Where is the spring that is to furnish water to the parched lip, when our stores shall fail; and where the field to give us its bread and nourishment? It is a fearful thing to be brought down to the dregs of life, by the failure of food and water, on the surface of the wide ocean, dying by inches, often without the consolations of the church, and ever without Christian sepulture. These are the fancies of the seaman, and he is only to be driven from them violently when duty demands extreme remedies for his disease."

"To me it seemeth, Don Christopher, that it will be time to reason thus, when our casks are drained, and the last biscuit is broken. Until then, I ask leave of your Excellency to apply the necessary logic to the *outside* of the heads of these varlets, instead of their insides, of which I much question the capacity to hold any good."

Columbus too well understood the hot nature of the young noble to make a serious reply; and they both stood some time leaning against the mizen-mast, watching the scene before them, and musing on the chances of their situation. It was night, and the figures of the watch, on the deck beneath, were visible only by a light that rendered it difficult to distinguish countenances. The men were grouped; and it was evident by the low but eager tones in which they conversed, that they discussed matters connected with the calm, and the risks they ran. The outlines of the Pinta and Niña were visible, beneath a firmament that was studded with brilliants, their lazy sails hanging in festoons, like the drapery of curtains, and their black hulls were as stationary as if they both lay moored in one of the rivers of Spain. It was a bland and gentle night, but the immensity of the solitude, the deep calm of the slumbering ocean, and even the occasional creaking of a spar, by recalling to the mind the actual presence of vessels so situated, rendered the scene solemn, almost to sublimity.

"Dost thou detect aught fluttering in the rigging, Luis?" the admiral cautiously inquired. "My ear deceiveth me, or I hear something on the wing. The sounds, moreover, are quick and slight, like those produced by birds of indifferent size."

"Don Christopher, you are right. There are little creatures perched on the upper yards, and that of a size like the smaller songsters of the land."

"Hark!" interrupted the admiral. "That is a joyous note, and of such a melody as might be met in one of the orange groves of Seville, itself! God be praised for this sign of the extent and unity of his kingdom, since land cannot well be distant, when creatures, gentle and frail as these, have so lately taken their flight from it!"

The presence of these birds soon became known to all on deck, and their songs brought more comfort than the most able mathematical demonstration, even though founded on modern learning, could have produced on the sensitive feelings of the common men.

"I told thee land was near," cried Sancho, turning with exultation to Martin Martinez, his constant disputant; "here thou hast the proof of it, in a manner that none but the traitor will deny. Thou hearest the songs of orchard birds—notes that would never come from the throats of the tired; and which sound as gaily as if the dear little feathered rogues were pecking at a fig or a grape in a field of Spain."

"Sancho is right!" exclaimed the seamen. "The air savors of land, too; and the sea hath a look of the land; and God is with us—blessed be his Holy name—and honor to our lord the king, and to our gracious mistress, Doña Isabella!"

From this moment concern seemed to leave the vessel, again. It was thought, even by the admiral himself, that the presence of birds so small, and which were judged to be so feeble of wing, was an unerring evidence that land was nigh; and land, too, of generous productions, and a mild, gentle climate; for these warblers, like the softer sex of the human family, best love scenes that most favor their gentle propensities and delicate habits.

Investigation has since proved that, in this particular, however plausible the grounds of error, Columbus was deceived. Men often mistake the powers of the inferior animals of creation, and at other times they overrate the extent of their instinct. In point of fact, a bird of light weight would be less liable to perish on the ocean, and in that low latitude, than a bird of more size, neither being aquatic. The sea-weed itself would furnish resting-places without number for the smaller animals, and, in some instances, it would probably furnish food. That birds, purely of the land, should take long flights at sea, is certainly improbable; but, apart from the consequence of gales, which often force even that heavy-winged animal the owl, hundreds of miles from the land, instinct is not infallible; whales being frequently found embayed in shallow waters, and birds sailing beyond the just limits of their habits. Whatever may have been the cause of the opportune appearance of these little inhabitants of the orchard on the spars of the Santa Maria, the effect was of the most auspicious kind on the spirits of the men. As long as they sang, no amateurs ever listened to the most brilliant passages from the orchestra with greater delight than those rude seamen listened to their warbling; and while they slept, it was with a security that had its existence in veneration and gratitude. The songs were renewed with the dawn, shortly after which the whole went off in a body, taking their flight toward the south-west. The next day brought a calm, and then an air so light, that the vessels could with difficulty make their way through the dense masses of weeds, that actually gave the ocean the appearance of vast inundated meadows. The current was now found to be from the west, and shortly after daylight a new source of alarm was reported by Sancho.

"The people have got a notion in their heads, Señor Almirante, which partaketh so much of the marvellous, that it findeth exceeding favor with such as love miracles more than they love God. Martin Martinez, who is a philosopher in the way of terror, maintaineth that this sea, into which we seem to be entering deeper and deeper, lieth over sunken islands, and that the weeds, which it would be idle to deny grow more abundant as we proceed, will shortly get to be so plentiful on the surface of the water, that the caravels will become unable to advance or to retreat."

"Doth Martin find any to believe this silly notion?"

"Señor Don Almirante, he doth; and for the plain reason that it is easier to find those who are ready to believe an absurdity, than to find those who will only believe truth. But the man is backed by some unlucky chances, that must come of the Powers of Darkness, more particularly as they can have no great wish to see your Excellency reach Cathay, with the intention of making a Christian of the Great Khan, and of planting the tree of the cross in his dominions. This calm sorely troubleth many, moreover, and the birds are beginning to be looked upon as creatures sent by Satan himself, to lead us whither we can never return. Some even believe we shall tread on shoals, and lie forever stranded wrecks in the midst of the wide ocean!"

"Go, bid the men prepare to sound; I will show them the folly of this idea, at least; and see that all are summoned to witness the experiment."

Columbus now repeated this order to the pilots, and the deep-sea was let go in the usual manner. Fathom after fathom of the line glided over the rail, the lead taking its unerring way toward the bottom, until so little was left as to compel the downward course to be arrested.

"Ye see, my friends, that we are yet full two hundred fathoms from the shoals ye so much dread, and as much more as the sea is deeper than our measurement. Lo! yonder, too, is a whale, spouting the water before him—a creature never seen except on the coasts of large islands or continents."

This appeal of Columbus, which was in conformity with the notions of the day, had its weight—his crew being naturally most under the influence of notions that were popular. It is now known, however, that whales frequent those parts of the ocean where their food is most abundant, and one of the best grounds for taking them, of late years, has been what is called the False Brazil Banks, which lie near the centre of the ocean. In a word, all those signs, that were connected with the movements of birds and fishes, and which appear to have had so much effect, not only on the common men of this great enterprise, but on Columbus himself, were of far less real importance than was then believed; navigators being so little accustomed to venture far from the land themselves, that they were not duly acquainted with the mysteries of the open ocean.

Notwithstanding the moments of cheerfulness and hope that intervened, distrust and apprehension were fast getting to be again the prevailing feelings among the mariners. Those who had been most disaffected from the first, seized every occasion to increase these apprehensions; and when the sun rose, Saturday, September 22d, on a calm sea, there were not a few in the vessels who were disposed to unite in making another demand on the admiral to turn the heads of the caravels toward the east.

"We have come some hundreds of leagues before a fair wind, into a sea that is entirely unknown to man, until we have reached a part of the ocean where the wind seems altogether to fail us, and where there is danger of our being bound up in immovable weeds, or stranded on sunken islands, without the means of procuring food or water!"

Arguments like these were suited to an age in which even the most learned were obliged to grope their way to accurate knowledge, through the mists of superstition and ignorance, and in which it was a prevailing weakness to put faith, on the one hand, in visible proofs of the miraculous power of God, and, on the other, in substantial evidences of the ascendency of evil spirits, as they were permitted to affect the temporal affairs of those they persecuted.

It was, therefore, most fortunate for the success of the expedition, that a light breeze sprang up from southward and westward, in the early part of the day just mentioned, enabling the vessels to gather way, and to move beyond the vast fields of weeds, that equally obstructed the progress of the caravels, and awakened the fears of their people. As it was an object to get clear of the floating obstacles that surrounded the vessels, the first large opening that offered was entered, and then the fleet was brought close upon a wind, heading as near as possible to the desired course. Columbus now believed himself to be steering west-north-west, when, in fact, he was sailing in a direction far nearer to his true course, than when his ships headed west by compass; the departure from the desired line of sailing, being owing to the variation in the needle. This circumstance alone, would seem to establish the fact, that Columbus believed in his own theory of the moving star, since he would hardly have steered west-and-by-south-half-south, with a fair wind, for many days in succession, as he is known to have done, when it was his strongest wish to proceed directly west. He was now heading up, within half a point of the latter course, though he and all with him, fancied they were running off nearly two points to leeward of the so much desired direction.

But these little variations were trifles as compared with the advantage that the admiral obtained over the fears of his followers by the shift of the wind, and the liberation from the weeds. By the first, the men saw a proof that the breezes did not always blow from the same quarter; and by the last, they ascertained that they had not actually reached a point where the ocean had become impassable. Although the wind was now favorable to return to the Canaries, no one any longer demanded that such a course should be adopted, so apt are we all to desire that which appears to be denied to us, and so ready to despise that which lies perfectly at our disposal.

This, indeed, was a moment when the feelings of the people appeared to be as variable as the light and baffling winds themselves. The Saturday passed away in the manner just mentioned, the vessels once more entering into large fields of weeds, just as the sun set. When the light returned, the airs headed them off to north-west and north-west-by-north, by compass, which was, in truth, steering north-west-by-west-half-west, and north-west-half-west. Birds abounded again, among which was a turtle-dove, and many living crabs were seen crawling among the weeds. All these signs would have encouraged the common men, had they not already so often proved deceptive.

"Señor," said Martin Martinez, to the admiral, when Columbus went among the crew to raise their drooping spirits, "we know not what to think! For days did the wind blow in the same direction, leading us on, as it might be, to our ruin; and then it hath deserted us in such a sea as mariners in the Santa Maria never before saw. A sea, looking like meadows on a river side, and which wanteth only kine and cow-herds, to be mistaken for fields a little overflowed by a rise of the water, is a fearful thing!"

"Thy meadows are the weeds of the ocean, and prove the richness of the nature that hath produced them; while thy breezes from the east, are what all who have ever made the Guinea voyage, well know to exist in latitudes so low. I see naught in either to alarm a bold seaman; and as for the bottom, we all know it hath not yet been found by many a long and weary fathom of line. Pepe, thou hast none of these weaknesses; but hast set thy heart on Cathay and a sight of the Great Khan?"

"Señor Almirante, as I swore to Monica, so do I swear to your Excellency; and that is to be true and obedient. If the cross is to be raised among the Infidels, my hand shall not be backward in doing its share toward the holy act. Still, Señor, none of us like this long unnatural calm. Here is an ocean that hath no waves, but a surface so smooth that we much distrust whether the waters obey the same laws, as they are known to do near Spain; for never before have I beheld a sea that hath so much the air of the dead! May it not be, Señor, that God hath placed a belt of this calm and stagnant water around the outer edges of the earth, in order to prevent the unheedy from looking into some of his sacred secrets?"

"Thy reasoning hath, at least, a savor of religion; and, though faulty, can scarce be condemned. God hath placed man on this earth, Pepe, to be its master, and to serve him by extending the dominion of his church, as well as by turning to the best account all the numberless blessings that accompany the great gift. As to the limits, of which thou speakest, they exist only in idea, the earth being a sphere, or a ball, to which there are no other edges than those thou seest everywhere on its surface."

"And as for what Martin saith," put in Sancho, who was never at fault for a fact, or for a reason, "concerning the winds, and the weeds, and the calms, I can only wonder where a seaman of his years hath been navigating so long, that these things should be novelties. To me, all this is as common as dish-water at Moguer, and so much a matter of course, that I should not have remarked it, but for the whinings of Martin and his fellows. When the Santa Catalina made the voyage to that far-off region, Ireland, we landed on the sea-weed, a distance of half a league or so from the coast; and as for the wind, it blew regularly four weeks from one quarter, and four weeks from the other; after which the people of the country said it would blow four weeks each way, transversely; but we did not remain long enough in those seas to enable me to swear to the two last facts."

"Hast thou not heard of shoals so wide that a caravel could never find its way out of them, if it once entered?" demanded Martinez, fiercely, for, much addicted to gross exaggerations himself, he little liked to be outdone; "and do not these weeds bespeak our near approach to such a danger, when the weeds themselves often are so closely packed as to come near to stop the ship?"

"Enough of this," said the admiral: "at times we have weeds, and then we are altogether free from them; these changes are owing to the currents; no doubt as soon as we have passed this meridian, we shall come to clear water again."

"But the calm, Señor Almirante," exclaimed a dozen voices. "This unnatural smoothness of the ocean frighteneth us! Never before did we see water so stagnant and immovable!"

"Call ye this stagnant and immovable?" exclaimed the admiral. "Nature herself arises to reproach your senseless fears, and to contradict your mistaken reasoning, by her own signs and portents!"

This was said as the Santa Maria's bows rose on a long low swell, every spar creaking at the motion, and the whole hull heaving and setting as the billow passed beneath it, washing the sides of the ship from the water line to its channels. At this moment there was not even a breath of air, and the seamen gazed about them with an astonishment that was increased and rendered extreme by dread. The ship had scarcely settled heavily into the long trough when a second wave lifted her again forward, and billow succeeded billow, each successive wave increasing in height, until the entire ocean was undulating, though only marked at distant intervals, and that slightly, by the foam of crests or combing seas. It took half an hour to bring this phenomenon up to its height, when all three vessels were wallowing in the seas, as mariners term it, their hulls falling off helplessly into the troughs, until the water fairly spouted from their low scuppers, as each rose by her buoyancy from some roll deeper than common. Fancying that this occurrence promised to be either a source of new alarm, or a means of appeasing the old one, Columbus took early measures to turn it to account, in the latter mode. Causing all the crew to assemble at the break of the poop, he addressed them, briefly, in the following words:

"Ye see, men, that your late fears about the stagnant ocean are rebuked, in this sudden manner, as it might be, by the hand of God himself, proving, beyond dispute, that no danger is to be apprehended from that source. I might impose on your ignorance, and insist that this sudden rising of the sea is a miracle wrought to sustain me against your rebellious repinings and unthinking alarms; but the cause in which I am engaged needs no support of this nature, that doth not truly come from heaven. The calms, and the smoothness of the water, and even the weeds of which ye complain, come from the vicinity of some great body of land; I think not a continent, as that must lie still further west, but of islands, either so large or so numerous, as to make a far-extended lee; while these swells are probably the evidence of wind at a distance, which hath driven up the ocean into mountainous waves, such as we often see them, and which send out their dying efforts, even beyond the limits of the gale. I do not say that this intervention, to appease your fears, doth not come of God, in whose hands I am; for this last do I fully believe, and for it am I fully grateful; but it cometh through the agencies of nature, and can in no sense be deemed providential, except as it demonstrateth the continuance of the divine care, as well as its surpassing goodness. Go, then, and be tranquil. Remember, if Spain be far behind ye, that Cathay now lieth at no great distance before ye; that each hour shorteneth that distance, as well as the time necessary to reach our goal. He that remaineth true and faithful, shall not repent his confidence; while he who unnecessarily disturbeth either himself or others, with silly doubts, may look forward to an exercise of authority that shall maintain the rights of their Highnesses to the duty of all their servants."

We record this speech of the great navigator with so much the more pleasure, as it goes fully to establish the fact that he did not believe the sudden rising of the seas, on this occasion, was owing to a direct miracle, as some of the historians and biographers seem inclined to believe; but rather to a providential interference of Divine Power, through natural means, in order to protect him against the consequences of the blind apprehensions of his followers. It is not easy, indeed, to suppose that a seaman as experienced as Columbus, could be ignorant of the natural cause of a circumstance so very common on the ocean, that those who dwell on its coast have frequent occasion to witness its occurrence.

CHAPTER XX

"'Ora pro nobis, Mater!' —what a spell
Was in those notes, with day's last glory dying
On the flush'd waters—seemed they not to swell
From the far dust wherein my sires were lying
With crucifix and sword?—Oh! yet how clear
Comes their reproachful sweetness to my ear!
'Ora' —with all the purple waves replying,
All my youth's visions rising in the strain—
And I had thought it much to bear the rack and chain!"

The Forest Sanctuary.

It may now be well to recapitulate, and to let the reader distinctly know how far the adventurers had actually advanced into the unknown waters of the Atlantic; what was their real, and what their supposed position. As has been seen, from the time of quitting Gomera, the admiral kept two reckonings, one intended for his own government, which came as near the truth as the imperfect means of the science of navigation that were then in use would allow, and another that was freely exhibited to the crew, and was purposely miscalculated in order to prevent alarm, on account of the distance that had been passed. As Columbus believed himself to be employed in the service of God, this act of deception would be thought a species of pious fraud, in that devout age; and it is by no means probable that it gave the conscience of the navigator any trouble, since churchmen, even, did not hesitate always about buttressing the walls of faith by means still less justifiable.

The long calms and light head-winds had prevented the vessels from making much progress for the few last days; and, by estimating the distance that was subsequently run in a course but a little south of west, it appears, notwithstanding all the encouraging signs of birds, fishes, calms, and smooth water, that on the morning of Monday, September 24th, or that of the fifteenth day after losing sight of Ferro, the expedition was about half-way across the Atlantic, counting from continent to continent, on the parallel of about 31 or 32 degrees of north latitude The circumstance of the vessels being so far north of the Canaries, when it is known that they had been running most of the time west, a little southerly, must be imputed to the course steered in the scant winds, and perhaps to the general set of the currents. With this brief explanation, we return to the daily progress of the ships.

The influence of the trades was once more felt, though in a very slight degree, in the course of the twenty-four hours that succeeded the day of the "miraculous seas," and the vessels again headed west by compass. Birds were seen as usual, among which was a pelican. The whole progress of the vessels was less than fifty miles, a distance that was lessened, as usual, in the public reckoning.

The morning of the 25th was calm, but the wind returned, a steady, gentle breeze from the south-east, when the day was far advanced, the caravels passing most of the hours of light floating near each other in a lazy indolence, or barely stirring the water with their stems, at a rate little, if any, exceeding that of a mile an hour.

The Pinta kept near the Santa Maria, and the officers and crews of the two vessels conversed freely with each other concerning their hopes and situation. Columbus listened to these dialogues for a long time, endeavoring to collect the predominant feeling from the more guarded expressions that were thus publicly delivered, and watching each turn of the expressions with jealous vigilance. At length it struck him that the occasion was favorable to producing a good effect on the spirits of his followers.

"What hast thou thought of the chart I sent thee three days since, good Martin Alonzo?" called out the admiral. "Dost thou see in it aught to satisfy thee that we are approaching the Indies, and that our time of trial draweth rapidly to an end?"

At the first sound of the admiral's voice, every syllable was hushed among the people; for, in spite of their discontent, and their disposition even to rise against him, in their extremity, Columbus had succeeded in creating a profound respect for his judgment and his person among all his followers.

"'Tis a rare and well-designed chart, Señor Don Christopher," answered the master of the Pinta, "and doth a fair credit to him who hath copied and enlarged, as well as to him who first projected it. I doubt that it is the work of some learned scholar, that hath united the opinions of all the greater navigators in his map."

"The original came from one Paul Toscanelli, a learned Tuscan, who dwelleth at Firenze in that country; a man of exceeding knowledge, and of an industry in investigation that putteth idleness to shame. Accompanying the chart he sent a missive that hath much profound and learned matter on the subject of the Indies, and touching those islands that thou seest laid down with so much particularity. In that letter he speaketh of divers places, as being so many wonderful exemplars of the power of man; more especially of the port of Zaiton, which sendeth forth no less than a hundred ships yearly, loaded with the single product of the pepper-tree. He saith, moreover, that an ambassador came to the Holy Father, in the time of Eugenius IV., of blessed memory, to express the desire of the Great Khan, which meaneth King of Kings, in the dialect of those regions, to be on friendly terms with the Christians of the west, as we were then termed; but of the east, as will shortly be our designation in that part of the world."

"This is surprising, Señor!" exclaimed Pinzon: "how is it known, or is it known at all, of a certainty?"

"Beyond a question; since Paul stateth, in his missive, that he saw much of this same ambassador, living greatly in his society, Eugenius deceasing as lately as 1477. From the ambassador, no doubt a wise and grave personage, since no other would have been sent so far on a mission to the Head of the Church; from this discreet person, then, did Toscanelli gain much pleasant information concerning the populousness and vast extent of those distant countries, the gorgeousness of the palaces, and the glorious beauty of the cities. He spoke of one town, in particular, that surpasseth all others of the known world; and of a single river that hath two hundred noble cities on its own banks, with marble bridges spanning the stream. The chart before thee, Martin Alonzo, showeth that the exact distance from Lisbon to the city of Quisay is just three thousand nine hundred miles of Italy, or about a thousand leagues, steering always in a due-west direction." [2]

"And doth the learned Tuscan say aught of the riches of those countries?" demanded Master Alonzo—a question that caused all within hearing to prick up their ears, afresh.

"That doth he, and in these precise and impressive words—'This is a noble country,' observed the learned Paul, in his missive, 'and ought to be explored by us, on account of its great riches, and the quantity of gold, silver, and precious stones, which might be obtained there.' He moreover described Quisay as being five-and-thirty leagues in circuit, and addeth that its name in the Castilian, is 'the City of Heaven.'"

"In which case," muttered Sancho, though in a tone so low that no one but Pepe heard him, "there is little need of our bearing thither the cross, which was intended for the benefit of man, and not of paradise."

"I see here two large islands, Señor Almirante," continued Pinzon, keeping his eyes on the chart, "one of which is called Antilla, and the other is the Cipango of which your Excellency so often speaketh."

"Even so, good Martin Alonzo, and thou also seest that they are laid down with a precision that must prevent any experienced navigator from missing his way, when in pursuit of them. These islands lie just two hundred and twenty-five leagues asunder."

"According to our reckoning, here, in the Pinta, noble Admiral, we cannot, then, be far from Cipango at this very moment."

"It would so seem by the reckonings, though I somewhat doubt their justness. It is a common error of pilots to run ahead of their reckonings, but in this instance, apprehension hath brought ye behind them. Cipango lieth many days' sail from the continent of Asia, and cannot, therefore, be far from this spot; still the currents have been adverse, and I doubt that it will be found that we are as near this island, good Martin Alonzo, as thou and thy companions imagine. Let the chart be returned, and I will trace our actual position on it, that all may see what reason there is to despond, and what reason to rejoice."

Pinzon now took the chart, rolled it together carefully, attached a light weight, and securing the whole with the end of a log-line, he hove it on board the Santa Maria, as a seaman makes a cast with the lead. So near were the vessels at the moment, that this communication was made without any difficulty; after which, the Pinta, letting fall an additional sail or two, flapped slowly ahead, her superiority, particularly in light winds, being at all times apparent.

Columbus now caused the chart to be spread over a table on the poop, and invited all who chose to draw near, in order that they might, with their own eyes, see the precise spot on the ocean where the admiral supposed the vessels to be. As each day's work was accurately laid down, and measured on the chart, by one as expert as the great navigator himself, there is little question that he succeeded in showing his people, as near as might be, and subject to the deduction in distance that was intentionally made, the longitude and latitude to which the expedition had then reached; and as this brought them quite near those islands which were believed to lie east of the continent of Asia, this tangible proof of their progress had far more effect than any demonstration that depended on abstract reasoning, even when grounded on premises that were true; most men submitting sooner to the authority of the senses, than to the influence of the mere mind. The seamen did not stop to inquire how it was settled that Cipango lay in the precise place where it had been projected on this famous chart, but, seeing it there, in black and white, they were disposed to believe it was really in the spot it appeared to be; and, as Columbus' reputation for keeping a ship's reckoning far surpassed that of any other navigator in the fleet, the facts were held to be established. Great was the joy, in consequence; and the minds of the people again passed from the verge of despair to an excess and illusion of hope, that was raised only to be disappointed.

That Columbus was sincere in all that related to this new delusion, with the exception of the calculated reduction of the true distance, is beyond a doubt. In common with the cosmographers of the age, he believed the circumference of the earth much less than actual measurement has since shown it to be; striking out of the calculation, at once, nearly the whole breadth of the Pacific Ocean. That this conclusion was very natural, will be seen by glancing at the geographical facts that the learned then possessed, as data for their theories.

It was known that the continent of Asia was bounded on the east by a vast ocean, and that a similar body of water bounded Europe on the west, leaving the plausible inference, on the supposition that the earth was a sphere, that nothing but islands existed between these two great boundaries of land. Less than half of the real circumference of the globe is to be found between the western and eastern verges of the old continent, as they were then known; but it was too bold an effort of the mind, to conceive that startling fact, in the condition of human knowledge at the close of the fifteenth century. The theories were consequently content with drawing the limits of the east and the west into a much narrower circle, finding no data for any freer speculation; and believing it a sufficient act of boldness to maintain the spherical formation of the earth at all. It is true, that the latter theory was as old as Ptolemy, and quite probably much older; but even the antiquity of a system begins to be an argument against it, in the minds of the vulgar, when centuries elapse, and it receives no confirmation from actual experiment. Columbus supposed his island of Cipango, or Japan, to lie about one hundred and forty degrees of longitude east of its actual position; and, as a degree of longitude in the latitude of Japan, or 35° north, supposing the surface of the earth to be perfectly spherical, is about fifty-six statute miles, it follows that Columbus had advanced this island, on his chart, more than seven thousand English miles toward the eastward, or a distance materially exceeding two thousand marine leagues.

All this, however, was not only hidden in mystery as regards the common men of the expedition, but it far out-stripped the boldest conceptions of the great navigator himself. Facts of this nature, notwithstanding, are far from detracting from the glory of the vast discoveries that were subsequently made, since they prove under what moral disadvantages the expedition was conceived, and under what a limited degree of knowledge it finally triumphed.

While Columbus was thus employed with the chart, it was a curious thing to witness the manner in which the seamen watched his smallest movement, studied the expression of his grave and composed countenance, and sought to read their fate in the contraction, or dilation, of his eyes. The gentlemen of the Santa Maria, and the pilots, stood at his elbow, and here and there some old mariner ventured to take his post at hand, where he could follow the slow progress of the pen, or note the explanation of a figure. Among these was Sancho, who was generally admitted to be one of the most expert seamen in the little fleet—in all things, at least, that did not require the knowledge of the schools. Columbus even turned to these men, and spoke to them kindly, endeavoring to make them comprehend a part of their calling, which they saw practised daily, without ever succeeding in acquiring a practical acquaintance with it, pointing out particularly the distance come, and that which yet remained before them. Others, again, the less experienced, but not the less interested among the crew, hung about the rigging, whence they could overlook the scene, and fancy they beheld demonstrations that came of theories which it as much exceeded their reasoning powers to understand, as it exceeded their physical vision to behold the desired Indies themselves. As men become intellectual, they entertain abstractions, leaving the dominion of the senses to take refuge in that of thought. Until this change arrives, however, we are all singularly influenced by a parade of positive things. Words spoken seldom produce the effect of words written; and the praise or censure that would enter lightly and unheeded into the ear, might even change our estimates of character, when received into the mind through the medium of the eye. Thus, the very seamen, who could not comprehend the reasoning of Columbus, fancied they understood his chart, and willingly enough believed that islands and continents must exist in the precise places where they saw them so plainly delineated.

After this exhibition, cheerfulness resumed its sway over the crew of the Santa Maria; and Sancho, who was generally considered as of the party of the admiral, was eagerly appealed to by his fellows, for many of the little circumstances that were thought to explain the features of the chart.

"Dost think, Sancho, that Cipango is as large as the admiral hath got the island on the chart?" asked one who had passed from the verge of despair to the other extreme; "that it lieth fairly, any eye may see, since its look is as natural as that of Ferro or Madeira."

"That hath he," answered Sancho, positively, "as one may see by its shape. Didst not notice the capes, and bays, and headlands, all laid down as plainly as on any other well-known coast? Ah! these Genoese are skilful navigators; and Señor Colon, our noble admiral, hath not come all this distance without having some notion in what roadstead he is to anchor."

In such conclusive arguments, the dullest minds of the crew found exceeding consolation; while among all the common people of the ship, there was not one who did not feel more confidence in the happy termination of the voyage, since he had this seeming ocular proof of the existence of land in the part of the ocean they were in.

When the discourse between the admiral and Pinzon ceased, the latter made sail on the Pinta, which vessel had slowly passed the Santa Maria, and was now a hundred yards, or more, ahead of her; neither going through the water at a rate exceeding a knot an hour. At the moment just mentioned, or while the men were conversing of their newly awakened hopes, a shout drew all eyes toward their consort, where Pinzon was seen on the poop, waving his cap in exultation, and giving the usual proofs of extravagant delight.

"Land!—Land! Señor!" he shouted. "I claim my reward! Land! Land!"

"In what direction, good Martin Alonzo?" asked Columbus, so eagerly that his voice fairly trembled. "In which quarter dost thou perceive this welcome neighbor?"

"Here, to the south-west," pointing in that direction—"a range of dim but noble mountains, and such as promise to satisfy the pious longings of the Holy Father himself!"

Every eye turned toward the south-west, and there, indeed, they fancied they beheld the long-sought proofs of their success. A faint, hazy mass was visible in the horizon, broken in outline, more distinctly marked than clouds usually are, and yet so obscure as to require a practised eye to draw it out of the obscurity of the void. This is the manner in which land often appears to seamen, in peculiar conditions of the atmosphere; others, under such circumstances, being seldom able to distinguish it at all. Columbus was so practised in all the phenomena of the ocean, that the face of every man in the Santa Maria was turned toward his, in breathless expectation of the result, as soon as the first glance had been given toward the point of the compass mentioned. It was impossible to mistake the expression of the admiral's countenance, which immediately became radiant with delight and pious exultation. Uncovering himself, he cast a look upward in unbounded gratitude, and then fell on his knees, to return open thanks to God. This was the signal of triumph, and yet, in their desolate situation, exultation was not the prevalent feeling of the moment. Like Columbus, the men felt their absolute dependence on God; and a sense of humble and rebuked gratitude came over every spirit, as it might be simultaneously.

Kneeling, the entire crews of the three vessels simultaneously commenced the chant of "Gloria in excelsis Deo!" lifting the voice of praise, for the first time since the foundations of the earth were laid, in that deep solitude of the ocean. Matins and vespers, it is true, were then habitually repeated in most Christian ships; but this sublime chant was now uttered to waves that had been praising their Maker, in their might and in their calm, for so many thousand years, for the first time in the voice of man.

"*Glory be to God on high!*" sang these rude mariners, with hearts softened by their escapes, dangers, and success, speaking as one man, though modulating their tones to the solemn harmony of a religious rite—"*and on ear h peace, good will toward men. We praise thee, we bless thee, we worship thee, we glorify thee, we give thanks to thee for thy great glory! O Lord God! Heavenly King! God the Father Almighty!*" &c., &c.

In this noble chant, which would seem to approach as near to the praises of angels as human powers can ever hope to rise, the voice of the admiral was distinct, and deep, but trembling with emotion.

When this act of pious gratitude was performed, the men ascended the rigging to make more certain of their success. All agreed in pronouncing the faintly delineated mass to be land, and the first sudden transport of unexpected joy was succeeded by the more regulated feelings of confirmed security. The sun set a little north of the dim mountains, and night closed around the scene, shadowing the ocean with as much gloom as is ever to be found beneath a tropical and cloudless sky. As the first watch was set, Columbus, who, whenever the winds would allow, had persevered in steering what he fancied to be a due-west course, to satisfy the longings of his people, ordered the vessels to haul up to south-west by compass, which was, in fact, heading south-west-by-south-southerly. The wind increased, and, as the admiral had supposed the land to be distant about twenty-five leagues, when last seen, all in the little fleet confidently relied on obtaining a full and complete view of it in the morning. Columbus himself entertained this hope, though he varied his course reluctantly, feeling certain that the continent would be met by sailing west, or what he thought to be west, though he could have no similar confidence as to making any island.

Few slept soundly that night—visions of oriental riches, and of the wonders of the East, crowding on the minds of even the least imaginative, converting their slumbers into dreams rendered uneasy by longings for gold, and anticipations of the wonders of the unknown East. The men left their hammocks, from hour to hour, to stand in the rigging, watching for some new proofs of their proximity to the much-desired islands, and straining their eyes in vain, in the hope of looking deeper into the obscurity in quest of objects that fancy had already begun to invest with forms. In the course of the night, the vessels ran in a direct line toward the south-west, seventeen of the twenty-five leagues that Columbus had supposed alone separated him from this new discovery; and just before the light dawned, every soul in the three vessels was stirring, in the eager hope of having the panorama of day open on such a sight, as they felt it to be but a slight grievance to have come so far, and to have risked so much, to behold.

"Yonder is a streak of light, glimmering in the east," cried Luis, in a cheerful voice; "and now, Señor Almirante, we may unite in terming you the honored of the earth!"

"All rests with God, my young friend," returned Columbus; "whether land is near us or not, it boundeth the western ocean, and to that boundary we must proceed. Thou art right, truly, friend Gutierrez; the light is beginning to shed itself along the eastern margin of the sea, and even to rise in an arch into the vault above it."

"Would that the sun rose, for this one day, in the west, that we might catch the first glimpse of our new possessions in that radiant field of heaven, which his coming rays are so gloriously illuminating above the track we have just passed!"

"That will not happen, Master Pedro, since Sol hath journeyed daily round this planet of ours, from east to west, since time began, and will so continue to journey until time shall cease. This *is* a fact on which our senses may be trusted, though they mislead us in so many other things."

So reasoned Columbus, a man whose mind had out-stripped the age, in his favorite study, and who was usually so calm and philosophical; simply because he reasoned in the fetters of habit and prejudice. The celebrated system of Ptolemy, that strange compound of truth and error, was the favorite astronomical law of the day. Copernicus, who was then but a mere youth, did not reduce the just conception of Pythagoras—just in outline, though fanciful in its connection with both cause and effect—to the precision of science for many years after the discovery of America; and it is a strong proof of the dangers which attended the advancement of thought, that he was rewarded for this vast effort of human reason, by excommunication from the church. the maledictions of which actually rested on his soul, if not on his body, until within a few years of the present moment! This single circumstance will show the reader how much our navigator had to overcome in achieving the great office he had assumed.

But all this time, the day is dawning, and the light is beginning to diffuse itself over the entire panorama of ocean and sky. As means were afforded, each look eagerly took in the whole range of the western horizon, and a chill of disappointment settled on every heart, as suspicion gradually became confirmation, that no land was visible. The vessels had passed, in the night, those bounds of the visible horizon, where masses of clouds had settled; and no one could any longer doubt that his senses had been deceived by some accidental peculiarity in the atmosphere. All eyes now turned again to the admiral, who, while he felt the disappointment in his inmost heart, maintained a dignified calm that it was not easy to disturb.

"These signs are not infrequent at sea, Señor," he said to those near him, speaking loud enough, nevertheless, to be heard by most of the crew, "though seldom as treacherous as they have now proved to be. All accustomed to the ocean have doubtless seen them often; and as physical facts, they must be taken as counting neither for nor against us. As omens, each person will consider them as he putteth his trust in God, whose grace and mercy to us all, is yet, by a million of times, unrequited, and still would be, were we to sing *Glory in excelsis*, from morn till night, as long as breath lasted for the sacred office."

"Still, our hope was so very strong, Don Christopher," observed one of the gentlemen, "that we find the disappointment hard to be borne. You speak of omens, Señor; are there any physical signs of our being near the land of Cathay?"

"Omens come of God, if they come at all. They are a species of miracles preceding natural events, as real miracles surpass them. I think this expedition cometh of God; and I see no irreverence in supposing that this late appearance of land may have been heaped along the horizon for an encouraging sign to persevere, and as a proof that our labors will be rewarded in the end. I cannot say, nevertheless, that any but natural means were used, for these deceptions are familiar to us mariners."

"I shall endeavor so to consider it, Señor Almirante," gravely returned the other, and the conversation dropped.

The non-appearance of the land, which had been so confidently hoped for, produced a deep gloom in the vessels, notwithstanding; again changing the joy of their people into despondency. Columbus continued to steer due west by compass, or west-by-south-southerly, in reality, until meridian, when, yielding to the burning wishes of those around him, he again altered his course to the south-west. This course was followed until the ships had gone far enough in that direction to leave no doubt that the people had been misled by clouds, the preceding evening. At night, when not the faintest hope remained, the vessels kept away due west again, running, in the course of the twenty-four hours, quite thirty-one leagues, which were recorded before the crew as twenty-four.

For several succeeding days no material changes occurred. The wind continued favorable, though frequently so light as to urge the vessels very slowly ahead, reducing the day's progress sometimes to little more than fifty of our English miles. The sea was calm, and weeds were again met, though in much smaller quantities than before. September 29th, or the fourth day after Pinzon had called out "land," another frigate-bird was seen; and as it was the prevalent notion among seamen that this bird never flew far from the shore, some faint hopes were momentarily revived by his passage. Two pelicans also appeared, and the air was so soft and balmy that Columbus declared nothing but nightingales were wanting, to render the nights as delicious as those of Andalusia.

In this manner did birds come and go, exciting hopes that were doomed to be disappointed; sometimes flying in numbers that would seem to forbid the idea that they could be straying on the waste of waters, without the certainty of their position. Again, too, the attention of the admiral and of the people, was drawn to the variation of the needle, all uniting in the opinion that the phenomenon was only to be explained by the movements of the star. At length the first day of October arrived, and the pilots of the admiral's vessel seriously set to work to ascertain the distance they had come. They had been misled, as well as the rest, by the management of Columbus, and they now approached the latter, as he stood at his usual post on the poop, in order to give the result of their calculations, with countenances that were faithful indexes of the concern they felt.

"We are not less than five hundred and seventy-eight leagues west of Ferro, Señor Almirante," commenced one of the two; "a fearful distance to venture into the bosom of an unknown ocean!"

"Thou say'st true, honest Bartolemeo," returned Columbus, calmly; "though the further we venture, the greater will be the honor. Thy reckoning is even short of the truth, since this of mine, which is no secret from our people, giveth even five hundred and eighty-four leagues, fully six more than thine. But, after all, this scarce equalleth a voyage from Lisbon to Guinea, and we are not men to be outdone by the seamen of Don John!"

"Ah! Señor Almirante, the Portuguese have their islands by the way, and the old world at their elbows; while we, should this earth prove not to be really a sphere, are hourly sailing toward its verge, and are running into untried dangers!"

"Go to, Bartolemeo! thou talkest like a river-man who hath been blown outside his bar by a strong breeze from the land, and who fancieth his risks greater than man ever yet endured, because the water that wetteth his tongue is salt. Let the men see this reckoning, fearlessly; and strive to be of cheer, lest we remember thy misgivings beneath the groves of Cathay."

"The man is sorely beset with dread," coolly observed Luis, as the pilots descended from the poop with a lingering step and a heavy heart. "Even your six short leagues added to the weight on his spirit. Five hundred and seventy-eight were frightful, but five hundred and eighty-four became burdensome to his soul!"

"What would he then have thought had he known the truth, of which, young count, even thou art ignorant?"

"I hope you do not distrust my nerves, Don Christopher, that this matter is kept a secret from me?"

"I ought not, I do believe, Señor de Llera; and yet one gets to be distrustful even of himself, when weighty concerns hang by a thread. Hast thou any real idea of the length of the road we have come?"

"Not I, by St. Iago! Señor. It is enough for me that we are far from the Doña Mercedes, and a league more or less counts but little. Should your theory be true, and the earth prove to be round, I have the consolation of knowing that we shall get back to Spain, in time, even by chasing the sun."

"Still thou hast some general notion of our true distance from Ferro, knowing that each day it is lessened before the people."

"To tell you the truth, Don Christopher, arithmetic and I have little feeling for each other. For the life of me, I never could tell the exact amount of my own revenues, in figures, though it might not be so difficult to come at their results, in another sense. If truth were said, however, I should think your five hundred and eighty leagues might fairly be set down at some six hundred and ten or twenty."

"Add yet another hundred and thou wilt not be far from the fact. We are, at this moment, seven hundred and seven leagues from Ferro, and fast drawing near to the meridian of Cipango. In another glorious week, or ten days at most, I shall begin seriously to expect to see the continent of Asia!"

"This is travelling faster than I had thought, Señor," answered Luis, carelessly; "but journey on; one of your followers will not complain, though we circle the earth itself."

CHAPTER XXI

"Pronounce what sea, what shore is this?
The gulf, the rock of Salamis?"

Byron.

The adventurers had now been twenty-three days out of sight of land, all of which time, with the exception of a few very immaterial changes in the wind, and a day or two of calms, they had been steadily advancing toward the west, with a southern variation that ranged between a fourth of a point and a point and a quarter, though the latter fact was unknown to them. Their hopes had been so often raised to be disappointed, that a sort of settled gloom now began to prevail among the common men, which was only relieved by irregular and uncertain cries of "land," as the clouds produced their usual deceptions in the horizon. Still their feelings were in that feverish state which admits of any sudden change; and as the sea continued smooth as a river, the air balmy, and the skies most genial, they were prevented from falling into despair. Sancho reasoned, as usual, among his fellows, resisting ignorance and folly, with impudence and dogmatism; while Luis unconsciously produced an effect on the spirits of his associates by his cheerfulness and confidence. Columbus, himself, remained calm, dignified, and reserved, relying on the justice of his theories, and continuing resolute to attain his object. The wind remained fair, as before, and in the course of the night and day of the 2d of October, the vessels sailed more than a hundred miles still further into that unknown and mysterious sea. The weeds now drifted westerly, which was a material change, the currents previously setting, in the main, in an opposite direction. The 3d proved even a still more favorable day, the distance made reaching to forty-seven leagues. The admiral now began to think seriously that he had passed the islands laid down in his chart, and, with the high resolution of one sustained by grand conceptions, he decided to stand on west, with the intention of reaching the shores of the Indies, at once. The 4th was a better day than either, the little fleet passing steadily ahead, without deviating from its course, until it had fairly made one hundred and eighty-nine miles, much the greatest day's work it had yet achieved. This distance, so formidable to men who began to count each hour and each league with uneasiness, was reckoned to all on board, but Luis, as only one hundred and thirty-eight miles.

Friday, October 5th, commenced even more favorably, Columbus finding his ship gliding though the water—there being no sea to cause her to reel and stagger—at the rate of about eight miles the hour, which was almost as fast as she had ever been known to go, and which would have caused this day's work to exceed the last, had not the wind failed in the night. As it was, however, fifty-seven more leagues were placed between Ferro and the position of the vessel; a distance that was reduced to forty-five, with the crew. The following day brought no material change, Providence appearing to urge them on at a speed that must soon solve the great problem which the admiral had been so long discussing with the learned. It was already dark, when the Pinta came sheering down upon the quarter of the Santa Maria, until she had got so near that her commander hailed without the aid of a trumpet.

"Is Señor Don Christopher at his post, as usual?" hurriedly demanded Pinzon, speaking like one who felt he had matter of weight upon his mind: "I see persons on the poop; but know not if his Excellency be among them."

"What wouldst thou, good Martin Alonzo?" answered the admiral: "I am here, watching for the shores of Cipango, or Cathay, whichever God, in his goodness, may be pleased first to give us."

"I see so many reasons, noble admiral, for changing our course more to the south, that I could not resist the desire to come down and say as much. Most of the late discoveries have been made in the southern latitudes, and we might do well to get more southing."

"Have we gained aught by changing our course in this direction? Thy heart seemeth bent on more southern climes, worthy friend; while to my feelings we are now in the very paradise of sweets, land only excepted. Islands *may* lie south, or even north of us; but a continent *must* lie west. Why abandon a certainty for an uncertainty? the greater for the less? Cipango, or Cathay, for some pleasant spot, fragrant with spices no doubt, but without a name, and which can never equal the glories of Asia, either as a discovery or as a conquest?"

"I would, Señor, I might prevail on you to steer more to the south!"

"Go to, Martin Alonzo, and forget thy cravings. My heart is in the west, and thither reason teacheth me to follow it. First hear my orders, and then go seek the Niña, that thy brother, the worthy Vicente Yañez, may obey them also. Should aught separate us in the night, it shall be the duty of all to stand manfully toward the west, striving to find our company; for it would be a sad, as well as a useless thing, to be wandering alone in this unknown ocean."

Pinzon, though evidently much displeased, was fain to obey, and after a short but a sharp and loud altercation with the admiral, the commander of the Pinta caused her to sheer toward the felucca to execute the order.

"Martin Alonzo beginneth to waver," Columbus observed to Luis. "He is a bold and exceeding skilful mariner, but steadiness of object is not his greatest quality. He must be restrained from following the impulses of his weakness, by the higher hand of authority. Cathay!—Cathay is my aim!"

After midnight the wind increased, and for two hours the caravels glanced through the smooth ocean at their greatest speed, which equalled nine English miles the hour. Few now undressed, except to change their clothes; and Columbus slumbered on the poop that night, using an old sail for his couch. Luis was his companion, and both were up and on the deck with the first appearance of dawn. A common feeling seemed to exist among all, that land was near, and that a great discovery was about to be made. An annuity of ten thousand maravedis had been promised by the sovereigns to him who should first descry land, and every eye was on the gaze, whenever opportunity permitted, to gain the prize.

As the light diffused itself downward toward the margin of the ocean, in the western horizon, all thought there was the appearance of land, and sail was eagerly crowded on the different vessels, in order to press forward as fast as possible, that their respective crews might enjoy the earliest and the best chances of obtaining the first view. In this respect, circumstances singularly balanced the advantages and disadvantages between the competitors. The Niña was the fastest vessel in light airs and smooth water, but she was also the smallest. The Pinta came next in general speed, holding a middle place in size, and beating her consorts with a fresh breeze; while the Santa Maria, the last in point of sailing, had the highest masts, and consequently swept the widest range of horizon.

"There is a good feeling uppermost to-day, Señor Don Christopher," said Luis, as he stood at the admiral's side, watching the advance of the light; "and if eyes can do it, we may hope for the discovery of land. The late run hath awakened all our hopes, and land we must have, even if we raise it from the bottom of the ocean."

"Yonder is Pepe, the dutiful husband of Monica, perched on our highest yard, straining his eyes toward the west, in the hope of gaining the reward!" said Columbus, smiling. "Ten thousand maravedis, yearly, would, in sooth, be some atonement to carry back to the grieved mother and the deserted boy!"

"Martin Alonzo is in earnest, also, Señor. See how he presseth forward in the Pinta; but Vicente Yañez hath the heels of him, and is determined to make his salutations first to the Great Khan, neglectful of the elder brother's rights."

"Señor!—Señores!" shouted Sancho from the spar on which he was seated as composedly as a modern lady would recline on her ottoman—"the felucca is speaking in signals."

"This is true," cried Columbus—"Vicente Yañez showeth the colors of the queen, and there goeth a lombarda to announce some great event!"

As these were the signals directed in the event that either vessel should discover land before her consorts, little doubt was entertained that the leading caravel had, at last, really announced the final success of the expedition. Still the recent and grave disappointment was remembered, and, though all devoutly poured out their gratitude in mental offerings, their lips were sealed until the result should show the truth. Every rag of canvas was set, however, and the vessels seemed to hasten their speed toward the west, like birds tired with an unusual flight, which make new efforts with their wearied wings as the prospect of alighting suddenly breaks on their keen vision and active instincts.

Hour passed after hour, however, and brought no confirmation of the blessed tidings. The western horizon looked heavy and clouded throughout the morning, it is true, often deceiving even the most practised eyes; but as the day advanced, and the vessels had passed more than fifty miles further toward the west, it became impossible to ascribe the hopes of the morning to another optical illusion. The depression of spirits that succeeded this new disappointment was greater than any that had before existed, and the murmurs that arose were neither equivocal nor suppressed. It was urged that some malign influence was leading the adventurers on, finally to abandon them to despair and destruction, in a wilderness of waters. This is the moment when, it has been said, Columbus was compelled to make conditions with his followers, stipulating to abandon the enterprise altogether, should it fail of success in a given number of days. But this weakness has been falsely ascribed to the great navigator, who never lost the fullest exercise of his authority, even in the darkest moments of doubt; maintaining his purpose, and asserting his power, with the same steadiness and calmness, in what some thought this distant verge of the earth, as he had done in the rivers of Spain. Prudence and policy at last dictated a change of course, however, which he was neither too obstinate nor too proud to submit to, and he accordingly adopted it of his own accord.

"We are now quite a thousand leagues from Ferro, by my private reckoning, friend Luis," said Columbus to his young companion, in one of their private conferences, which took place after nightfall, "and it is really time to expect the continent of Asia. Hitherto I have looked for naught but islands, and not with much expectation of seeing even them, though Martin Alonzo and the pilots have been so sanguine in their hopes. The large flocks of birds, however, that have appeared to-day, would seem to invite us to follow their flights—land, out of doubt, being their aim. I shall accordingly change our course more to the south, though not as far as Pinzon desireth, Cathay being still my goal."

Columbus gave the necessary orders, and the two other caravels were brought within hail of the Santa Maria, when their commanders were directed to steer west-south-west. The reason for this change was the fact that so many birds had been seen flying in that direction. The intention of the admiral was to pursue this course for two days. Notwithstanding this alteration, no land was visible in the morning; but, as the wind was light, and the vessels had only made five leagues since the course was changed, the disappointment produced less despondency than usual. In spite of their uncertainty, all in the vessels now rioted in the balmy softness of the atmosphere, which was found so fragrant that it was delicious to breathe it. The weeds, too, became more plenty, and many of them were as fresh as if torn from their native rocks only a day or two previously. Birds, that unequivocally belonged to the land, were also seen in considerable numbers, one of which was actually taken; while ducks abounded, and another pelican was met. Thus passed the 8th of October, the adventurers filled with hope, though the vessels only increased their distance from Europe some forty miles in the course of the twenty-four hours. The succeeding day brought no other material change than a shift of wind, which compelled the admiral to alter his course to west-by-north, for a few hours. This caused him some uneasiness, for it was his wish to proceed due west, or west-southerly; though it afforded considerable relief to many among his people, who had been terrified by the prevalence of the winds in one direction. Had the variation still existed, this would have been, in fact, steering the very course the admiral desired to go: but by this time, the vessels were in a latitude and longitude where the needle resumed its powers and became faithful to its direction. In the course of the night, the trades also resumed their influence; and early on the morning of the 10th, the vessels again headed toward the west-south-west, by compass, which was, in truth, the real course, or as near to it as might be.

Such was the state of things when the sun rose on the morning of the 10th October, 1492. The wind had freshened, and all three of the vessels were running free the whole day, at a rate varying from five knots to nine. The signs of the proximity of land had been so very numerous of late, that, at every league of ocean they passed over, the adventurers had the strongest expectations of discovering it, and nearly every eye in all three of the ships was kept constantly bent on the western horizon, in the hope of its owner's being the first to make the joyful announcement of its appearance. The cry of "land" had been so frequent of late, however, that Columbus caused it to be made known that he who again uttered it causelessly, should lose the reward promised by the sovereigns, even should he happen to be successful in the end. This information induced more caution, and not a tongue betrayed its master's eagerness on this all-engrossing subject, throughout the anxious and exciting days of the 8th, 9th, and 10th October. But, their progress in the course of the 10th exceeding that made in the course of both the other days, the evening sky was watched with a vigilance even surpassing that which had attended any previous sunset. This was the moment most favorable for examining the western horizon, the receding light illuminating the whole watery expanse in that direction, in a way to give up all its secrets to the eye.

"Is that a hummock of land?" asked Pepe of Sancho, in a low voice, as they lay together on a yard, watching the upper limb of the sun, as it settled, like a glimmering star, beneath the margin of the ocean; "or is it some of this misguiding vapor that hath so often misled us of late?"

"'Tis neither, Pepe," returned the more cool and experienced Sancho; "but a rise of the sea, which is ever thus tossing itself upward on the margin of the ocean. Didst ever see a calm so profound, that the water left a straight circle on the horizon? No—no—there is no land to be seen in the west to-night; the ocean, in that quarter, looking as blank as if we stood on the western shore of Ferro, and gazed outward into the broad fields of the Atlantic. Our noble admiral may have the truth of his side, Pepe; but, as yet, he hath no other evidence of it than is to be found in his reasons."

"And dost thou, too, take sides against him, Sancho, and say that he is a madman who is willing to lead others to destruction, as well as himself, so that he die an admiral in fact, and a viceroy in fancy?"

"I take sides against no man whose doblas take sides with me, Pepe; for that would be quarrelling with the best friend that both the rich and poor can make, which is gold. Don Christopher is doubtless very learned, and one thing hath he settled to my satisfaction, even though neither he nor any of us ever see a single jewel of Cathay, or pluck a hair from the beard of the Great Khan, and that is, that this world is round; had it been a plain, all this water would not be placed at the outer side, since it would clearly run off, unless dammed up by land. Thou canst conceive that, Pepe?"

"That do I; it is reasonable and according to every man's experience. Monica thinketh the Genoese a saint!"

"Harkee, Pepe; thy Monica is no doubt an uncommonly sensible woman, else would she never have taken thee for a husband, when she might have chosen among a dozen of thy fellows. I once thought of the girl myself, and might have told her so, had she seen fit to call me a saint, too, which she did not, seeing that she used a very different epithet. But, admitting the Señor Colon to be a saint, he would be none the better admired for it, inasmuch as I never yet met with a saint, or even with a virgin that could understand the bearings and distances of a run as short as that from Cadiz to Barcelona."

"Thou speakest irreverently, Sancho, of virgins and saints, seeing that they know every thing" —

"Ay, every thing but that. Our Lady of Rabida does not know south-east-and-by-southe-half-southe, from north-west-and-by-noathe-half-noathe. I have tried her, in this matter, and I tell thee she is as ignorant of it as thy Monica is ignorant of the manner in which the Duchess of Medina Sidonia saluteth the noble duke, her husband, when he returneth from hawking."

"I dare say the duchess would not know, either, what to say, were she in Monica's place, and were she called on to receive me, as Monica will be, when we return from this great expedition. If I have never hawked, neither hath the duke ever sailed for two-and-thirty days, in a west course from Ferro, and this, too, without once seeing land!"

"Thou say'st true, Pepe; nor hast thou ever yet done this and returned to Palos. But what meaneth all this movement on deck? Our people seem to be much moved by some feeling, while I can swear it is not from having discovered Cathay, or from having seen the Great Khan, shining like a carbuncle, on his throne of diamonds."

"It is rather that they do not see him thus, that the men are moved. Dost not hear angry and threatening words from the mouths of the troublesome ones?"

"By San Iago! were I Don Christopher, but I would deduct a dobla from the wages of each of the rascals, and give the gold to such peaceable men as you and me, Pepe, who are willing to starve to death, ere we will go back without a sight of Asia."

"'Tis something of this sort, of a truth, Sancho. Let us descend, that his Excellency may see that he hath some friends among the crew."

As Sancho assented to this proposition, he and Pepe stood on the deck in the next minute. Here, indeed, the people were found in a more mutinous state than they had been since the fleet left Spain. The long continuation of fair winds, and pleasant weather, had given them so much reason to expect a speedy termination of their voyage, that nearly the whole crew were now of opinion it was due to themselves to insist on the abandonment of an expedition that seemed destined to lead to nothing but destruction. The discussion was loud and angry, even one or two of the pilots inclining to think, with their inferiors, that further perseverance would certainly be useless, and might be fatal. When Sancho and Pepe joined the crowd, it had just been determined to go in a body to Columbus, and to demand, in terms that could not be misconceived, the immediate return of the ships to Spain. In order that this might be done with method, Pedro Alonzo Niño, one of the pilots, and an aged seaman called Juan Martin, were selected as spokesmen. At this critical moment, too, the admiral and Luis were seen descending from the poop, with an intent to retire to their cabin, when a rush was made aft, by all on deck, and twenty voices were heard simultaneously crying—

"Señor—Don Christopher—Your Excellency—Señor Almirante!"

Columbus stopped, and faced the people with a calmness and dignity that caused the heart of Niño to leap toward his mouth, and which materially checked the ardor of most of his followers.

"What would ye?" demanded the admiral, sternly. "Speak! Ye address a friend."

"We come to ask our precious lives, Señor," answered Juan Martin, who thought his insignificance might prove a shield—"nay, what is more, the means of putting bread into the mouths of our wives and children. All here are weary of this profitless voyage, and most think if it last any longer than shall be necessary to return, it will be the means of our perishing of want."

"Know ye the distance that lieth between us and Ferro, that ye come to me with this blind and foolish request? Speak, Niño; I see that thou art also of their number, notwithstanding thy hesitation."

"Señor," returned the pilot, "we are all of a mind. To go further into this blank and unknown ocean, is tempting God to destroy us, for our wilfulness. It is vain to suppose that this broad belt of water hath been placed by Providence around the habitable earth for any other purpose than to rebuke those who audaciously seek to be admitted to mysteries beyond their understanding. Do not all the churchmen, Señor—the pious prior of Santa Maria de Rabida, your own particular friend, included—tell us constantly of the necessity of submitting to a knowledge we can never equal, and to believe without striving to lift a veil that covers incomprehensible things?"

"I might retort on thee, honest Niño, with thine own words," answered Columbus, "and bid thee confide in those whose knowledge thou canst never equal, and to follow submissively where thou art totally unfitted to lead. Go to; withdraw with thy fellows, and let me hear no more of this."

"Nay, Señor," cried two or three in a breath, "we cannot perish without making our complaints heard. We have followed too far already, and, even now, may have gone beyond the means of a safe return. Let us, then, turn the heads of the caravels toward Spain, this night, lest we never live to see that blessed country again."

"This toucheth on revolt! Who among ye dare use language so bold, to your admiral?"

"All of us, Señor," answered twenty voices together. "Men need be bold, when their lives would be forfeited by silence."

"Sancho, art thou, too, of the party of these mutineers? Dost thou confess thy heart to be Spain-sick, and thy unmanly fears to be stronger than thy hopes of imperishable glory and thy longings for the riches and pleasures of Cathay?"

"If I do, Señor Don Almirante, set me to greasing masts, and take me from the helm, forever, as one unfit to watch the whirlings of the north star. Sail with the caravels, into the hall of the Great Khan, and make fast to his throne, and you will find Sancho at his post, whether it be at the helm or at the lead. He was born in a ship-yard, and hath a natural desire to know what a ship can do."

"And thou, Pepe? Hast thou so forgotten thy duty as to come with this language to thy commander? to the admiral and viceroy of thy sovereign, the Doña Isabella?"

"Viceroy over what?" exclaimed a voice from the crowd, without permitting Pepe to answer. "A viceroy over sea-weed, and one that hath tunny-fish, and whales, and pelicans, for subjects! We tell you, Señor Colon, that this is no treatment for Castilians, who require more substantial discoveries than fields of weeds, and islands of clouds!"

"Home!—Home!—Spain!—Spain!—Palos!—Palos!" cried nearly all together, Sancho and Pepe having quitted the throng and ranged themselves at the side of Columbus. "We will no further west, which is tempting God; but demand to be carried back whence we came, if, indeed, it be not already too late for so happy a deliverance."

Mercedes Of Castile; Or, The Voyage To Cathay | 275

"To whom speak ye in this shameless manner, graceless knaves?" exclaimed Luis, unconsciously laying a hand where it had been his practice to carry a rapier. "Get ye gone, or" —

"Be tranquil, friend Pedro, and leave this matter with me," interrupted the admiral, whose composure had scarce been deranged by the violent conduct of his subordinates. "Listen to what I have to say, ye rude and rebellious men, and let it be received as my final answer to any and all such demands as ye have just dared to make. This expedition hath been sent forth by the two sovereigns, your royal master and mistress, with the express design of crossing the entire breadth of the vast Atlantic, until it might reach the shores of India. Now, let what will happen, these high expectations shall not be disappointed; but westward we sail, until stopped by the land. For this determination, my life shall answer. Look to it, that none of yours be endangered by resistance to the royal orders, or by disrespect and disobedience to their appointed substitute; for, another murmur, and I mark the man that uttereth it, for signal punishment. In this ye have my full determination, and beware of encountering the anger of those whose displeasure may prove more fatal than these fancied dangers of the ocean.

"Look at what ye have before you, in the way of fear, and then at what ye have before ye, in the way of hope. In the first case, ye have every thing to dread from the sovereigns' anger, should ye proceed to a violent resistance of their authority; or, what is as bad, something like a certainty of your being unable to reach Spain, for want of food and water, should ye revolt against your lawful leaders and endeavor to return. For this, it is now too late. The voyage east must, as regards time, be double that we have just made, and the caravels are beginning to be lightened in their casks. Land, and land in this region, hath become necessary to us. Now look at the other side of the picture. Before ye, lieth Cathay, with all its riches, its novelties, and its glories! A region more wonderful than any that hath yet been inhabited by man, and occupied by a race as gentle as they are hospitable and just. To this must be added the approbation of the sovereigns, and the credit that will belong to the meanest mariner that hath manfully stood by his commander in achieving so great an end."

"If we will obey three days longer, Señor, will you then turn toward Spain, should no land be seen?" cried a voice from the crowd.

"Never," returned Columbus, firmly. "To India am I bound, and for India will I steer, though another month be needed to complete the journey. Go, then, to your posts or your hammocks, and let me hear no more of this."

There was so much natural dignity in the manner of Columbus, and when he spoke in anger, his voice carried so much of rebuke with it, that it exceeded the daring of ordinary men to presume to answer when he commanded silence. The people sullenly dispersed, therefore, though the disaffection was by no means appeased. Had there been only a single vessel in the expedition, it is quite probable that they would have proceeded to some act of violence; but, uncertain of the state of feeling in the Pinta and the Niña, and holding Martin Alonzo Pinzon in as much habitual respect as they stood in awe of Columbus, the boldest among them were, for the present, fain to give vent to their dissatisfaction in murmurs, though they secretly meditated decided measures, as soon as an opportunity for consultation and concert with the crews of the other vessels might offer.

"This looketh serious, Señor," said Luis, as soon as he and the admiral were alone again in their little cabin, "and, by St. Luke! it might cool the ardor of these knaves, did your Excellency suffer me to cast two or three of the most insolent of the vagabonds into the sea."

"Which is a favor that some among them have actually contemplated conferring upon thee and me," answered Columbus.

"Sancho keepeth me well informed of the feeling among the people, and it is now many days since he hath let me know this fact. We will proceed peaceably, if possible, Señor Gutierrez, or de Muños, whichever name thou most affectest, as long as we can; but should there truly arise an occasion to resort to force, thou wilt find that Christofero Colombo knoweth how to wield a sword as well as he knoweth how to use his instruments of science."

"How far do you really think us from land, Señor Almirante? I ask from curiosity, and not from dread; for though the ship floated on the very verge of the earth, ready to fall off into vacuum, you should hear no murmur from me."

"I am well assured of this, young noble," returned Columbus, affectionately squeezing the hand of Luis, "else wouldst thou not be here. I make our distance from Ferro exceed a thousand marine leagues; this is about the same as that at which I have supposed Cathay to lie from Europe, and it is, out of question, sufficiently far to meet with many of the islands that are known to abound in the seas of Asia. The public reckoning maketh the distance a little more than eight hundred leagues; but, in consequence of the favorable currents of which we have lately had so much, I doubt if we are not fully eleven hundred from the Canaries, at this moment, if not even further. We are doubtless a trifle nearer to the Azores, which are situated further west, though in a higher latitude."

"Then you think, Señor, that we may really expect land, ere many days?"

"So certain do I feel of this, Luis, that I should have little apprehension of complying with the terms of these audacious men, but for the humiliation. Ptolemy divided the earth into twenty-four hours, of fifteen degrees each, and I place but some five or six of these hours in the Atlantic. Thirteen hundred leagues, I feel persuaded, will bring us to the shores of Asia, and eleven of these thirteen hundred leagues do I believe we have come."

"To-morrow may then prove an eventful day, Señor Almirante; and now to our cots, where I shall dream of a fairer land than Christian eye ever yet looked upon, with the fairest maiden of Spain—nay, by San Pedro! of Europe—beckoning me on!"

Columbus and Luis now sought their rest. In the morning, it was evident by the surly looks of the people, that feelings like a suppressed volcano were burning in their bosoms, and that any untoward accident might produce an eruption. Fortunately, however, signs, of a nature so novel, soon appeared, as to draw off the attention of the most disaffected from their melancholy broodings. The wind was fresh, as usual fair, and, what was really a novelty since quitting Ferro, the sea had got up, and the vessels were riding over waves which removed that appearance of an unnatural calm that had hitherto alarmed the men with its long continuance. Columbus had not been on deck five minutes, when a joyful cry from Pepe drew all eyes toward the yard on which he was at work. The seaman was pointing eagerly at some object in the water, and rushing to the side of the vessel, all saw the welcome sign that had caught his gaze. As the ship lifted on a sea, and shot ahead, a rush of a bright fresh green was passed, and the men gave a loud shout, for all well knew that this plant certainly came from some shore, and that it could not have been long torn from the spot of its growth.

"This is truly a blessed omen!" said Columbus; "rushes cannot grow without the light of heaven, whatever may be the case with weeds."

This little occurrence changed, or at least checked, the feelings of the disaffected. Hope once more resumed its sway, and all who could, ascended the rigging to watch the western horizon. The rapid motion of the vessels, too, added to this buoyancy of feeling, the Pinta and Niña passing and repassing the admiral, as it might be in pure wantonness. A few hours later, fresh weeds were met, and about noon Sancho announced confidently that he had seen a fish which is known to live in the vicinity of rocks. An hour later, the Niña came sheering up toward the admiral, with her commander in the rigging, evidently desirous of communicating some tidings of moment.

"What now, good Vicente Yañez?" called out Columbus; "thou seemest the messenger of welcome news!"

"I think myself such, Don Christopher," answered the other. "We have just passed a bush bearing roseberries, quite newly torn from the tree! This is a sign that cannot deceive us."

"Thou say'st true, my friend. To the west!—to the west! Happy will he be whose eyes first behold the wonders of the Indies!"

It would not be easy to describe the degree of hope and exultation that now began to show itself among the people. Good-natured jests flew about the decks, and the laugh was easily raised where so lately all had been despondency and gloom. The minutes flew swiftly by, and every man had ceased to think of Spain, bending his thoughts again on the as yet unseen west.

A little later, a cry of exultation was heard from the Pinta, which was a short distance to windward and ahead of the admiral. As this vessel shortened sail and hove-to, lowering a boat, and then immediately kept away, the Santa Maria soon came foaming up under her quarter, and spoke her.

"What now, Martin Alonzo?" asked Columbus, suppressing his anxiety in an appearance of calmness and dignity. "Thou and thy people seem in an ecstasy!"

"Well may we be so! About an hour since, we passed a piece of the cane-plant, of the sort of which sugar is made in the East, as travellers say, and such as we often see in our own ports. But this is a trifling symptom of land compared to the trunk of a tree that we have also passed. As if Providence had not yet dealt with us with sufficient kindness, all these articles were met floating near each other; and we have thought them of sufficient value to lower a boat, that we might possess them."

"Lay thy sails to the mast, good Martin Alonzo, and send thy prizes hither, that I may judge of their value."

Pinzon complied, and the Santa Maria being hove-to, at the same time, the boat soon touched her side. Martin Alonzo made but one bound from the thwart to the gunwale of the ship, and was soon on the deck of the admiral. Here he eagerly displayed the different articles that his men tossed after him, all of which had been taken out of the sea, not an hour before.

"See, noble Señores," said Martin Alonzo, almost breathless with haste to display his treasures—"this is a sort of board, though of unknown wood, and fashioned with exceeding care: here is also another piece of cane: this is a plant that surely cometh from the land; and most of all, this is a walking-stick, fashioned by the hand of man, and that, too, with exceeding care!"

"All this is true," said Columbus, examining the different articles, one by one; "God, in his might and power, be praised for these comfortable evidences of our near approach to a new world! None but a malignant Infidel can now doubt of our final success."

"These things have questionless come from some boat that hath been upset, which will account for their being so near each other in the water," said Martin Alonzo, willing to sustain his physical proofs by a plausible theory. "It would not be wonderful were drowned bodies near."

"Let us hope not, Martin Alonzo," answered the admiral; "let us fancy naught so melancholy. A thousand accidents may have thrown these articles together, into the sea; and once there, they would float in company for a twelvemonth, unless violently separated. But come they whence they may, to us, they are infallible proofs that not only land is near, but land which is the abiding-place of men."

It is not easy to describe the enthusiasm that now prevailed in all the vessels. Hitherto they had met with only birds, and fishes, and weeds, signs that are often precarious; but here was such proof of their being in the neighborhood of their fellow-creatures, as it was not easy to withstand. It was true, articles of this nature might drift, in time, even across the vast distance they had come; but it was not probable that they would drift so far in company. Then, the berries were fresh, the board was of an unknown wood, and the walking-stick, in particular, if such indeed was its use, was carved in a manner that was never practised in Europe. The different articles passed from hand to hand, until all in the ship had examined them; and every thing like doubt vanished before this unlooked-for confirmation of the admiral's predictions. Pinzon returned to his vessel, sail was again made, and the fleet continued to steer to the west-south-west, until the hour of sunset.

Something like a chill of disappointment again came over the more faint-hearted of the people, however, as they once more, or for the thirty-fourth time since quitting Gomera, saw the sun sink behind a watery horizon. More than a hundred vigilant eyes watched the glowing margin of the ocean, at this interesting moment, and though the heavens were cloudless, naught was visible but the gloriously tinted vault, and the outline of water, broken into the usual ragged forms of the unquiet element.

The wind freshened as evening closed, and Columbus having called his vessels together, as was usual with him at that hour, he issued new orders concerning the course. For the last two or three days they had been steering materially to the southward of west, and Columbus, who felt persuaded that his most certain and his nearest direction from land to land, was to traverse the ocean, if possible, on a single parallel of latitude, was anxious to resume his favorite course, which was what he fancied to be due west. Just as night drew around the mariners, accordingly, the ships edged away to the required course, and ran off at the rate of nine miles the hour, following the orb of day as if resolute to penetrate into the mysteries of his nightly retreat, until some great discovery should reward the effort.

Immediately after this change in the course, the people sang the vesper hymn, as usual, which, in that mild sea, they often deferred until the hour when the watch below sought their hammocks. That night, however, none felt disposed to sleep; and it was late when the chant of the seamen commenced, with the words of *"Salve fac Regina."* It was a solemn thing to hear the songs of religious praise mingling with the sighings of the breeze and the wash of the waters, in that ocean solitude; and the solemnity was increased by the expectations of the adventurers and the mysteries that lay behind the curtain they believed themselves about to raise. Never before had this hymn sounded so sweetly in the ears of Columbus, and Luis found his eyes suffusing with tears, as he recalled the soft thrilling notes of Mercedes' voice, in her holy breathings of praise at this hour. When the office ended, the admiral called the crew to the quarter-deck, and addressed them earnestly from his station on the poop.

"I rejoice, my friends," he said, "that you have had the grace to chant the vesper hymn in so devout a spirit, at a moment when there is so much reason to be grateful to God for his goodness to us throughout this voyage. Look back at the past and see if one of you, the oldest sailor of your number, can recall any passage at sea, I will not say of equal length, for that no one here hath ever before made, but any equal number of days at sea, in which the winds have been as fair, the weather as propitious, or the ocean as calm, as on this occasion. Then what cheering signs have encouraged us to persevere! God is in the midst of the ocean, my friends, as well as in his sanctuaries of the land. Step by step, as it were, hath he led us on, now filling the air with birds, now causing the sea to abound with unusual fishes, and then spreading before us fields of plants, such as are seldom met far from the rocks where they grew. The last and best of his signs hath he given us this day. My own calculations are in unison with these proofs, and I deem it probable that we reach the land this very night. In a few hours, or when we shall have run the distance commanded by the eye, as the light left us, I shall deem it prudent to shorten sail; and I call on all of you to be watchful, lest we unwittingly throw ourselves on the strange shores. Ye know that the sovereigns have graciously promised ten thousand maravedis, yearly, and for life, to him who shall first discover land: to this rich reward I will add a doublet of velvet, such as it would befit a grandee to wear. Sleep not, then;

but, at the turn of the night, be all vigilance and watchfulness. I am now most serious with ye, and look for land this very blessed night."

These encouraging words produced their full effect, the men scattering themselves in the ship, each taking the best position he could, to earn the coveted prizes. Deep expectation is always a quiet feeling, the jealous senses seeming to require silence and intensity of concentration, in order to give them their full exercise. Columbus remained on the poop, while Luis, less interested, threw himself on a sail, and passed the time in musing on Mercedes, and in picturing to himself the joyful moment when he might meet her again, a triumphant and successful adventurer.

The death-like silence that prevailed in the ship, added to the absorbing interest of that important night. At the distance of a mile was the little Niña, gliding on her course with a full sail; while half a league still further in advance, was to be seen the shadowy outline of the Pinta, which preceded her consorts, as the swiftest sailer with a fresh breeze. Sancho had been round to every sheet and brace, in person, and never before had the admiral's ship held as good way with her consorts as on that night, all three of the vessels appearing to have caught the eager spirit of those they contained, and to be anxious to outdo themselves. At moments the men started, while the wind murmured through the cordage, as if they heard unknown and strange voices from a mysterious world; and fifty times, when the waves combed upon the sides of the ship, did they turn their heads, expecting to see a crowd of unknown beings, fresh from the eastern world, pouring in upon their decks.

As for Columbus, he sighed often; for minutes at a time would he stand looking intently toward the west, like one who strove to penetrate the gloom of night, with organs exceeding human powers. At length he bent his body forward, gazed intently over the weather railing of the ship, and then, lifting his cap, he seemed to be offering up his spirit in thanksgiving or prayer. All this Luis witnessed where he lay: at the next instant he heard himself called.

"Pero Gutierrez—Pedro de Muños—Luis—whatever thou art termed," said Columbus, his fine masculine voice trembling with eagerness—"come hither, son; tell me if thine eyes accord with mine. Look in this direction— here, more on the vessel's beam; seest thou aught uncommon?"

"I saw a light, Señor; one that resembled a candle, being neither larger nor more brilliant; and to me it appeared to move, as if carried in the hand, or tossed by waves."

"Thy eyes did not deceive thee; thou seest it doth not come of either of our consorts, both of which are here on the bow."

"What do you, then, take this light to signify, Don Christopher?"

"Land! It is either on the land itself, rendered small by distance, or it cometh of some vessel that is a stranger to us, and which belongeth to the Indies. There is Rodrigo Sanchez of Segovia, the comptroller of the fleet, beneath us; descend, and bid him come hither."

Luis did as required, and presently the comptroller was also at the admiral's side. Half an hour passed, and the light was not seen again; then it gleamed upward once or twice, like a torch, and finally disappeared. This circumstance was soon known to all in the ship, though few attached the same importance to it as Columbus himself.

"This is land," quietly observed the admiral, to those near his person: "ere many hours we may expect to behold it. Now ye may pour out your souls in gratitude and confidence, for in such a sign there can be no deception. No phenomenon of the ocean resembleth that light; and my reckoning placeth us in a quarter of the world where land *must* exist, else is the earth no sphere."

Notwithstanding this great confidence on the part of the admiral, most of those in the ship did not yet feel the same certainty in the result, although all felt the strongest hopes of falling in with land next day. Columbus saying no more on the subject, the former silence was soon resumed, and, in a few minutes, every eye was again turned toward the west, in anxious watchfulness. In this manner the time passed away, the ships driving ahead with a speed much exceeding that of their ordinary rate of sailing, until the night had turned, when its darkness was suddenly illuminated by a blaze of light, and the report of a gun from the Pinta came struggling up against the fresh breeze of the trades.

"There speaketh Martin Alonzo!" exclaimed the admiral; "and we may be certain that he hath not given the signal idly. Who sitteth on the top-gallant yard, there, on watch for wonders ahead?"

"Señor Don Almirante, it is I," answered Sancho. "I have been here since we sang the vesper hymn."

"Seest thou aught unusual, westward? Look vigilantly, for we touch on mighty things!"

"Naught, Señor, unless it be that the Pinta is lessening her canvas, and the Niña is already closing with our fleet consort—nay, I now see the latter shortening sail also!"

"For these great tidings, all honor and praise be to God! These are proofs that no false cry hath this time misled their judgments. We will join our consorts, good Bartolemeo, ere we take in a single inch of canvas."

Every thing was now in motion on board the Santa Maria, which went dashing ahead for another half hour, when she came up with the two other caravels, both of which had hauled by the wind, under short canvas, and were forging slowly through the water, on different tacks, like coursers cooling themselves after having terminated a severe struggle by reaching the goal.

"Come hither, Luis," said Columbus, "and feast thine eyes with a sight that doth not often meet the gaze of the best of Christians."

The night was far from dark, a tropical sky glittering with a thousand stars, and even the ocean itself appearing to emit a sombre, melancholy light. By the aid of such assistants it was possible to see several miles, and more especially to note objects on the margin of the ocean. When the young man cast his eyes to leeward, as directed by Columbus, he very plainly perceived a point where the blue of the sky ceased, and a dark mound rose from the water, stretching for a few leagues southward, and then terminated, as it had commenced, by a union between the watery margin of the ocean and the void of heaven. The intermediate space had the defined outline, the density, and the hue of land, as seen at midnight.

"Behold the Indies!" said Columbus; "the mighty problem is solved! This is doubtless an island, but a continent is near. Laud be to God!"

CHAPTER XXII

"There is a Power, whose care
Teaches thy way along that pathless coast—
The desert and illimitable air—
Lone wandering, but not lost."

Bryant.

The two or three hours that succeeded, were hours of an extraordinary and intense interest. The three vessels stood hovering off the dusky shore, barely keeping at a safe distance, stripped of most of their canvas, resembling craft that cruised leisurely at a given point, indifferent to haste or speed. As they occasionally and slowly passed each other, words of heart-felt congratulation were exchanged; but no noisy or intemperate exultation was heard on that all-important night. The sensations excited in the adventurers, by their success, were too deep and solemn for any such vulgar exhibition of joy; and perhaps there was not one among them all who did not, at that moment, inwardly confess his profound submission to, and absolute dependence on a Divine Providence.

Columbus was silent. Emotions like his seldom find vent in words; but his heart was overflowing with gratitude and love. He believed himself to be in the further east, and to have reached that part of the world by sailing west; and it is natural to suppose that he expected the curtain of day would rise on some of those scenes of oriental magnificence which had been so eloquently described by the Polos and other travellers in those remote and little-known regions. That this or other islands were inhabited, the little he had seen sufficiently proved; but, as yet, all the rest was conjecture of the wildest and most uncertain character. The fragrance of the land, however, was very perceptible in the vessels, thus affording an opportunity to two of the senses to unite in establishing their success.

At length the long wished-for day approached, and the eastern sky began to assume the tints that precede the appearance of the sun. As the light diffused itself athwart the dark blue ocean, and reached the island, the outlines of the latter became more and more distinct; then objects became visible on its surface, trees, glades, rocks, and irregularities, starting out of the gloom, until the whole picture was drawn in the gray, solemn colors of morning. Presently the direct rays of the sun touched it, gilding its prominent points, and throwing others into shadow. It then became apparent that the discovery was that of an island of no great extent, well wooded, and of a verdant and pleasant aspect. The land was low, but possessed an outline sufficiently graceful to cause it to seem a paradise in the eyes of men who had seriously doubted whether they were ever to look on solid ground again. The view of his mother earth is always pleasant to the mariner who has long gazed on nothing but water and sky; but thrice beautiful did it now seem to men who not only saw in it their despair cured, but their most brilliant hopes revived. From the position of the land near him, Columbus did not doubt that he had passed another island, on which the light had been seen, and, from his known course, this conjecture has since been rendered almost certain.

The sun had scarcely risen, when living beings were seen rushing out of the woods, to gaze in astonishment at the sudden appearance of machines, that were at first mistaken by the untutored islanders, for messengers from heaven. Shortly after, Columbus anchored his little fleet, and landed to take possession in the name of the two sovereigns.

As much state was observed on this occasion as the limited means of the adventurers would allow. Each vessel sent a boat, with her commander. The admiral, attired in scarlet, and carrying the royal standard, proceeded in advance, while Martin Alonzo, and Vicente Yañez Pinzon, followed, holding banners bearing crosses, the symbol of the expedition, with letters representing the initials of the two sovereigns, or F. and Y., for Fernando and Ysabel.

The forms usual to such occasions were observed on reaching the shore. Columbus took possession, rendered thanks to God for the success of the expedition, and then began to look about him in order to form some estimate of the value of his discovery. [3]

No sooner were the ceremonies observed, than the people crowded round the admiral, and began to pour out their congratulations for his success, with their contrition for their own distrust and disaffection. The scene has often been described as a proof of the waywardness and inconstancy of human judgments; the being who had so lately been scowled on as a reckless and selfish adventurer, being now regarded as little less than a God. The admiral was no more elated by this adulation, than he had been intimidated by the previous dissatisfaction, maintaining his calmness of exterior and gravity of demeanor, with those who pressed around him, though a close observer might have detected the gleaming of triumph in his eye, and the glow of inward rapture on his cheek.

"These honest people are as inconstant in their apprehensions, as they are extreme in their rejoicings," said Columbus to Luis, when liberated a little from the throng; "yesterday they would have cast me into the sea, and to-day they are much disposed to forget God, himself, in his unworthy creature. Dost not see, that the men who gave us most concern, on account of their discontent, are now the loudest in their applause?"

"This is but nature, Señor; fear flying from panic to exultation. These knaves fancy they are praising you, when they are, in truth, rejoicing in their own escape from some unknown but dreaded evil. Our friends Sancho and Pepe seem not to be thus overwhelmed, for while the last is gathering flowers from this shore of India, the first seems to be looking about him with commendable coolness, as if he might be calculating the latitude and longitude of the Great Khan's doblas."

Columbus smiled, and, accompanied by Luis, he drew nearer to the two men mentioned, who were a little apart from the rest of the group. Sancho was standing with his hands thrust into the bosom of his doublet, regarding the scene with the coolness of a philosopher, and toward him the admiral first directed his steps.

"How is this, Sancho of the ship-yard-gate?" said the great navigator; "thou lookest on this glorious scene as coolly as thou wouldst regard a street in Moguer, or a field in Andalusia?"

"Señor Don Almirante, the same hand made both. This is not the first island on which I have landed; nor are yonder naked savages the first men I have seen who were not dressed in scarlet doublets."

"But hast thou no feeling for success—no gratitude to God for this vast discovery? Reflect, my friend, we are on the confines of Asia, and yet have we come here by holding a western course."

"That the last is true, Señor, I will swear myself, having held the tiller in mine own hands no small part of the way. Do you think, Señor Don Almirante, that we have come far enough in this direction to have got to the back side of the earth, or to stand, as it might be, under the very feet of Spain?"

"By no means. The realms of the Great Khan will scarcely occupy the position you mean."

"Then, Señor, what will there be to prevent the doblas of that country from falling off into the air, leaving us our journey for our pains?"

"The same power that will prevent our caravels from dropping out of the sea, and the water itself from following. These things depend on natural laws, my friend, and nature is a legislator that will be respected."

"It is all Moorish to me," returned Sancho, rubbing his eye-brows. "Here we are, of a verity, if not actually beneath the feet of Spain, standing, as it might be, on the side of the house; and yet I find no more difficulty in keeping on an even keel, than I did in Moguer—by Santa Clara! less, in some particulars, good solid Xeres wine being far less plenty here than there."

"Thou art no Moor, Sancho, although thy father's name be a secret. And thou, Pepe, what dost thou find in those flowers to draw thy attention so early from all these wonders?"

"Señor, I gather them for Monica. A female hath a more delicate feeling than a man, and she will be glad to see with what sort of ornaments God hath adorned the Indies."

"Dost thou fancy, Pepe, that thy love can keep those flowers in bloom, until the good caravel shall recross the Atlantic?" demanded Luis, laughing.

"Who knoweth, Señor Gutierrez? A warm heart maketh a thriving nursery. You would do well, too, if you prefer any Castilian lady to all others, to bethink you of her beauty, and gather some of these rare plants to deck her hair."

Columbus now turned away, the natives seeming disposed to approach the strangers, while Luis remained near the young sailor, who still continued to collect the plants of the tropics. In a minute our hero was similarly employed; and long ere the admiral and the wondering islanders had commenced their first parley, he had arranged a gorgeous *bouquet*, which he already fancied in the glossy dark hair of Mercedes.

The events of a public nature that followed, are too familiar to every intelligent reader to need repetition here. After passing a short time at San Salvador, Columbus proceeded to other islands, led on by curiosity, and guided by real or fancied reports of the natives, until the 28th, when he reached that of Cuba. Here he imagined, for a time, that he had found the continent, and he continued coasting it, first in a north-westerly, and then in a south-easterly direction, for near a month. Familiarity with the novel scenes that offered soon lessened their influence, and the inbred feelings of avarice and ambition began to resume their sway in the bosoms of several of those who had been foremost in manifesting their submission to the admiral, when the discovery of land so triumphantly proved the justice of his theories, and the weakness of their own misgivings. Among others who thus came under the influence of their nature, was Martin Alonzo Pinzon, who, finding himself almost entirely excluded from the society of the young Count of Llera, in whose eyes he perceived he filled but a very subordinate place, fell back on his own local importance, and began to envy Columbus a glory that he now fancied he might have secured for himself. Hot words had passed between the admiral and himself, on more than one occasion, before the land was made, and every day something new occurred to increase the coldness between them.

It forms no part of this work to dwell on the events that followed, as the adventurers proceeded from island to island, port to port, and river to river. It was soon apparent that very important discoveries had been made; and the adventurers were led on day by day, pursuing their investigations, and following directions that were ill comprehended, but which, it was fancied, pointed to mines of gold. Everywhere they met with a gorgeous and bountiful nature, scenery that fascinated the eye, and a climate that soothed the senses; but, as yet, man was found living in the simplest condition of the savage state. The delusion of being in the Indies was general, and every intimation that fell from those untutored beings, whether by word or sign, was supposed to have some reference to the riches of the east. All believed that, if not absolutely within the kingdom of the Great Khan, they were at least on its confines. Under such circumstances, when each day actually produced new scenes, promising still greater novelties, few bethought them of Spain, unless it were in connection with the glory of returning to her, successful and triumphant. Even Luis dwelt less intently in his thoughts on Mercedes, suffering her image, beautiful as it was, to be momentarily supplanted by the unusual spectacles that arose before his physical sight in such constant and unwearied succession. Little substantial, beyond the fertile soil and genial climate, offered, it is true, in the way of realizing all the bright expectations of the adventurers in connection with pecuniary advantages; but each moment was fraught with hope, and no one knew what a day would bring forth.

Two agents were at length sent into the interior to make discoveries, and Columbus profited by the occasion to careen his vessels. About the time this mission was expected to return, Luis sallied forth with a party of armed men to meet it, Sancho making one of his escort. The ambassadors were met on their way back at a short day's march from the vessels, accompanied by a few of the natives, who were following with intense curiosity, expecting at each moment to see their unknown visitors take their flight toward heaven. A short halt was made for the purpose of refreshing themselves, after the two parties had joined; and Sancho, as reckless of danger on the land as on the ocean, stalked into a village that lay near the halting place. Here he endeavored to make himself as agreeable to the inhabitants as one of his appearance very well could, by means of signs. Sancho figured in this little hamlet under some such advantages as those that are enjoyed in the country by a great man from town; the spectators not being, as yet, sufficiently sophisticated to distinguish between the cut of a doublet and the manner of wearing it, as between a clown and a noble. He had not been many minutes playing the grandee among these simple beings, when they seemed desirous of offering to him some mark of particular distinction. Presently, a man appeared, holding certain dark-looking and dried leaves, which he held out to the hero of the moment in a deferential manner, as a Turk would offer his dried sweet-meats, or an American his cake. Sancho was about to accept the present, though he would greatly have preferred a dobla, of which he had not seen any since the last received from the admiral, when a forward movement was made by most of the Cubans, who humbly, and with emphasis, uttered the word "tobacco" — "tobacco." On this hint, the person who held forth the offering drew back, repeated the same word in an apologizing manner, and set about making what, it was now plain was termed a "tobacco," in the language of that country. This was soon effected, by rolling up the leaves in the form of a rude segar, when a "tobacco," duly manufactured, was offered to the seaman. Sancho took the present, nodded his head condescendingly, repeated the words himself, in the best manner he could, and thrust the "tobacco" into his pocket. This movement evidently excited some surprise among the spectators, but, after a little consultation, one of them lighted an end of a roll, applied the other to his mouth, and began to puff forth volumes of a fragrant light smoke, not only to his own infinite satisfaction, but seemingly to that of all around him. Sancho attempted an imitation, which resulted, as is common with the tyro in this accomplishment, in his reeling back to his party with the pallid countenance of an opium-chewer, and a nausea that he had not experienced since the day he first ventured beyond the bar of Saltes, to issue on the troubled surface of the Atlantic.

This little scene might be termed the introduction of the well-known American weed into civilized society, the misapprehension of the Spaniards, touching the appellation, transferring the name of the roll to the plant itself. Thus did Sancho, of the ship-yard-gate, become the first Christian tobacco smoker, an accomplishment in which he was so soon afterward rivalled by some of the greatest men of his age, and which has extended down to our own times.

On the return of his agents, Columbus again sailed, pushing his way along the north shore of Cuba. While struggling against the trades, with a view to get to the eastward, he found the wind too fresh, and determined to bear up for a favorite haven in the island of Cuba, that he had named Puerto del Principe. With this view a signal was made to call the Pinta down, that vessel being far to windward; and, as night was near, lights were carried in order to enable Martin Alonzo to close with his commander. The next morning, at the dawn of day, when Columbus came on deck, he cast a glance around him, and beheld the Niña, hove-to under his lee, but no signs of the other caravel.

"Have none seen the Pinta?" demanded the admiral, hastily, of Sancho, who stood at the helm.

"Señor, I did, as long as eyes could see a vessel that was striving to get out of view. Master Martin Alonzo hath disappeared in the eastern board, while we have been lying-to, here, in waiting for him to come down."

Columbus now perceived that he was deserted by the very man who had once shown so much zeal in his behalf, and who had given, in the act, new proof of the manner in which friendship vanishes before self-interest and cupidity. There had been among the adventurers many reports of the existence of gold mines, obtained from the descriptions of the natives; and the admiral made no doubt that his insubordinate follower had profited by the superior sailing of his caravel, to keep the wind, in the expectation to be the first to reach the Eldorado of their wishes. As the weather still continued unfavorable, however, the Santa Maria and the Niña returned to port, where they waited for a change. This separation occurred on the 21st of November, at which moment the expedition had not advanced beyond the north coast of Cuba.

From this time until the sixth of the following month, Columbus continued his examination of this noble island, when he crossed what has since been termed the "windward passage," and first touched on the shores of Hayti. All this time, there had been as much communication as circumstances would allow, with the aborigines, the Spaniards making friends wherever they went, as a consequence of the humane and prudent measures of the admiral. It is true that violence had been done, in a few instances, by seizing half a dozen individuals in order to carry them to Spain, as offerings to Doña Isabella; but this act was easily reconcilable to usage in that age, equally on account of the deference that was paid to the kingly authority, and on the ground that the seizures were for the good of the captives' souls.

The adventurers were more delighted with the bold, and yet winning aspect of Hayti, than they had been with even the adjacent island of Cuba. The inhabitants were found to be handsomer and more civilized than any they had yet seen, while they retained the gentleness and docility that had proved so pleasing to the admiral. Gold, also, was seen among them in considerable quantities; and the Spaniards set on foot a trade of some extent, in which the usual incentive of civilized man was the great aim of one side, and hawk's-bells appear to have been the principal desideratum with the other.

In this manner, and in making hazardous advances along the coast, the admiral was occupied until the 20th of the month, when he reached a point that was said to be in the vicinity of the residence of the Great Cacique of all that portion of the island. This prince, whose name, as spelt by the Spaniards, was Guacanagari, had many tributary caciques, and was understood, from the half-intelligible descriptions of his subjects, to be a monarch that was much beloved. On the 22d, while still lying in the Bay of Acúl, where the vessels had anchored two days previously, a large canoe was seen entering the haven. It was shortly after announced to the admiral that this boat contained an ambassador from the Great Cacique, who brought presents from his master, with a request that the vessels would move a league or two further east, and anchor off the town inhabited by the prince himself. The wind preventing an immediate compliance, a messenger was despatched with a suitable answer, and the ambassador returned. Fatigued with idleness, anxious to see more of the interior, and impelled by a constitutional love of adventure, Luis, who had struck up a hasty friendship with a young man called Mattinao, who attended the ambassador, asked permission to accompany him, taking his passage in the canoe. Columbus gave his consent to this proposal with a good deal of reluctance, the rank and importance of our hero inducing him to avoid the consequences of any treachery or accident. The importunity of Luis finally prevailed, however, and he departed with many injunctions to be discreet, being frequently admonished of the censure that would await the admiral in the event of any thing serious occurring. As a precaution, too, Sancho Mundo was directed to accompany the young man, in this chivalrous adventure, in the capacity of an esquire.

No weapon more formidable than a blunt arrow having yet been seen in the hands of the natives, the young Count de Llera declined taking his mail, going armed only with a trusty sword, the temper of which had been tried on many a Moorish corslet and helm, in his foot encounters, and protected by a light buckler. An arquebuse had been put into his hand, but he refused it, as a weapon unsuited to knightly hands, and as betraying a distrust that was not merited by the previous conduct of the natives. Sancho, however, was less scrupulous, and accepted the weapon. In order, moreover, to divert the attention of his followers from a concession that the admiral felt to be a departure from his own rigid laws, Luis and his companions landed, and entered the canoe at a point concealed from the vessels, in order that their absence might not be known. It is owing to these circumstances, as well as to the general mystery that was thrown about the connection of the young grandee with the expedition, that the occurrences we are about to relate were never entered by the admiral in his journal, and have consequently escaped the prying eyes of the various historians who have subsequently collected so much from that pregnant document.

CHAPTER XXIII

"Thou seemest to fancy's eye
An animated blossom born in air;
Which breathes and bourgeons in the golden sky,
And sheds its odors there."

Sutermeister.

Notwithstanding his native resolution, and an indifference to danger that amounted to recklessness, Luis did not find himself alone with the Haytians without, at least, a lively consciousness of the novelty of his situation. Still, nothing occurred to excite uneasiness, and he continued his imperfect communications with his new friends, occasionally throwing in a remark to Sancho, in Spanish, who merely wanted encouragement to discourse by the hour. Instead of following the boat of the Santa Maria, on board which the ambassador had embarked, the canoe pushed on several leagues further east, it being understood that Luis was not to present himself in the town of Guacanagari, until after the arrival of the ships, when he was to rejoin his comrades stealthily, or in a way not to attract attention.

Our hero would not have been a true lover, had he remained indifferent to the glories of the natural scenery that lay spread before his eyes, as he thus coasted the shores of Española. The boldness of the landscape, as in the Mediterranean, was relieved by the softness of a low latitude, which throws some such witchery around rocks and promontories, as a sunny smile lends to female beauty. More than once did he burst out into exclamations of delight, and as often did Sancho respond in the same temper, if not exactly in the same language; the latter conceiving it to be a sort of duty to echo all that the young noble said, in the way of poetry.

"I take it, Señor Conde," observed the seaman, when they had reached a spot several leagues beyond that where the launch of the ship had put to shore; "I take it for granted, Señor Conde, that your Excellency knoweth whither these naked gentry are paddling, all this time. They seem in a hurry, and have a port in their minds, if it be not in view."

"Art thou uneasy, friend Sancho, that thou puttest thy question thus earnestly?"

"If I am, Don Luis, it is altogether on account of the family of Bobadilla, which would lose its head, did any mishap befall your Excellency. What is it to Sancho, of the ship-yard-gate, whether he is married to some princess in Cipango, and gets to be adopted by the Great Khan, or whether he is an indifferent mariner out of Moguer? It is very much as if one should offer him the choice between wearing a doublet and eating garlic, and going naked on sweet fruits and a full stomach. I take it, Señor, your Excellency would not willingly exchange the castle of Llera for the palace of this Great Cacique?"

"Thou art right, Sancho; even rank must depend on the state of society in which we live. A Castilian noble cannot envy a Haytian sovereign."

"More especially, since my lord, the Señor Don Almirante, hath publicly proclaimed that our gracious lady, the Doña Isabella, is henceforth and forever to be queen over him," returned Sancho, with a knowing glance of the eye. "Little do these worthy people understand the honor that is in store for them, and least of all, his Highness, King Guacanagari!"

"Hush, Sancho, and keep thy unpleasant intimations in thine own breast. Our friends turn the head of the canoe toward yonder river's mouth, and seem bent on landing."

By this time, indeed, the natives had coasted as far as they intended, and were turning in toward the entrance of a small stream, which, taking its rise among the noble mountains that were grouped inland, found its way through a smiling valley to the ocean. This stream was neither broad nor deep, but it contained far more than water sufficient for any craft used by the natives. Its banks were fringed with bushes; and as they glided up it, Luis saw fifty sites where he thought he could be content to pass his life, provided, always, that it might possess the advantage of Mercedes' presence. It is scarcely necessary to add, too, that in all these scenes he fancied his mistress attired in the velvets and laces that were then so much used by high-born dames, and that he saw her natural grace, embellished by the courtly ease and polished accessories of one who lived daily, if not hourly, in the presence of her royal mistress.

As the canoe shut in the coast, by entering between the two points that formed the river's mouth, Sancho pointed out to the young noble a small fleet of canoes, that was coming down before the wind from the eastward, apparently bound, like so many more they had seen that day, to the Bay of Acúl, on a visit to the wonderful strangers. The natives in the canoe also beheld this little flotilla, which was driving before the wind under cotton sails, and by their smiles and signs showed that they gave it the same destination. About this time, too, or just as they entered the mouth of the stream, Mattinao drew from under a light cotton robe, that he occasionally wore, a thin circlet of pure gold, which he placed upon his head, in the manner of a coronet. This, Luis knew, was a token that he was a cacique, one of those who were tributary to Guacanagari, and he arose to salute him at this evidence of his rank, an act that was imitated by all of the Haytians also. From this assumption of state, Luis rightly imagined that Mattinao had now entered within the limits of a territory that acknowledged his will. From the moment that the young cacique threw aside his incognito, he ceased to paddle, but, assuming an air of authority and dignity, he attempted to converse with his guest in the best manner their imperfect means of communication would allow. He often pronounced the word, Ozema, and Luis inferred from the manner in which he used it, that it was the name of a favorite wife, it having been already ascertained by the Spaniards, or at least it was thought to be ascertained, that the caciques indulged in polygamy, while they rigidly restricted their subjects to one wife.

The canoe ascended the river several miles, until it reached one of those tropical valleys in which nature seems to expend her means of rendering this earth inviting. While the scenery had much of the freedom of a wilderness, the presence of man for centuries had deprived it of all its ruder and more savage features. Like those who tenanted it, the spot possessed the perfection of native grace, unfettered and uninvaded by any of the more elaborate devices of human expedients. The dwellings were not without beauty, though simple as the wants of their owners; the flowers bloomed in midwinter, and the generous branches still groaned with the weight of their nutritious and palatable fruits.

Mattinao was received by his people with an eager curiosity, blended with profound respect. His mild subjects crowded around Luis and Sancho, with some such wonder as a civilized man would gaze at one of the prophets, were he to return to earth in the flesh. They had heard of the arrival of the ships, but they did not the less regard their inmates as visitors from heaven. This, probably, was not the opinion of the more elevated in rank, for, even in the savage state, the vulgar mind is far from being that of the favored few. Whether it was owing to this greater facility of character, and to habits that more easily adapted themselves to the untutored notions of the Indians, or to their sense of propriety, Sancho soon became the favorite with the multitude; leaving the Count of Llera more especially to the care of Mattinao, and the principal men of his tribe. Owing to this circumstance, the two Spaniards were soon separated, Sancho being led away by the *oi polloi* to a sort of square in the centre of the village, leaving Don Luis in the habitation of the cacique.

No sooner did Mattinao find himself in the company of our hero, and that of two of his confidential chiefs, than the name of Ozema was repeated eagerly among the Indians. A rapid conversation followed, a messenger was despatched, Luis knew not whither, and then the chiefs took their departure, leaving the young Castilian alone with the cacique. Laying aside his golden band, and placing a cotton robe about his person, which had hitherto been nearly naked, Mattinao made a sign for his companion to follow him, and left the building. Throwing the buckler over his shoulder, and adjusting the belt of his sword in a way that the weapon should not incommode him in walking, Luis obeyed with as much confidence as he would have followed a friend along the streets of Seville.

Mattinao led the way through a wilderness of sweets, where tropical plants luxuriated beneath the branches of trees loaded with luscious fruits, holding his course by a foot-path which lay on the banks of a torrent that flowed from a ravine, and poured its waters into the river below. The distance he went might have been half a mile. Here he reached a cluster of rustic dwellings that occupied a lovely terrace on a hill-side, where they overlooked the larger town below the river, and commanded a view of the distant ocean. Luis saw at a glance that this sweet retreat was devoted to the uses of the gentler sex, and he doubted not that it formed a species of seraglio, set apart for the wives of the young cacique. He was led into one of the principal dwellings, where the simple but grateful refreshments used by the natives, were again offered to him.

The intercourse of a month had not sufficed to render either party very familiar with the language of the other. A few of the commoner words of the Indians had been caught by the Spaniards, and perhaps Luis was one of the most ready in their use; still, it is highly probable, he was oftener wrong than right, even when he felt the most confident of his success. But the language of friendship is not easily mistaken, and our hero had not entertained a feeling of distrust from the time he left the ships, down to the present moment.

Mattinao had despatched a messenger to an adjacent dwelling when he entered that in which Luis was now entertained, and when sufficient time had been given for the last to refresh himself, the cacique arose, and by a courteous gesture, such as might have become a master of ceremonies in the court of Isabella, he again invited the young grandee to follow. They took their way along the terrace, to a house larger than common, and which evidently contained several subdivisions, as they entered into a sort of anteroom. Here they remained but a minute; the cacique, after a short parley with a female, removing a curtain ingeniously made of sea-weed, and leading the way to an inner apartment. It had but a single occupant, whose character Luis fancied to be announced in the use of the single word "Ozema," that the cacique uttered in a low, affectionate tone, as they entered. Luis bowed to this Indian beauty, as profoundly as he could have made his reverence to a high-born damsel of Spain; then, recovering himself, he fastened one long, steady look of admiration on the face of the curious but half-frightened young creature who stood before him, and exclaimed, in such tones as only indicate rapture, admiration, and astonishment mingled—

"Mercedes!"

The young cacique repeated this name in the best manner he could, evidently mistaking it for a Spanish term to express admiration, or satisfaction; while the trembling young thing, who was the subject of all this wonder, shrunk back a step, blushed, laughed, and muttered in her soft, low, musical voice, "Mercedes," as the innocent take up and renew any source of their harmless pleasures. She then stood, with her arms folded meekly on her bosom, resembling a statue of wonder. But it may be necessary to explain why, at a moment so peculiar, the thoughts and tongue of Luis had so suddenly resorted to his mistress. In order to do this, we shall first attempt a short description of the person and appearance of Ozema, as was, in fact, the name of the Indian beauty.

All the accounts agree in describing the aborigines of the West Indies as being singularly well formed, and of a natural grace in their movements, that extorted a common admiration among the Spaniards. Their color was not unpleasant, and the inhabitants of Hayti, in particular, were said to be very little darker than the people of Spain. Those who were but little exposed to the bright sun of that climate, and who dwelt habitually beneath the shades of groves, or in the retirement of their dwellings, like persons of similar habits in Europe, might, by comparison, have even been termed fair. Such was the fact with Ozema, who, instead of being the wife of the young cacique, was his only sister. According to the laws of Hayti, the authority of a cacique was transmitted through females, and a son of Ozema was looked forward to, as the heir of his uncle. Owing to this fact, and to the circumstance that the true royal line, if a term so dignified can be applied to a state of society so simple, was reduced to these two individuals, Ozema had been more than usually fostered by the tribe, leaving her free from care, and as little exposed to hardships, as at all comported with the condition of her people. She had reached her eighteenth year, without having experienced any of those troubles and exposures which are more or less the inevitable companions of savage life; though it was remarked by the Spaniards, that all the Indians they had yet seen seemed more than usually free from evils of this character. They owed this exception to the generous quality of the soil, the genial warmth of the climate, and the salubrity of the air. In a word, Ozema, in her person, possessed just those advantages that freedom from restraint, native graces, and wild luxuriance, might be supposed to lend the female form, under the advantages of a mild climate, a healthful and simple diet, and perfect exemption from exposure, care, or toil. It would not have been difficult to fancy Eve such a creature, when she first appeared to Adam, fresh from the hands of her divine Creator, modest, artless, timid, and perfect.

The Haytians used a scanty dress, though it shocked none of their opinions to go forth in the garb of nature. Still, few of rank were seen without some pretensions to attire, which was worn rather as an ornament, or a mark of distinction, than as necessary either to usage or comfort. Ozema, herself, formed no exception to the general rule. A cincture of Indian cloth, woven in gay colors, circled her slender waist, and fell nearly as low as her knees; a robe of spotless cotton, inartificially made, but white as the driven snow, and of a texture so fine that it might have shamed many of the manufactures of our own days, fell like a scarf across a shoulder, and was loosely united at the opposite side, dropping in folds nearly to the ground. Sandals, of great ingenuity and beauty, protected the soles of feet that a queen might have envied; and a large plate of pure gold, rudely wrought, was suspended from her neck by a string of small, but gorgeous shells. Bracelets of the latter were on her pretty wrists, and two light bands of gold encircled ankles that were as faultless as those of the Venus of Naples. In that region, the fineness of the hair was thought the test of birth, with better reason than many imagine the feet and hands to be, in civilized life. As power and rank had passed from female to female in her family, for several centuries, the hair of Ozema was silken, soft, waving, exuberant, and black as jet. It covered her shoulders, like a glorious mantle, and fell as low as her simple cincture. So light and silken was this natural veil, that its ends waved in the gentle current of air that was rather breathing than blowing through the apartment.

Although this extraordinary creature was much the loveliest specimen of young-womanhood that Luis had seen among the wild beauties of the islands, it was not so much her graceful and well-rounded form, or even the charms of face and expression, that surprised him, as a decided and accidental resemblance to the being he had left in Spain, and who had so long been the idol of his heart. This resemblance alone had caused him to utter the name of his mistress, in the manner related. Could the two have been placed together, it would have been easy to detect marked points of difference between them, without being reduced to compare the intellectual and thoughtful expression of our heroine's countenance, with the wondering, doubting, half-startled look of Ozema: but still the general likeness was so strong, that no person who was familiar with the face of one could fail to note it on meeting with the other. Side by side, it would have been discovered that the face of Mercedes had the advantage in finesse and delicacy; that her features and brow were nobler; her eye more illuminated by the intelligence within; her smile more radiant with thought and the feelings of a cultivated woman; her blush more sensitive, betraying most of the consciousness of conventional habits; and that the expression generally was much more highly cultivated, than that which sprung from the artless impulses and limited ideas of the young Haytian. Nevertheless, in mere beauty, in youth, and tint, and outline, the disparity was scarcely perceptible, while the resemblance was striking; and, on the score of animation, native frankness, ingenuousness, and all that witchery which ardent and undisguised feeling lends to woman, many might have preferred the confiding *abandon* of the beautiful young Indian, to the more trained and dignified reserve of the Castilian heiress. What in the latter was earnest, high-souled, native, but religious enthusiasm, in the other was merely the outpourings of unguided impulses, which, however feminine in their origin, were but little regulated in their indulgence.

"Mercedes!" exclaimed our hero, when this vision of Indian loveliness unexpectedly broke on his sight. "Mercedes!" repeated Mattinao; "Mercedes!" murmured Ozema, recoiling a step, blushing, laughing, and then resuming her innocent confidence, as she several times uttered the same word, which she also mistook for an expression of admiration, in her own low, melodious voice.

Conversation being out of the question, there remained nothing for the parties but to express their feelings by signs and acts of amity. Luis had not come on his little expedition unprovided with presents. Anticipating an interview with the wife of the cacique, he had brought up from the village below, several articles that he supposed might suit her untutored fancy. But the moment he beheld the vision that actually stood before him, they all seemed unworthy of such a being. In one of his onsets against the Moors, he had brought off a turban of rich but light cloth, and he had kept it as a trophy, occasionally wearing it, in his visits to the shore, out of pure caprice, and as a sort of ornament that might well impose on the simple-minded natives. These vagaries excited no remarks, as mariners are apt to indulge their whims in this manner, when far from the observations of those to whom they habitually defer. This turban was on his head at the moment he entered the apartment of Ozema, and, overcome with the delight of finding so unexpected a resemblance, and, possibly, excited by so unlooked-for an exhibition of feminine loveliness, he gallantly unrolled it, threw out the folds of rich cloth, and cast it over the shoulders of the beautiful Ozema as a mantle.

The expressions of gratitude and delight that escaped this unsophisticated young creature, were warm, sincere, and undisguised. She cast the ample robe on the ground before her, repeated the word "Mercedes," again and again, and manifested her pleasure with all the warmth of a generous and ingenuous nature. If we were to say that this display of Ozema was altogether free from the child-like rapture that was, perhaps, inseparable from her ignorance, it would be attributing to her benighted condition the experience and regulated feelings of advanced civilization; but, notwithstanding the guileless simplicity with which she betrayed her emotions, her delight was not without much of the dignity and tone that usually mark the conduct of the superior classes all over the world. Luis fancied it as graceful as it was *naive* and charming. He endeavored to imagine the manner in which the Lady of Valverde might receive an offering of precious stones from the gracious hands of Doña Isabella, and he even thought it very possible that the artless grace of Ozema was not far behind what he knew would be the meek self-respect, mingled with grateful pleasure, that Mercedes could not fail to exhibit.

While thoughts like these were passing through his mind, the Indian girl laid aside her own less enticing robe, without a thought of shame, and then she folded her faultless form in the cloth of the turban. This was no sooner done, with a grace and freedom peculiar to her unfettered mind, than she drew the necklace of shells from her person, and advancing a step or two toward our hero, extended the offering with a half-averted face, though the laughing and willing eyes more than supplied the place of language. Luis accepted the gift with suitable eagerness, nor did he refrain from using the Castilian gallantry of kissing the pretty hand from which he took the bauble.

The cacique, who had been a pleased spectator of all that passed, now signed for the count to follow him, leading the way toward another dwelling. Here Don Luis was introduced to other young females, and to two or three children, the former of whom, he soon discovered, were the wives of Mattinao, and the latter his offspring. By dint of gestures, a few words, and such other means of explanation as were resorted to between the Spaniards and the natives, he now succeeded in ascertaining the real affinity which existed between the cacique and Ozema. Our hero felt a sensation like pleasure when he discovered that the Indian beauty was not married; and he was fain to refer the feeling, perhaps justly, to a sort of jealous sensitiveness that grew out of her resemblance to Mercedes.

The remainder of that, and the whole of the three following days, were passed by Luis with his friend, the cacique, in this, the favorite and sacred residence of the latter. Of course our hero was, if any thing, a subject of greater interest to all his hosts, than they could possibly be to him. They took a thousand innocent liberties with his person: examining his dress, and the ornaments he wore, not failing to compare the whiteness of his skin with the redder tint of that of Mattinao. On these occasions Ozema was the most reserved and shy, though her look followed every movement, and her pleased countenance denoted the interest she felt in all that concerned the stranger. Hours at a time, did Luis lie stretched on fragrant mats near this artless and lovely creature, studying the wayward expression of her features, in the fond hope of seeing stronger and stronger resemblances to Mercedes, and sometimes losing himself in that which was peculiarly her own. In the course of the time passed in these dwellings, efforts were made by the count to obtain some useful information of the island; and whether it was owing to her superior rank, or to a native superiority of mind, or to a charm of manner, he soon fancied that the cacique's beautiful sister succeeded better in making him understand her meaning, than either of the wives of Mattinao, or the cacique himself. To Ozema, then, Luis put most of his questions; and ere the day had passed, this quick-witted and attentive girl had made greater progress in opening an intelligible understanding between the adventurers and her countrymen, than had been accomplished by the communications of the two previous months. She caught the Spanish words with a readiness that seemed instinctive, pronouncing them with an accent that only rendered them prettier and softer to the ear.

Luis de Bobadilla was just as good a Catholic as a rigid education, a wandering life, and the habits of the camp would be apt to make one of his rank, years, and temperament. Still, that was an age in which most laymen had a deep reverence for religion; whether they actually submitted to its purifying influence or not. If there were any free-thinkers, at all, they existed principally among those who passed their lives in their closets, or were to be found among the churchmen, themselves; who often used the cowl as a hood to conceal their infidelity. His close association with Columbus, too, had contributed to strengthen our hero's tendency to believe in the constant supervision of Providence; and he now felt a strong inclination to fancy that this extraordinary facility of Ozema's in acquiring languages, was one of its semi-miraculous provisions, made with a view to further the introduction of the religion of the cross among her people. Often did he flatter himself, as he sat gazing into the sparkling, and yet mild eyes of the girl, listening to her earnest efforts to make him comprehend her meaning, that he was to be the instrument of bringing about this great good, through so young and charming an agent. The admiral had also enjoined on him the importance of ascertaining, if possible, the position of the mines, and he had actually succeeded in making Ozema comprehend his questions on a subject that was all-engrossing with most of the Spaniards. Her answers were less intelligible, but Luis thought they never could be sufficiently full; flattering himself, the whole time, that he was only laboring to comply with the wishes of Columbus.

The day after his arrival, our hero was treated to an exhibition of some of the Indian games. These sports have been too often described to need repetition here; but, in all their movements and exercises, which were altogether pacific, the young princess was conspicuous for grace and skill. Luis, too, was required to show his powers, and being exceedingly athletic and active, he easily bore away the palm from his friend Mattinao. The young cacique manifested neither jealousy nor disappointment at this result, while his sister laughed and clapped her hands with delight, when he was outdone, even at his own sports, by the greater strength or greater efforts of his guest. More than once, the wives of Mattinao seemed to utter gentle reproaches at this exuberance of feeling, but Ozema answered with smiling taunts, and Luis thought her, at such moments, more beautiful than even imagination could draw, and perhaps with justice; for her cheeks were flushed, her eyes became as brilliant as ornaments of jet, and the teeth that were visible between lips like cherries, resembled rows of ivory. We have said that the eyes of Ozema were black, differing, in this particular, from the deep-blue, melancholy orbs of the enthusiastic Mercedes; but still they were alike, so often uttering the same feelings, more especially touching matters in which Luis was concerned. More than once, during the trial of strength, did the young man fancy that the expression of the rapture which fairly danced in the eyes of Ozema, was the very counterpart of that of the deep-seated delight which had so often beamed on him, from the glances of Mercedes, in the tourney; and, at such times, it struck him that the resemblance between the two was so strong as, after some allowance had been made for dress, and other sufficiently striking circumstances, to render them almost identical.

The reader is not to suppose from this, that our hero was actually inconstant to his ancient love. Far from it. Mercedes was too deeply enshrined in his heart—and Luis, with all his faults, was as warm-hearted and true-hearted a cavalier as breathed—to be so easily dispossessed. But he was young, distant from her he had so long adored, and was, withal, not altogether insensible to admiration so artlessly and winningly betrayed by the Indian girl. Had there been the least immodest glance, any proof that art or design lay at the bottom of Ozema's conduct, he would at once have taken the alarm, and been completely disenthralled from his temporary delusion; but, on the contrary, all was so frank and natural with this artless girl; when she most betrayed the hold he had taken of her imagination, it was done with a simplicity so obvious, a *naïveté* so irrepressible, and an ingenuousness so clearly the fruit of innocence, that it was impossible to suspect artifice. In a word, our hero merely showed that he was human, by yielding in a certain degree to a fascination that, under the circumstances, might well have made deeper inroads on the faith even of men who enjoyed much better reputations for stability of purpose.

In situations of so much novelty, time flies swiftly, and Luis himself was astonished when, on looking back, he remembered that he had now been several days with Mattinao, most of which period had actually been passed in what might not inaptly be termed the seraglio of the cacique. Sancho of the ship-yard-gate had not been in the least neglected all this time. He had been a hero, in his own circle, as well as the young noble, nor had he been at all forgetful of his duty on the subject of searching for gold. Though he had neither acquired a single word of the Haytian language, nor taught a syllable of Spanish to even one of the laughing nymphs who surrounded him, he had decorated the persons of many of them with hawk's-bells, and had contrived to abstract from them, in return, every ornament that resembled the precious metal, which they possessed. This transfer, no doubt, was honestly effected, however, having been made on that favorite principle of the free trade theorists, which maintains that trade is merely an exchange of equivalents; overlooking all the adverse circumstances which may happen, just at the moment, to determine the standard of value. Sancho had his notions of commerce as well as the modern philosophers, and, as he and Luis occasionally met during their sojourn with Mattinao, he revealed a few of his opinions on this interesting subject, in one of their interviews.

"I perceive thou hast not forgotten thy passion for doblas, friend Sancho," said Luis, laughing, as the old seaman exhibited the store of dust and golden plates he had collected; "there is sufficient of the metal in thy sack to coin a score of them, each having the royal countenances of our lord the King, and our lady the Queen!"

"Double that, Señor Conde; just double that; and all for the price of some seventeen hawk's-bells, that cost but a handful of maravedis. By the mass! this is a most just and holy trade, and such as it becomes us Christians to carry on. Here are these savages, they think no more of gold than your Excellency thinks of a dead Moor, and to be revenged on them, I hold a hawk's-bell just as cheap. Let them think as poorly as they please of their ornaments and yellow dust, they will find me just as willing to part with the twenty hawk's-bells that remain. Let them barter away, they will find me as ready as they possibly can be, to give nothing for nothing."

"Is this quite honest, Sancho, to rob an Indian of his gold, in exchange for a bauble that copper so easily purchaseth? Remember thou art a

Castilian, and henceforth give *two* hawk's-bells, where thou hast hitherto given but *one*."

"I never forget my birth, Señor, for happily the ship-yard of Moguer is in old Spain. Is not the value of a thing to be settled by what it will bring in the market? ask any of our traders and they will tell you this, which is clear as the sun in the heavens. When the Venetians lay before Candia, grapes, and figs, and Greek wine, could be had for the asking in that island, while western articles commanded any price. Oh, nothing is plainer than the fact that every thing hath its price, and it is real trade to give one worthless commodity for another."

"If it be honest to profit by the ignorance of another," answered Luis, who had a nobleman's contempt for commerce, "then it is just to deceive the child and the idiot."

"God forbid, and especially St. Andrew, my patron, that I should do any thing so wicked. Hawk's-bells are of more account than gold, in Hayti, Señor, and happening to know it, I am willing to part with the precious things for the dross. You see I am generous instead of being avaricious, for all parties are in Hayti, where the value of, the articles must be settled. It is true, that after running great risks at sea, and undergoing great pains and chances, by carrying this gold to Spain, I may be requited for my trouble, and get enough benefit to make an honest livelihood. I hope Doña Isabella will have so much feeling for these, her new subjects, as to prevent their ever going into the shipping business—a most laborious and dangerous calling, as we both well know."

"And why art thou so particular in desiring this favor in behalf of these poor islanders, and that, too, Sancho, at the expense of thine own bones?"

"Simply, Señor," answered the knave, with a cunning leer, "lest it unsettle trade, which ought to be as free and unencumbered as possible. Here, now, if we Spaniards come to Hayti, we sell-one hawk's-bell for a dobla in gold; whereas, were we to give these savages the trouble to come to Spain, a dobla of their gold would buy a hundred hawk's-bells! No—no—it is right as it is; and may a double allowance of purgatory be the lot of him who wishes to throw any difficulties in the way of a good, honest, free, and civilizing trade, say I."

Sancho was thus occupied in explaining his notions of free trade—the great mystification of modern philanthropists—when there arose such a cry in the village of Mattinao, as is only heard in moments of extreme jeopardy and sudden terror. The conversation took place in the grove, about midway between the town and the private dwellings of the cacique; and so implicit had become the confidence the two Spaniards reposed in their friends, that neither had any other arms about his person, than those furnished by nature. Luis had left both sword and buckler, half an hour earlier, at the feet of Ozetna, who had been enacting a mimic hero, with his weapons, for their mutual diversion; while Sancho had found the arquebuse much too heavy to be carried about for a plaything. The last was deposited in the room where he had taken up his comfortable quarters.

"Can this mean treachery, Señor?" exclaimed Sancho. "Have these blackguards found out the true value of hawk's-bells, after all, and do they mean to demand the balance due them?"

"My life on it, Mattinao and all his people are true, Sancho. This uproar hath a different meaning—hark! is not that the cry of 'Caonabo!'"

"The very same, Señor! That is the name of the Carib cacique, who is the terror of all these tribes."

"Thy arquebuse, Sancho, if possible; then join me at the dwellings above. Ozema and the wives of our good friend must be defended, at every hazard!"

Luis had no sooner given these orders, than he and Sancho separated, the latter running toward the town, which, by this time, was a scene of wild tumult, while our hero, slowly and sullenly, retired toward the private dwellings of the cacique, occasionally looking back, as if he longed to plunge into the thickest of the fray. Twenty times did he wish for his favorite charger and a stout lance, when, indeed, it would not have been an extraordinary feat for a knight of his prowess to put to flight a thousand enemies like those who now menaced him. Often had he singly broken whole ranks of Christian foot-soldiers, and it is well known that solitary individuals, when mounted, subsequently drove hundreds of the natives before them.

The alarm reached the dwelling of Mattinao before our hero. When he entered the house of Ozema, he found its mistress surrounded by fifty females, some of whom had already ascended from the town below, each of whom was eagerly uttering the terrible name of "Caonabo." Ozema herself was the most collected of them all, though it was apparent that, from some cause, she was an object of particular solicitude from those around her. As Luis entered the apartment, the wives of Mattinao were pressing around the princess; and he soon gathered from their words and entreaties, that they urged her to fly, lest she should fall into the hands of the Carib chief. He even fancied, and he fancied it justly, that the rest of the females supposed the seizure of the cacique's beautiful sister to be the real object of the sudden attack. This conjecture in no manner lessened Luis' ardor in the defence. The moment Ozema caught sight of him, she flew to his side, clasping her hands, and uttering the name of "Caonabo," in a tone that would have melted a heart of stone. At the same time, her eyes spoke a language of hope, confidence, and petition that was not necessary to enlist our hero's resolution on her side. In a moment, the sword of the young cavalier was in his hand, and the buckler on his arm. He then assured the princess of his zeal, in the best manner he could, by placing the buckler before her throbbing breast, and waving the sword, as in defiance of her enemies: no sooner was this pledge given, than every other female disappeared, some flying to the rescue of their children, and all endeavoring to find places of concealment. By this singular and unexpected desertion, Luis found himself, for the first time since they had met, alone with Ozema.

To remain in the house would be to suffer the enemy to approach unseen, and the shrieks and cries sufficiently announced that, each moment, the danger grew nearer Luis accordingly made a sign for the girl to follow him, first rolling the turban into a bundle and placing it on her arm, that it might serve her, at need, as a species of shield against the hostile arrows. While he was thus employed, Ozema's head fell upon his breast, and the excited girl burst into tears. This display of weakness, however, lasted but a moment, when she aroused herself, smiled through her tears, pressed the arm of Luis convulsively, and became the Indian heroine again. They then left the building together.

Luis soon perceived that his retreat from the house had not been made a moment too soon. The family of Mattinao had already disappeared, and a strong party of the invaders was in full view, rushing madly up the grove, silent, but evidently bent on seizing their prey. He felt Ozema, who clung to his arm, tremble violently, and then he heard her murmuring—

"Caonabo—no—no—no!"

The young Indian princess had caught the Spanish monosyllable of dissent, and Luis understood this exclamation to express her strong disinclination to become a wife of the Carib chief. His resolution to protect her or to die, was in no manner lessened by this involuntary betrayal of her feelings, which he could not but think might have some connection with himself; for, while our hero was both honorable and generous, he was human, and, consequently, well disposed to take a favorable view of his own powers of pleasing. It was only in connection with Mercedes, that Luis de Bobadilla was humble.

A soldier almost from childhood, the young count looked hastily around him for a position that would favor his means of defence, and which would render his arms the most available. Luckily, one offered so near him, that it required but a minute to occupy it. The terrace lay against a precipice of rocks, and a hundred feet from the house, was a spot where the face of this precipice was angular, throwing forward a wall on each side to some distance, while the cliff above overhung the base sufficiently to remove all danger from falling stones. In the angle were several large fragments of rock that would afford shelter against arrows, and, there being a sufficient space of greensward before them, on which a knight might well display his prowess when in possession of this position, our hero felt himself strong, if not impregnable, since he could be assailed only in front. Ozema was stationed behind one of the fragments of the fallen rocks, her person only half concealed, however, concern for Luis, and curiosity as related to her enemies, equally inducing her to expose her head and beautiful bust.

Luis was scarcely in possession of this post, ere a dozen Indians were drawn up in a line at the distance of fifty yards in his front. They were armed with bows, war-clubs, and spears. Being without other defensive armor than his buckler, the young man would have thought his situation sufficiently critical, did he not know that the archery of the natives was any thing but formidable. Their arrows would kill, certainly, when shot at short distances, and against the naked skin, but it might be questioned if they would penetrate the stout velvet in which Luis was encased, and fifty yards was not near enough to excite undue alarm. The young man did not dare to retreat to the rocks, as a clear space was indispensable for the free use of his good sword, and to that weapon alone he looked for his eventual triumph.

It was, perhaps, fortunate for our hero that Caonabo himself was not with the party which beleaguered him. That redoubtable chieftain, who had been led to a distance in pursuit of the flying females, under a belief that she he sought was among them, would doubtless have brought the matter to an immediate issue by a desperate charge, when numbers might have prevailed against courage and skill. The actual assailants chose a different course, and began to poise their bows. One of the most skilful among them drew an arrow to the head, and let it fly. The missile glanced from the buckler of the knight, and struck the hill behind him, as lightly as if the parties had been at their idle sports. Another followed, and Luis turned it aside with his sword, disdaining to raise his shield against such a trifle. This cool manner of receiving their assaults caused the Indians to raise a shout, whether in admiration or rage, Luis could not tell.

The next attack was more judicious, being made on a principle that Napoleon is said to have adopted in directing discharges of his artillery. All those who had bows, some six or eight, drew their arrows together, and the weapons came rattling on the buckler of the assailed in a single flight. It was not easy to escape altogether from such a combined assault, and our hero received one or two bruises from glancing arrows, though no blood followed the blows. A second attempt of the same nature was about to be made, when the alarmed girl rushed from her place of concealment, and, like the Pocahontas of our own history, threw herself before Luis, with her arms meekly placed on her bosom. As soon as she appeared, there was a cry of "Ozema"—"Ozema," among the assailants, who were not Caribs, as all will understand who are familiar with the island history, but milder Haytians, governed by a Carib chief.

In vain Luis endeavored to persuade the devoted girl to withdraw. She thought his life in danger, and no language, had he been able to exert his eloquence on the occasion, could have induced her to leave him exposed to such a danger. As the Indians were endeavoring to obtain chances at the person of Luis without killing the princess, he saw there remained no alternative but a retreat behind the fragment of rock. Just as he obtained this temporary security, a fierce-looking warrior joined the assailants, who immediately commenced a vociferous explanation of the actual state of the attack.

"Caonabo?" demanded Luis, of Ozema, pointing toward the new-comer.

The girl shook her head, after taking an anxious look at the stranger's face, at the same time clinging to our hero's arm, with seductive dependence.

"No—no—no—" she said, eagerly. "No Caonabo—no—no—no."

Luis understood the first part of this answer to mean that the stranger was not the Carib chief; and the last to signify Ozema's strong and settled aversion to becoming his wife.

The consultation among the assailants was soon ended. Six of them then poised their war-clubs and spears, and made a rush for the citadel of the besieged. When they were within twenty feet of his cover, our hero sprang lightly forward on the sward to meet his foes. Two of the spears he received on his buckler, severing both shafts with a single blow of his keen and highly-tempered sword. As he recovered from the effort, with an upward cut he met the raised arm of the club-man most in advance. Hand and club fell at his feet with the skilful touch. Making a sweep with the weapon in his front, its point seamed the breasts of the two astonished spears-men, whose distance alone saved them from more serious injuries.

This rapid and unlooked-for execution struck the assailants with awe and dread. Never before had they witnessed the power of metal as used in war; and the sudden amputation of the arm struck them as something miraculous. Even the ferocious Carib fell back in dismay, and Luis felt hopes of victory. This was the first occasion on which the Spaniards had come to blows with the mild inhabitants of the islands they had discovered, though it is usual with the historians to refer to an incident of still latter occurrence, as the commencement of strife, the severe privacy which has ever been thrown over the connection of Don Luis with the expedition, having completely baffled their slight and superficial researches. Of course, the efficiency of a weapon like that used by our hero, was as novel to the Haytians as it was terrific.

At this instant a shout among the assailants, and the appearance of a fresh body of the invaders, with a tall and commanding chief at their head, announced the arrival of Caonabo in person. This warlike cacique was soon made acquainted with the state of affairs, and it was evident that the prowess of our hero struck him as much with admiration as with wonder. After a few minutes, he directed his followers to fall back to a greater distance, and, laying aside his club, he advanced fearlessly toward Luis, making signs of amity.

When the two adversaries met, it was with mutual respect and confidence. The Carib made a short and vehement speech, in which the only word that was intelligible to our hero, was the name of the beautiful young Indian. By this time Ozema had also advanced, as if eager to speak, and her rude suitor turned to her, with an appeal that was passionate, if not eloquent. He laid his hand frequently on his heart, and his voice became soft and persuasive. Ozema replied earnestly, and in the quick manner of one whose resolution was settled. At the close of her speech, the color mounted to the temples of the ardent girl, and, as if purposely to make her meaning understood by our hero, she ended by saying, in Spanish—

"Caonabo—no—no—no!—Luis—Luis!"

The aspect of the hurricane of the tropics is not darker, or more menacing, than the scowl with which the Carib chief heard this unequivocal rejection of his suit, accompanied, as it was, by so plain a demonstration in favor of the stranger. Waving his hand in defiance, he strode back to his people, and issued orders for a fresh assault.

This time, a tempest of arrows preceded the rush, and Luis was fain to seek his former cover behind the rocks. Indeed, this was the only manner in which he could save the life of Ozema; the devoted girl resolutely persevering in standing before his body, in the hope it would shield him from his enemies. There had been some words of reproach from Caonabo to the Carib chief who had retreated from the first attack, and the air was yet filled with arrows, as this man rushed forward, singly, to redeem his name. Luis met him, firm as the rock behind him. The shock was violent, and the blow that fell on the buckler would have crushed an arm less inured to such rude encounters; but it glanced obliquely from the shield, and the club struck the earth with the weight of a beetle. Our hero saw that all now depended on a deep impression. His sword flashed in the bright sun, and the head of the Carib tumbled by the side of his club, actually leaving the body erect for an instant, so keen was the weapon, and so dexterous had been the blow.

Twenty savages were on the spring, but they stopped like men transfixed, at this unexpected sight. Caonabo, however, undaunted even when most surprised, roared out his orders like a maddened bull, and the wavering crowd was again about to advance, when the loud report of an arquebuse was heard, followed by the whistling of its deadly missives. A second Haytian fell dead in his tracks. It exceeded the powers of savage endurance to resist this assault, which, to their uninstructed minds, appeared to come from heaven. In two minutes, neither Caonabo nor any of his followers were visible. As they rushed down the hill, Sancho appeared from a cover, carrying the arquebuse, which he had taken the precaution to reload.

The circumstances did not admit of delay. Not a being of Mattinao's tribe was to be seen in any direction; and Luis made no doubt that they had all fled. Determined to save Ozema at every hazard, he now took his way to the river, in order to escape in one of the canoes. In passing through the town, it was seen that not a house had been plundered; and the circumstance was commented on by the Spaniards, Luis pointing it out to his companion.

"Caonabo—no—no—no—Ozema!—Ozema!" was the answer of the girl, who well knew the real object of the inroad.

A dozen canoes lay at the landing, and five minutes sufficed for the fugitives to enter one and to commence their retreat. The current flowed toward the sea, and in a couple of hours they were on the ocean. As the wind blew constantly from the eastward, Sancho soon rigged an apology for a sail, and an hour before the sun set, the party landed on a point that concealed them from the bay; Luis being mindful of the admiral's injunction, to conceal his excursion, lest others might claim a similar favor.

CHAPTER XXIV

"Three score and ten I can remember well,
Within the volume of which time I have seen
Hours dreadful, and things strange, but this sore sight
Hath trifled former knowings."

Macbeth.

A sight that struck our hero with a terror and awe, almost as great as those experienced by the ignorant Haytians at the report and effect of the arquebuse, awaited him, as he came in view of the anchorage. The Santa Maria, that vessel of the admiral, which he had left only four days before in her gallant array and pride, lay a stranded wreck on the sands, with fallen masts, broken sides, and all the other signs of nautical destruction. The Niña was anchored in safety, it is true, at no great distance, but a sense of loneliness and desertion came over the young man, as he gazed at this small craft, which was little more than a felucca, raised to the rank of a ship for the purposes of the voyage. The beach was covered with stores, and it was evident that the Spaniards and the people of Guacanagari toiled in company, at the construction of a sort of fortress; an omen that some great change had come over the expedition. Ozema was immediately left in the house of a native, and the two adventurers hurried forward to join their friends, and to ask an explanation of what they had seen.

Columbus received his young friend kindly, but in deep affliction. The manner in which the ship was lost has been often told, and Luis learned that the Niña being too small to carry all away, a colony was to be left in the fortress, while the remainder of the adventurers hastened back to Spain. Guacanagari had shown himself full of sympathy, and was kindness itself, while every one had been too much occupied with the shipwreck to miss our hero, or to hearken to rumors of an event as common as an inroad from a Carib chief, to carry off an Indian beauty. Perhaps, the latter event was still too recent to have reached the shores.

The week that succeeded the return of Luis was one of active exertion. The Santa Maria was wrecked on the morning of Christmas day, 1492, and on that of the 4th of January following, the Niña was ready to depart on her return voyage. During this interval, Luis had seen Ozema but once, and then he had found her sorrowing, mute, and resembling a withered flower, that retained its beauty even while it drooped. On the evening of the third, however, while lingering near the new-finished fortress, he was summoned by Sancho to another interview. To the surprise of our hero, he found the young cacique with his sister.

Although language was wanting, on this occasion, the parties easily understood each other. Ozema was no longer sorrowful, and borne down with grief: the smile and the laugh came easily from her young and buoyant spirits, and Luis thought he had never seen her so winning and lovely. She had arranged her scanty toilet with Indian coquetry, and the bright, warm color of her cheeks added new lustre to her brilliant eyes. Her light, agile form, a model of artless grace, seemed so ethereal as scarce to touch the earth. The secret of this sudden change was not long hid from Luis. The brother and sister, after discussing all their dangers and escapes, and passing in review the character and known determination of Caonabo, had come to the conclusion that there was no refuge for Ozema but in flight. What most determined the brother to consent that his sister should accompany the strangers to their distant home, it would be useless to inquire; but the motive of Ozema herself, can be no secret to the reader. It was known that the admiral was desirous of carrying to Spain a party of natives; and three females, one of whom was of Ozema's rank, had already consented to go. This chieftain's wife was not only known to Ozema, but she was a kinswoman. Every thing seemed propitious to the undertaking; and as a voyage to Spain was still a mystery to the natives, who regarded it as something like an extended passage from one of their islands to another, no formidable difficulties presented themselves to the imagination of either the cacique or his sister.

This proposition took our hero by surprise. He was both flattered and pleased at the self-devotion of Ozema, even while it troubled him. Perhaps there were moments when he a little distrusted himself. Still Mercedes reigned in his heart, and he shook off the feeling as a suspicion that a true knight could not entertain without offering an insult to his own honor. On second thoughts, there were fewer objections to the scheme than he at first fancied; and, after an hour's discussion, he left the place to go and consult the admiral.

Columbus was still at the fortress, and he heard our hero gravely and with interest. Once or twice Luis' eyes dropped under the searching glance of his superior; but, on the whole, he acquitted himself of the task he had undertaken, with credit.

"The sister of a cacique, thou say'st, Don Luis," returned the admiral, thoughtfully. "The virgin sister of a cacique!"

"Even so, Don Christopher; and of a grace, birth, and beauty, that will give our Lady, the Queen, a most exalted idea of the merits of our discovery."

"Thou wilt remember, Señor Conde, that naught but purity may be offered to purity. Doña Isabella is a model for all queens, and mothers, and wives; and I trust nothing to offend her angelic mind can ever come from her favored servants. There has been no deception practised on this wild girl, to lead her into sin and misery?"

"Don Christopher, you can scarce think this of me. Doña Mercedes herself is not more innocent than the girl I mean, nor could her brother feel more solicitude in her fortunes, than I feel. When the king and queen have satisfied their curiosity, and dismissed her, I propose to place her under the care of the Lady of Valverde."

"The rarer the specimens that we take, the better, Luis. This will gratify the sovereigns, and cause them to think favorably of our discoveries, as thou say'st. It might be done without inconvenience. The Niña is small, of a verity, but we gain much in leaving this large party behind us. I have given up the principal cabin to the other females, since thou and I can fare rudely for a few weeks. Let the girl come, and see thou to her comfort and convenience."

This settled the matter. Early next morning Ozema embarked, carrying with her the simple wealth of an Indian princess, among which the turban was carefully preserved. Her relative had an attendant, who sufficed for both. Luis paid great attention to the accommodations, in which both comfort and privacy were duly respected. The parting with Mattinao was touchingly tender, for the domestic affections appear to have been much cultivated among these simple-minded and gentle people; but the separation, it was supposed, would be short, and Ozema had, again and again, assured her brother that her repugnance to Caonabo, powerful cacique as he might be, was unconquerable. Each hour increased it, strengthening her resolution never to become his wife. The alternative was to secrete herself in the island, or to make this voyage to Spain; and there was glory as well as security in the latter. With this consolation, the brother and sister parted.

Columbus had intended to push his discoveries much further, before he returned to Europe; but the loss of the Santa Maria, and the desertion of the Pinta, reduced him to the necessity of bringing the expedition to a close, lest, by some untoward accident, all that had actually been achieved should be forever lost to the world. Accordingly, in the course of the 4th of January, 1493, he made sail to the eastward, holding his course along the shores of Hayti. His great object now was to get back to Spain before his remaining little bark should fail him, when his own name would perish with the knowledge of his discoveries. Fortunately, however, on the 6th, the Pinta was seen coming down before the wind, Martin Alonzo Pinzon having effected one of the purposes for which he had parted company, that of securing a quantity of gold, but failed in discovering any mines, which is believed to have been his principal motive.

It is not important to the narrative to relate the details of the meeting that followed. Columbus received the offending Pinzon with prudent reserve, and, hearing his explanations, he directed him to prepare the Pinta for the return passage. After wooding and watering accordingly, in a bay favorable to such objects, the two vessels proceeded to the eastward in company; still following the north shore of Hayti, Española, or Little Spain, as the island had been named by Columbus. [4]

It was the 16th of the month, ere the adventurers finally took their leave of this beautiful spot. They had scarcely got clear of the land, steering a north-easterly course, when the favorable winds deserted them, and they were again met by the trades. The weather was moderate, however, and by keeping the two vessels on the best tack, by the 10th of February, the admiral, making sundry deviations from a straight course, however, had stretched across the track of ocean in which these constant breezes prevailed, and reached a parallel of latitude as high as Palos, his port. In making this long slant, the Niña, contrary to former experience, was much detained by the dull sailing of the Pinta, which vessel, having sprung her after-mast, was unable to bear a press of sail. The light breeze also favored the first, which had ever been deemed a fast craft in smooth water and gentle gales.

Most of the phenomena of the outward passage were observed on the homeward; but the tunny-fish no longer excited hopes, nor did the sea-weed awaken fears. These familiar objects were successfully, but slowly passed, and the variable winds were happily struck again in the first fortnight. Here the traverses necessarily became more and more complicated, until the pilots, unused to so long and difficult a navigation, in which they received no aids from either land or water, got confused in their reckonings, disputing hotly among themselves concerning their true position.

"Thou hast heard to-day, Luis," said the admiral, smiling, in one of his renewed conferences with our hero, "the contentions of Vicente Yañez, with his brother, Martin Alonzo, and the other pilots, touching our distance from Spain. These constant shifts of wind have perplexed the honest mariners, and they fancy themselves in any part of the Atlantic, but that in which they really are!"

"Much depends on you, Señor; not only our safety, but the knowledge of our great discoveries."

"Thou say'st true, Don Luis. Vicente Yañez, Sancho Ruiz, Pedro Alonzo Niño, and Bartolemeo Roldan, to say nothing of the profound calculators in the Pinta, place the vessels in the neighborhood of Madeira, which is nearer to Spain, by a hundred and fifty leagues, than the truth would show. These honest people have followed their wishes, rather than their knowledge of the ocean and the heavens."

"And you, Don Christopher, where do you place the caravels, since there is no motive to conceal the truth?"

"We are south of Flores, young Count, fully twelve degrees west of the Canaries, and in the latitude of Nafé, in Africa. But I would that they should be bewildered, until the right of possession to our discoveries be made a matter of certainty. Not one of these men now doubts his ability to do all I have done, and yet neither is able to grope his way back again, after crossing this track of water to Asia!"

Luis understood the admiral, and the size of the vessels rendering the communication of secrets hazardous, the conversation changed.

Up to this time, though the winds were often variable, the weather had been good. A few squalls had occurred, as commonly happens at sea, but they had proved to be neither long nor severe. All this was extremely grateful to Columbus, who, now he had effected the great purpose for which he might have been said to live, felt some such concern lest the important secret should be lost to the rest of mankind, as one who carries a precious object through scenes of danger experiences for the safety of his charge. A change, however, was at hand, and at the very moment when the great navigator began to hope the best, he was fated to experience the severest of all his trials.

As the vessels advanced north, the weather became cooler, as a matter of course, and the winds stronger. During the night of the 11th of February, the caravels made a great run on their course, gaining more than a hundred miles between sunset and sunrise. The next morning many birds were in sight, from which fact Columbus believed himself quite near the Azores, while the pilots fancied they were in the immediate vicinity of Madeira. The following day the wind was less favorable, though strong, and a heavy sea had got up. The properties of the little Niña now showed themselves to advantage, for, ere the turn of the day, she had to contend with such a struggle of the elements, as few in her had ever before witnessed. Fortunately, all that consummate seamanship could devise to render her safe and comfortable had been done, and she was in as perfect a state of preparation for a tempest, as circumstances would allow. The only essential defect was her unusual lightness, since, most of her stores as well as her water being nearly exhausted, her draught of water was materially less than it should have been. The caravel was so small, that this circumstance, which is of little consequence to the safety of large vessels, got to be one of consideration in a craft whose means of endurance did not place her above the perils of squalls. The reader will understand the distinction better when he is told that ships of size can only lose their spars by sudden gusts of wind, seldom being thrown on their beam ends, as it is termed, unless by the power of the waves; whereas, smaller craft incur the risk of being capsized, when the spread of their canvas is disproportioned to their stability. Although the seamen of the Niña perceived this defect in their caravel, which, in a great measure, proceeded from the consumption of the fresh water, they hoped so soon to gain a haven, that no means had been taken to remedy the evil.

Such was the state of things, as the sun set on the night of the 12th of February, 1493. As usual, Columbus was on the poop, vessels of all sizes then carrying these clumsy excrescences, though this of the Niña was so small as scarcely to deserve the name. Luis was at his side, and both watched the aspect of the heavens and the ocean in grave silence. Never before had our hero seen the elements in so great commotion, and the admiral had just remarked that even he had not viewed many nights as threatening. There is a solemnity about a sunset at sea, when the clouds appear threatening, and the omens of a storm are brooding, that is never to be met with on the land. The loneliness of a ship, struggling through a waste of dreary-looking water, contributes to the influence of the feelings that are awakened, as there appears to be but one object on which the wild efforts of the storm can expend themselves. All else seem to be in unison to aid the general strife; ocean, heavens, and the air, being alike accessories in the murky picture. When the wintry frowns of February are thrown around all, the gloomy hues of the scene are deepened to their darkest tints.

"This is a brooding nightfall, Don Luis," Columbus remarked, just as the last rays that the sun cast upward on the stormy-looking clouds disappeared from their ragged outlines—"I have rarely seen another as menacing."

"One has a double confidence in the care of God, while sailing under your guidance, Señor; first in his goodness, and next in the knowledge of his agent's skilfulness."

"The power of the Almighty is sufficient to endue the feeblest mortal with all fitting skill, when it is his divine will to spare; or to rob the most experienced of their knowledge, when his anger can only be appeased by the worldly destruction of his creatures."

"You look upon the night as portentous, Don Christopher!"

"I *have* seen omens as ill, though very seldom. Had not the caravel this burdensome freight, I might view our situation less anxiously."

"You surprise me, sir Admiral! the pilots have regretted that our bark is so light."

"True, as to material substance; but it beareth a cargo of knowledge, Luis, that it would be grievous to see wasted on these vacant waters. Dost thou not perceive how fast and gloomily the curtain of night gathereth about us, and the manner in which the Niña is rapidly getting to be our whole world? Even the Pinta is barely distinguishable, like a shapeless shadow on the foaming billows, serving rather as a beacon to warn us of our own desolation, than as a consort to cheer us with her presence and companionship."

"I have never known you thus moody, excellent Señor, on account of the aspect of the weather!"

"'Tis not usual with me, young lord; but my heart is loaded with its glorious secret. Behold!—dost thou remark that further sign of the warring of the elements?"

The admiral, as he spoke, was standing with his face toward Spain, while his companion's gaze was fastened on the portentous-looking horizon of the west, around which still lingered sufficient light to render its frowns as chilling as they were visible. He had not seen the change that drew the remark from Columbus, but, turning quickly, he asked an explanation. Notwithstanding the season, the horizon at the north-east had been suddenly illuminated by a flash of lightning, and even while the admiral was relating the fact, and pointing out the quarter of the heavens in which the phenomenon had appeared, two more flashes followed each other in quick succession.

"Señor Vicente"—called out Columbus, leaning forward in a way to overlook a group of dusky figures that was collected on the half-deck beneath him—"Is Señor Vicente Yañez of your number?"

"I am here, Don Christopher, and note the omen. It is the sign of even more wind."

"We shall be visited with a tempest, worthy Vicente; and it will come from that quarter of the heavens, or its opposite. Have we made all sure in the caravel?"

"I know not what else is to be done, Señor Almirante. Our canvas is at the lowest, every thing is well lashed, and we carry as little aloft as can be spared. Sancho Ruiz, look you to the tarpaulings, lest we ship more water than will be safe."

"Look well to our light, too, that our consort may not part from us in the darkness. This is no time for sleep, Vicente—place your most trusty men at the tiller."

"Señor, they are selected with care. Sancho Mundo, and young Pepe of Moguer, do that duty, at present; others as skilled await to relieve them, when their watch ends."

"'Tis well, good Pinzon—neither you nor I can close an eye to-night."

The precautions of Columbus were not uncalled-for. About an hour after the unnatural flashes of lightning had been seen, the wind rose from the south-west, favorably as to direction, but fearfully as to force. Notwithstanding his strong desire to reach port, the admiral found it prudent to order the solitary sail that was set, to be taken in; and most of the night the two caravels drove before the gale, under bare poles, heading to the north-east. We say both, for Martin Alonzo, practised as he was in stormy seas, and disposed as he was to act only for himself, now the great problem was solved, kept the Pinta so near the Niña, that few minutes passed without her being seen careering on the summit of a foaming sea, or settling bodily into the troughs, as she drove headlong before the tempest; keeping side by side with her consort, however, as man clings to man in moments of dependency and peril.

Thus passed the night of the 13th, the day bringing with it a more vivid picture of the whole scene, though it was thought that the wind somewhat abated in its force as the sun arose. Perhaps this change existed only in the imaginations of the mariners, the light usually lessening the appearance of danger, by enabling men to face it. Each caravel, however, set a little canvas, and both went foaming ahead, hurrying toward Spain with their unlooked-for tidings. As the day advanced, the fury of the gale sensibly lessened; but as night drew on again, it returned with renewed force, more adverse, and compelling the adventurers to take in every rag of sail they had ventured to spread. Nor was this the worst. The caravels, by this time, had driven up into a tract of ocean where a heavy cross-sea was raging, the effects of some other gale that had recently blown from a different quarter. Both vessels struggled manfully to lay up to their course, under these adverse circumstances; but they began to labor in a way to excite uneasiness in those who comprehended the fullest powers of the machines, and who knew whence the real sources of danger were derived. As night approached, Columbus perceived that the Pinta could not maintain her ground, the strain on her after-mast proving too severe to be borne, even without an inch of canvas spread. Reluctantly did he order the Niña to edge away toward her consort, separation, at such a moment, being the evil next to positive destruction.

In this manner the night of the 14th drew around our lone and sea-girt adventurers. What had been merely menace and omens the previous night, were now a dread reality. Columbus, himself, declared he had never known a bark to buffet a more furious tempest, nor did he affect to conceal from Luis the extent of his apprehensions. With the pilots, and before the crew, he was serene, and even cheerful; but when alone with our hero, he became frank and humble. Still was the celebrated navigator always calm and firm. No unmanly complaint escaped him, though his very soul was saddened at the danger his great discoveries ran of being forever lost.

Such was the state of feeling that prevailed with the admiral, as he sat in his narrow cabin, in the first hours of that appalling night, watching for any change, relieving or disastrous, that might occur. The howling of the winds, which fairly scooped up, from the surface of the raging Atlantic, the brine in sheets, was barely audible amid the roar and rush of the waters. At times, indeed, when the caravel sunk helplessly between two huge waves, the fragment of sail she still carried would flap, and the air seemed hushed and still; and then, again, as the buoyant machine struggled upward, like a drowning man who gains the surface by frantic efforts, it would seem as if the columns of air were about to bear her off before them, as lightly as the driving spray. Even Luis, albeit little apt to take alarm, felt that their situation was critical, and his constitutional buoyancy of spirits had settled down in a thoughtful gravity, that was unusual with him. Had a column of a thousand hostile Moors stood before our hero, he would have thought rather of the means of overturning it than of escape; but this warring of the elements admitted of no such relief. It appeared actually like contending with the Almighty. In such scenes, indeed, the bravest find no means of falling back on their resolution and intrepidity; for the efforts of man seem insignificant and bootless as opposed to the will and power of God.

"'Tis a wild night, Señor," our hero observed calmly, preserving an exterior of more unconcern than he really felt. "To me this surpasseth all I have yet witnessed of the fury of a tempest."

Columbus sighed heavily; then he removed his hands from his face, and glanced about him, as if in search of the implements he wanted.

"Count of Llera," he answered, with dignity, "there remaineth a solemn duty to perform. There is parchment in the draw on your side of this table, and here are the instruments for writing. Let us acquit ourselves of this important trust while time is yet mercifully given us, God alone knowing how long we have to live."

Luis did not blanch at these portentous words, but he looked earnest and grave. Opening the draw, he took out the parchment and laid it upon the table. The admiral now seized a pen, beckoning to his companion to take another, and both commenced writing as well as the incessant motion of the light caravel would allow. The task was arduous, but it was clearly executed. As Columbus wrote a sentence, he repeated it to Luis, who copied it word for word, on his own piece of parchment. The substance of this record was the fact of the discoveries made, the latitude and longitude of Española, with the relative positions of the other islands, and a brief account of what he had seen. The letter was directed to Ferdinand and Isabella. As soon as each had completed his account, the admiral carefully enveloped his missive in a covering of waxed cloth, Luis imitating him in all things. Each then took a large cake of wax, and scooping a hole in it, the packet was carefully secured in the interior, when it was covered with the substance that had been removed. Columbus now sent for the cooper of the vessel, who was directed to inclose each cake in a separate barrel. These vessels abound in ships; and, ere many minutes, the two letters were securely inclosed in the empty casks. Each taking a barrel, the admiral and our hero now appeared again on the half-deck. So terrific was the night that no one slept, and most of the people of the Niña, men as well as officers, were crowded together on the gratings near the main-mast, where alone, with the exception of the still more privileged places, they considered themselves safe from being swept overboard. Indeed, even here they were constantly covered with the wash of the sea, the poop itself not being protected from rude visits of this nature.

As soon as the admiral was seen again, his followers crowded round him, solicitous to hear his opinion, and anxious to learn his present object. To have told the truth would have been to introduce despair where hope had already nearly ceased; and, merely intimating that he performed a religious vow, Columbus, with his own hands, cast his barrel into the hissing ocean. That of Luis was placed upon the poop, in the expectation that it would float, should the caravel sink.

Three centuries and a half have rolled by since Columbus took this wise precaution, and no tidings have ever been obtained of that cask. Its buoyancy was such that it might continue to float for ages. Covered with barnacles, it may still be drifting about the waste of waters, pregnant with its mighty revelations. It is possible, it may have been repeatedly rolled upon some sandy beach, and as frequently swept off again; and it may have been passed unheeded on a thousand occasions, by different vessels, confounded with its vulgar fellows that are so often seen drifting about the ocean. Had it been found, it would have been opened; and had it been opened by any civilized man, it is next to impossible that an occurrence of so much interest should have been totally lost.

This duty discharged, the admiral had leisure to look about him. The darkness was now so great, that, but for the little light that was disengaged from the troubled water, it would have been difficult to distinguish objects at the length of the caravel. No one, who has merely been at sea in a tall ship, can form any just idea of the situation of the Niña. This vessel, little more than a large felucca, had actually sailed from Spain with the latine rig, that is so common to the light coasters of southern Europe; a rig that had only been altered in the Canaries. As she floated in a bay, or a river, her height above the water could not have exceeded four or five feet, and now that she was struggling with a tempest, in a cross sea, and precisely in that part of the Atlantic where the rake of the winds is the widest, and the tumult of the waters the greatest, it seemed as if she were merely some aquatic animal, that occasionally rose to the surface to breathe. There were moments when the caravel appeared to be irretrievably sinking into the abyss of the ocean; huge black mounds of water rising around her in all directions, the confusion in the waves having destroyed all the ordinary symmetry of the rolling billows. Although so much figurative language has been used, in speaking of mountainous waves, it would not be exceeding the literal truth to add, that the Niña's yards were often below the summits of the adjacent seas, which were tossed upward in so precipitous a manner, as to create a constant apprehension of their falling in cataracts on her gratings; for midship-deck, strictly speaking, she had none. This, indeed, formed the great source of danger; since one falling wave might have filled the little vessel, and carried her, with all in her, hopelessly to the bottom. As it was, the crests of seas were constantly tumbling inboard, or shooting athwart the hull of the caravel, in sheets of glittering foam, though happily, never with sufficient power to overwhelm the buoyant fabric. At such perilous instants, the safety of the craft depended on the frail tarpaulings. Had these light coverings given way, two or three successive waves would infallibly have so far filled the hold, as to render the hull water-logged; when the loss of the vessel would have followed as an inevitable consequence.

The admiral had ordered Vicente Yañez to carry the foresail close reefed, in the hope of dragging the caravel through this chaos of waters, to a part of the ocean where the waves ran more regularly. The general direction of the seas, too, so far as they could be said to have a general direction at all, had been respected, and the Niña had struggled onward—it might be better to say, waded onward—some five or six leagues, since the disappearance of the day, and found no change. It was getting to be near midnight, and still the surface of the ocean presented the same wild aspect of chaotic confusion.

Vicente Yañez approached the admiral, and declared that the bark could no longer bear the rag of sail she carried.

"The jerk, as we rise on the sea, goes near to pull the stern out of the craft," he said. "and the backward flap, as we settle into the troughs, is almost as menacing. The Niña will bear the canvas no longer, with safety."

"Who has seen aught of Martin Alonzo within the hour?" demanded Columbus, looking anxiously in the direction in which the Pinta ought to be visible. "Thou hast lowered the lantern, Vicente Yañez."

"It would stand the hurricane no longer. From time to time it hath been shown, and each signal hath been answered by my brother."

"Let it be shown once more. This is a moment when the presence of a friend gladders the soul, even though he be helpless as ourselves."

The lantern was hoisted, and, after a steady gaze, a faint and distant light was seen glimmering in the rack of the tempest. The experiment was repeated, at short intervals, and as often was the signal answered, at increasing distances, until the light of their consort was finally lost altogether.

"The Pinta's mast is too feeble to bear even its gear, in such a gale," observed Vicente Yañez; "and my brother hath found it impossible to keep as near the wind as we have done. He goes off more to leeward."

"Let the foresail be secured," answered Columbus, "as thou say'st. Our feeble craft can no longer bear these violent surges."

Vicente Yañez now mustered a few of his ablest men, and went forward himself to see this order executed. At the same moment the helm was righted, and the caravel slowly fell off, until she got dead before the gale. The task of gathering in the canvas was comparatively easy, the yard being but a few feet above the deck, and little besides the clews being exposed. Still it required men of the firmest nerve and the readiest hands to venture aloft at such an instant. Sancho took one side of the mast and Pepe the other, both manifesting such qualities as mark the perfect seaman only.

The caravel was now drifting at the mercy of the winds and waves, the term scudding being scarcely applicable to the motion of a vessel so low, and which was so perfectly sheltered from the action of the wind by the height of the billows. Had the latter possessed their ordinary regularity, the low vessel must have been pooped; but, in a measure, her exemption from this calamity was owing to an irregularity that was only the source of a new danger. Still, the Niña drove ahead, and that swiftly, though not with the velocity necessary to outstrip the chasing water, had the waves followed with their customary order and regularity. The cross seas defeated this; wave meeting wave, actually sending those crests, which otherwise would have rolled over in combing foam, upward in terrific *jets d'eau*.

This was the crisis of the danger. There was an hour when the caravel careered amid the chaotic darkness with a sort of headlong fury, not unfrequently dashing forward with her broadside to the sea, as if the impatient stern was bent on overtaking the stem, and exposing all to the extreme jeopardy of receiving a flood of water on the beam. This imminent risk was only averted by the activity of the man at the helm, where Sancho toiled with all his skill and energy, until the sweat rolled from his brow, as if exposed again to the sun of the tropics. At length the alarm became so great and general, that a common demand was made to the admiral to promise the customary religious oblations. For this purpose, all but the men at the helm assembled aft, and preparations were made to cast lots for the penance.

"Ye are in the hands of God, my friends," said Columbus, "and it is meet that ye all confess your dependence on his goodness, placing your security on his blessings and favor alone. In this cap which ye see in the hands of the Señor de Muños, are the same number of peas that we are of persons. One of these peas bears the mark of the Holy Cross, and he who shall draw forth this blessed emblem, stands pledged to make a pilgrimage to Santa Maria de Guadalupe, bearing a waxen taper of five pounds weight. As the chiefest sinner among you, no less than as your admiral, the first trial shall be mine."

Here Columbus put his hand into the cap, and on drawing forth a pea, and holding it to the lantern, it was found to bear on its surface the mark he had mentioned.

"This is well, Señor," said one of the pilots; "but replace the pea, and let the chance be renewed for a still heavier penance, and that at a shrine which is most in request with all good Christians; I mean that of our Lady of Loretto. One pilgrimage to that shrine is worth two to any other."

In moments of emergency, the religious sentiment is apt to be strong; and this proposition was seconded with warmth. The admiral cheerfully consented; and when all had drawn, the marked pea was found in the hands of a common seaman, of the name of Pedro de Villa; one who bore no very good name for either piety or knowledge.

"'Tis a weary and costly journey," grumbled the chosen penitent, "and cannot cheaply be made."

"Heed it not, friend Pedro," answered Columbus; "the bodily pains shall limit thy sufferings. for the cost of the journey shall be mine. This night groweth more and more terrific, good Bartolemeo Roldan."

"That doth it, Señor Admiral, and I am little content with such a pilgrim as Pedro here, although it may seem as if heaven itself directed the choice. A mass in Santa Clara de Moguer, with a watcher all night in that chapel, will be of more account than your distant journeys made by such an one as he."

This opinion wanted not for supporters among the seamen of Moguer, and a third trial was made to determine the person. Again the pea was withdrawn from the cap by the admiral. Still the danger did not diminish, the caravel actually threatening to roll over amid the turbulence of the waves.

"We are too light, Vicente Yañez," said Columbus, "and, desperate as the undertaking seemeth, we must make an effort to fill our empty casks with sea-water. Let hose be carefully introduced beneath the tarpaulings, and send careful hands below to make sure that the water does not get into the hold instead of the casks."

This order was obeyed, and several hours passed in efforts to execute this duty. The great difficulty was in protecting the men who raised the water from the sea, for, while the whole element was raging in such confusion around them, it was no easy matter to secure a single drop in a useful manner. Patience and perseverance, however, prevailed in the end, and, ere the light returned, so many empty casks had been filled, as evidently to aid the steadiness of the vessel. Toward morning it rained in torrents, and the wind shifted from south to west, losing but little of its force, however. At this juncture the foresail was again got on the bark, and she was dragged by it, through a tremendous sea, a few miles to the eastward.

When the day dawned, the scene was changed for the better. The Pinta was nowhere to be seen, and most in the Niña believed she had gone to the bottom. But the clouds had opened a little, and a sort of mystical brightness rested on the ocean, which was white with foam, and still hissing with fury. The waves, however, were gradually getting to be more regular, and the seamen no longer found it necessary to lash themselves to the vessel, in order to prevent being washed overboard. Additional sail was got on the caravel, and, as her motion ahead increased, she became steadier, and more certain in all her movements.

CHAPTER XXV

"For now, from sight of land diverted clear,
They drove uncertain o'er the pathless deep;
Nor gave the adverse gale due course to steer,
Nor durst they the design'd direction keep:
The gathering tempest quickly raged so high,
The wave-encompass'd boat but faintly reach'd my eye."

Vision of Patience.

Such was the state of things on the morning of the 15th, and shortly after the sun arose, the joyful cry of land was heard from aloft. It is worthy of being mentioned that this land was made directly ahead, so accurate were all the admiral's calculations, and so certain did he feel of his position on the chart. A dozen opinions, however, prevailed among the pilots and people concerning this welcome sight; some fancying it the continent of Europe, while others believed it to be Madeira. Columbus, himself, publicly announced it to be one of the Azores.

Each hour was lessening the distance between this welcome spot of earth and the adventurers, when the gale chopped directly round, bringing the island dead to windward. Throughout a long and weary day the little bark kept turning up against the storm, in order to reach this much-desired haven, but the heaviness of the swell and the foul wind made their progress both slow and painful. The sun set in wintry gloom, again, and the land still lay in the wrong quarter, and apparently at a distance that was unattainable. Hour after hour passed, and still, in the darkness, the Niña was struggling to get nearer to the spot where the land had been seen. Columbus never left his post throughout all these anxious scenes, for to him it seemed as if the fortunes of his discoveries were now suspended, as it might be, by a hair. Our hero was less watchful, but even he began to feel more anxiety in the result, as the moment approached when the fate of the expedition was to be decided.

As the sun arose, every eye turned inquiringly around the watery view, and, to the common disappointment, no land was visible. Some fancied all had been illusion, but the admiral believed they had passed the island in the darkness, and he hove about, with a view to stand further south. This change in the course had not been made more than an hour or two, when land was again dimly seen astern, and in a quarter where it could not have been previously perceived. For this island the caravel tacked, and until dark she was beating up for it, against a strong gale and a heavy sea. Night again drew around her, and the land once more vanished in the gloom.

At the usual hour of the previous night, the people of the Niña had assembled to chant the *salve fac, regina,* or the evening hymn to the Virgin, for it is one of the touching incidents of this extraordinary voyage, that these rude sailors first carried with them into the unknown wastes of the Atlantic the songs of their religion, and the Christian's prayers. While thus employed, a light had been made to leeward, which was supposed to be on the island first seen, thus encouraging the admiral in his belief that he was in the centre of a group, and that by keeping well to windward, he would certainly find himself in a situation to reach a port in the morning. That morning, however, had produced no other change than the one noted, and he was now preparing to pass another night, or that of the 17th, in uncertainty, when the cry of land ahead suddenly cheered the spirits of all in the vessel.

The Niña stood boldly in, and before midnight she was near enough to the shore to let go an anchor; so heavy were both wind and sea, however, that the cable parted, thus rejecting them, as it were, from the regions to which they properly belonged. Sail was made. and the effort to get to windward renewed, and by daylight the caravel was enabled to run in and get an anchorage on the north side of the island. Here the wearied and almost exhausted mariners learned that Columbus was right, as usual, and that they had reached the island of St. Mary, one of the Azores.

It does not belong to this tale to record all the incidents that occurred while the Niña lay at this port. They embraced an attempt to seize the caravel, on the part of the Portuguese, who, as they had been the last to harass the admiral on his departure from the old world, were the first to beset him on his return. All their machinations failed, however, and after having the best portion of his crew in their power, and actually having once sailed from the island without the men, the admiral finally arranged the matter, and took his departure for Spain, with all his people on board, on the 24th of the month.

Providence seemed to favor the passage of the adventurers, for the first few days; the wind being favorable and the sea smooth. Between the morning of the 24th and the evening of the 26th, the caravel had made nearly a hundred leagues directly on her course to Palos, when she was met by a foul wind and another heavy sea. The gale now became violent again, though sufficiently favorable to allow them to steer east, a little northerly, occasionally hauling more ahead. The weather was rough, but as the admiral knew he was drawing in with the continent of Europe, he did not complain, cheering his people with the hopes of a speedy arrival. In this manner the time passed until the turn of the day, Saturday, March 2d, when Columbus believed himself to be within a hundred miles of the coast of Portugal, the long continuance of the scant southerly winds having set him thus far north.

The night commenced favorably, the caravel struggling ahead through a tremendous sea that was sweeping down from the south, having the wind abeam, blowing so fresh as to cause the sails to be reduced within manageable size. The Niña was an excellent craft, as had been thoroughly proved, and she was now steadier than when first assailed by the tempests, her pilots having filled still more of the casks than they had been able to do during the late storm.

"Thou hast lived at the helm, Sancho Mundo, since the late gales commenced," said the admiral, cheerfully, as, about the last hour of the first watch, he passed near the post of the old mariner. "It is no small honor to hold that station in the cruel gales we have been fated to endure."

"I so consider it, Señor Don Almirante; and I hope their illustrious and most excellent Highnesses, the two sovereigns, will look upon it with the same eyes, so far as the weight of the duty is concerned."

"And why not as respects the honor, friend Sancho?" put in Luis, who had become a sworn friend of the seaman, since the rescue of the rocks.

"Honor, Señor Master Pedro, is cold food, and sits ill on a poor man's stomach. One dobla is worth two dukedoms to such a man as I am, since the dobla would help to gain me respect, whereas the dukedoms would only draw down ridicule upon my head. No, no—Master Pedro, your worship, give me a pocket full of gold, and leave honors to such as have a fancy for them. If a man must be raised in the world, begin at the beginning, or lay a solid foundation; after which he may be made a knight of St. James, if the sovereigns have need of his name to make out their list."

"Thou art too garrulous for a helmsman, Sancho, though so excellent otherwise," observed the admiral, gravely. "Look to thy course; doblas will not be wanting, when the voyage is ended."

"Many thanks, Señor Almirante; and, as a proof that my eyes are not shut, even though the tongue wags, I will just desire your Excellency, and the pilots, to study that rag of a cloud that is gathering up here, at the south-west, and ask yourselves if it means evil or good."

"By the mass! the man is right, Don Christopher!" exclaimed Bartolemeo Roldan, who was standing near; "that is a most sinister-looking cloud, and is not unlike those that give birth to the white squalls of Africa."

"See to it—see to it—good Bartolemeo," returned Columbus, hastily. "We have, indeed, counted too much on our good fortune, and have culpably overlooked the aspect of the heavens. Let Vicente Yañez and all our people be called; we may have need of them."

Columbus now ascended to the poop, where he got a wider and a better view of the ocean and the skies. The signs were, indeed, as portentous as they had been sudden in their appearance. The atmosphere was filled with a white mist, that resembled a light smoke, and the admiral had barely time to look about him, when a roar that resembled the trampling of a thousand horses passing a bridge at full speed, came rushing down with the wind. The ocean was heard hissing, as is usual at such moments, and the tempest burst upon the little bark, as if envious demons were determined she should never reach Spain with the glorious tidings she bore.

A report like that of a heavy discharge of musketry, was the first signal that the squall had struck the Niña. It came from the rent canvas, every sail having given way at the same instant. The caravel heeled until the water reached her masts, and there was a breathless instant, when the oldest seaman feared that she would be forced over entirely upon her side. Had not the sails split, this calamity might truly have occurred. Sancho, too, had borne the tiller up in season, and when the Niña recovered from the shock, she almost flew out of the water as she drove before the blast.

This was the commencement of a new gale, which even surpassed in violence that from which they had so recently escaped. For the first hour, awe and disappointment almost paralyzed the crew, as nothing was or could be done to relieve them from the peril they were in. The vessel was already scudding—the last resource of seamen—and even the rags of the canvas were torn, piece by piece, from the spars, sparing the men the efforts that would have been necessary to secure them. In this crisis, again the penitent people resorted to their religious rites; and again it fell to the lot of the admiral to make a visit to some favorite shrine. In addition, the whole crew made a vow to fast on bread and water, the first Saturday after they should arrive.

"It is remarkable, Don Christopher," said Luis, when the two were again alone on the poop, "it is remarkable that these lots should fall so often on you. Thrice have you been selected by Providence to be an instrument of thankfulness and penitence. This cometh of your exceeding faith!"

"Say, rather, Luis, that it cometh of my exceeding sins. My pride, alone, should draw down upon me stronger rebukes than these. I fear me, I had forgotten that I was merely an agent chosen by God, to work his own great ends, and was falling into the snares of Satan, by fancying that I, of my own wisdom and philosophy, had done this great exploit, which cometh so truly of God."

"Do you believe us in danger, Señor?"

"Greater hazard besets us now, Don Luis, than hath befallen us since we left Palos. We are driving toward the continent, which cannot be thirty leagues distant; and, as thou seest, the ocean is becoming more troubled every hour. Happily, the night is far advanced, and with the light we may find the means of safety."

The day did reappear as usual; for whatever disturbances occur on its surface, the earth continues its daily revolutions in the sublimity of its vastness, affording, at each change, to the mites on its surface, the indubitable proofs that an omnipotent power reigns over all its movements. The light, however, brought no change in the aspects of the ocean and sky. The wind blew furiously, and the Niña struggled along amid the chaos of waters, driving nearer and nearer to the continent that lay before her.

About the middle of the afternoon, signs of land became quite apparent, and no one doubted the vicinity of the vessel to the shores of Europe. Nevertheless, naught was visible but the raging ocean, the murky sky, and the sort of supernatural light with which the atmosphere is so often charged in a tempest. The spot where the sun set, though known by means of the compass, could not be traced by the eye; and again night closed on the wild, wintry scene, as if the little caravel was abandoned by hope as well as by day. To add to the apprehensions of the people, a high cross sea was running; and, as ever happens with vessels so small, in such circumstances, tons' weight of water were constantly falling inboard, threatening destruction to the gratings and their frail coverings of tarred cloth.

"This is the most terrible night of all, son Luis," said Columbus, about an hour after the darkness had drawn around them. "If we escape this night, well may we deem ourselves favored of God!"

"And yet you speak calmly, Señor; as calmly as if your heart was filled with hope."

"The seaman that cannot command his nerves and voice, even in the utmost peril, hath mistaken his calling. But I *feel* calm, Luis, as well as *seem* calm. God hath us in his keeping, and will do that which most advanceth his own holy will. My boys—my two poor boys trouble me sorely; but even the fatherless are not forgotten!"

"If we perish, Señor, the Portuguese will remain masters of our secret: to them only is it now known, ourselves excepted, since, for Martin Alonzo, I should think, there is little hope."

"This is another source of grief; yet have I taken such steps as will probably put their Highnesses on the maintenance of their rights. The rest must be trusted to heaven."

At that moment was heard the startling cry of "land." This word, which so lately would have been the cause of sudden bursts of joy, was now the source of new uneasiness. Although the night was dark, there were moments when the gloom opened, as it might be, for a mile or two around the vessel, and when objects as prominent as a coast could be seen with sufficient distinctness. Both Columbus and our hero hastened to the forward part of the caravel, at this cry, though even this common movement was perilous, in order to obtain the best possible view of the shore. It was, indeed, so near, that all on board heard, or fancied they heard, the roar of the surf against the rocks. That it was Portugal, none doubted, and to stand on in the present uncertainty of their precise position, or without a haven to enter, would be inevitable destruction. There remained only the alternative to ware with the caravel's head off shore, and endeavor to keep an offing until morning. Columbus had no sooner mentioned this necessity, than Vicente Yañez set about its execution in the best manner circumstances would allow.

Hitherto the wind had been kept a little on the starboard quarter, the caravel steering east, a point or two north, and it was now the aim to lay her head so far round as to permit her to steer north, a point or two west. By the manner in which the coast appeared to trend, it was thought that this variation in the direction might keep them, for a few hours, at a sufficient distance from the shore. But this manœuvre could not be effected without the aid of canvas, and an order was issued to set the foresail. The first flap of the canvas, as it was loosened to the gale, was tremendous, the jerk threatening to tear the fore-mast from its step, and then all was still as death forward, the hull sinking so low behind a barrier of water, as actually to becalm the sail. Sancho and his associate seized the favorable moment to secure the clews, and, as the little bark struggled upward again, the canvas filled with some such shock as is felt at the sudden checking of a cable. From this moment the Niña drew slowly off to sea again, though her path lay through such a scene of turbulent water, as threatened, at each instant, to overwhelm her.

Mercedes Of Castile; Or, The Voyage To Cathay | 331

"Luis!" said a soft voice, at our hero's elbow, as the latter stood clinging to the side of the door of the cabin appropriated to the females—"Luis—Hayti better—Mattinao better—much bad, Luis!"

It was Ozema, who had risen from her pallet to look out upon the appalling view of the ocean. During the mild weather of the first part of the passage, the intercourse between Luis and the natives on board had been constant and cheerful. Though slightly incommoded by her situation, Ozema had always received his visits with guileless delight, and her progress in Spanish had been such as to astonish even her teacher. Nor were the means of communication confined altogether to the advance of Ozema, since Luis, in his endeavors to instruct her, had acquired nearly as many words of her native tongue, as he had taught her of his own. In this manner they conversed, resorting to both dialects for terms, as necessity dictated. We shall give a free translation of what was said, endeavoring, at the same time, to render the dialogue characteristic and graphic.

"Poor Ozema!" returned our hero, drawing her gently to a position where he could support her against the effects of the violent motion of the caravel—"thou must regret Hayti, indeed, and the peaceful security of thy groves!"

"Caonabo there, Luis."

"True, innocent girl; but even Caonabo is not as terrible as this anger of the elements."

"No—no—no—Caonabo much bad. Break Ozema's heart. No Caonabo—no Hayti."

"Thy dread of the Carib chief, dear Ozema, hath upset thy reason, in part. Thou hast a God, as well as we Christians, and, like us, must put thy trust in him; he alone can now protect thee."

"What protect?"

"Care for thee, Ozema. See that thou dost not come to harm. Look to thy safety and welfare."

"Luis protect Ozema. So promise Mattinao—so promise Ozema—so promise heart."

"Dear girl, so will I, to the extent of my means. But what can I do against this tempest?"

"What Luis do against Caonabo?—Kill him—cut Indians—make him run away!"

"This was easy to a Christian knight, who carried a good sword and buckler, but it is impossible against a tempest. We have only one hope, and that is to trust in the Spaniard's God."

"Spaniards great—have great God."

"There is but one God, Ozema, and he ruleth all, whether in Hayti or in Spain. Thou rememberest what I have told thee of his love, and of the manner of his death, that we might all be saved, and thou didst then promise to worship him, and to be baptized when we should reach my country."

"God!—Ozema do, what Ozema say. Love Luis' God already."

"Thou hast seen the holy cross, Ozema, and hast promised me to kiss it, and bless it."

"Where cross? See no cross—up in heaven?—or where? Show Ozema cross, now—Luis' cross—cross Luis love."

The young man wore the parting gift of Mercedes near his heart, and raising a hand he withdrew the small jewel, pressed it to his own lips with pious fervor, and then offered it to the Indian girl.

"See"—he said—"this is a cross; we Spaniards revere and bless it. It is our pledge of happiness."

"That Luis' God?" enquired Ozema, in a little surprise.

"Not so, my poor benighted girl"—

"What benighted?" interrupted the quick-witted Haytian, eagerly, for no term that the young man could or did apply to her, fell unheeded on her vigilant and attentive ear.

"Benighted means those who have never heard of the cross, or of its endless mercies."

"Ozema no benighted now," exclaimed the other, pressing the bauble to her bosom. "Got cross—keep cross—no benighted again, never. Cross, Mercedes"—for, by one of those mistakes that are not unfrequent in the commencement of all communications between those who speak different tongues, the young Indian had caught the notion, from many of Luis' involuntary exclamations, that "Mercedes" meant all that was excellent.

"I would, indeed, that she of whom thou speakest had thee in her gentle care, that she might lead thy pure soul to a just knowledge of thy Creator! That cross cometh of Mercedes, if it be not Mercedes herself, and thou dost well in loving it, and in blessing it. Place the chain around thy neck, Ozema, for the precious emblem may help in preserving thee, should the gale throw us on the coast ere morning. *That cross is a sign of undying love.*"

The girl understood enough of this, especially as the direction was seconded by a little gentle aid, on the part of our hero, to comply, and the chain was soon thrown around her neck, with the holy emblem resting on her bosom. The change in the temperature, as well as a sense of propriety, had induced the admiral to cause ample robes of cotton to be furnished all the females, and Ozema's beautiful form was now closely enveloped in one, and beneath its folds she had hidden the jewel, which she fondly hugged to her heart, as a gift of Luis. Not so did the young man himself view the matter. He had merely meant to lend, in a moment of extreme peril, that which the superstitious feeling of the age seriously induced him to fancy might prove a substantial safeguard. As Ozema was by no means expert in managing the encumbrance of a dress to which she was unaccustomed, even while native taste had taught her to throw it around her person gracefully, the young man had half unconsciously assisted in placing the cross in its new position, when a violent roll of the vessel compelled him to sustain the girl by encircling her waist with an arm. Partly yielding to the motion of the caravel, which was constantly jerking even the mariners from their feet, and probably as much seduced by the tenderness of her own heart, Ozema did not rebuke this liberty—the first our hero had ever offered, but stood, in confiding innocence, upheld by the arm that, of all others, it was most grateful to her feelings to believe destined to perform that office for life. In another moment, her head rested on his bosom, and her face was turned upward, with the eyes fastened on the countenance of the young noble.

"Thou art less alarmed at this terrific storm, Ozema, than I could have hoped. Apprehension for thee has made me more miserable than I could have thought possible, and yet thou seemest not to be disturbed."

"Ozema no unhappy—no want Hayti—no want Mattinao—no want any thing—Ozema happy now. Got cross."

"Sweet, guileless innocent, may'st thou never know any other feelings!—confide in thy cross."

"Cross, Mercedes—Luis, Mercedes. Luis and Ozema keep cross forever."

It was, perhaps, fortunate for this high-prized happiness of the girl, that the Niña now took a plunge that unavoidably compelled our hero to release his hold of her person, or to drag her with him headlong toward the place where Columbus stood, sheltering his weather-beaten form from a portion of the violence of the tempest. When he recovered his feet, he perceived that the door of the cabin was closed, and that Ozema was no longer to be seen.

"Dost thou find our female friends terrified by this appalling scene, son Luis?" Columbus quietly demanded, for, though his own thoughts had been much occupied by the situation of the caravel, he had noted all that had just passed so near him. "They are stout of heart, but even an amazon might quail at this tempest."

"They heed it not, Señor, for I think they understand it not. The civilized man is so much their superior, that both men and women appear to have every confidence in our means of safety. I have just given Ozema a cross, and bade her place her greatest reliance on that."

"Thou hast done well; it is now the surest protector of us all. Keep the head of the caravel as near to the wind as may be, Sancho, when it lulls, every inch off shore being so much gained in the way of security."

The usual reply was made, and then the conversation ceased; the raging of the elements, and the fearful manner in which the Niña was compelled to struggle literally to keep on the surface of the ocean, affording ample matter for the reflections of all who witnessed the scene.

In this manner passed the night. When the day broke, it opened on a scene of wintry violence. The sun was not visible that day, the dark vapor driving so low before the tempest, as to lessen the apparent altitude of the vault of heaven one-half, but the ocean was an undulating sheet of foam. High land soon became visible nearly abeam of the caravel, and all the elder mariners immediately pronounced it to be the rock of Lisbon. As soon as this important fact was ascertained, the admiral wore with the head of the caravel in-shore, and laid his course for the mouth of the Tagus. The distance was not great, some twenty miles perhaps; but the necessity of facing the tempest, and of making sail, on a wind, in such a storm, rendered the situation of the caravel more critical than it had been in all her previous trials. At that moment, the policy of the Portugese was forgotten, or held to be entirely a secondary consideration, a port or shipwreck appearing to be the alternative. Every inch of their weatherly position became of importance to the navigators, and Vicente Yañez placed himself near the helm to watch its play with the vigilance of experience and authority. No sail but the lowest could be carried, and these were reefed as closely as their construction would allow.

In this manner the tempest-tossed little bark struggled forward, now sinking so low in the troughs that land, ocean, and all but the frowning billows, with the clouds above their heads, were lost to view; and now rising, as it might be, from the calm of a sombre cavern, into the roaring, hissing, and turbulence of a tempest. These latter moments were the most critical. When the light hull reached the summit of a wave, falling over to windward by the yielding of the element beneath her, it seemed as if the next billow must inevitably overwhelm her; and yet, so vigilant was the eye of Vicente Yañez, and so ready the hand of Sancho, that she ever escaped the calamity. To keep the wash of the sea entirely out, was, however, impossible; and it often swept athwart the deck, forward, like the sheets of a cataract, that part of the vessel being completely abandoned by the crew.

"All now depends on our canvas," said the admiral, with a sigh; "if that stand, we are safer than when scudding, and I think God is with us. To me it seemeth as if the wind was a little less violent than in the night."

"Perhaps it is, Señor. I believe we gain on the place you pointed out to me."

"It is yon rocky point. *That* weathered, and we are safe. That not weathered, and we see our common grave."

"The caravel behaveth nobly, and I will still hope."

An hour later, and the land was so near that human beings were seen moving on it. There are moments when life and death may be said to be equally presented to the seaman's sight. On one side is destruction; on the other security. As the vessel drew slowly in toward the shore, not only was the thunder of the surf upon the rocks audible, but the frightful manner in which the water was tossed upward in spray, gave additional horrors to the view. On such occasions, it is no uncommon thing to see *jets d'eau* hundreds of feet in height, and the driving spray is often carried to a great distance inland, before the wind. Lisbon has the whole rake of the Atlantic before it, unbroken by island or headland; and the entire coast of Portugal is one of the most exposed of Europe. The south-west gales, in particular, drive across twelve hundred leagues of ocean, and the billows they send in upon its shores, are truly appalling. Nor was the storm we are endeavoring to describe, one of common occurrence. The season had been tempestuous, seldom leaving the Atlantic any peace; and the surges produced by one gale had not time to subside, ere another drove up the water in a new direction, giving rise to that irregularity of motion which most distresses a vessel, and which is particularly hazardous to small ones.

"She looks up better, Don Christopher!" exclaimed Luis, as they got within musket-shot of the desired point; "another ten minutes of as favorable a slant, and we do it!"

"Thou art right, son," answered the admiral, calmly. "Were any calamity to throw us ashore on yonder rocks, two planks of the Niña would not hold together five minutes. Ease her—good Vicente Yañez—ease her, quite a point, and let her go through the water. All depends on the canvas, and we can spare that point. She moves, Luis! Regard the land, and thou wilt now see our motion."

"True, Señor, but the caravel is drawing frightfully near the point!"

"Fear not; a bold course is often the safest. It is a deep shore, and we need but little water."

No one now spoke. The caravel was dashing in toward the point with appalling speed, and every minute brought her perceptibly nearer to the cauldron of water that was foaming around it. Without absolutely entering within this vortex, the Niña flew along its edge, and, in five minutes more, she had a direct course up the Tagus open before her. The mainsail was now taken in, and the mariners stood fearlessly on, certain of a haven and security.

Thus, virtually, ended the greatest marine exploit the world has ever witnessed. It is true that a run round to Palos was subsequently made, but it was insignificant in distance, and not fruitful in incidents. Columbus had effected his vast purpose, and his success was no longer a secret. His reception in Portugal is known, as well as all the leading occurrences that took place at Lisbon. He anchored in the Tagus on the 4th of March, and left it again on the 13th. On the morning of the 14th, the Niña was off Cape St. Vincent, when she hauled in to the eastward, with a light air from the north. At sunrise on the 15th she was again off the bar of Saltes, after an absence of only two hundred and twenty-four days.

CHAPTER XXVI

"One evening-tide, as with her crones she sate,
Making sweet solace of some scandal new,
A boisterous noise came thund'ring at the gate,
And soon a sturdie boy approached in view;
With gold far glitter and were his vestments blue,
And pye-shaped hat, and of the silver sheen
An huge broad buckle glaunst in either shoe,
And round his necke an Indian kerchiefe clean,
And in his hand a switch;—a jolly wight I ween."

Mickle.

Notwithstanding the noble conceptions that lay at the bottom of the voyage we have just related, the perseverance and self-devotion that were necessary to its accomplishment, and the magnificence of the consequences that were dependent on its success, it attracted very little attention, amid the stirring incidents and active selfishness of the age, until the result was known. Only a month before the arrangement was made with Columbus, the memorable edict of the two sovereigns, for the expulsion of the Jews, had been signed; and this uprooting of so large a portion of the Spanish nation was, of itself, an event likely to draw off the eyes of the people from an enterprise deemed as doubtful, and which was sustained by means so insignificant, as that of the great navigator. The close of the month of July had been set as the latest period for the departure of these persecuted religionists; and thus, at the very time, almost on the very day, when Columbus sailed from Palos, was the attention of the nation directed toward what might be termed a great national calamity. The departure was like the setting forth from Egypt, the highways being thronged with the moving masses, many of which were wandering they knew not whither.

The king and queen had left Granada in May, and after remaining two months in Castile, they passed into Aragon, about the commencement of August, in which kingdom they happened to be when the expedition sailed. Here they remained throughout the rest of the season, settling affairs of importance, and, quite probably, disposed to avoid the spectacle of the misery their Jewish edict had inflicted, Castile having contained much the greater portion of that class of their subjects. In October, a visit was paid to the turbulent Catalans; the court passing the entire winter in Barcelona. Nor did momentous events cease to occupy them while in this part of their territories. On the 7th of December an attempt was made on the life of Ferdinand; the assassin inflicting a severe, though not a fatal wound, by a blow on the neck. During the critical weeks in which the life of the king was deemed to be in danger, Isabella watched at his bed-side, with the untiring affection of a devoted wife; and her thoughts dwelt more on her affections than on any worldly aggrandisement. Then followed the investigation into the motives of the criminal; conspiracies ever being distrusted in such cases, although history would probably show that much the greater part of these wicked attempts on the lives of sovereigns, are more the results of individual fanaticism, than of any combined plans to destroy.

Isabella, whose gentle spirit grieved over the misery her religious submission had induced her to inflict on the Jews, was spared the additional sorrow of mourning for a husband, taken away by means so violent. Ferdinand gradually recovered. All these occurrences, together with the general cares of the state, had served to divide the thoughts of even the queen from the voyage; while the politic Ferdinand, in his mind, had long since set down the gold expended in the outfit as so much money lost.

The balmy spring of the south opened as usual, and the fertile province of Catalonia had already become delightful with the fresh verdure of the close of March. The king had, for some weeks, resumed his usual occupations, and Isabella, relieved from her conjugal fears, had again fallen into the quiet current of her duties and her usual acts of beneficence. Indisposed to the gorgeousness of her station by the recent events, and ever pining for the indulgence of the domestic affections, this estimable woman, notwithstanding the strong natural disposition she had always felt for that sort of life, had lived more among her children and confidants, of late, than had been even her wont. Her earliest friend, the Marchioness of Moya, as a matter of course, was ever near her person, and Mercedes passed most of her time either in the immediate presence of her royal mistress, or in that of her children.

There had been a small reception one evening, near the close of the month; and Isabella, glad to escape from such scenes, had withdrawn to her private apartments, to indulge in conversation in the circle she so much loved. It was near the hour of midnight, the king being at work, as usual, in an adjoining closet. There were present, besides the members of the royal family and Doña Beatriz with her lovely niece, the Archbishop of Granada, Luis de St. Angel, and Alonzo de Quintanilla, the two last of whom had been summoned by the prelate, to discuss some question of clerical finance before their illustrious mistress. All business, however, was over, and Isabella was rendering the circle agreeable, with the condescension of a princess and the gentle grace of a woman.

"Are there fresh tidings from the unfortunate and deluded Hebrews, Lord Archbishop?" demanded Isabella, whose kind feelings ever led her to regret the severity which religious dependence on her confessors had induced her to sanction. "Our prayers should surely attend them, notwithstanding our policy and duty have demanded their expulsion."

"Señora," answered Fernando de Talavera, "they are doubtless serving Mammon among the Moors and Turks, as they served him in Spain. Let not your Highness' gracious mind be disturbed on account of these descendants of the enemies and crucifiers of Christ, who, if they suffer at all, do but suffer justly, for the unutterable sin of their forefathers. Let us rather inquire, my gracious mistress, of the Señores St. Angel and Quintanilla here, what hath become of their favorite Colon, the Genoese; and when they look for his return, dragging the Great Khan, a captive, by the beard!"

"We know naught of him, holy prelate," put in de St. Angel, briskly, "since his departure from the Canaries."

"The Canaries!" interrupted the queen, in a little surprise. "Hath aught been received, that cometh from that quarter?"

"By report only, Señora. Letters have not reached any in Spain, that I can learn, but there is a rumor from Portugal, that the admiral touched at Gomera and the Grand Canary, where it would seem he had his difficulties, and whence he shortly after departed, holding a western course; since which time no tidings have been received from either of the caravels."

"By which fact, Lord Archbishop," added Quintanilla, "we can perceive that trifles are not likely to turn the adventurers back."

"I'll warrant ye, Señores, that a Genoese adventurer who holdeth their Highnesses' commission as an admiral, will be in no unseemly haste to get rid of the dignity!" rejoined the prelate, laughing, without much deference to his mistress' concessions in Columbus' favor. "One does not see rank, authority, and emolument, carelessly thrown aside, when they may be retained by keeping aloof from the power whence they spring."

"Thou art unjust to the Genoese, holy sir, and judgest him harshly," observed the queen. "Truly, I did not know of these tidings from the Canaries, and I rejoice to hear that Colon hath got thus far in safety. Hath not the past been esteemed a most boisterous winter among mariners, Señor de St. Angel?"

"So much so, your Highness, that I have heard the seamen here, in Barcelona, swear that, within the memory of man, there hath not been another like it. Should ill-luck wait upon Colon, I trust this circumstance may be remembered as his excuse; though I doubt if he be very near any of our tempests and storms."

"Not he!" exclaimed the bishop, triumphantly. "It will be seen that he hath been safely harbored in some river of Africa; and we shall have some question yet to settle about him with Don John of Portugal."

"Here is the king to give us his opinion," interposed Isabella. "It is long since I have heard him mention the name of Colon. Have you entirely forgotten our Genoese admiral, Don Fernando?"

"Before I am questioned on subjects so remote," returned the king, smiling, "let me inquire into matters nearer home. How long is it that your Highness holdeth court, and giveth receptions, past the hour of midnight?"

"Call you this a court, Señor? Here are but our own dear children, Beatriz and her niece, with the good archbishop, and those two faithful servants of your own."

"True; but you overlook the ante-chambers, and those who await your pleasure without."

"None can await without at this unusual hour; surely you jest, my lord."

"Then your own page, Diego de Ballesteros, hath reported falsely. Unwilling to disturb your privacy, at this unseasonable hour, he hath come to me, saying that one of strange conduct and guise is in the palace, insisting on an interview with the queen, let it be late or early. The accounts of this man's deportment are so singular, that I have ordered him to be admitted, and have come myself to witness the interview. The page telleth me that he swears all hours are alike, and that night and day are equally made for our uses."

"Dearest Don Fernando, there may be treason in this!"

"Fear not, Isabella; assassins are not so bold, and the trusty rapiers of these gentlemen will prove sufficient for our protection—Hist! there are footsteps, and we must appear calm, even though we apprehend a tumult."

The door opened, and Sancho Mundo stood in the royal presence. The air and appearance of so singular a being excited both astonishment and amusement, and every eye was fastened on him in wonder; and this so much the more, because he had decked his person with sundry ornaments from the imaginary Indies, among which were one or two bands of gold. Mercedes alone detected his profession by his air and attire, and she rose involuntarily, clasping her hands with energy, and suffering a slight exclamation to escape her. The queen perceived this little pantomime, and it at once gave a right direction to her own thoughts.

"I am Isabella, the queen," she said, prising, without any further suspicion of danger; "and thou art a messenger from Colon, the Genoese?"

Sancho, who had found great difficulty in gaining admittance, now that his end was obtained, took matters with his native coolness. His first act was to fall on his knees, as he had been particularly enjoined by Columbus to do. He had caught the habit of using the weed of Hayti and Cuba, from the natives, and was, in fact, the first seaman who ever chewed tobacco. The practice had already got to be confirmed with him, and before he answered, or as soon as he had taken this, for him, novel position, he saw fit to fill a corner of his mouth with the attractive plant. Then, giving his wardrobe a shake, for all the decent clothes he owned were on his person, he disposed himself to make a suitable reply.

"Señora—Doña—your Highness," he answered, "any one might have seen that at a glance. I am Sancho Mundo, of the ship-yard-gate; one of your Highness' Excellency's most faithful subjects and mariners, being a native and resident of Moguer."

"Thou comest from Colon, I say?"

"Señora, I do; many thanks to your Royal Grace for the information. Don Christopher hath sent me across the country from Lisbon, seeing that the wily Portuguese would be less likely to distrust a simple mariner, like myself, than one of your every-day-booted couriers. 'Tis a weary road, and there is not a mule between the stables of Lisbon and the palace of Barcelona, fit for a Christian to bestride."

"Then, hast thou letters? One like thee can scarcely bear aught else."

"Therein, your Grace's Highness, Doña Reyña, is mistaken; though I am far from bearing half the number of doblas I had at starting. Mass! the innkeepers took me for a grandee, by the manner in which they charged!"

"Give the man gold, good Alonzo—he is one that liketh his reward ere he will speak."

Sancho coolly counted the pieces that were put into his hand, and, finding them greatly to exceed his hopes, he had no longer any motive for prevarication.

"Speak, fellow!" cried the king. "Thou triflest where thou owest thy duty and obedience."

The sharp, quick voice of Ferdinand had much more effect on the ear of Sancho, than the gentler tones of Isabella, notwithstanding his rude nature had been impressed with the matronly beauty and grace of the latter.

"If your Highness would condescend to let me know what you wish to hear, I will speak in all gladness."

"Where is Colon?" demanded the queen.

"At Lisbon, lately, Señora, though I think now at Palos de Moguer, or in that neighborhood."

"Whither hath he been?"

"To Cipango, and the territories of the Great Khan; forty days' sail from Gomera, and a country of marvellous beauty and excellence!"

"Thou canst not—darest not trifle with me! Can we put credit in thy words?"

"If your Highness only knew Sancho Mundo, you would not feel this doubt. I tell you, Señora, and all these noble cavaliers and dames, that Don Christopher Colon hath discovered the other side of the earth, which we now know to be round, by having circled it; and that he hath found out that the north star journeyeth about in the heavens, like a gossip spreading her news; and that he hath taken possession of islands as large as Spain, in which gold groweth, and where the holy church may employ itself in making Christians to the end of time."

"The letter—Sancho—give me the letter. Colon would scarce send thee as a verbal expositor."

The fellow now undid sundry coverings of cloth and paper, until he reached the missive of Columbus, when, without rising from his knees, he held it out toward the queen, giving her the trouble to move forward several paces to receive it. So unexpected and astounding were the tidings, and so novel the whole scene, that no one interfered, leaving Isabella to be the sole actor, as she was, virtually, the sole speaker. Sancho having thus successfully acquitted himself of a task that had been expressly confided to him on account of his character and appearance, which, it was thought, would prove his security from arrest and plunder, settled down quietly on his heels, for he had been directed not to rise until ordered; and drawing forth the gold he had received, he began coolly to count it anew. So absorbing was the attention all gave to the queen, that no one heeded the mariner or his movements. Isabella opened the letter, which her looks devoured, as they followed line after line. As was usual with Columbus, the missive was long, and it required many minutes to read it. All this time not an individual moved, every eye being fastened on the speaking countenance of the queen. There, were seen the heightening flush of pleasure and surprise, the glow of delight and wonder, and the look of holy rapture. When the letter was ended, Isabella turned her eyes upward to heaven, clasped her hands with energy, and exclaimed —

"Not unto us, O Lord, but to Thee, be all the honor of this wonderful discovery, all the benefits of this great proof of thy goodness and power!"

Thus saying, she sunk into a seat and dissolved in tears. Ferdinand uttered a slight ejaculation at the words of his royal consort; and then he gently took the letter from her unresisting hand, and read it with great deliberation and care. It was not often that the wary King of Aragon was as much affected, in appearance at least, as on this occasion. The expression of his face, at first, was that of wonder; eagerness, not to say avidity, followed; and when he had finished reading, his grave countenance was unequivocally illuminated by exultation and joy.

"Good Luis de St. Angel!" he cried, "and thou, honest Alonzo de Quintanilla, these must be grateful tidings to you both. Even thou, holy prelate, wilt rejoice that the church is like to have acquisitions so glorious — albeit no favorer of the Genoese of old. Far more than all our expectations are realized, for Colon hath truly discovered the Indies; increasing our dominions, and otherwise advancing our authority in a most unheard-of manner."

It was unusual to see Don Ferdinand so excited, and he seemed conscious himself that he was making an extraordinary exhibition, for he immediately advanced to the queen, and, taking her hand, he led her toward his own cabinet. In passing out of the saloon, he indicated to the three nobles that they might follow to the council. The king made this sudden movement more from habitual wariness than any settled object, his mind being disturbed in a way to which he was unaccustomed, while caution formed a part of his religion, as well as of his policy. It is not surprising, therefore, that when he and the party he invited to follow him had left the room, there remained only the princesses, the Marchioness of Moya, and Mercedes. No sooner had the king and queen disappeared, than the royal children retired to their own apartments, leaving our heroine, her guardian, and Sancho, the sole occupants of the saloon. The latter still remained on his knees, scarce heeding what had passed, so intently was he occupied with his own situation, and his own particular sources of satisfaction.

"Thou canst rise, friend," observed Doña Beatriz; "their Highnesses are no longer present."

At this intelligence, Sancho quitted his humble posture, brushed his knees with some care, and looked about him with the composure that he was wont to exhibit in studying the heavens at sea.

"Thou wert of Colon's company, friend, by the manner in which thou hast spoken, and the circumstance that the admiral hath employed thee as his courier?"

"You may well believe that, Señora, your Excellency, for most of my time was passed at the helm, which was within three fathoms of the very spot that Don Christopher and the Señor de Muños loved so well that they never quitted it, except to sleep, and not always then."

"Hadst thou a Señor de Muños of thy party?" resumed the Marchioness, making a sign to her ward to control her feelings.

"That had we, Señora, and a Señor Gutierrez, and a certain Don Somebody Else, and they all three did not occupy more room than one common man. Prithee, honorable and agreeable Señora, is there one Doña Beatriz de Cabrera, the Marchioness of Moya, a lady of the illustrious house of Bobadilla, anywhere about the court of our gracious queen?"

"I am she, and thou hast a message for me, from this very Señor de Muños, of whom thou hast spoken."

"I no longer wonder that there are great lords with their beautiful ladies, and poor sailors with wives that no one envies! Scarce can I open my mouth, but it is known what I wish to say, which is knowledge to make one party great and the other party little! Mass!—Don Christopher, himself, will need all his wit, if he journeyeth as far as Barcelona!"

"Tell us of this Pedro de Muños; for thy message is to me."

"Then, Señora, I will tell you of your own brave nephew, the Conde de Llera, who goeth by two other names in the caravel, one of which is supposed to be a sham, while the other is still the greatest deception of the two."

"Is it, then, known who my nephew really is? Are many persons acquainted with his secret?"

"Certainly, Señora; it is known, firstly, to himself; secondly, to Don Christopher; thirdly, to me; fourthly, to Master Alonzo Pinzon, if he be still in the flesh, as most probably he is not. Then it is known to your ladyship; and this beautiful Señorita must have some suspicions of the matter."

"Enough—I see the secret is not public; though, how one of thy class came to be of it, I cannot explain. Tell me of my nephew:—did he, too, write? if so, let me, at once, peruse his letter."

"Señora, my departure took Don Luis by surprise, and he had no time to write. The admiral had given the princes and princesses, that we brought from Española, in charge to the Conde, and he had too much to do to be scribbling letters, else would he have written sheets to an aunt as respectable as yourself."

"Princes and princesses!—What mean you, friend, by such high-sounding terms?"

"Only that we have brought several of these great personages to Spain, to pay their respects to their Highnesses. We deal with none of the common fry, Señora, but with the loftiest princes, and the most beautiful princesses of the east."

"And dost thou really mean that persons of this high rank have returned with the admiral?"

"Out of all question, lady, and one of a beauty so rare, that the fairest dames of Castile need look to it, if they wish not to be outdone. She, in particular, is Don Luis' friend and favorite."

"Of whom speakest thou?" demanded Doña Beatriz, in the lofty manner in which she was wont to insist on being answered directly. "What is the name of this princess, and whence doth she come?"

"Her name, your Excellency, is Doña Ozema de Hayti, of a part of which country her brother, Don Mattinao, is cacique or king, Señora Ozema being the heiress, or next of kin. Don Luis and your humble servant paid that court a visit"—

"Thy tale is most improbable, fellow—art thou one whom Don Luis would be likely to select as a companion on such an occasion?"

"Look at it as you will, Señora, it is as true as that this is the court of Don Ferdinand and Doña Isabella. You must know, illustrious Marchioness, that the young count is a little given to roving about among us sailors, and on one occasion, a certain Sancho Mundo, of Moguer, happened to be of the same voyage; and thus we became known to each other. I kept the noble's secret, and he got to be Sancho's friend. When Don Luis went to pay a visit to Don Mattinao, the cacique, which word meaneth 'your Highness,' in the eastern tongue, Sancho must go with him, and Sancho went. When King Caonabo came down from the mountains to carry off the Princess Doña Ozema for a wife, and the princess was unwilling to go, why there remained nothing to be done, but for the Conde de Llera and his friend Sancho of the ship-yard-gate, to fight the whole army in her defence, which we did, gaining as great a victory as Don Fernando, our sovereign master, ever gained over the Moors."

"Carrying off the princess yourselves, as would seem! Friend Sancho, of the ship-yard-gate, if that be thy appellation, this tale of thine is ingenious, but it lacketh probability. Were I to deal justly by thee, honest Sancho, it would be to order thee the stripes thou merietst so well, as a reward for this trifling."

"The man speaketh as he hath been taught," observed Mercedes, in a low, unsteady voice; "I fear, Señora, there is too much truth in his tale!"

"You need fear nothing, beautiful Señorita," put in Sancho, altogether unmoved at the menace implied by the words of the Marchioness, "since the battle hath been fought, the victory hath been gained, and both the heroes escaped uninjured. This illustrious Señora, to whom I can forgive any thing, as the aunt of the best friend I have on earth—any thing *spoken*, I mean— will remember that the Haytians know nothing of arquebuses, by means of which we defeated Caonabo, and also, that many is the column of Moors that Don Luis hath broken singly, and by means of his own good lance."

"Ay, fellow," answered Doña Beatriz, "but that hath been in the saddle, behind plaits of steel, and with a weapon that hath overturned even Alonzo de Ojeda!"

"Hast thou truly brought away with thee the princess thou hast named?" asked Mercedes, earnestly.

"I swear to it, Señora and Señorita, illustrious ladies both, by the holy mass, and all the saints in the calendar! A princess, moreover, surpassing in beauty the daughters of our own blessed queen, if the fair ladies who passed out of this room, even now, are they, as I suspect."

"Out upon thee, knave!" cried the indignant Beatriz—"I will no more of this, and marvel that my nephew should have employed one of so loose a tongue, on any of his errands. Go to, and learn discretion ere the morning, or the favor of even thy admiral will not save thy bones. Mercedes, we will seek our rest—the hour is late."

Sancho was immediately left alone, and in a minute a page appeared to show him to the place where he was to pass the night. The old mariner had grumbled a little to himself, concerning the spirit of Don Luis' aunt, counted anew his gold, and was about to take possession of his pallet, when the same page reappeared to summon him to another interview. Sancho, who knew little distinction between night and day, made no objections, especially when he was told that his presence was required by the lovely Señorita, whose gentle, tremulous voice had so much interested him, in the late interview. Mercedes received her rude guest in a small saloon of her own, after having parted from her guardian for the night. As he entered, her face was flushed, her eye bright, and her whole demeanor, to one more expert in detecting female emotions, would have betrayed intense anxiety.

"Thou hast had a long and weary journey, Sancho," said our heroine, when alone with the seaman, "and, I pray thee, accept this gold, as a small proof of the interest with which I have heard the great tidings of which thou hast been the bearer."

"Señorita!" exclaimed Sancho, affecting indifference to the doblas that fell into his hand—"I hope you do not think me mercenary! the honor of being the messenger, and of being admitted to converse with such illustrious ladies, more than pays me for any thing I could do."

"Still, thou may'st need money for thy wants, and wilt not refuse that which a lady offereth."

"On that ground, I would accept it, Doña Señorita, even were it twice as much."

So saying, Sancho placed the money, with a suitable resignation, by the side of that which he had previously received by order of the queen. Mercedes now found herself in the situation that they who task their powers too much, are often fated to endure; in other words, now she had at command the means of satisfying her own doubts, she hesitated about using them.

"Sancho," Mercedes at length commenced, "thou hast been with the Señor Colon, throughout this great and extraordinary voyage, and must know much that it will be curious for us, who have lived quietly in Spain, to hear. Is all thou hast said about the princes and princesses true?"

"As true, Señorita, as such things need be for a history. Mass!—Any one who hath been in a battle, or seen any other great adventure, and then cometh to hear it read of, afterward, will soon learn to understand the difference between the thing itself, and the history that may be given of it. Now, I was"—

"Never mind thy other adventures, good Sancho; tell me only of this. Are there really a Prince Mattinao, and a Princess Ozema his sister, and have both accompanied the admiral to Spain?"

"I said not that, beautiful Señorita, for Don Mattinao remained behind to rule his people. It is only his handsome sister, who hath followed Don Christopher and Don Luis to Palos."

"Followed!—Do the admiral and the Conde de Llera possess such influence over royal ladies, as to induce them to abandon their native country and to *follow* them to a foreign land?"

"Ay, Señorita, that might seem out of rule in Castile, or Portugal, or even in France. But Hayti is not yet a Christian country, and a princess there may not be more than a noble lady in Castile, and, in the way of wardrobe, perhaps, not even as much. Still, a princess is a princess, and a handsome princess is a handsome princess. Doña Ozema, here, is a wonderful creature, and beginneth already to prattle your pure Castilian, and she had been brought up at Toledo, or Burgos. But Don Luis is a most encouraging master, and no doubt made great head-way, during the time he was living in her palace, as it might be alone with her, before that incarnate devil Don Caonabo came down with his followers to seize the lady."

"Is this lady a Christian princess, Sancho?"

"Heaven bless your own pure soul, Doña Señorita, she can boast of but little in that way; still, she hath made something of a beginning, as I see she now weareth a cross—one small in size, it is true, but precious in material, as, indeed it ought to be, seeing that it is a present from one as noble and rich as the Count of Llera."

"A cross, say'st thou, Sancho!" interrupted Mercedes, almost gasping for breath, yet so far subduing her feelings as to prevent the old seaman from detecting them; "hath Don Luis succeeded in inducing her to accept of a cross?"

"That hath he, Señorita—one of precious stones, that he once wore at his own neck."

"Knowest thou the stones?—was it of turquoise, embellished with the finest gold?"

"For the gold I can answer, lady, though my learning hath never reached as high as the precious stones. The heavens of Hayti, however, are not bluer than the stones of that cross. Doña Ozema calls it 'Mercedes,' by which I understand that she looketh for the mercies of the crucifixion to help her benighted soul."

"Is this cross, then, held so common, that it hath gotten to be the subject of discourse even for men of thy class?"

"Hearkee, Señorita; a man like me is more valued, on board a caravel, in a tossing sea, than he is likely to be here, in Barcelona, on solid ground. We went to Cipango to set up crosses, and to make Christians; so that all hath been in character. As for the Lady Ozema, she taketh more notice of me than of another, as I was in the battle that rescued her from Caonabo, and so she showed me the cross the day we anchored in the Tagus, or just before the admiral ordered me to bring his letter to her Highness. Then it was that she kissed the cross, and held it to her heart, and said it was 'Mercedes.'"

"This is most strange, Sancho! Hath this princess attendants befitting her rank and dignity?"

"You forget, Señorita, that the Niña is but a small craft, as her name signifieth, and there would be no room for a large train of lords and ladies. Don Christopher and Don Luis are honorable enough to attend on any princess; and for the rest, the Doña Ozema must wait until our gracious queen can command her a retinue befitting her birth. Besides, my lady, these Haytian dames are simpler than our Spanish nobles, half of them thinking clothes of no great use in that mild climate."

Mercedes looked offended and incredulous; but her curiosity and interest were too active, to permit her to send the man away without further question.

"And Don Luis de Bobadilla was ever with the admiral?" she said; "ever ready to support him, and foremost in all hazards?"

"Señorita, you describe the count as faithfully as if you had been present from first to last. Had you but seen him dealing out his blows upon Caonabo's followers, and the manner in which he kept them all at bay, with the Doña Ozema near him, behind the rocks, it would have drawn tears of admiration from your own lovely eyes."

"The Doña Ozema near him—behind rocks—and assailants held at bay!"

"Si, Señora; you repeat it all like a book. It was much as you say, though the Lady Ozema did not content herself with being behind the rocks, for, when the arrows came thickest, she rushed before the count, compelling the enemy to withhold, lest they should slay the very prize they were battling for; thereby saving the life of her knight."

"Saving his life!—the life of Luis—of Don Luis de Bobadilla—an Indian princess?"

"It is just as you say, and a most noble girl she is, asking pardon for speaking so light of one of her high rank. Time and again, since that day, hath the young count told me, that the arrows came in such clouds, that his honor might have been tarnished by a retreat, or his life been lost, but for the timely resolution of the Doña Ozema. She is a rare creature, Señorita, and you will love her as a sister, when you come to see and know her."

"Sancho," said our heroine, blushing like the dawn, "thou saidst that the Conde de Llera bade thee speak of him to his aunt; did he mention no one else?"

"No one, Señorita."

"Art certain, Sancho? Bethink thee well—did he mention no other name to thee?"

"Not that I can swear. It is true, that either he or old Diego, the helmsman, spoke of one Clara that keepeth an *hosteria*, here in Barcelona, as a place famous for its wine; but I think it more likely to have been Diego than the count, as one thinketh much of these matters, and the other would not be apt to know aught of Clara."

"Thou canst retire, Sancho," said Mercedes, in a faint voice. "We will say more to thee in the morning."

Sancho was not sorry to be dismissed, and he gladly returned to his pallet, little dreaming of the mischief he had done by the mixture of truth and exaggeration that he had been recounting.

CHAPTER XXVII

"Mac-Homer, too, in prose or song,
By the state-papers of Buffon,
To deep researches led;
A Gallo-Celtic scheme may botch,
To prove the Ourang race were Scotch,
Who from the Highlands fled."

Lord John Townshend.

The intelligence of the return of Columbus, and of the important discoveries he had made, spread through Europe like wild-fire. It soon got to be, in the general estimation, the great event of the age. For several years afterward, or until the discovery of the Pacific by Balboa, it was believed that the Indies had been reached by the western passage; and, of course, the problem of the earth's spherical shape was held to be solved by actual experiment. The transactions of the voyage, the wonders seen, the fertility of the soil of the east, the softness of its climate, its treasures in gold, spices, and pearls, and the curious things that the admiral had brought as proofs of his success, were all the themes of the hour. Men never wearied in discussing the subjects. For many centuries had the Spaniards been endeavoring to expel the Moors from the peninsula; but as that much-desired event had been the result of time and a protracted struggle, even its complete success seemed tame and insignificant compared with the sudden brilliancy that shone around the western discoveries. In a word, the pious rejoiced in the hope of spreading the gospel; the avaricious feasted their imaginations on untold hoards of gold; the politic calculated the increase of the power of Spain; the scientific exulted in the triumph of mind over prejudice and ignorance, while they hoped for still greater accessions of knowledge; and the enemies of Spain wondered, and deferred, even while they envied.

The first few days that succeeded the arrival of Columbus' courier, were days of delight and curiosity. Answers were sent soliciting his early presence, high honors were proffered to him, and his name filled all mouths, as his glory was in the heart of every true Spaniard. Orders were issued to make the necessary outfits for a new voyage, and little was talked of but the discovery and its consequences. In this manner passed a month, when the admiral arrived at Barcelona, attended by most of the Indians he had brought with him from the islands. His honors were of the noblest kind, the sovereigns receiving him on a throne placed in a public hall, rising at his approach, and insisting on his being seated himself, a distinction of the highest nature, and usually granted only to princes of royal blood. Here the admiral related the history of his voyage, exhibited the curiosities he had brought with him, and dwelt on his hopes of future benefits. When the tale was told, all present knelt, and *Te Deum* was chanted by the usual choir of the court; even Ferdinand's stern nature dissolving into tears of grateful joy, at this unlooked-for and magnificent behest of heaven.

For a long time, Columbus was the mark of every eye; nor did his honors and consideration cease untill he left Spain, in command of the second expedition to the east, as the voyage was then termed.

A few days previously to the arrival of the admiral at court, Don Luis de Bobadilla suddenly appeared in Barcelona. On ordinary occasions, the movements of one of the rank and peculiarities of the young grandee would have afforded a topic for the courtiers, that would not soon have been exhausted, but the all-engrossing theme of the great voyage afforded him a screen. His presence, however, could not escape notice; and it was whispered, with the usual smiles and shrugs, that he had entered the port in a caravel, coming from the Levant; and it was one of the received pleasantries of the hour to say, in an undertone, that the young Conde de Llera had also made the *eastern* voyage. All this gave our hero little concern, and he was soon pursuing his ordinary life, when near the persons of the sovereigns. The day that Columbus was received in state, he was present in the hall, attired in the richest vestments, and no noble of Spain did more credit to his lineage, or his condition, than Don Luis, by his mien and carriage. It was remarked that Isabella smiled on him, during the pageant; but the head of more than one wary observer was shaken, as its owner remarked how grave the queen's favorite appeared, for an occasion so joyous; a fact that was attributed to the unworthy pursuits of her truant nephew. No one, that day, gazed at Luis with more delight than Sancho, who lingered at Barcelona to share in the honors of his chief, and who, in virtue of his services, was permitted to take his place among the courtiers themselves. Not a little admiration was excited by the manner in which he used the novel weed, called tobacco; and some fifteen or twenty of his neighbors were nauseated by their efforts to emulate his indulgence and satisfaction. One of his exploits was of a character so unusual, and so well illustrates the feeling of the hour, that it may be well to record it in detail.

The reception was over, and Sancho was quitting the hall with the rest of the crowd, when he was accosted by a man apparently of forty, well attired, and of agreeable manner, who desired the honor of his presence at a slight entertainment, of which several had been prepared for the admiral and his friends. Sancho, nothing loth, the delights of distinction being yet so novel, cheerfully complied, and he was quickly led to a room of the palace, where he found a party of some twenty young nobles assembled to do him honor; for happy was he that day in Barcelona who could get even one of the meanest of Columbus' followers to accept of his homage. No sooner did the two enter the room, than the young Castilian lords crowded around them, covering Sancho with protestations of admiration, and addressing eager questions, a dozen at a time, to his companion, whom they styled "Señor Pedro," "Señor Matir," and occasionally "Señor Pedro Matir." It is scarcely necessary to add, that this person was the historian who has become known to us of these latter days as "Peter Martyr," an Italian, to whose care and instruction Isabella had entrusted most of the young nobles of the court. The present interview had been got up to indulge the natural curiosity of the youthful lords, and Sancho had been chosen for the occasion, on the principle that when the best is denied us, we must be content to accept information of an inferior quality.

"Congratulate me, Señores," cried Peter Martyr, as soon as he could find an opportunity to speak, "since my success surpasseth our own hopes. As for the Liguirian, himself, and all of high condition about him, they are in the hands of the most illustrious of Spain, for this day; but here is a most worthy pilot, no doubt the second in authority on board one of the caravels, who consenteth to do us honor, and to partake of our homely cheer. I drew him from a crowd of applicants, and have not yet had an opportunity to inquire his name, which he is about to give us of his own accord."

Sancho never wanted for self-possession, and had far too much mother-wit to be either clownish or offensively vulgar, though the reader is not now to be told that he was neither qualified to be an academician, nor had the most profound notions of natural philosophy. He assumed an air of suitable dignity, therefore, and, somewhat practised in his new vocation by the thousand interrogatories he had answered in the last month, he disposed himself to do credit to the information of a man who had visited the Indies.

"I am called Sancho Mundo, Señores, at your service—sometimes Sancho of the ship-yard-gate, though I would prefer now to be called Sancho of the Indies, unless, indeed, it should suit his Excellency Don Christopher to take that appellation—his claim being somewhat better than mine."

Here several protested that his claims were of the highest order; and then followed sundry introductions to Sancho of the ship-yard-gate, of several young men of the first families in Castile; for, though the Spaniards have not the same mania for this species of politeness as the Americans, the occasion was one in which native feeling got the ascendency of conventional reserve. After this ceremony, and the Mendozas, Guzmans, Cerdas, and Toledos, present, felt honored in knowing this humble seaman, the whole party repaired to the banqueting-room, where a table was spread that did credit to the cooks of Barcelona. During the repast, although the curiosity of the young men made some inroads on their breeding in this particular, no question could induce Sancho to break in upon the duty of the moment, for which he entertained a sort of religious veneration. Once, when pushed a little more closely than common, he laid down his knife and fork, and made the following solemn reply:

"Señores," he said. "I look upon food as a gift from God to man, and hold it to be irreverent to converse much, when the bounties of the table invite us to do homage to this great dispenser. Don Christopher is of this way of thinking, I know, and all his followers imitate their beloved and venerated chief. As soon as I am ready to converse, Señores Don Hidalgos, you shall be told of it, and then God help the ignorant and silly!"

After this admonition, there remained nothing to be said until Sancho's appetite was satisfied, when he drew a little back from the table, and announced his readiness to proceed.

"I profess to very little learning, Señor Pedro Martir," he said; "but what I have seen I have seen, and that which is known, is as well known by a mariner, as by a doctor of Salamanca. Ask your questions, then, o' heaven's sake, and expect such answers as a poor but honest man can give."

The learned Peter Martyr was fain to make the best of his subject, for at that moment, any information that came from what might be termed first hands, was greedily received; he proceeded, therefore, to his inquiries, as simply and as directly as he had been invited to do.

"Well, Señor," commenced the man of learning, "we are willing to obtain knowledge on any terms. Prithee, tell us, at once, which of all the wonderful things that you witnessed on this voyage, hath made the deepest impression on your mind, and striketh you as the most remarkable!"

"I know nothing to compare with the whiffling of the north star," said Sancho, promptly. "That star hath always been esteemed among us seamen, as being immovable as the cathedral of Seville; but, in this voyage, it hath been seen to change its place, with the inconstancy of the winds."

"That is, indeed, miraculous!" exclaimed Peter Martyr, who scarcely knew how to take the intelligence; "perhaps there is some mistake, Master Sancho, and you are not accustomed to sidereal investigations."

"Ask Don Christopher; when the phernomerthon, as the admiral called it, was first observed, we talked the matter over together, and came to the conclusion, that nothing in this world was as permanent as it seemed to be. Depend on it, Señor Don Pedro, the north star flits about like a weathercock."

"I shall inquire into this of the illustrious admiral; but, next to this star, Master Sancho, what deem you most worthy of observation? I speak now of ordinary things, leaving science to future discussion."

This was too grave a question to be lightly answered, and while Sancho was cogitating the matter, the door opened, and Luis de Bobadilla entered the room, in a blaze of manly grace and rich attire. A dozen voices uttered his name, and Peter Martyr rose to receive him, with a manner in which kindness of feeling was blended with reproof.

"I asked this honor, Señor Conde," he said, "though you have now been beyond my counsel and control some time, for it appeared to me that one fond of voyages as yourself, might find a useful lesson, as well as enjoy a high satisfaction, in listening to the wonders of an expedition as glorious as this of Colon's. This worthy seaman, a pilot, no doubt, much confided in by the admiral, hath consented to share in our poor hospitalities on this memorable day, and is about to give us many interesting facts and incidents of the great adventure. Master Sancho Mundo, this is Don Luis de Bobadilla, Conde de Llera, a grandee of high lineage, and one that is not unknown to the seas, having often traversed them in his own person."

"It is quite unnecessary to tell me that, Señor Pedro," answered Sancho, returning Luis' gay and graceful salutation, with profound, but awkward respect, "since I see it at a glance. His Excellency hath been in the east, as well as Don Christopher and myself, though we went different ways, and neither party went as far as Cathay. I am honored in your acquaintance, Don Luis, and shall just say that the noble admiral will bring navigation more in fashion than it hath been of late years. If you travel in the neighborhood of Moguer, I beg you will not pass the door of Sancho Mundo without stopping to inquire if he be within."

"That I most cheerfully promise, worthy master," said Luis, laughing, and taking a seat, "even though it lead me to the ship-yard-gate. And now, Señor Pedro, let me not interrupt the discourse, which I discovered was most interesting as I entered."

"I have been thinking of this matter, Señores," resumed Sancho, gravely, "and the fact that appears most curious to me, next to the whiffling of the north star, is the circumstance that there are no doblas in Cipango. Gold is not wanting, and it seemeth passing singular that a people should possess gold, and not bethink them of the convenience of striking doblas, or some similar coin."

Peter Martyr and his young pupils laughed at this sally, and then the subject was pushed in another form.

"Passing by this question, which belongeth rather to the policy of states than to natural phenomena," continued Peter Martyr, "what most struck you as remarkable, in the way of human nature?"

"In that particular, Señor, I think the island of the women may be set down as the most extraordinary of all the phernomerthons we fell in with. I have known women shut themselves up in convents; and men, too; but never did I hear, before this voyage, of either shutting themselves up in islands!"

"And is this true?" inquired a dozen voices—"did you really meet with such an island, Señor!"

"I believe we saw it at a distance, Señores; and I hold it to be lucky that we went no nearer, for I find the gossips of Moguer troublesome enough, without meeting a whole island of them. Then there is the bread that grows like a root—what think *you* of that, Señor Don Luis? Is it not a most curious dish to taste of?"

"Nay, Master Sancho, that is a question of your own putting, and it must be one of your own answering. What know I of the wonders of Cipango, since Candia lieth in an opposite course? Answer these matters for thyself, friend."

"True, illustrious Conde, and I humbly crave your pardon. It is, indeed, the duty of him that seeth to relate, as it is the duty of him that seeth not to believe. I hope all here will perform their several duties."

"Do these Indians eat flesh as remarkable as their bread?" inquired a Cerda.

"That do they, noble sir, seeing that they eat each other. Neither I nor Don Christopher was invited to any of their feasts of this sort; for, I suppose, they were well convinced we would not go; but we had much information touching them, and by the nearest calculation I could make, the consumption of men in the island of Bohio must be about equal to that of beeves in Spain."

The speaker was interrupted by twenty exclamations of disgust, and Peter Martyr shook his head like one who distrusted the truth of the account. Still, as he had not expected any very profound philosophy or deep learning in one of Sancho's character, he pursued the conversation.

"Know you any thing of the rare birds the admiral exhibited to their Highnesses to-day?" he asked.

"Señor, I am well acquainted with several, more particularly with the parrots. They are sensible birds, and, I doubt not, might answer some of the questions that are put to me by many here, in Barcelona, to their perfect satisfaction."

"Thou art a wag, I see, Señor Sancho, and lovest thy joke," answered the man of learning, with a smile. "Give way to thy fancy, and if thou canst not improve us with thy science, at least amuse us with thy conceits."

"San Pedro knows that I would do any thing to oblige you, Señores; but I was born with such a love of truth in my heart, that I know not how to embellish. What I see I believe, and having been in the Indies, I cannot shut my eyes to their wonders. There was the sea of weeds, which was no every-day miracle, since I make no doubt that the devils piled all these plants on the water to prevent us from carrying the cross to the poor heathens who dwell on the other side of them. We got through that sea more by our prayers, than by means of the winds."

The young men looked at Peter Martyr, to ascertain how he received this theory, and Peter Martyr, if tinctured with the superstition of the age, was not disposed to swallow all that it pleased Sancho to assert, even though the latter had made a voyage to the Indies.

"Since you manifest so much curiosity, Señores, on the subject of Colon, now Admiral of the Ocean Sea, by their Highnesses' honorable appointment, I will, in a measure, relieve your minds on the subject, by recounting what I know," said Luis, speaking calmly, but with dignity. "Ye know that I was much with Don Christopher before he sailed, and that I had some little connection with bringing him back to Santa Fé, even when he had left the place, as was supposed for the last time. This intimacy hath been renewed since the arrival of the great Genoese at Barcelona, and hours have we passed together in private, discoursing on the events of the last few months. What I have thus learned I am ready to impart, if ye will do me the grace to listen."

The whole company giving an eager assent, Luis now commenced a general narrative of the voyage, detailing all the leading circumstances of interest, and giving the reasons that were most in favor at the time, concerning the different phenomena that had perplexed the adventurers. He spoke more than an hour; proceeding consecutively from island to island, and dilating on their productions, imaginary and real. Much that he related, proceeded from the misconceptions of the admiral, and misinterpretations of the signs and language of the Indians, as a matter of course; but it was all told clearly, in elegant, if not in eloquent language, and with a singular air of truth. In short, our hero palmed upon his audience the results of his own observation, as the narrative of the admiral, and more than once was he interrupted by bursts of admiration at the vividness and graphic beauties of his descriptions. Even Sancho listened with delight, and when the young man concluded, he rose from his chair, and exclaimed heartily—

"Señores, you may take all this as so much gospel! Had the noble Señor witnessed, himself, that which he hath so well described, it could not have been truer, and I look on myself to be particularly fortunate to have heard this history of the voyage, which henceforth shall be my history, word for word; for as my patron saint shall remember me, naught else will I tell to the gossips of Moguer, when I get back to that blessed town of my childhood."

Sancho's influence was much impaired by the effects of Luis' narrative, which Peter Martyr pronounced to be one that would have done credit to a scholar who had accompanied the expedition. A few appeals were made to the old seaman, to see if he would corroborate the statements he had just heard, but his protestations became so much the louder in behalf of the accuracy of the account.

It was wonderful how much reputation the Conde de Llera obtained by this little deception. To be able to repeat, with accuracy and effect, language that was supposed to have fallen from the lips of Columbus, was a sort of illustration; and Peter Martyr, who justly enjoyed a high reputation for intelligence, was heard sounding the praises of our hero in all places, his young pupils echoing his words with the ardor and imitation of youth! Such, indeed, was the vast reputation obtained by the Genoese, that one gained a species of reflected renown by being thought to live in his confidence, and a thousand follies of the Count of Llera, real or imaginary, were forgotten in the fact that the admiral had deemed him worthy of being the repository of facts and feelings such as he had related. As Luis, moreover, was seen to be much in the company of Don Christopher, the world was very willing to give the young man credit for qualities, that, by some unexplained circumstance, had hitherto escaped its notice. In this manner did Luis de Bobadilla reap some advantages, of a public character, from his resolution and enterprise, although vastly less than would have attended an open admission of all that occurred. How far, and in what manner, these qualities availed him in his suit with Mercedes, will appear in our subsequent pages.

CHAPTER XXVIII

"Each look, each motion, waked a new-born grace,
That o'er her form its transient glory cast:
Some lovelier wonder soon usurp'd the place,
Chased by a charm still lovelier than the last."

Mason.

The day of the reception of Columbus at Barcelona, had been one of tumultuous feelings and of sincere delight, with the ingenuous and pure-minded Queen of Castile. She had been the moving spirit of the enterprise, as it was connected with authority and means, and never was a sovereign more amply rewarded, by a consciousness of the magnitude of the results that followed her well-meant and zealous efforts.

When the excitement and bustle of the day were over, Isabella retired to her closet, and there, as was usual with her on all great occasions, she poured out her thankfulness on her knees, entreating the Divine Providence to sustain her under the new responsibilities she felt, and to direct her steps aright, equally as a sovereign and as a Christian woman. She had left the attitude of prayer but a few minutes, and was seated with her head leaning on her hand, in deep meditation, when a slight knock at the door called her attention. There was but one person in Spain who would be likely to take even this liberty, guarded and modest as was the tap; rising, she turned the key and admitted the king.

Isabella was still beautiful. Her form, always of admirable perfection, still retained its grace. Her eyes had lost but little of their lustre, and her smile, ever sweet and beneficent, failed not to reflect the pure and womanly impulses of her heart. In a word, her youthful beauty had been but little impaired by the usual transition to the matronly attractions of a wife and a mother; but this night, all her youthful charms seemed to be suddenly renewed. Her cheek was flushed with holy enthusiasm; her figure dilated with the sublimity of the thoughts in which she had been indulging; and her eyes beamed with the ennobling hopes of religious enthusiasm. Ferdinand was struck with this little change, and he stood admiring her, for a minute, in silence, after he had closed the door.

"Is not this a most wonderful reward, for efforts so small, my husband and love?" exclaimed the queen, who fancied the king's thoughts similar to her own; "a new empire thus cheaply purchased, with riches that the imagination cannot tell, and millions of souls to be redeemed from eternal woe, by means of a grace that must be as unexpected to themselves, as the knowledge of their existence hath been to us!"

"Ever thinking, Isabella, of the welfare of souls! But thou art right; for what are the pomps and glories of the world to the hopes of salvation, and the delights of heaven! I confess Colon hath much exceeded all my hopes, and raised such a future for Spain, that the mind scarce knoweth where to place the limits to its pictures."

"Think of the millions of poor Indians that may live to bless our sway, and to feel the influence and consolations of holy church!"

"I trust that our kinsman and neighbor, Dom Joao, will not give us trouble in this matter. Your Portuguese have so keen an appetite for discoveries, that they little relish the success of other powers; and, it is said, many dangerous and wicked proposals were made to the king, even while our caravels lay in the Tagus."

"Colon assureth me, Fernando, that he doubteth if these Indians have now any religious creed, so that our ministers will have no prejudices to encounter, in presenting to their simple minds the sublime truths of the gospel!"

"No doubt the admiral hath fully weighed these matters. It is his opinion, that the island he hath called Española wanteth but little of being of the full dimensions of Castile, Leon, Aragon, Granada, and, indeed, of all our possessions within the peninsula!"

"Didst thou attend to what he said, touching the gentleness and mildness of the inhabitants? And wert thou not struck with the simple, confiding aspects of those he hath brought with him? Such a people may readily be brought, first, as is due, to worship the one true and living God, and next, to regard their sovereigns as kind and benignant parents."

"Authority can ever make itself respected; and Don Christopher hath assured me, in a private conference, that a thousand tried lances would overrun all that eastern region. We must make early application to the Holy Father to settle such limits between us and Don John, as may prevent disputes, hereafter, touching our several interests. I have already spoken to the cardinal on this subject, and he flattereth me with the hope of having the ear of Alexander."

"I trust that the means of disseminating the faith of the cross will not be overlooked in the negotiation; for it paineth me to find churchmen treating of worldly things, to the utter neglect of those of their Great Master."

Don Ferdinand regarded his wife intently for an instant, without making any reply. He perceived, as often happened in questions of policy, that their feelings were not exactly attuned, and he had recourse to an allusion that seldom failed to draw the thoughts of Isabella from their loftier aspirations to considerations more worldly, when rightly applied.

"Thy children, Doña Isabella, will reap a goodly heritage by the success of this, our latest and greatest stroke of policy! Thy dominions and mine will henceforth descend in common to the same heir; then this marriage in Portugal may open the way to new accessions of territory; Granada is already secured to thine, by our united arms; and here hath Providence opened the way to an empire in the east, that promiseth to outdo all that hath yet been performed in Europe."

"Are not my children thine, Fernando? Can good happen to one, without its equally befalling the other? I trust they will learn to understand why so many new subjects and such wide territories are added to their possessions, and will ever remain true to their highest and first duty, that of spreading the gospel, that the sway of the one Catholic church may the more speedily be accomplished."

"Still it may be necessary to secure advantages that are offered in a worldly shape, by worldly means."

"Thou say'st true, my lord; and it is the proper care of loving parents to look well to the interest of their offspring in this, as in all other particulars."

Isabella now lent a more willing ear to the politic suggestions of her consort, and they passed an hour in discussing some of the important measures that it was thought their joint interests required should be immediately attended to. After this, Ferdinand saluted his wife affectionately, and withdrew to his own cabinet, to labor, as usual, until his frame demanded rest.

Isabella sat musing for a few minutes after the king had retired, and then she took a light and proceeded through certain private passages, with which she was familiar, to the apartment of her daughters. Here she spent an hour, indulging in the affections and discharging the duties of a careful mother, when, embracing each in turn, she gave her blessings, and left the place in the same simple manner as she had entered. Instead, however, of returning to her own part of the palace, she pursued her way in an opposite direction, until, reaching a private door, she gently tapped. A voice within bade her enter, and complying, the Queen of Castile found herself alone with her old and tried friend, the Marchioness of Moya. A quiet gesture forbade all the usual testimonials of respect, and knowing her mistress' wishes in this particular, the hostess received her illustrious guest, much as she would have received an intimate of her own rank in life.

"We have had so busy and joyful a day, Daughter-Marchioness," the queen commenced, quietly setting down the little silver lamp she carried, "that I had near forgotten a duty which ought not to be overlooked. Thy nephew, the Count de Llera, hath returned to court, bearing himself as modestly and as prudently, as if he had no share in the glory of this great success of Colon's!"

"Señora, Luis is here, but whether prudent or modest, I leave for others, who may be less partial, to say."

"To me such seemeth to be his deportment, and a young mind might be pardoned some exultation at such a result. But I have come to speak of Don Luis and thy ward. Now that thy nephew hath given me this high proof of his perseverance and courage, there can remain no longer any reason for forbidding their union. Thou know'st that I hold the pledged word of Doña Mercedes, not to marry without my consent, and this night will I make her happy as I feel myself, by leaving her mistress of her own wishes; nay, by letting her know that I desire to see her Countess of Llera, and that right speedily."

"Your Highness is all goodness to me and mine," returned the Marchioness, coldly. "Mercedes ought to feel deeply grateful that her royal mistress hath a thought for her welfare, when her mind hath so many greater concerns to occupy it."

"It is that, my friend, that hath brought me hither at this late hour. My soul is truly burdened with gratitude, and ere I sleep, were it possible, I would fain make all as blessed as I feel myself. Where is thy ward?"

"She left me for the night, but as your Highness entered. I will summon her to hear your pleasure."

"We will go to her, Beatriz; tidings such as I bring, should not linger on weary feet."

"It is her duty, and it would be her pleasure to pay all respect, Señora."

"I know that well, Marchioness, but it is my pleasure to bear this news myself," interrupted the queen, leading the way to the door. "Show thou the way, which is better known to thee than to another. We go with little state and ceremony, as thou seest, like Colon going forth to explore his unknown seas, and we go bearers of tidings as grateful to thy ward, as those the Genoese bore to the benighted natives of Cipango. These corridors are our trackless seas, and all these intricate passages, the hidden ways we are to explore."

"Heaven grant your Highness make not some discovery as astounding as that which the Genoese hath just divulged. For myself, I scarce know whether to believe all things, or to grant faith to none."

"I wonder not at thy surprise; it is a feeling that hath overcome all others, through the late extraordinary events," answered the queen, evidently misconceiving the meaning of her friend's words. "But we have still another pleasure in store: that of witnessing the joy of a pure female heart which hath had its trials, and which hath borne them as became a Christian maiden."

Doña Beatriz sighed heavily, but she made no answer. By this time they were crossing the little saloon in which Mercedes was permitted to receive her female acquaintances, and were near the door of her chamber. Here they met a maid, who hastened onward to inform her mistress of the visit she was about to receive. Isabella was accustomed to use a mother's liberties with those she loved, and, opening the door, without ceremony, she stood before our heroine, ere the latter could advance to meet her.

"Daughter," commenced the queen, seating herself, and smiling benignantly on the startled girl, "I have come to discharge a solemn duty. Kneel thou here, at my feet, and listen to thy sovereign as thou wouldst listen to a mother."

Mercedes gladly obeyed, for, at that moment, any thing was preferable to being required to speak. When she had knelt, the queen passed an arm affectionately round her neck, and drew her closer to her person, until, by a little gentle violence, the face of Mercedes was hid in the folds of Isabella's robe.

"I have all reason to extol thy faith and duty, child," said the queen, as soon as this little arrangement to favor the feelings of Mercedes, had been considerately made; "thou hast not forgotten thy promise, in aught; and my object, now, is to leave thee mistress of thine own inclinations, and to remove all impediments to their exercise. Thou hast no longer any pledge with thy sovereign; for one who hath manifested so much discretion and delicacy, may be surely trusted with her own happiness."

Mercedes continued silent, though Isabella fancied that she felt a slight shudder passing convulsively through her delicate frame.

"No answer, daughter? Is it more preferable to leave another arbitress of thy fate, than to exercise that office for thyself? Well, then, as thy sovereign and parent, I will substitute command for consent, and tell thee it is my wish and desire that thou becomest, as speedily as shall comport with propriety and thy high station, the wedded wife of Don Luis de Bobadilla, Conde de Llera."

"No—no—no—Señora—never—never"—murmured Mercedes, her voice equally stifled by her emotions, and by the manner in which she had buried her face in the dress of the queen.

Isabella looked at the Marchioness of Moya in wonder. Her countenance did not express either displeasure or resentment, for she too well knew the character of our heroine to suspect caprice, or any weak prevarication in a matter that so deeply touched the feelings; and the concern she felt was merely overshadowed at the suddenness of the intelligence, by a feeling of ungovernable surprise.

"Canst thou explain this, Beatriz?" the queen at length inquired. "Have I done harm, where I most intended good? I am truly unfortunate, for I appear to have deeply wounded the heart of this child, at the very moment I fancied I was conferring supreme happiness!"

"No—no—no—Señora," again murmured Mercedes, clinging convulsively to the queen's knees. "Your Highness hath wounded no one— *would* wound no one—*can* wound no one—you are all gracious goodness and thoughtfulness."

"Beatriz, I look to thee for the explanation! Hath aught justifiable occurred to warrant this change of feeling?"

"I fear, dearest Señora, that the feelings continue too much as formerly, and that the change is not in this young and unpractised heart, but in the fickle inclinations of man."

A flash of womanly indignation darted from the usually serene eyes of the queen, and her form assumed all of its native majesty.

"Can this be true?" she exclaimed. "Would a subject of Castile *dare* thus to trifle with his sovereign—thus to trifle with one sweet and pure as this girl—thus to trifle with his faith with God! If the reckless Conde thinketh to do these acts of wrongfulness with impunity, let him look to it! Shall I punish him that merely depriveth his neighbor of some paltry piece of silver, and let him escape who woundeth the soul? I wonder at thy calmness, Daughter-Marchioness; thou, who art so wont to let an honest indignation speak out in the just language of a fearless and honest spirit!"

"Alas! Señora, my beloved mistress, my feelings have had vent already, and nature will no more. This boy, moreover, is my brother's son, and when I would fain arouse a resentment against him, such as befitteth his offence, the image of that dear brother, whose very picture he is, hath arisen to my mind in a way to weaken all its energy."

"This is most unusual! A creature so fair—so young—so noble—so rich—every way so excellent, to be so soon forgotten! Canst thou account for it by any wandering inclination, Lady of Moya?"

Isabella spoke musingly, and, as one of her high rank is apt to overlook minor considerations, when the feelings are strongly excited, she did not remember that Mercedes was a listener. The convulsive shudder that again shook the frame of our heroine, however, did not fail to remind her of this fact, and the queen could not have pressed the Princess Juana more fondly to her heart, than she now drew the yielding form of our heroine.

"What would you, Señora?" returned the marchioness, bitterly. "Luis, thoughtless and unprincipled boy as he is, hath induced a youthful Indian princess to abandon home and friends, under the pretence of swelling the triumph of the admiral, but really, in obedience to a wandering fancy, and in submission to those evil caprices, that make men what, in sooth, they are, and which so often render unhappy women their dupes and their victims."

"An Indian princess, say'st thou? The admiral made one of that rank known to us, but she was already a wife, and far from being one to rival Doña Mercedes of Valverde."

"Ah! dearest Señora, she of whom you speak will not compare with her I mean—Ozema—for so is the Indian lady called—Ozema is a different being, and is not without high claims to personal beauty. Could mere personal appearances justify the conduct of the boy, he would not be altogether without excuse."

"How know'st thou this, Beatriz?"

"Because, your Highness, Luis hath brought her to the palace, and she is, at this moment, in these very apartments. Mercedes hath received her like a sister, even while the stranger hath unconsciously crashed her heart."

"*Here*, say'st thou, Marchioness? Then can there be no vicious union between the thoughtless young man and the stranger. Thy nephew would not thus presume to offend virtue and innocence."

"Of that we complain not, Señora. 'Tis the boyish inconstancy and thoughtless cruelty of the count, that hath awakened my feelings against him. Never have I endeavored to influence my ward to favor his suit, for I would not that they should have it in their power to say I sought a union so honorable and advantageous to our house; but now do I most earnestly desire her to steel her noble heart to his unworthiness."

"Ah! Señora—my guardian," murmured Mercedes, "Luis is not so *very* culpable. Ozema's beauty, and my own want of the means to keep him true, are alone to blame."

"Ozema's beauty!" slowly repeated the queen. "Is this young Indian, then, so very perfect, Beatriz, that thy ward need fear or envy her? I did not think that such a being lived!"

"Your Highness knoweth how it is with men. They love novelties, and are most captivated with the freshest faces. San Iago!—Andres de Cabrera hath caused me to know this, though it were a crime to suppose any could teach this hard lesson to Isabella of Trastamara."

"Restrain thy strong and impetuous feelings, Daughter-Marchioness," returned the queen, glancing her eye at the bowed form of Mercedes, whose head was now buried in her lap; "truth seldom asserts its fullest power when the heart is overflowing with feeling. Don Andres hath been a loyal subject, and doth justice to thy merit; and, as to my lord the king, he is the father of my children, as well as thy sovereign. But, touching this Ozema—can I see her, Beatriz?"

"You have only to command, Señora, to see whom you please. But Ozema is, no doubt, at hand, and can be brought into your presence as soon as it may please your Highness to order it done."

"Nay, Beatriz, if she be a princess, and a stranger in the kingdom, there is a consideration due to her rank and to her position. Let Doña Mercedes go and prepare her to receive us; I will visit her in her own apartment. The hour is late, but she will overlook the want of ceremony in the desire to do her service."

Mercedes did not wait a second bidding, but, rising from her knees, she hastened to do as the queen had suggested. Isabella and the marchioness were silent some little time, when left to themselves; then the former, as became her rank, opened the discourse.

"It is remarkable, Beatriz, that Colon should not have spoken to me of this princess!" she said. "One of her condition ought not to have entered Spain with so little ceremony."

"The admiral hath deemed her the chosen subject of Luis' care, and hath left her to be presented to your Highness by my recreant nephew. Ah, Señora! is it not wonderful, that one like Mercedes could be so soon supplanted by a half-naked, unbaptized, benighted being, on whom the church hath never yet smiled, and whose very soul may be said to be in jeopardy of instantaneous condemnation?"

"That soul must be cared for, Beatriz, and that right quickly. Is the princess really of sufficient beauty to supplant a creature as lovely as the Doña Mercedes?"

"It is not that, Señora—it is not that. But men are fickle—and they so love novelties! Then is the modest restraint of cultivated manners less winning to them, than the freedom of those who deem even clothes superfluous. I mean not to question the modesty of Ozema; for, according to her habits, she seemeth irreproachable in this respect; but the ill-regulated fancy of a thoughtless boy may find a momentary attraction in her unfettered conduct and half-attired person, that is wanting to the air and manners of a high-born Spanish damsel, who hath been taught rigidly to respect herself and her sex."

"This may be true, as toucheth the vulgar, Beatriz, but such unworthy motives can never influence the Conde de Llera. If thy nephew hath really proved the recreant thou supposest, this Indian princess must be of more excellence than we have thought."

"Of that, Señora, you can soon judge for yourself; here is the maiden of Mercedes to inform us that the Indian is ready to receive the honor that your Highness intendeth."

Our heroine had prepared Ozema to meet the queen. By this time, the young Haytian had caught so many Spanish words, that verbal communication with her was far from difficult, though she still spoke in the disconnected and abrupt manner of one to whom the language was new. She understood perfectly that she was to meet that beloved sovereign, of whom Luis and Mercedes had so often spoken with reverence; and accustomed, herself, to look up to caciques greater than her brother, there was no difficulty in making her understand that the person she was now about to receive was the first of her sex in Spain. The only misconception which existed, arose from the circumstance that Ozema believed Isabella to be the queen of all the Christian world, instead of being the queen of a particular country; for, in her imagination, both Luis and Mercedes were persons of royal station.

Although Isabella was prepared to see a being of surprising perfection of form, she started with surprise, as her eye first fell on Ozema. It was not so much the beauty of the young Indian that astonished her, as the native grace of her movements, the bright and happy expression of her countenance, and the perfect self-possession of her mien and deportment.

Ozema had got accustomed to a degree of dress that she would have found oppressive at Hayti; the sensitiveness of Mercedes, on the subject of female propriety, having induced her to lavish on her new friend many rich articles of attire, that singularly, though wildly, contributed to aid her charms. Still the gift of Luis was thrown over one shoulder, as the highest-prized part of her wardrobe, and the cross of Mercedes rested on her bosom, the most precious of all her ornaments.

"This is wonderful, Beatriz!" exclaimed the queen, as she stood at one side of the room, while Ozema bowed her body in graceful reverence on the other; "can this rare being really have a soul that knoweth naught of its God and Redeemer! But let her spirit be benighted as it may, there is no vice in that simple mind, or deceit in that pure heart."

"Señora, all this is true. Spite of our causes of dissatisfaction, my ward and I both love her already, and could take her to our hearts forever; one as a friend, and the other as a parent."

"Princess," said the queen, advancing with quiet dignity to the spot where Ozema stood, with downcast eyes and bended body, waiting her pleasure, "thou art welcome to our dominions. The admiral hath done well in not classing one of thy evident claims and station among those whom he hath exhibited to vulgar eyes. In this he hath shown his customary judgment, no less than his deep respect for the sacred office of sovereigns."

"Almirante!" exclaimed Ozema, her looks brightening with intelligence, for she had long known how to pronounce the well-earned title of Columbus; "Almirante, Mercedes—Isabella, Mercedes—Luis, Mercedes, Señora Reyña."

"Beatriz, what meaneth this? Why doth the princess couple the name of thy ward with that of Colon, with mine, and even with that of the young Count of Llera?"

"Señora, by some strange delusion, she hath got to think that Mercedes is the Spanish term for every thing that is excellent or perfect, and thus doth she couple it with all that she most desireth to praise. Your Highness must observe that she even united Luis and Mercedes, a union that we once fondly hoped might happen, but which now would seem to be impossible; and which she herself must be the last really to wish."

"Strange delusion!" repeated the queen; "the idea hath had its birth in some particular cause, for things like this come not of accidents; who but thy nephew, Beatriz, would know aught of thy ward, or who but he would have taught the princess to deem her very name a sign of excellence?"

"Señora!" exclaimed Mercedes, the color mounting to her pale cheek, and joy momentarily flashing in her eyes, "can this be so?"

"Why not, daughter? We may have been too hasty in this matter, and mistaken what are truly signs of devotion to thee, for proofs of fickleness and inconstancy."

"Ah! Señora! but this can never be, else would not Ozema so love him."

"How know'st thou, child, that the princess hath any other feeling for the count than that which properly belongeth to one who is grateful for his care, and for the inexpressible service of being made acquainted with the virtues of the cross? Here is some rash error, Beatriz."

"I fear not, your Highness. Touching the nature of Ozema's feelings, there can be no misconception, since the innocent and unpractised creature hath not art sufficient to conceal them. That her heart is all Luis', we discovered in the first few hours of our intercourse; and it is too pure, unsought, to be won. The feeling of the Indian is not merely admiration, but it is such a passionate devotion, as partaketh of the warmth of that sun, which, we are told, glows with a heat so genial in her native clime."

"*Could* one see so much of Don Luis, Señora," added Mercedes, "under circumstances to try his martial virtues, and so long daily be in communion with his excellent heart, and not come to view him as far above all others?"

"Martial virtues—excellent heart!"—slowly repeated the queen, "and yet so regardless of the wrong he doeth! He is neither knight nor cavalier worthy of the sex, if what thou thinkest be true, child."

"Nay, Señora," earnestly resumed the girl, whose diffidence was yielding to the wish to vindicate our hero, "the princess hath told us of the manner in which he rescued her from her greatest enemy and persecutor, Caonabo, a headstrong and tyrannical sovereign of her island, and of his generous self-devotion in her behalf."

"Daughter, do thou withdraw, and, first calling on Holy Maria to intercede for thee, seek the calm of religious peace and submission, on thy pillow. Beatriz, I will question the princess alone."

The marchioness and Mercedes immediately withdrew, leaving Isabella with Ozema, in possession of the room. The interview that followed lasted more than an hour, that time being necessary to enable the queen to form an opinion of the stranger's explanations, with the imperfect means of communication she possessed. That Ozema's whole heart was Luis', Isabella could not doubt. Unaccustomed to conceal her preferences, the Indian girl was too unpractised to succeed in such a design, had she even felt the desire to attempt it; but, in addition to her native ingenuousness, Ozema believed that duty required her to have no concealments from the sovereign of Luis, and she laid bare her whole soul in the simplest and least disguised manner.

"Princess," said the queen, after the conversation had lasted some time, and Isabella believed herself to be in possession of the means of comprehending her companion, "I now understand your tale. Caonabo is the chief, or, if thou wilt, the king of a country adjoining thine own; he sought thee for a wife, but being already married to more than one princess, thou didst very properly reject his unholy proposals. He then attempted to seize thee by violence. The Conde de Llera was on a visit to thy brother at the time" —

"Luis — Luis" — the girl impatiently interrupted, in her sweet, soft voice — "Luis no Conde — Luis."

"True, princess, but the Conde de Llera and Luis de Bobadilla are one and the same person. Luis, then, if thou wilt, was present in thy palace, and he beat back the presumptuous cacique, who, not satisfied with fulfilling the law of God by the possession of one wife, impiously sought, in thy person, a second, or a third, and brought thee off in triumph. Thy brother, next, requested thee to take shelter, for a time, in Spain, and Don Luis, becoming thy guardian and protector, hath brought thee hither to the care of his aunt?"

Ozema bowed her head in acknowledgment of the truth of this statement, most of which she had no difficulty in understanding, the subject having, of late, occupied so much of her thoughts.

"And, now, princess," continued Isabella, "I must speak to thee with maternal frankness, for I deem all of thy birth my children while they dwell in my realms, and have a right to look to me for advice and protection. Hast thou any such love for Don Luis as would induce thee to forget thine own country, and to adopt his in its stead?"

"Ozema don't know what 'adopt his,' means," observed the puzzled girl.

"I wish to inquire if thou wouldst consent to become the wife of Don Luis de Bobadilla?"

"Wife" and "husband" were words of which the Indian girl had early learned the signification, and she smiled guilelessly, even while she blushed, and nodded her assent.

"I am, then, to understand that thou expectest to marry the count, for no modest young female like, thee, would so cheerfully avow her preference, without having that hope ripened in her heart, to something like a certainty."

"Si, Señora—Ozema, Luis' wife."

"Thou meanest, princess, that Ozema expecteth shortly to wed the count—shortly to become his wife!"

"No—no—no—Ozema *now* Luis' wife. Luis marry Ozema, already."

"Can this be so?" exclaimed the queen, looking steadily into the face of the beautiful Indian to ascertain if the whole were not an artful deception. But the open and innocent face betrayed no guilt, and Isabella felt compelled to believe what she had heard. In order, however, to make certain of the fact, she questioned and cross-questioned Ozema, for near half an hour longer, and always with the same result.

When the queen arose to withdraw, she kissed the princess, for so she deemed this wild creature of an unknown and novel state of society, and whispered a devout prayer for the enlightenment of her mind, and for her future peace. On reaching her own apartment, she found the Marchioness of Moya in attendance, that tried friend being unable to sleep until she had learned the impressions of her royal mistress.

"'Tis even worse than we had imagined, Beatriz," said Isabella, as the other closed the door behind her. "Thine heartless, inconstant nephew hath already wedded the Indian, and she is, at this moment, his lawful wife."

"Señora, there must be some mistake in this! The rash boy would hardly dare to practise this imposition on me, and that in the very presence of Mercedes."

"He would sooner place his wife in thy care, Daughter-Marchioness, than make the same disposition of one who had fewer claims on him. But there can be no mistake. I have questioned the princess closely, and no doubt remaineth in my mind, that the nuptials have been solemnized by religious rites. It is not easy to understand all she would wish to say, but that much she often and distinctly hath affirmed."

"Your Highness—can a Christian contract marriage with one that is yet unbaptized?"

"Certainly not, in the eye of the church, which is the eye of God. But I rather think Ozema hath received this holy rite, for she often pointed to the cross she weareth, when speaking of the union with thy nephew. Indeed, from her allusions, I understood her to say that she became a Christian, ere she became a wife."

"And that blessed cross, Señora, was a gift of Mercedes to the reckless, fickle-minded boy; a parting gift in which the holy symbol was intended to remind him of constancy and faith!"

"The world maketh so many inroads into the hearts of men, Beatriz, that they know not woman's reliance and woman's fidelity. But to thy knees, and bethink thee of asking for grace to sustain thy ward, in this cruel, but unavoidable extremity."

Isabella now turned to her friend, who advanced and raised the hand of her royal mistress to her lips. The queen, however, was not content with this salutation, warm as it was; passing an arm around the neck of Doña Beatriz, she drew her to her person, and imprinted a kiss on her forehead.

"Adieu, Beatriz—true friend as thou art!" she said. "If constancy hath deserted all others, it hath still an abode in thy faithful heart."

With these words the queen and the marchioness separated, each to find her pillow, if not her repose.

CHAPTER XXIX

"Now, Gondarino, what can you put on now
That may deceive us?
Have ye more strange illusions, yet more mists,
Through which the weak eye may be led to error?
What can ye say that may do satisfaction
Both for her wronged honor and your ill?"

Beaumont and Fletcher.

The day which succeeded the interview related in the preceding chapter, was that which Cardinal Mendoza had selected for the celebrated banquet given to Columbus. On this occasion, most of the high nobility of the court were assembled in honor of the admiral, who was received with a distinction which fell little short of that usually devoted to crowned heads. The Genoese bore himself modestly, though nobly, in all these ceremonies; and, for the hour, all appeared to delight in doing justice to his great exploits, and to sympathize in a success so much surpassing the general expectation. Every eye seemed riveted on his person, every ear listened eagerly to the syllables as they fell from his lips, every voice was loud and willing in his praise.

As a matter of course, on such an occasion, Columbus was expected to give some account of his voyage and adventures. This was not an easy task, since it was virtually asserting how much his own perseverance and spirit, his sagacity and skill, were superior to the knowledge and enterprise of the age. Still, the admiral acquitted himself with dexterity and credit, touching principally on those heads which most redounded to the glory of Spain, and the lustre of the two crowns.

Among the guests was Luis de Bobadilla. The young man had been invited on account of his high rank, and in consideration of the confidence and familiarity with which he was evidently treated by the admiral. The friendship of Columbus was more than sufficient to erase the slightly unfavorable impressions that had been produced by Luis' early levities, and men quietly submitted to the influence of the great man's example, without stopping to question the motive or the end. The consciousness of having done that which few of his station and hopes would ever dream of attempting, gave to the proud mien and handsome countenance of Luis, a seriousness and elevation that had not always been seated there, and helped to sustain him in the good opinion that he had otherwise so cheaply purchased. The manner in which he had related to Peter Martyr and his companions the events of the expedition, was also remembered, and, without understanding exactly why, the world was beginning to associate him, in some mysterious manner, with the great western voyage. Owing to these accidental circumstances, our hero was actually reaping some few of the advantages of his spirit, though in a way he had never anticipated; a result by no means extraordinary, men as often receiving applause, or reprobation, for acts that were never meditated, as for those for which reason and justice would hold them rigidly responsible.

"Here is a health to my lord, their Highnesses' Admiral of the Ocean Sea," cried Luis de St. Angel, raising his cup so that all at the board might witness the act. "Spain oweth him her gratitude for the boldest and most beneficial enterprise of the age, and no good subject of the two sovereigns will hesitate to do him honor for his services."

The bumper was drunk, and the meek acknowledgments of Columbus listened to in respectful silence.

"Lord Cardinal," resumed the free-speaking accountant of the church's revenues, "I look upon the church's cure as doubled by these discoveries, and esteem the number of souls that will be rescued from perdition by the means that will now be employed to save them, as forming no small part of the lustre of the exploit, and a thing not likely to be forgotten at Rome."

"Thou say'st well, good de St. Angel," returned the cardinal, "and the Holy Father will not overlook God's agent, or his assistants. Knowledge came from the east, and we have long looked forward to the time when, purified by revelation and the high commission that we hold direct from the source of all power, it would be rolled backward to its place of beginning; but we now see that its course is still to be westward, reaching Asia by a path that, until this great discovery, was hid from human eyes."

Although so much apparent sympathy ruled at the festival, the human heart was at work, and envy, the basest, and perhaps the most common of our passions, was fast swelling in more than one breast. The remark of the cardinal produced an exhibition of the influence of this unworthy feeling that might otherwise have been smothered. Among the guests was a noble of the name of Juan de Orbitello, and he could listen no longer, in silence, to the praises of those whose breath he had been accustomed to consider fame.

"Is it so certain, holy sir," he said, addressing his host, "that God would not have directed other means to be employed, to effect this end, had these of Don Christopher failed? Or, are we to look upon this voyage as the only known way in which all these heathen could be rescued from perdition?"

"No one may presume, Señor, to limit the agencies of heaven," returned the cardinal, gravely; "nor is it the office of man to question the means employed, or to doubt the power to create others, as wisdom may dictate. Least of all, should laymen call in question aught that the church sanctioneth."

"This I admit, Lord Cardinal," answered the Señor de Orbitello, a little embarrassed, and somewhat vexed at the implied rebuke of the churchman's remarks, "and it was the least of my intentions to do so. But you, Señor Don Christopher, did you deem yourself an agent of heaven in this expedition?"

"I have always considered myself a most unworthy instrument, set apart for this great end, Señor," returned the admiral, with a grave solemnity that was well suited to impose on the spectators. "From the first, I have felt this impulse, as being of divine origin, and I humbly trust heaven is not displeased with the creature it hath employed."

"Do you then imagine, Señor Almirante, that Spain could not produce another, fitted equally with yourself, to execute this great enterprise, had any accident prevented either your sailing or your success?"

The boldness, as well as the singularity of this question, produced a general pause in the conversation, and every head was bent a little forward in expectation of the reply. Columbus sat silent for more than a minute; then, reaching forward, he took an egg, and holding it up to view, he spoke mildly, but with great gravity and earnestness of manner.

"Señores," he said, "is there one here of sufficient expertness to cause this egg to stand on its end? If such a man be present, I challenge him to give us an exhibition of his skill."

The request produced a good deal of surprise; but a dozen immediately attempted the exploit, amid much laughter and many words. More than once, some young noble thought he had succeeded, but the instant his fingers quitted the egg, it rolled upon the table, as if in mockery of his awkwardness.

"By Saint Luke, Señor Almirante, but this notable achievement surpasseth our skill," cried Juan de Orbitello. "Here is the Conde de Llera, who hath slain so many Moors, and who hath even unhorsed Alonzo de Ojeda, in a tourney, can make nothing of his egg, in the way you mention."

"And yet it will no longer be difficult to him, or even to you, Señor, when the art shall be exposed."

Saying thus, Columbus tapped the smaller end of his egg lightly on the table, when, the shell being forced in, it possessed a base on which it stood firmly and without tremor. A murmur of applause followed this rebuke, and the Lord of Orbitello was fain to shrink back into an insignificance, from which it would have been better for him never to have emerged. At this precise instant a royal page spoke to the admiral, and then passed on to the seat of Don Luis de Bobadilla.

"I am summoned hastily to the presence of the queen, Lord Cardinal," observed the admiral, "and look to your grace for an apology for my withdrawing. The business is of weight, by the manner of the message, and you will pardon my now quitting the board, though it seem early."

The usual reply was made; and, bowed to the door by his host and all present, Columbus quitted the room. Almost at the same instant, he was followed by the Conde de Llera.

"Whither goest thou, in this hurry, Don Luis?" demanded the admiral, as the other joined him. "Art thou in so great haste to quit a banquet such as Spain hath not often seen, except in the palaces of her kings?"

"By San Iago! nor there, neither, Señor," answered the young man, gaily, "if King Ferdinand's board be taken as the sample. But I quit this goodly company in obedience to an order of Doña Isabella, who hath suddenly summoned me to her royal presence."

"Then, Señor Conde, we go together, and are like to meet on the same errand. I, too, am hastening to the apartments of the queen."

"It gladdens my heart to hear this, Señor, as I know of but one subject on which a common summons should be sent to us. This affair toucheth on my suit, and, doubtless, you will be required to speak of my bearing in the voyage."

"My mind and my time have been so much occupied, of late, with public cares, Luis, that I have not had an occasion to question you of this. How fareth the Lady of Valverde, and when will she deign to reward thy constancy and love?"

"Señor, I would I could answer the last of these questions with greater certainty, and the first with a lighter heart. Since my return I have seen Doña Mercedes but thrice; and though she was all gentleness and truth, my suit for the consummation of my happiness hath been coldly and evasively answered by my aunt. Her Highness is to be consulted, it would seem; and the tumult produced by the success of the voyage hath so much occupied her, that there hath been no leisure to wait on trifles such as those that lead to the felicity of a wanderer like myself."

"Then is it like, Luis, that we are indeed summoned on this very affair; else, why should thou and I be brought together in a manner so unusual and so sudden."

Our hero was not displeased to fancy this, and he entered the apartments of the queen with a step as elastic, and a mien as bright, as if he had come to wed his love. The Admiral of the Ocean Sea, as Columbus was now publicly called, had not long to wait in ante-chambers, and, ere many minutes, he and his companion were ushered into the presence.

Isabella received her guests in private, there being no one in attendance but the Marchioness of Moya, Mercedes, and Ozema. The first glances of their eyes told Columbus and Luis that all was not right. Every countenance denoted that its owner was endeavoring to maintain a calmness that was assumed. The queen herself was serene and dignified, it is true, but her brow was thoughtful, her eye melancholy, and her cheek slightly flushed. As for Doña Beatriz, sorrow and indignation struggled in her expressive face, and Luis saw, with concern, that her look was averted from him in a way she always adopted when he had seriously incurred her displeasure. Mercedes' lips were pale as death, though a bright spot, like vermilion, was stationary on each cheek; her eyes were downcast, and all her mien was humbled and timid. Ozema alone seemed perfectly natural; still, her glances were quick and anxious, though a gleam of joy danced in her eyes, and even a slight exclamation of delight escaped her, as she beheld Luis, whom she had seen but once since her arrival in Barcelona, already near a month.

Isabella advanced a step or two, to meet the admiral, and when the last would have kneeled, she hurriedly prevented the act by giving him her hand to kiss.

"Not so—not so—Lord Admiral," exclaimed the queen; "this is homage unsuited to thy high rank and eminent services. If we are thy sovereigns, so are we also thy friends. I fear my lord cardinal will scarce pardon the orders I sent him, seeing that it hath deprived him of thy society somewhat sooner than he may have expected."

"His Eminence, and all his goodly company, have that to muse on, Señora, that may yet occupy them some time," returned Columbus, smiling in his grave manner; "doubtless, they will less miss me than at an ordinary time. Were it otherwise, both I, and this young count, would not scruple to quit even a richer banquet, to obey the summons of your Highness."

"I doubt it not, Señor, but I have desired to see thee, this night, on a matter of private, rather than of public concernment. Doña Beatriz, here, hath made known to me the presence at court, as well as the history of this fair being, who giveth one an idea so much more exalted of thy vast discoveries that I marvel she should ever have been concealed. Know'st thou her rank, Don Christopher, and the circumstances that have brought her to Spain?"

"Señora, I do; in part through my own observation, and in part from the statements of Don Luis de Bobadilla. I consider the rank of the Lady Ozema to be less than royal, and more than noble, if our opinions will allow us to imagine a condition between the two; though it must always be remembered that Hayti is not Castile; the one being benighted under the cloud of heathenism, and the other existing in the sunshine of the church and civilization."

"Nevertheless, Don Christopher, station is station, and the rights of birth are not impaired by the condition of a country. Although it hath pleased him already, and will still further please the head of the church, to give us rights, in our characters of Christian princes, over these caciques of India, there is nothing unusual or novel in the fact. The relation between the suzerain and the lieges is ancient and well established; and instances are not wanting, in which powerful monarchs have held certain of their states by this tenure, while others have come direct from God. In this view, I feel disposed to consider the Indian lady as more than noble, and have directed her to be treated accordingly. There remaineth only to relate the circumstances that have brought her to Spain."

"These can better come from Don Luis than from me, Señora; he being most familiar with the events."

"Nay, Señor, I would hear them from thine own lips. I am already possessed of the substance of the Conde de Llera's story."

Columbus looked both surprised and pained, but he did not hesitate about complying with the queen's request.

"Hayti hath its greater and its lesser princes, or caciques, your Highness," he added; "the last paying a species of homage, and owing a certain allegiance to the first, as hath been said" —

"Thou seest, Daughter-Marchioness, this is but a natural order of government, prevailing equally in the east and in the west!"

"Of the first of these was Guacanagari, of whom I have already related so much to your Highness," continued Columbus; "and of the last, Mattinao, the brother of this lady. Don Luis visited the Cacique Mattinao, and was present at an inroad of Caonabo, a celebrated Carib chief, who would fain have made a wife of her who now stands in this illustrious presence. The conde conducted himself like a gallant Castilian cavalier, routed the foe, saved the lady, and brought her in triumph to the ships. Here it was determined she should visit Spain, both as a means of throwing more lustre on the two crowns, and of removing her, for a season, from the attempts of the Carib, who is too powerful and warlike to be withstood by a race as gentle as that of Mattinao's."

"This is well, Señor, and what I have already heard; but how happeneth it, that Ozema did not appear with the rest of thy train, in the public reception of the town?"

"It was the wish of Don Luis it should be otherwise, and I consented that he and his charge should sail privately from Palos, with the expectation of meeting me in Barcelona. We both thought the Lady Ozema too superior to her companions, to be exhibited to rude eyes as a spectacle."

"There was delicacy, if there were not prudence in the arrangement," the queen observed, a little drily. "Then, the Lady Ozema hath been some weeks solely in the care of the Conde de Llera."

"I so esteem it, your Highness, except as she hath been placed under the guardianship of the Marchioness of Moya."

"Was this altogether discreet, Don Christopher, or as one prudent as thou shouldst have consented to?"

"Señora!" exclaimed Luis, unable to restrain his feelings longer.

"Forbear, young sir," commanded the queen. "I shall have occasion to question thee presently, when thou may'st have a need for all thy readiness, to give the fitting answers. Doth not thy discretion rebuke thy indiscretion in this matter, Lord Admiral?"

"Señora, the question, like its motive, is altogether new to me; I have the utmost reliance on the honor of the count, and then did I know that his heart hath long been given to the fairest and worthiest damsel of Spain; besides, my mind hath been so much occupied with the grave subjects of your Highness' interests, that it hath had but little opportunity to dwell on minor things."

"I believe thee, Señor, and thy pardon is secure. Still, for one so experienced, it was a sore indiscretion to trust to the constancy of a fickle heart, when placed in the body of a light-minded and truant boy. And, now, Conde de Llera, I have that to say to thee, which thou may'st find it difficult to answer. Thou assentest to all that hath hitherto been said?"

"Certainly, Señora. Don Christopher can have no motive to misstate, even were he capable of the meanness. I trust our house hath not been remarkable in Spain, for recreant and false cavaliers."

"In that I fully agree. If thy house hath had the misfortune to produce one untrue and recreant heart, it hath the glory"—glancing at her friend—"of producing others that might equal the constancy of the most heroic minds of antiquity. The lustre of the name of Bobadilla doth not altogether depend on the fidelity and truth of its head—nay, hear me, sir, and speak only when thou art ready to answer my questions. Thy thoughts, of late, have been bent on matrimony?"

"Señora, I confess it. Is it an offence to dream of the honorable termination of a suit that hath been long urged, and which I had dared to hope was finally about to receive your own royal approbation?"

"It is, then, as I feared, Beatriz!" exclaimed the queen; "and this benighted but lovely being hath been deceived by the mockery of a marriage; for no subject of Castile would dare thus to speak of wedlock, in my presence, with the consciousness that his vows had actually and lawfully been given to another. Both the church and the prince would not be thus braved, by even the greatest profligate of Spain!"

"Señora, your Highness speaketh most cruelly, even while you speak in riddles!" cried Luis. "May I presume to ask if I am meant in these severe remarks?"

"Of whom else should we be speaking, or to whom else allude? Thou must have the inward consciousness, unprincipled boy, of all thy unworthiness; and yet thou darest thus to brave thy sovereign—nay, to brave that suffering and angelic girl, with a mien as bold as if sustained by the purest innocence!"

"Señora, I am no angel, myself, however willing to admit Doña Mercedes to be one; neither am I a saint of perfect purity, perhaps—in a word, I am Luis de Bobadilla—but as far from deserving these reproaches, as from deserving the crown of martyrdom. Let me humbly demand my offence?"

"Simply that thou hast either cruelly deceived, by a feigned marriage, this uninstructed and confiding Indian princess, or hast insolently braved thy sovereign with the professions of a desire to wed another, with thy faith actually plighted at the altar, to another. Of which of these crimes thou art guilty, thou know'st best, thyself."

"And thou, my aunt—thou, Mercedes—dost thou, too, believe me capable of this?"

"I fear it is but too true," returned the marchioness, coldly; "the proof is such that none but an Infidel could deny belief."

"Mercedes?"

"No, Luis," answered the generous girl, with a warmth and feeling that broke down the barriers of all conventional restraint—"I do not think thee base as this—I do not think thee base at all; merely unable to restrain thy wandering inclinations. I know thy heart too well, and thine honor too well, to suppose aught more than a weakness that thou wouldst fain subdue, but canst not."

"God and the Holy Virgin be blessed for this!" cried the count, who had scarcely breathed while his mistress was speaking. "Any thing but thy entertaining so low an opinion of me, may be borne!"

"There must be an end of this, Beatriz; and I see no surer means, than by proceeding at once to the facts," said the queen. "Come hither, Ozema, and let thy testimony set this matter at rest, forever."

The young Indian, who comprehended Spanish much better than she expressed herself in the language, although far from having even a correct understanding of all that was said, immediately complied, her whole soul being engrossed with what was passing, while her intelligence was baffled in its attempts thoroughly to comprehend it. Mercedes alone had noted the workings of her countenance, as Isabella reproved, or Luis made his protestations, and they were such as completely denoted the interest she felt in our hero.

"Ozema," resumed the queen, speaking slowly, and with deliberate distinctness, in order that the other might get the meaning of her words as she proceeded. "Speak—art thou wedded to Luis de Bobadilla, or not?"

"Ozema, Luis' wife," answered the girl, laughing and blushing. "Luis, Ozema's husband."

"This is plain as words can make it, Don Christopher, and is no more than she hath already often affirmed, on my anxious and repeated inquiries. How and when did Luis wed thee, Ozema?"

"Luis wed Ozema with religion—with Spaniard's religion. Ozema wed Luis with love and duty—with Hayti manner."

"This is extraordinary, Señora," observed the admiral, "and I would gladly look into it. Have I your Highness' permission to inquire into the affair, myself?"

"Do as thou wilt, Señor," returned the queen, coldly. "My own mind is satisfied, and it behoveth my justice to act speedily."

"Conde de Llera, dost thou admit, or dost thou deny, that thou art the husband of the Lady Ozema?" demanded Columbus, gravely.

"Lord Admiral, I deny it altogether. Neither have I wedded her, nor hath the thought of so doing, with any but Mercedes, ever crossed my mind."

This was said firmly, and with the open frankness that formed a principal charm in the young man's manner.

"Hast thou, then, wronged her, and given her a right to think that thou didst mean wedlock?"

"I have not. Mine own sister would not have been more respected than hath Ozema been respected by me, as is shown by the fact that I have hastened to place her in the care of my dear aunt, and in the company of Doña Mercedes."

"This seemeth reasonable, Señora; for man hath ever that much respect for virtue in your sex, that he hesitateth to offend it even in his levities."

"In opposition to all these protestations, and to so much fine virtue, Señor Colon, we have the simple declaration of one untutored in deception—a mind too simple to deceive, and of a rank and hopes that would render such a fraud as unnecessary as it would be unworthy. Beatriz, thou dost agree with me, and it cannot find an apology for this recreant knight, even though he were once the pride of thy house?"

"Señora, I know not. Whatever may have been the failings and weaknesses of the boy—and heaven it knows that they have been many—deception and untruth have never made a part. I have even ascribed the manner in which he hath placed the princess in my immediate care, to the impulses of a heart that did not wish to conceal the errors of the head, and to the expectation that her presence in my family might sooner bring me to a knowledge of the truth. I could wish that the Lady Ozema might be questioned more closely, in order that we make certain of not being under the delusion of some strange error."

"This is right," observed Isabella, whose sense of justice ever inclined her to make the closest examination into the merits of every case that required her decision. "The fortune of a grandee depends on the result, and it is meet he enjoy all fair means of vindicating himself from so heinous an offence. Sir Count, thou canst, therefore, question her, in our presence, touching all proper grounds of inquiry."

"Señora, it would ill become a knight to put himself in array against a lady, and she, too, of the character and habits of this stranger," answered Luis, proudly; coloring as he spoke, with the consciousness that Ozema was utterly unable to conceal her predilection in his favor. "If such an office is, indeed, necessary, its functions would better become another."

"As the stern duty of punishing must fall on me," the queen calmly observed, "I will then assume this unpleasant office. Señor Almirante, we may not shrink from any obligation that brings us nearer to the greatest attribute of God, his justice. Princess, thou hast said that Don Luis hath wedded thee, and that thou considerest thyself his wife. When and where didst thou meet him before a priest?"

So many attempts had been made to convert Ozema to Christianity, that she was more familiar with the terms connected with religion than with any other part of the language, though her mind was a confused picture of imaginary obligations, and of mystical qualities. Like all who are not addicted to abstractions, her piety was more connected with forms than with principles, and she was better disposed to admit the virtue of the ceremonies of the church than the importance of its faith. The question of the queen was understood, and, therefore, it was answered without guile, or a desire to deceive.

"Luis wed Ozema with Christian's cross," she said, pressing to her heart the holy emblem that the young man had given to her in a moment of great peril, and in a manner the reader already knows. "Luis think he about to die—Ozema think she about to die—both wish to die man and wife, and Luis wed with the cross, like good Spanish Christian. Ozema wed Luis in her heart, like Hayti lady, in her own country."

"Here is some mistake—some sad mistake, growing out of the difference of language and customs," observed the admiral. "Don Luis hath not been guilty of this deception. I witnessed the offering of that cross, which was made at sea, during a tempest, and in a way to impress me favorably with the count's zeal in behalf of a benighted soul. There was no wedlock there; nor could any, but one who hath confounded our usages, through ignorance, imagine more than the bestowal of a simple emblem, that it was hoped might be useful, in extremity, to one that had not enjoyed the advantages of baptism and the church's offices."

"Don Luis, dost thou confirm this statement, and also assert that thy gift was made solely with this object?" asked the queen.

"Señora, it is most true. Death was staring us in the face; and I felt that this poor wanderer, who had trusted herself to our care, with the simple confidence of a child, needed some consolation; none seemed so meet, at the moment, as that memorial of our blessed Redeemer, and of our own redemption. To me it seemed the preservative next to baptism."

"Hast thou never stood before a priest with her, nor in any manner abused her guileless simplicity?"

"Señora, it is not my nature to deceive, and every weakness of which I have been guilty in connexion with Ozema shall be revealed. Her beauty and her winning manners speak for themselves, as doth her resemblance to Doña Mercedes. The last greatly inclined me to her, and, had not my heart been altogether another's, it would have been my pride to make the princess my wife. But we met too late for that; and even the resemblance led to comparisons, in which one, educated in infidelity and ignorance, must necessarily suffer. That I have had moments of tenderness for Ozema, I will own; but that they ever supplanted, or came near supplanting, my love for Mercedes, I do deny. If I have any fault to answer for, to the Lady Ozema, it is because I have not always been able to suppress the feelings that her likeness to the Doña Mercedes, and her own ingenuous simplicity—chiefly the former—have induced. Never otherwise, in speech or act, have I offended against her."

"This soundeth upright and true, Beatriz. Thou know'st the count better than I, and can easier say how far we ought to confide in these explanations."

"My life on their truth, my beloved mistress! Luis is no hypocrite, and I rejoice!—oh! how exultingly do I rejoice!—at finding him able to give this fair vindication of his conduct. Ozema, who hath heard of our form of wedlock, and hath seen our devotion to the cross, hath mistaken her position, as she hath my nephew's feelings, and supposed herself a wife, when a Christian girl would not have been so cruelly deceived."

"This really hath a seeming probability, Señores," continued the queen, with her sex's sensitiveness to her sex's delicacy of sentiment, not to say to her sex's rights—"This toucheth of a lady's—nay, of a princess' feelings, and must not be treated of openly. It is proper that any further explanations should be made only among females, and I trust to your honor, as cavaliers and nobles, that what hath this night been said, will never be spoken of amid the revels of men. The Lady Ozema shall be my care; and, Count of Llera, thou shalt know my final decision to-morrow, concerning Doña Mercedes and thyself."

As this was said with a royal, as well as with a womanly dignity, no one presumed to demur, but, making the customary reverences, Columbus and our hero left the presence. It was late before the queen quitted Ozema, but what passed in this interview will better appear in the scenes that are still to be given.

CHAPTER XXX

"When sinking low the sufferer wan
Beholds no arm outstretch'd to save,
Fair, as the bosom of the swan
That rises graceful o'er the wave,
I've seen your breast with pity heave,
And *therefore* love you, sweet Genevieve!"

Coleridge.

When Isabella found herself alone with Ozema and Mercedes (for she chose that the last should be present), she entered on the subject of the marriage with the tenderness of a sensitive and delicate mind, but with a sincerity that rendered further error impossible. The result showed how naturally and cruelly the young Indian beauty had deceived herself. Ardent, confiding, and accustomed to be considered the object of general admiration among her own people, Ozema had fancied that her own inclinations had been fully answered by the young man. From the first moment they met, with the instinctive quickness of a woman, she perceived that she was admired, and, as she gave way to the excess of her own feelings, it was almost a necessary consequence of the communications she held with Luis, that she should think they were reciprocated. The very want of language in words, by compelling a substitution of one in looks and acts, contributed to the mistake; and it will be remembered that, if Luis' constancy did not actually waver, it had been sorely tried. The false signification she attached to the word "Mercedes," largely aided in the delusion, and it was completed by the manly tenderness and care with which our hero treated her on all occasions. Even the rigid decorum that Luis invariably observed, and the severe personal respect which he maintained toward his charge, had their effect on her feelings; for, wild and unsophisticated as had been her training, the deep and unerring instinct of the feeble, told her the nature of the power she was wielding over the strong.

Then came the efforts to give her some ideas of religion, and the deep and lamentable mistakes which imperfectly explained, and worse understood subtleties, left on her plastic mind. Ozema believed that the Spaniards worshipped the cross. She saw it put foremost in all public ceremonies, knelt to, and apparently appealed to, on every occasion that called for an engagement more solemn than usual. Whenever a knight made a vow, he kissed the cross of his sword-hilt. The mariners regarded it with reverence, and even the admiral had caused one to be erected as a sign of his right to the territory that had been ceded to him by Guacanagari. In a word, to her uninstructed imagination, it seemed as if the cross were used as a pledge for the fidelity of all engagements. Often had she beheld and admired the beautiful emblem worn by our hero; and, as the habits of her own people required the exchange of pledges of value as a proof of wedlock, she fancied, when she received this much-valued jewel, that she received the sign that our hero took her for a wife, at a moment when death was about to part them forever. Further than this, her simplicity and affections did not induce her to reason or to believe.

It was an hour before Isabella elicited all these facts and feelings from Ozema, though the latter clearly wished to conceal nothing; in truth, had nothing to conceal. The painful part of the duty remained to be discharged. It was to undeceive the confiding girl, and to teach her the hard lesson of bitterness that followed. This was done, however, and the queen, believing it best to remove all delusion on the subject, finally succeeded in causing her to understand that, before the count had ever seen herself, his affections were given to Mercedes, who was, in truth, his betrothed wife. Nothing could have been gentler, or more femininely tender, than the manner in which the queen made her communication; but the blow struck home, and Isabella, herself, trembled at the consequences of her own act. Never before had she witnessed the outbreaking of feeling in a mind so entirely unsophisticated, and the images of what she then saw, haunted her troubled slumbers for many succeeding nights.

As for Columbus and our hero, they were left mainly in the dark, as to what had occurred, for the following week. It is true, Luis received a kind and encouraging note from his aunt, the succeeding day, and a page of Mercedes' silently placed in his hand the cross that he had so long worn; but, beyond this, he was left to his own conjectures. The moment for explanation, however, arrived, and the young man received a summons to the apartment of the marchioness.

Luis did not, as he expected, meet his aunt on reaching the saloon, which he found empty. Questioning the page who had been his usher, he was desired to wait for the appearance of some one to receive him. Patience was not a conspicuous virtue in our hero's character, and he excited himself by pacing the room, for near half an hour, ere he discovered a single sign that his visit was remembered. Just as he was about to summon an attendant, however, again to announce his presence, a door was slowly opened, and Mercedes stood before him.

The first glance that the young man cast upon his betrothed, told him that she was suffering under deep mental anxiety. The hand which he eagerly raised to his lips trembled, and the color came and went on her cheeks, in a way to show that she was nearly overcome. Still she rejected the glass of water that he offered, putting it aside with a faint smile, and motioning her lover to take a chair, while she calmly placed herself on a *tabouret*—one of the humble seats she was accustomed to occupy in the presence of the queen.

"I have asked for this interview, Don Luis," Mercedes commenced, as soon as she had given herself time to command her feelings, "in order that there may no longer be any reasons for mistaking our feelings and wishes. You have been suspected of having married the Lady Ozema; and there was a moment when you stood on the verge of destruction, through the displeasure of Doña Isabella."

"But, blessed Mercedes, *you* never imputed to me this act of deception and unfaithfulness?"

"I told you truth, Señor—for that I knew you too well. I felt certain that, whenever Luis de Bobadilla had made up his mind to the commission of such a step, he would also have the manliness and courage to avow it. *I* never, for an instant, believed that you had wedded the princess."

"Why, then, those cold and averted looks?—eyes that sought the floor, rather than the meeting of glances that love delights in; and a manner which, if it hath not absolutely displayed aversion, hath at least manifested a reserve and distance that I had never expected to witness from thee to me?"

Mercedes' color changed, and she made no answer for a minute, during which little interval she had doubts of her ability to carry out her own purpose. Rallying her courage, however, the discourse was continued in the same manner as before.

"Hear me, Don Luis," she resumed, "for my history will not be long. When you left Spain, at my suggestion, to enter on this great voyage, you loved *me*—of that grateful recollection no earthly power can deprive me! Yes, you then loved *me*, and me *only*. We parted, with our troth plighted to each other; and not a day went by, during your absence, that I did not pass hours on my knees, beseeching heaven in behalf of the admiral and his followers."

"Beloved Mercedes! It is not surprising that success crowned our efforts; such an intercessor could not fail to be heard!"

"I entreat you, sir, to hear me. Until the eventful day which brought the tidings of your return, no Spanish wife could have felt more concern for him on whom she had placed all her hopes, than I felt for you. To me, the future was bright and filled with hope, if the present was loaded with fear and doubt. The messenger who reached the court, first opened my eyes to the sad realities of the world, and taught me the hard lesson the young are ever slow to learn—that of disappointment. It was then I first heard of Ozema—of your admiration of her beauty—your readiness to sacrifice your life in her behalf!"

"Holy Luke! Did that vagabond, Sancho, dare to wound thy ear, Mercedes, with an insinuation that touched the strength or the constancy of my love for thee?"

"He related naught but the truth, Luis, and blame him not. I was prepared for some calamity by his report, and I bless God that it came on me by such slow degrees, and with the means of preparation to bear it. When I beheld Ozema, I no longer wondered at thy change of feeling—scarce blamed it. Her beauty, I do think, thou might'st have withstood; but her unfeigned devotion to thyself, her innocence, her winning simplicity, and her modest joyousness and nature, are sufficient to win a lover from any Spanish maiden"—

"Mercedes!"

"Nay, Luis, I have told thee that I blame thee not. It is better that the blow come now, than later, when I should not be able to bear it. There is something which tells me that, as a wife, I should sink beneath the weight of blighted affections; but, now, there are open to me the convent and the espousals of the Son of God. Do not interrupt me, Luis," she added, smiling sweetly, but with an effort that denoted how difficult it was to seem easy. "I have to struggle severely to speak at all, and to an argument I am altogether unequal. Thou hast not been able to control thy affections; and to the strange novelties that have surrounded Ozema, as well as to her winning ingenuousness, I owe my loss, and she oweth her gain. It is the will of Heaven, and I strive to think it is to my everlasting advantage. Had I really wedded thee, the tenderness that is even now swelling in my heart—I wish not to conceal it—might have grown to such a strength as to supplant the love I owe to God; it is, therefore, doubtless, better as it is. If happiness on earth is not to be my lot, I shall secure happiness hereafter. Nay, all happiness here will not be lost; I can still pray for thee, as well as for myself—and thou and Ozema, of all earthly beings, will ever be uppermost in my thoughts."

"This is so wonderful, Mercedes—so cruel—so unreasonable—and so unjust, that I cannot credit my ears!"

"I have said that I blame thee not. The beauty and frankness of Ozema are more than sufficient to justify thee, for men yield to the senses, rather than to the heart, in bestowing their love. Then"—Mercedes blushed crimson as she continued—"a Haytian maid may innocently use a power, that it would ill become a Christian damsel to employ. And, now, we will come to facts that press for a decision. Ozema hath been ill—is still ill—dangerously so, as her Highness and my guardian believe—even as the physicians say—but it is in thy power, Luis, to raise her, as it might be, from the grave. See her—say but the word that will confer happiness—tell her, if thou hast not yet wedded her after the manner of Spain, that thou wilt—nay, let one of the holy priests, who are in constant attendance on her, to prepare the way for baptism, perform the ceremony this very morning, and we shall presently see the princess, again, the smiling, radiant, joyous creature she was, when thou first placed her in our care."

"And this thou say'st to me, Mercedes, calmly and deliberately, as if thy words express thy very wishes and feelings!"

"Calmly I may *seem* to say it, Luis," answered our heroine, in a smothered tone, "and deliberately I *do* say it. Marry me, loving another better, thou canst not; and why not, then, follow whither thy heart leadeth. The dowry of the princess shall not be small, for the convent recluse hath little need of gold, and none of lands."

Luis gazed earnestly at the enthusiastic girl, who in his eyes never appeared more lovely; then, rising, he paced the room for three or four minutes, like one who wished to keep down mental agony by physical action. When he had obtained a proper command of himself, he returned to his seat, and taking the unresisting hand of Mercedes, he replied to her extraordinary proposal.

"Watching over the sick couch of thy friend, and too much brooding on this subject, love, hath impaired thy judgment. Ozema hath no hold on my heart, in the way thou fanciest—never had, beyond a passing and truant inclination"—

"Ah! Luis, those 'passing and truant inclinations.' None such"—pressing both her hands on her own heart—"have ever found a place here!"

"Thy education and mine, Mercedes—thy habits and mine—nay, thy nature and the ruder elements of mine, are not, *cannot* be the same. Were they so, I should not worship thee as I now do. But didst thou not exist, the certainty that I should wed Ozema would not give me happiness—but thou existing, and beloved as thou art, it would entail on me a misery that even my buoyant nature could not endure. In no case can I ever be the husband of the Indian."

Although a gleam of happiness illumined the face of Mercedes for a moment, her high principles and pure intentions soon suppressed the momentary and unbidden triumph, and, even with a reproving manner, she made her answer.

"Is this just to Ozema? Hath not her simplicity been deluded by those 'passing and truant inclinations,' and doth not honor require that thy acts now redeem the pledges that have been given by, at least, thy manner?"

"Mercedes—beloved girl, hearken to me. Thou must know that, with all my levities and backslidings, I am no coxcomb. Never hath my manner said aught that the heart did not confirm, and never hath the heart been drawn toward any but thee. In this, is the great distinction that I make between thee and all others of thy sex. Ozema's is not the only form, her's are not the only charms that may have caught a truant glance from my eyes, or extorted some unmeaning and bootless admiration, but thou, love, art enshrined here, and seemest already a part of myself. Didst thou know how often thy image hath proved a monitor stronger than conscience; on how many occasions the remembrance of thy virtues and thy affections hath prevailed, when even duty, and religion, and early lessons would have been forgotten, thou wouldst understand the difference between the love I bear *thee*, and what thou hast so tauntingly repeated as truant and passing inclinations."

"Luis, I ought not to listen to these alluring words, which come from a goodness of heart that would spare me present pain, only to make my misery in the end the deeper. If thou hast never felt otherwise, why was the cross that I gave thee at parting, bestowed on another?"

"Mercedes, thou knew'st not the fearful circumstances under which I parted with that cross. Death was staring us in the face, and I gave it as a symbol that might aid a heathen soul in its extremity. That the gift, or rather that the thing I lent, was mistaken for a pledge of matrimony, is an unhappy misconception, that your own knowledge of Christian usages will tell you I could not foresee; otherwise I might now claim thee for my wife, in consequence of having first bestowed it on me."

"Ah! Luis; when I gave thee that cross, I did wish to be understood as plighting my faith to thee forever!"

"And when thou didst send it back to me, now within the week, how was it thy wish to be understood?"

"I sent it to thee, Luis, in a moment of reviving hope, and by the order of the queen. Her Highness is now firmly thy friend, and would fain see us united, but for the melancholy condition of Ozema, to whom all has been explained—all, as I fear, except the real state of thy feelings toward us both."

"Cruel girl! Am I, then, never to be believed—never again to be happy? I swear to thee, dearest Mercedes, that thou alone hast my whole heart—that with thee, I could be contented in a hovel, and that without thee I should be miserable on a throne. Thou wilt believe this, when thou see'st me a wretch, wandering the earth, reckless alike of hopes and objects, perhaps of character, because thou alone canst make me, and keep me the man I ought to be. Bethink thee, Mercedes, of the influence thou canst have— must have—*wilt* have on one of my temperament and passions. I have long looked upon thee as my guardian angel, one that can mould me to thy will, and rule me when all others fail. With thee—the impatience produced by thy doubts excepted—am I not ever tractable and gentle? Hath Doña Beatriz ever exercised a tithe of thy power over me, and hast thou ever failed to tame even my wildest and rashest humors?"

"Luis—Luis—no one that knew it, ever doubted of thy heart!" Mercedes paused, and the working of her countenance proved that the earnest sincerity of her lover had already shaken her doubts of his constancy. Still, her mind reverted to the scenes of the voyage, and her imagination portrayed the couch of the stricken Ozema. After a minute's delay, she proceeded, in a low, humbled tone—"I will not deny that it is soothing to my heart to hear this language, to which, I fear, I listen too readily," she said. "Still, I find it difficult to believe that thou canst ever forget one who hath even braved the chances of death, in order to shelter thy body from the arrows of thy foes."

"Believe not this, beloved girl; thou wouldst have done that thyself, in Ozema's place, and so I shall ever consider it."

"I should have the wish, Luis," Mercedes continued, her eyes suffused with tears, "but I might not have the power!"

"Thou wouldst—thou wouldst—I know thee too well to doubt it."

"I could envy Ozema the occasion, were it not sinful! I fear thou wilt think of this, when thy mind shall have tired with attractions that have lost their novelty."

"Thou wouldst not only have done it, but thou wouldst have done it far better. Ozema, moreover, was exposed in her own quarrel, whilst thou wouldst have exposed thyself in mine."

Mercedes again paused, and appeared to muse deeply. Her eyes had brightened under the soothing asseverations of her lover, and, spite of the generous self-devotion with which she had determined to sacrifice all her own hopes to what she had imagined would make her lover happy, the seductive influence of requited affection was fast resuming its power.

"Come with me, then, Luis, and behold Ozema," she at length continued. "When thou see'st her, in her present state, thou wilt better understand thine own intentions. I ought not to have suffered thee thus to revive thy ancient feelings in a private interview, Ozema not being present; it is like forming a judgment on the hearing of only one side. And, Luis"—her heightened color, the effect of feeling, not of shame, rendered the girl surpassingly beautiful—"and, Luis, if thou shouldst find reason to change thy language after visiting the princess, however hard I may find it to be borne, thou wilt be certain of my forgiveness for all that hath passed, and of my prayers"—

Sobs interrupted Mercedes, and she stopped an instant to wipe away her tears, rejecting Luis' attempt to fold her in his arms, in order to console her, with a sensitive jealousy of the result; a feeling, however, in which delicacy had more weight than resentment. When she had dried her eyes, and otherwise removed the traces of her agitation, she led the way to the apartment of Ozema, where the presence of the young man was expected.

Luis started on entering the room; a little on perceiving that the queen and the admiral were present, and more at observing the inroads that disappointment had made on the appearance of Ozema. The color of the latter was gone, leaving a deadly paleness in its place; her eyes possessed a brightness that seemed supernatural, and yet her weakness was so evident as to render it necessary to support her, in a half-recumbent posture, on pillows. An exclamation of unfeigned delight escaped her when she beheld our hero, and then she covered her face with both her hands, in childish confusion, as if ashamed at betraying the pleasure she felt. Luis behaved with manly propriety, for, though his conscience did not altogether escape a few twinges, at the recollection of the hours he had wasted in Ozema's society, and at the manner in which he had momentarily submitted to the influence of her beauty and seductive simplicity, on the whole he stood self-acquitted of any thing that might fairly be urged as a fault, and most of all, of any thought of being unfaithful to his first love, or of any design to deceive. He took the hand of the young Indian respectfully, and he kissed it with an openness and warmth that denoted brotherly tenderness and regard, rather than passion, or the emotion of a lover. Mercedes did not dare to watch his movements, but she observed the approving glance that the queen threw at her guardian, when he had approached the couch on which Ozema lay. This glance she interpreted into a sign that the count had acquitted himself in a manner favorable to her own interests.

"Thou findest the Lady Ozema weak and changed," observed the queen, who alone would presume to break a silence that was already awkward. "We have been endeavoring to enlighten her simple mind on the subject of religion, and she hath, at length, consented to receive the holy sacrament of baptism. The lord archbishop is even now preparing for the ceremony in my oratory, and we have the blessed prospect of rescuing this one precious soul from perdition."

"Your Highness hath ever the good of all your people at heart," said Luis, bowing low to conceal the tears that the condition of Ozema had drawn from his eyes. "I fear this climate of ours ill agrees with the poor Haytians, generally, for I hear that the sick among them, at Seville and Palos, offer but little hope of recovery."

"Is this so, Don Christopher?"

"Señora, I believe it is only too true. Care hath been had, however, to their souls, as well as to their bodies, and Ozema is the last of her people, now in Spain, to receive the holy rite of Christian baptism."

"Señora," said the marchioness, coming from the couch, with surprise and concern in her countenance, "I fear our hopes are to be defeated after all! The Lady Ozema hath just whispered me, that Luis and Mercedes must first be married in her presence, ere she will consent to be admitted within the pale of the church herself."

"This doth not denote the right spirit, Beatriz—and, yet, what can be done with a mind so little illuminated with the light from above. 'Tis merely a passing caprice, and will be forgotten when the archbishop shall be ready."

"I think not, Señora. Never have I seen her so decided and clear. In common, we find her gentle and tractable, but this hath she thrice said, in a way to cause the belief of her perfect seriousness."

Isabella now advanced to the couch, and spoke long and soothingly to the invalid. In the meantime, the admiral conversed with the marchioness, and Luis again approached our heroine. The evidences of emotion were plain in both, and Mercedes scarce breathed, not knowing what to expect. But a few low words soon brought an assurance that could not fail to bring happiness, spite of her generous efforts to feel for Ozema—that the heart of our hero was all her own. From this moment Mercedes dismissed every doubt, and she regarded Luis as had so long been her wont.

As is usual in the presence of royalty, the conversation was carried on in a low tone; and a quarter of an hour elapsed before a page announced that the oratory, or little chapel, was ready, opening a door that communicated directly with it, as he entered.

"This wilful girl persisteth, Daughter-Marchioness," said the queen, advancing from the side of the couch, "and I know not what to answer. It is cruel to deny her the offered means of grace, and yet it is a sudden and unseemly request to make of thy nephew and thy ward!"

"As for the first, dearest Señora, never distrust his forgiveness; though I much doubt the possibility of prevailing on Mercedes. Her very nature is made up of religion and female decorum."

"It is, indeed, scarce right to think of it. A Christian maiden should have time to prepare her spirit for the holy sacrament of marriage, by prayer."

"And yet, Señora, many wed without it! The time hath been when Don Ferdinand of Aragon and Doña Isabella might not have hesitated for such a purpose."

"That time never was, Beatriz. Thou hast a habit of making me look back to our days of trial and youth, whenever thou wouldst urge on me some favorite but ill-considered wish of thine own. Dost really think thy ward would overlook the want of preparation and time?"

"I know not what she might feel disposed to overlook, Señora; but I do know that if there be one woman in Spain who is at all times ready in *spirit*, for the most sacred rites of the church, it is your Highness; and, if there be another, it is my ward."

"Go to—go to—good Beatriz; flattery sitteth ill on thee. None are always ready, and all have an unceasing need for watchfulness. Bid Doña Mercedes follow to my closet; I will converse with her on this subject. At least, there shall be no unfeminine and unseemly surprise."

So saying, the queen withdrew. She had hardly reached her closet, before our heroine entered, with a doubtful and timid step. As soon as her eyes met those of her sovereign, Mercedes burst into tears, and falling on her knees, she again buried her face in the robe of Doña Isabella. This outbreak of feeling was soon subdued, however, and then the girl stood erect, waiting her sovereign's pleasure.

"Daughter," commenced the queen, "I trust there is no longer any misapprehension between thee and the Conde de Llera. Thou know'st the views of thy guardian and myself, and may'st, in a matter like this, with safety defer to our cooler heads and greater experience. Don Luis loveth thee, and hath never loved the princess, though it would not be out of character did an impetuous young man, who hath been much exposed to temptation, betray some transient and passing feeling toward one of so much nature and beauty."

"Luis hath admitted all, Señora; inconstant he hath never been, though he may have had his weaknesses."

"'Tis a hard lesson to learn, child, even in this stage of thy life," said the queen, gravely; "but it would have been harder were it deferred until the nearer tenderness of a wife had superseded the impulses of the girl. Thou hast heard the opinions of the learned; there is little hope that the Princess Ozema can long survive."

"Ah! Señora, 'tis a cruel fate! To die among strangers, in the flower of her beauty, and with a heart crushed by the weight of unrequited love!"

"And yet, Mercedes, if heaven open on her awaking eyes, when the last earthly scene is over, the transition will be most blessed; and they who mourn her loss, would do wiser to rejoice. One so youthful and so innocent; whose pure mind hath been laid bare to us, as it might be, and which we have found wanting in nothing beside the fruits of a pious instruction, can have little to apprehend on the score of personal errors. All that is required for such a being, is to place her within the covenant of God's grace, by obtaining the rite of baptism, and there is not a bishop of the church that could depart with brighter hopes for the future."

"That holy office is my lord archbishop about to administer, as I hear, Señora."

"*That* somewhat dependeth on thee, daughter. Listen, and be not hasty in thy decision, which may touch on the security of a human soul."

The queen now related to Mercedes the romantic request of Ozema, placing it before her listener in terms so winning and gentle, that it produced less surprise and alarm than she herself had anticipated.

"Doña Beatriz hath a proposal that may, at first, appear plausible, but which reflection will not sanction. Her design was to cause the count actually to wed Ozema"—Mercedes started, and turned pale—"in order that the last hours of the young stranger might be soothed by the consciousness of being the wife of the man she idolized; but I have found serious objections to the scheme. What is thy opinion, daughter?"

"Señora, could I believe—as lately I did, but now do not—that Luis had such a preference for the princess as might lead him, in the end, to the happiness of that mutual affection without which wedlock must be a curse instead of a blessing, I would be the last to object; nay, I think I could even beg the boon of your Highness on my knees, for she who so truly loveth can only seek the felicity of its object. But I am assured the count hath not the affection for the Lady Ozema that is necessary to this end; and would it not be profane, Señora, to receive the church's sacraments under vows that the heart not only does not answer to, but against which it is actually struggling?"

"Excellent girl! These are precisely my own views, and in this manner have I answered the marchioness. The rites of the church may not be trifled with, and we are bound to submit to sorrows that may be inflicted, after all, for our eternal good; though it be harder to bear those of others than to bear our own. It remaineth only to decide on this whim of Ozema's, and to say if thou wilt now be married, in order that she may be baptized."

Notwithstanding the devotedness of feeling with which our heroine loved Luis, it required a strong struggle with her habits and her sense of propriety to take this great step so suddenly, and with so little preparation. The wishes of the queen, however, prevailed; for Isabella felt a deep responsibility on her own soul, in letting the stranger depart without being brought within the pale of the church. When Mercedes consented, she despatched a messenger to the marchioness, and then she and her companion both knelt, and passed near an hour together, in the spiritual exercises that were usual to the occasion. In this mood, did these pure-minded females, without a thought to the vanities of the toilet, but with every attention to the mental preparations of which the case admitted, present themselves at the door of the royal chapel, through which Ozema had just been carried, still stretched on her couch. The marchioness had caused a white veil to be thrown over the head of Mercedes, and a few proper but slight alterations had been made in her attire, out of habitual deference to the altar and its ministers.

About a dozen persons, deemed worthy of confidence, were present, already; and just as the bride and bridegroom were about to take their places, Don Ferdinand hastily entered, carrying in his hand some papers which he had been obliged to cease examining, in order to comply with the wishes of his royal consort. The king was a dignified prince; and when it suited him, no sovereign enacted his part more gracefully or in better taste. Motioning the archbishop to pause, he directed Luis to kneel. Throwing over the shoulder of the young man the collar of one of his own orders, he said—

"Now, arise, noble sir, and ever do thy duty to thy Heavenly Master, as thou hast of late discharged it toward us."

Isabella rewarded her husband for this act of grace by an approving smile, and the ceremony immediately proceeded. In the usual time, our hero and heroine were pronounced man and wife, and the solemn rites were ended. Mercedes felt, in the warm pressure with which Luis held her to his heart, that she now understood him; and, for a blissful instant, Ozema was forgotten, in the fulness of her own happiness. Columbus had given away the bride—an office that the king had assigned to him, though he stood at the bridegroom's side himself, with a view to do him honor, and even so far condescended as to touch the canopy that was held above the heads of the new-married couple. But Isabella kept aloof, placing herself near the couch of Ozema, whose features she watched throughout the ceremony. She had felt no occasion for public manifestations of interest in the bride, their feelings having so lately been poured out together in dear and private communion. The congratulations were soon over, and then Don Ferdinand, and all but those who were in the secret of Ozema's history, withdrew.

The queen had not desired her husband, and the other attendants, to remain and witness the baptism of Ozema, out of a delicate feeling for the cor dition of a female stranger, whom her habits and opinions had invested with a portion of the sacred rights of royalty. She had noted the intensity of feeling with which the half-enlightened girl watched the movements of the archbishop and the parties, and the tears had forced themselves from her own eyes, at witnessing the struggle between love and friendship, that was portrayed in every lineament of her pale, but still lovely countenance.

"Where cross?" Ozema eagerly demanded, as Mercedes stooped to fold the wasted form of the young Indian in her arms, and to kiss her cheek. "Give cross—Luis no marry with cross—give Ozema cross."

Mercedes, herself, took the cross from the bosom of her husband, where it had lain near his heart, since it had been returned to him, and put it in the hands of the princess.

"No marry with cross, then," murmured the girl, the tears suffusing her eyes, so as nearly to prevent her gazing at the much-prized bauble. "Now, quick, Señora, and make Ozema Christian."

The scene was getting to be too solemn and touching for many words, and the archbishop, at a sign from the queen, commenced the ceremony. It was of short duration; and Isabella's kind nature was soon quieted with the assurance that the stranger, whom she deemed the subject of her especial care, was put within the covenant for salvation that had been made with the visible church.

"Is Ozema Christian now?" demanded the girl, with a suddenness and simplicity, that caused all present to look at each other with pain and surprise.

"Thou hast, now, the assurance that God's grace will be offered to thy prayers, daughter," answered the prelate. "Seek it with thy heart, and thy end, which is at hand, will be more blessed."

"Christian no marry heathen?—Christian marry Christian?"

"This hast thou been often told, my poor Ozema," returned the queen; "the rite could not be duly solemnized between Christian and heathen."

"Christian marry first lady he love best?"

"Certainly. To do otherwise would be a violation of his vow, and a mockery of God."

"So Ozema think—but he can marry second wife—inferior wife—lady he love next. Luis marry Mercedes, first wife, because he love best—then he marry Ozema, second wife—lower wife—because he love next best— Ozema Christian, now, and no harm. Come, archbishop; make Ozema Luis' second wife."

Isabella groaned aloud, and walked to a distant part of the chapel, while Mercedes burst into tears, and sinking on her knees, she buried her face in the cloth of the couch, and prayed fervently for the enlightening of the soul of the princess. The churchman did not receive this proof of ignorance in his penitent, and of her unfitness for the rite he had just administered, with the same pity and indulgence.

"The holy baptism thou hast just received, benighted woman," he said, sternly, "is healthful, or not, as it is improved. Thou hast just made such a demand, as already loadeth thy soul with a fresh load of sin, and the time for repentance is short. No Christian can have two wives at the same time, and God knoweth no higher or lower, no first or last, between those whom his church hath united. Thou canst not be a second wife, the first still living."

"No would be to Caonabo—to Luis, yes. Fifty, hundred wife to dear Luis! No possible?"

"Self-deluded and miserable girl, I tell thee no. No—no—no—never— never—never. There is such a taint of sin in the very question, as profaneth this holy chapel, and the symbols of religion by which it is filled. Ay, kiss and embrace thy cross, and bow down thy very soul in despair, for" —

"Lord Archbishop," interrupted the Marchioness of Moya, with a sharpness of manner that denoted how much her ancient spirit was aroused, "there is enough of this. The ear thou wouldst wound, at such a moment, is already deaf, and the pure spirit hath gone to the tribunal of another, and, as I trust, a milder judge. Ozema is dead!"

It was, indeed, true. Startled by the manner of the prelate—bewildered with the confusion of ideas that had grown up between the dogmas that had been crowded on her mind, of late, and those in which she had been early taught; and physically paralyzed by the certainty that her last hope of a union with Luis was gone, the spirit of the Indian girl had deserted its beautiful tenement, leaving on the countenance of the corpse a lovely impression of the emotions that had prevailed during the last moments of its earthly residence.

Thus fled the first of those souls that the great discovery was to rescue from the perdition of the heathen. Casuists may refine, the learned dilate, and the pious ponder, on its probable fate in the unknown existence that awaited it: but the meek and submissive will hope all from the beneficence of a merciful God. As for Isabella, she received a shock from the blow that temporarily checked her triumph at the success of her zeal and efforts. Little, however, did she foresee, that the event was but a type of the manner in which the religion of the cross was to be abused and misunderstood; a sort of practical prognostic of the defeat of most of her own pious and gentle hopes and wishes.

CHAPTER XXXI

"A perfect woman, nobly planned
To warn, to comfort, and command;
And yet a spirit still, and bright,
With something of an angel light."

Wordsworth.

The lustre that was thrown around the voyage of Columbus, brought the seas into favor. It was no longer deemed an inferior occupation, or unsuited to nobles to engage in enterprises on its bosom; and that very propensity of our hero, which had so often been mentioned to his prejudice in former years, was now frequently named to his credit. Though his real connection with Columbus is published, for the first time, in these pages, the circumstance having escaped the superficial investigations of the historians, it was an advantage to him to be known as having manifested what might be termed a maritime disposition, in an age when most of his rank and expectations were satisfied with the adventures of the land. A sort of fashion was got up on behalf of the ocean; and the cavalier who had gazed upon its vast and unbroken expanse, beyond the view of his mother earth, regarded him who had not, much as he who had won his spurs looked down upon him who had suffered the proper period of life to pass without making the effort. Many of the nobles whose estates touched the Mediterranean or the Atlantic, fitted out small coasters—the yachts of the fifteenth century—and were met following the sinuosities of the glorious coasts of that part of the world, endeavoring to derive a satisfaction from a pursuit that it seemed meritorious to emulate. That all succeeded who attempted thus to transfer the habits of courts and castles to the narrow limits of xebecs and feluccas, it would be hazarding too much to assert; but there is little doubt that the spirit of the period was sustained by the experiments, and that men were ashamed to condemn that, which it was equally the policy and the affectation of the day to extol. The rivalry between Spain and Portugal, too, contributed to the feeling of the times; and there was soon greater danger of the youth who had never quitted his native shores, being pointed out for his want of spirit, than that the adventurer should be marked for his eccentric and vagrant instability.

In the meanwhile, the seasons advanced, and events followed, in their usual course, from cause to effect. About the close of the month of September, the ocean, just without that narrow and romantic pass that separates Europe from Africa, while it connects the transcendent Mediterranean with the broader wastes of the Atlantic, was glittering with the rays of the rising sun, which, at the same time, was gilding the objects that rose above the surface of the blue waters. The latter were not numerous, though a dozen different sails were moving slowly on their several courses, impelled by the soft breezes of the season. Of these, our business is with one alone, which it may be well to describe in a few general terms.

The rig of the vessel in question was latine, perhaps the most picturesque of all that the ingenuity of man has invented as the accessory of a view, whether given to the eye by means of the canvas, or in its real dimensions and substance. Its position, too, was precisely that which a painter would have chosen as the most favorable to his pencil, the little felucca running before the wind, with one of its high pointed sails extended on each side, resembling the pinions of some enormous bird that was contracting its wings as it settled toward its nest. Unusual symmetry was apparent in the spars and rigging; while the hull, which was distinguished by lines of the fairest proportions, had a neatness and finish that denoted the yacht of a noble.

The name of this vessel was the "Ozema," and she carried the Count of Llera with his youthful bride. Luis, who had acquired much of the mariner's skill, in his many voyages, directed the movements in person, though Sancho Mundo strutted around her decks with an air of authority, being the titular, if not the real patron of the craft.

"Ay—ay—good Bartolemeo, lash that anchor well," said the last, as he inspected the forecastle, in his hourly rounds; "for fair as may be the breezes, and mild as is the season, no one can know what humor the Atlantic may be in, when it fairly waketh up. In the great voyage to Cathay, nothing could have been more propitious than our outward passage, and nothing savor more of devils incarnate, than the homeward. Doña Mercedes maketh an excellent sailor, as ye all may see; and no one can tell which way, or how far, the humor of the conde may carry him, when he hath once taken his departure. I tell ye, fellows, that glory and gold may alight upon ye all, any minute, in the service of such a noble; and I hope none of ye have forgotten to come provided with hawk's-bells, which are as remarkable for assembling doblas, as the bells of the Seville cathedral are for assembling Christians."

"Master Mundo," called out our hero, from the quarter-deck, "let there be a man sent to the extremity of the fore-yard, and bid him look along the sea to the north and east of us."

This command interrupted one of Sancho's self-glorifying discourses, and compelled him to see the order executed. When the seaman who was sent aloft, had "shinned" his way to the airy and seemingly perilous position he had been told to occupy, an inquiry went up from the deck, to demand what he beheld.

"Señor Conde," answered the fellow, "the ocean is studded with sails, in the quarter your Excellency hath named, looking like the mouth of the Tagus, at the first of a westerly wind."

"Canst thou tell them, and let me know their numbers?" called out Luis.

"By the mass, Señor," returned the man, after taking time to make his count, "I see no less than sixteen—nay, now I see another, a smaller just opening from behind a carrack of size—seventeen, I make them in all."

"Then are we in season, love!" exclaimed Luis, turning toward Mercedes with delight—"once more shall I grasp the hand of the admiral, ere he quitteth us again for Cathay. Thou seemest glad as myself, that our effort hath not failed."

"That which gladdeneth thee, Luis, is sure to gladden me," returned the bride; "where there is but one interest, there ought to be but one wish."

"Beloved—beloved Mercedes—thou wilt make me every thing thou canst desire. This heavenly disposition of thine, and this ready consenting to voyage with me, will be sure to mould me in such a way that I shall be less myself than thee."

"As yet, Luis," returned the young wife, smiling, "the change promiseth to be the other way, since thou art much likelier to make me a rover, than I to make thee a fixture of the castle of Llera."

"Thou comest not out upon the sea, Mercedes, contrary to thine own wishes?" demanded Luis, with the earnest quickness of one who was fearful he might unconsciously have done an act of indiscretion.

"No, dearest Luis, so far from it, that I have come with satisfaction, apart from the pleasure I have had in obliging thee. Fortunately, I feel no indisposition from the motion of the felucca, and the novelty is of the most agreeable and exciting kind."

To say that Luis rejoiced to hear this on more accounts than one, is but to add that he still found a pleasure in the scenes of the ocean.

In half an hour the vessel of the admiral was visible from the Ozema's deck, and ere the sun had reached the meridian, the little felucca was gliding into the centre of the fleet, holding her course toward the carrack of Columbus. The usual hailing passed, when, apprised of the presence of Mercedes, the admiral gallantly repaired on board the Ozema, to pay his respects in person. The scenes through which they had passed together, had created in Columbus a species of paternal regard for Luis, in which Mercedes shared, through the influence of her noble conduct during the events that occurred at Barcelona. He met the happy pair, therefore, with dignified affection, and his reception partook of the feelings that the count and countess so fully reciprocated.

Nothing could be more striking to one who had an opportunity of witnessing both, than the contrast between the means with which the Genoese sailed on this, and on his former voyage. Then he had set forth neglected, almost forgotten, in three vessels, ill-found, and worse manned, while now, the ocean was whitened with his canvas, and he was surrounded by no inconsiderable portion of the chivalry of Spain. As soon as it was known that the Countess of Llera was in the felucca that had stopped the fleet, boats put off from most of the vessels, and Mercedes held a sort of court on the broad Atlantic; her own female attendants, among whom were two or three of the rank of ladies, assisting her in doing proper honor to the cavaliers who thronged the deck. The balmy influence of the pure air of the ocean, contributed to the happiness of the moment; and, for an hour, the Ozema presented a scene of gaiety and splendor, such as had never before been witnessed by any person present.

"Beautiful Countess," cried one, who had been a rejected suitor of our heroine, "you see to what acts of desperation your cruelty hath driven me, who am going forth on an adventure to the furthest east. It is well for Don Luis that I did not make this venture before he won your favor; as no damsel in Spain is expected, henceforth, to withstand the suit of one of the admiral's followers."

"It may be as you say, Señor," returned Mercedes, her heart swelling with the consciousness that he whom she had chosen had made this same boasted adventure, while others shrunk from its hazard, and when its result was still a mystery in the unknown future—"It may be as you say; but one of moderate wishes, like myself, must be content with these unambitious voyages along the coast, in which, happily, a wife may be her husband's companion."

"Lady," cried the gallant and reckless Alonzo de Ojeda, in his turn, "Don Luis caused me to roll upon the earth, in the tourney, by a fair and manly effort, that hath left no rancor behind it; but I shall outdo him now, since he is content to keep the shores of Spain in view, leaving to us the glory of seeking the Indies, and of reducing the Infidels to the sway of the two sovereigns!"

"It is a sufficient honor to my husband, Señor, that he can boast of the success you name, and he must rest satisfied with the reputation acquired in that one deed."

"Countess, a year hence you would love him better, did he come forth with us, and show his spirit among the people of the Grand Khan!"

"Thou see'st, Don Alonzo, that the illustrious admiral doth not altogether despise him as it is. They seek a private interview in my cabin together; an attention Don Christopher would not be apt to pay a recreant, or a laggard."

"'Tis surprising!" resumed the rejected suitor; "the favor of the conde with our noble admiral hath surprised us all, at Barcelona. Can it be, de Ojeda, that they have met in some of their earlier nautical wanderings?"

"By the mass! Señor," cried Alonzo, laughing, "if Don Luis ever met the admiral, as he met me in the lists, I should think one interview would answer for the rest of their days!"

In this manner did the discourse proceed, some speaking in levity, some in more sober mood, and all in amity. While this was passing on deck, Columbus had, indeed, retired to a cabin with our hero.

"Don Luis," said the admiral, when they were seated near each other, and alone, "thou know'st the regard I bear thee, and I feel certain that thou returnest it with an equal degree of esteem. I now go forth from Spain, on a far more perilous adventure than that in which thou wert my companion. Then I sailed concealed in contempt, and veiled from human eyes by ignorance and pity; now, have I left the old world, followed by malignancy and envy. These facts am I too old not to have seen, and foreseen. In my absence, many will be busy with my name. Even they who now shout at my heels will become my calumniators, revenging themselves for past adulation by present detraction. The sovereigns will be beset with lies, and any disappointment in the degree of success will be distorted into crimes. I leave friends behind me, too—friends, such as Juan Perez, de St. Angel, Quintanilla, and thyself. On ye, then, do I greatly rely, not for favors, but for the interest of truth and justice."

"Señor, you may count upon my small influence under all circumstances. I have seen you in the day of trial, and it exceedeth ordinary misrepresentations to weaken my faith in you."

"This did I believe, Luis, even before it was so warmly and sincerely said," returned the admiral, squeezing the young man's hand with fervor. "I doubt if Fonseca, who hath now so much power in the affairs of India, is truly my friend. Then, there is one of thy blood and name, who hath already regarded me with unfavorable eyes, and whom I distrust exceedingly, should an occasion offer in which he might do me injury."

"I know him well, Don Christopher, and account him as doing no credit to the house of Bobadilla."

"He hath credit, nevertheless, with the king, which is of more importance, just now!"

"Ah! Señor, to that wily and double-faced monarch, you must look for nothing generous. So long as Doña Isabella's ear can be kept open to the truth, there is nothing to fear, but Don Ferdinand groweth each day more worldly and temporizing. Mass!—that one who, in youth, was so bold and manly a knight, should in his age betray so many of the meannesses that would disgrace a Moor! My noble aunt, however, is a host in herself, and will ever remain true to you, as she commenced."

"God overruleth all, and it were sinful to distrust either his wisdom or justice. And now, Luis, one word touching thyself. Providence hath made thee the guardian of the happiness of such a being as is seldom found this side the gates of heaven. The man who is blessed with a virtuous and amiable wife, like her thou hast wedded, should erect an altar in his heart, on which he ought to make daily, nay, hourly sacrifices of gratitude to God for the boon; since of all earthly blessings, he enjoyeth the richest, the purest, and the most lasting, should he not be unmindful of his own riches. But a woman like Doña Mercedes is a creature as delicate as she is rare. Let her equanimity check thy impetuosity; her purity rebuke the less refined elements of thy composition; her virtue stimulate thine own; her love keep thine in an unceasing flame, and her tenderness be a constant appeal to thy manly indulgence and protection. Fulfil all thy duties as a Spanish grandee, son, and seek felicity in the partner of thy bosom, and in love to God."

The admiral now gave Luis his blessing, and, taking leave of Mercedes in the same solemn manner, he hastened to his carrack. Boat after boat quitted the felucca, many calling out their leave-takings even after they were at a distance. In a few minutes, the heavy yards swung around, and the fleet was again sweeping off toward the south-west, holding its way, as was then fancied, toward the distant shores of India. For an hour the Ozema lay where she had been left by Columbus, as if gazing at her retiring friends; then her canvas filled, and she hauled up toward that bight of the coast, at the bottom of which lay the port of Palos de Moguer.

The afternoon was deliciously balmy, and when the felucca drew in with the land, the surface of the sea was as smooth as that of an inland lake. There was just wind enough to cool the air, and to propel the little vessel three or four knots through the water. The day apartment occupied by our hero and heroine, was on the quarter-deck. It was formed, on the exterior, by a tarpauling, bent like the tilt of a wagon, while the interior was embellished with a lining of precious stuffs that converted it into a beautiful little saloon. In front, a canvas bulkhead protected it from the gaze of the crew; and, toward the stearn a rich curtain fell, when it became necessary to shut out the view. The latter was now carelessly festooned, permitting the eye to range over a broad expanse of the ocean, and to watch the glories of the setting sun.

Mercedes reclined on a luxurious couch, gazing on the ocean, and Luis touched a guitar, seated on a stool at her feet. He had just played a favorite national air, which he had accompanied with his voice, and had laid aside the instrument. when he perceived that his young wife did not listen, with her usual fondness and admiration, to his music.

"Thou art thoughtful, Mercedes," he said, leaning forward to read the melancholy expression of those eyes that were so often glowing with enthusiasm.

"The sun is setting in the direction of the land of poor Ozema, Luis," Mercedes answered, a slight tremor pervading her voice; "the circumstance, in connection with the sight of this boundless ocean, that so much resembleth eternity, hath led me to think of her end. Surely—surely—a creature so innocent can never be consigned to eternal misery, because her unenlightened mind and impassioned feelings were unable to comprehend all the church's mysteries!"

"I would that thou thought'st less on this subject, love; thy prayers, and the masses that have been said for her soul, should content thee; or, if thou wilt, the last can be repeated, again and again."

"We will offer still more," returned the young wife, scarce speaking above her breath, while the tears fell down her cheeks. "The best of us will need masses, and *we* owe this to poor Ozema. Didst thou bethink thee, to intercede again with the admiral, to do all service to Mattinao, on reaching Española?"

"That hath been attended to, and so dismiss the subject from thy mind. The monument is already erected at Llera, and we may feel regret for the loss of the sweet girl, but can scarce mourn for her. Were I not Luis de Bobadilla, thy husband, dearest, I could think her the subject of envy, rather than of pity."

"Ah! Luis, thy flattery is too pleasing to bring reproof, but it is scarce seemly. Even the happiness I feel, in being assured of thy love—that our fortunes, fate, name, interests are one—is, in truth, but misery, compared with the seraphic joys of the blessed; and to such joys I could wish Ozema's spirit might be elevated."

"Doubt it not, Mercedes; she hath all that her goodness and innocence can claim. Mass! If she even have half that I feel, in holding thee thus to my heart, she is no subject for grief, and thou say'st she hath, or wilt have, ten-fold more."

"Luis—Luis—speak not thus! We will have other masses said at Seville, as well as at Burgos and Salamanca."

"As thou wilt, love. Let them be said yearly, monthly, weekly, forever, or as long as the churchmen think they may have virtue."

Mercedes smiled her gratitude, and the conversation became less painful, though it continued to be melancholy. An hour passed in this manner, during which, the communion was of the sweet character that pervades the intercourse of those who love tenderly. Mercedes had already acquired a powerful command over the headlong propensities and impetuous feelings of her husband, and was gradually moulding him, unknown to herself, to be the man that was necessary to her own feelings. In this change, which was the result of influence, and not of calculation or design, she was aided by the manly qualities of our hero, which were secretly persuading him that he had now the happiness of another in his keeping, as well as his own. This is an appeal that a really generous mind seldom withstands, and far oftener produces the correction of minor faults, than any direct management, or open rebukes. Perhaps Mercedes' strongest arm, however, was her own implicit confidence in her husband's excellence, Luis feeling a desire to be that which she so evidently thought him; an opinion that his own conscience did not, in the fullest extent, corroborate.

Just as the sun had set, Sancho came to announce that he had let go the anchor.

"Here we are, Señor Conde—here we are, at last, Señora Doña Mercedes, lying off the town of Palos, and within a hundred yards of the very spot where Don Christopher and his gallant companions departed for the discovery of the Indies—God bless him a hundred-fold, and all who went with him. The boat is ready to take you to the shore, Señora; and there, if you do not find Seville, or Barcelona, cathedrals and palaces, you will find Palos, and Santa Clara, and the ship-yard-gate—three places that are, henceforth, to be more renowned than either: Palos, as having sent forth the expedition; Santa Clara, as having saved it from destruction, by vows fulfilled at its altars; and the gate, for having had the ship of the admiral built within it."

"And other great events, good Sancho!" put in the count.

"Just so, your Excellency; and for other great events. Am I to land you, lady?"

Mercedes assented, and in ten minutes she and her husband were walking on the beach, within ten yards of the very spot where Columbus and Luis had embarked the previous year. The firm sands were now covered with people, walking in the cool of the evening. Most of them were of the humbler classes, this being the only land, we believe, in which the population of countries that possess a favorable climate, do not thus mingle in their public promenades, at that witching hour.

Luis and his beautiful wife had landed merely for exercise and relaxation, well knowing that the felucca possessed better accommodations than any hosteria of Palos; and they fell into the current of the walkers. Before them was a group of young matrons, who were conversing eagerly, and sufficiently loud to be overheard. Our hero and heroine instantly ceased their own discourse, when they found that the subject was the voyage to Cathay.

"This day," said one of the party, in a tone of authority, "did Don Christopher sail from Cadiz; the sovereigns deeming Palos too small a port for the equipment of so great an enterprise. You may depend on what I tell ye, good neighbors; my husband, as you all well know, holding an appointment in the admiral's own ship."

"You are to be envied, neighbor, that he is in so good repute with so great a man!"

"How could he be otherwise, seeing that he was with him before, when few had courage to be his companions, and was ever faithful to his orders. 'Monica'—nay, it was '*good* Monica'—said the admiral to me, with his own mouth, 'thy Pepe is a true-hearted mariner, and hath conducted to my entire satisfaction. He shall be made the boatswain of my own carrack, and thou, and thy posterity, to the latest antiquity, may boast that you belong to so good a man.' These were his words; and what he said, he did—Pepe being now a boatswain. But the *paters* and *aves* that I said to reach this good fortune, would pave this beach!"

Luis now stepped forward and saluted the party, making curiosity to know the particulars of the first departure, his excuse. As he expected, Monica did not recognize him in his present rich attire, and she willingly related all she knew, and not a little more. The interview showed how completely this woman had passed from despair to exultation, reducing the general and more public change of sentiment, down to the individual example of a particular case.

"I have heard much of one Pinzon," added Luis, "who went forth as pilot of a caravel in the voyage; what hath become of him?"

"Señor, he is dead!" answered a dozen voices, Monica's, however, so far getting the ascendency, as to tell the story. "He was once a great man in this quarter; but now his name is lost, like his life. He was untrue, and died of grief, it is said, when he found the Niña lying in the river, when he expected to have had all the glory to himself."

Luis had been too much engrossed with his own feelings to have heard this news before, and he continued his walk, musing and sad.

"So much for unlawful hopes, and designs that God doth not favor!" he exclaimed, when they had walked a considerable distance. "Providence hath, I think, been of the admiral's side; and certainly, my love, it hath been of mine."

"This is Santa Clara," observed Mercedes. "Luis, I would enter, and return a thanksgiving at its altars for thy safety and return, and offer a prayer for the future success of Don Christopher."

They both entered the church, and they knelt together at the principal altar; for, in that age, the bravest warriors were not as much ashamed, as in our own times, of publicly acknowledging their gratitude to, and their dependence on God. This duty performed, the happy pair returned silently to the beach, and went off to the felucca.

Early in the morning, the Ozema sailed for Malaga again, Luis being fearful he might be recognized if he continued at Palos. Their port was reached in safety; and shortly after the party arrived at Valverde, the principal estate of Mercedes, where we shall leave our hero and heroine in the enjoyment of a felicity that was as great as could be produced by the connection between manly tenderness on one side, and purity of feeling and disinterested womanly love on the other.

At a late day, there were other Luis de Bobadillas in Spain, among her gallant and noble, and other Mercedes', to cause the hearts of the gay and aspiring to ache; but there was only one Ozema. She appeared at court, in the succeeding reign, and, for a time, blazed like a star that had just risen in a pure atmosphere. Her career, however, was short, dying young and lamented; since which time, the name itself has perished. It is, in part, owing to these circumstances, that we have been obliged to drag so much of our legend from the lost records of that eventful period.

[1] Note—The authorities differ as to which of the English princes was the suitor of Isabella; Edward IV. himself, Clarence, or Richard. Isabella was the grand-daughter of Catherine of Lancaster, who was a daughter of John of Gaunt.

[2] Note.—It is worthy of remark that the city of Philadelphia stands, as near as may be, in the position that the honest Paul Toscanelli supposed to have been occupied by "the famous city of Quisay."

[3] It is a singular fact that the position and name of the precise island that was first fallen in with, on this celebrated voyage, remain to this day, if not a matter of doubt, at least a matter of discussion. By most persons, some of the best authorities included, it is believed that the adventurers made Cat Island, as the place is now called, though the admiral gave it the appellation of San Salvador; while others contend for what is now termed Turk's Island. The reason given for the latter opinion is the position of the island, and the course subsequently steered in order to reach Cuba. Muñoz is of opinion that it was Watling's Island, which lies due east of Cat Island, at the distance of a degree of longitude, or a few hours' run. As respects Turk's Island, the facts do not sustain the theory. The course steered, after quitting the island, was not west, but south-west; and we find Columbus anxious to get south to reach the island of Cuba, which was described to him by the natives, and which he believed to be Cipango. No reason is given by Muñoz for his opinion; but Watling's Island does not answer the description of the great navigator, while it is so placed as to have lain quite near his course, and was doubtless passed unseen in the darkness. It is thought the light so often observed by Columbus was on this island.

[4] The fortunes of this beautiful island furnish a remarkable proof of the manner in which abusse are made, by the providence of God, to produce their own punishments. This island, which is about two-thirds the size of the state of New York, was the seat of Spanish authority, in the New World, for many years. The mild aborigines, who were numerous

and happy when discovered, were literally exterminated by the cruelties of their new masters; and it was found necessary to import negroes from Africa, to toil in the cane-fields. Toward the middle of the sixteenth century, it is said that two hundred of the aborigines were not to be found in the island, although Ovando had decoyed no less than forty thousand from the Bahamas, to supply the places of the dead, as early as 1518! At a later day, Española passed into the hands of the French, and all know the terrible events by which it has gone into the exclusive possession of the descendants of the children of Africa. All that has been said of the influence of the white population of this country, as connected with our own Indians, sinks into insignificance, as compared with these astounding facts.